MATTHEW BOURNE
and his Adventures
in Motion Pictures

MATTHEW BOURNE

and his Adventures
in Motion Pictures

In conversation with
ALASTAIR MACAULAY

faber and faber
LONDON·NEW YORK

First published in 1999
by Faber and Faber Limited
3 Queen Square London WC1N 3AU
Published in the United States by Faber and Faber Inc.
a division of Farrar, Straus and Giroux Inc., New York

Photoset by Parker Typesetting Service, Leicester
Printed in England by Clays Ltd, St Ives plc

© Matthew Bourne and Alastair Macaulay, 1999

Matthew Bourne and Alastair Macaulay are hereby identified
as authors of this work in accordance with
Section 77 of the Copyright, Designs and Patents Act 1988

A CIP record for this book
is available from the British Library
ISBN 0–571–19706–X

The publishers wish to express their gratitude to
the Friends of Adventures in Motion Pictures
for the generous financial assistance
they have provided.

2 4 6 8 10 9 7 5 3 1

For June and Jim Bourne
and for Judith Sharp and Roderick Smith

Contents

List of Illustrations

Photographs courtesy of the generosity of AMP.

1 Bourne, aged about fifteen, in an amateur piece *Mr Bojangles* (c. 1974).
2 Bourne and Emma Gladstone performing for Transitions Dance Company in 1986 in Ashley Page's *The Organizing Principle*.
3 From Bourne's BA course; choreographic coursework, 1984.
4 From Bourne's choreographic notebooks, 1984/85.
5 Bourne as the Rt Hon Remnant Blight in Jacob Marley's *Does Your Crimplene Go All Crusty When You Rub?* (1987). Photograph: Chris Nash.
6 *Buck and Wing*. From Bourne's notes.
7 One of the pages of advertisements for male underwear used by Bourne as source material for *Spitfire* (1988)
8 *Spitfire* (1988). From Bourne's notebook.
9 *Spitfire*. From Bourne's notebook.
10 *Spitfire*. David Waring, Keith Brazil, Joachim Chandler and Matthew Bourne. Photograph: Chris Nash.
11 *The Infernal Galop*: Keith Brazil as the Merman in 'Fruits de Mer'. Photograph: Chris Nash.
12 One of Brassaï's classic photographs of Paris used as source material for *The Infernal Galop*. Photograph: Brassaï, 1932
13 *The Infernal Galop* (1992 revival). Scott Ambler, Ally Fitzpatrick, Matthew Bourne, Etta Murfitt, Andrew George and Simon Murphy. Photograph: Chris Nash.
14 *Town & Country* (1991): Matthew Bourne and Scott Ambler in 'Dearest Love' in the 'Town' section. Photograph: Michael Daks.
15 *Town & Country*. Ally Fitzpatrick, Matthew Bourne, Ben Wright,

ix

Introduction

Late in 1998, Matthew Bourne's *Swan Lake* opened on Broadway and entered the syllabus for Dance A level in Britain. This book is conceived both for those who have only discovered his work recently through such productions as *Swan Lake* (whether in the theatre or on video) and for those who will be making some academic study of his work. It is neither a biography nor a critical study, but it tells the story of how Matthew Bourne and his company, Adventures in Motion Pictures, have risen to such eminence. It also allows Matthew Bourne to speak at length both about his work and about the wider world of dance and the performing arts. The openness and detail with which he has discussed the creation of his works is surely unprecedented among choreographers to date.

When Matthew and I first met, in 1982, we were both in our twenties. He was just beginning a three-year BA in Dance Theatre at the Laban Centre for Movement and Dance in London; I was beginning my third year as lecturer in dance history on that course. In those days, it was the only BA in dance in Britain, and it was still a young course, entering its fifth year. I do not think that any of us teachers were confident that any of our students at that stage would make names for themselves in the world of dance. When one of the 1981 BA graduates, Annelies Stoffel, became a member of the small-scale but influential Extemporary Dance Theatre, there was considerable excitement and pride.

In fact, the Laban Centre of that era proved fertile ground. Many of our students found permanent employment in dance, and a few of them did indeed make names for themselves, as dancers, choreographers and even critics. The group of BA students who graduated in 1983, two years before Matthew, included the critic Sophie Constanti, who has reviewed dance for several British newspapers (*Guardian, Financial Times, Independent, Evening Standard*). The next year produced the choreographers Lea Anderson (founder of The Cholmondeleys and The Featherstonehaughs) and Claire (Williams) Russ, and the dancer Teresa Barker (between 1992 and 1998 a member of Adventures in Motion Pictures). Of the students in Matthew Bourne's year – graduating in 1985 – Catherine (White) Malone went on to dance professionally for several British dance companies; David Massingham became choreographer to his own dance company; Jonathan Thrift became principal A level examiner in Dance; and several others have become successful and influential teachers. There was another, non-BA, three-year Dance Theatre course that also produced some eminent students – notably John Heath, who, as Jacob Marley, was to contribute to Adventures in Motion Picture's early seasons.

In Matthew's very first term, I taught nineteenth-century ballet history to the students, and so he was at once plunged into the context, composition and meanings of *La Sylphide, Swan Lake* and *The Nutcracker* – all of which he has gone on to rechoreograph during the 1990s. 'The two Freds' – Astaire and Ashton – were areas of twentieth-century dance history I taught with particular love; Matthew has said in recent years that they are his two favourite choreographers. Dance history mattered to Matthew, and he took it as his optional subject during Part Two of his course; his special study was on Astaire's choreography.

While I was teaching dance history, I was also working as a busy dance critic. I often encountered my students at London dance performances and became involved in many passionate and analytical conversations. I remember, for example, that in 1984 Matthew was one of several students I met in the audiences both for Frederick Ashton's *Varii Capricci* at the Royal Ballet and for Ian Spink's *Further and Further into Night* for Second Stride (both of these works crop up in the conversations in this book). I also remember how I would enthuse to the students about the ballerina Lynn Seymour – not only in the Ashton and Mac-Millan roles which are central to her reputation, but also in her revelatory accounts of such classics as *The Sleeping Beauty*. I spoke of her performances, scores of which I had attended between 1975 and 1978, in the past tense; it seemed to us then that her career on stage might well be over. How ironic it is therefore that, more than a dozen years later,

Lynn Seymour wrote to Matthew, after she had begun to perform in his *Swan Lake*, to thank him for making her feel like the Sleeping Beauty reawakened.

When I was able to, I would also watch performances of the students' own choreography. Inevitably, the general level of these seemed undistinguished to a critic accustomed to watching the world's leading dance companies; but here and there would emerge touching signs of original talent. In spring 1984, when I first saw performances of choreography by Matthew's group, his was the offering that most impressed me; and the two pieces he showed during his third year more than confirmed my view. I still remember, in the first piece, one particular step that showed an unusual feeling for movement; in the second, a wonderfully exuberant grasp of changing ensemble patterns and structures; in the third, ardently percussive, syncopated rhythm. As it happens, his choreography teachers did not think him the best of the bunch, and I take some pride in being the first to single him out, responding to his work as a critic rather than as a teacher.

Perhaps the best thing a teacher can do is simply encourage each student to see what his or her potential is. Some students fulfil their potential, others do not. I have encouraged other student choreographers or critics who then made little headway. The fact that Matthew progressed – as this book describes – to greater achievements says much, not about those who encouraged him along the way, but about Matthew himself. I have remained friends with quite a number of the students in his group, and it is my impression that Matthew has changed less, not more, than any of his classmates. The career he has had is due to the fact that he has remained true to himself; and due also to the fact that his parents, June and Jim Bourne, have at every stage given him support (to a remarkable degree), but never pressure.

Neither Matthew nor I would like readers to assume that I am his tame critic or that he is the Trilby to my Svengali. Some notes are appropriate here on this friendship between choreographer and critic, or between ex-student and ex-teacher.

Of the seven founder-members of Adventures in Motion Pictures in 1987, three had been my students for three years, and five were my friends. Around that time, Emma Gladstone (now Assistant Director of the Place Theatre) and Matthew shared a flat only a street away from mine, and there were many happy breakfasts at the Café Dôme on

Saturday mornings – the same Café Dôme where I met Matthew for breakfast after first seeing his *Swan Lake* in 1995 and where I often met him, again for breakfast, during the preparation of this book in summer and autumn 1998.

It was, I think, always understood that I would put criticism above friendship if the choice had to arise. But I took care not to review AMP's early performances, and it was gratifying to see how quickly it attracted attention from others. *Greenfingers*, one of the early works Matthew made for AMP, was privately dedicated to me. There have been numerous AMP productions that I have never reviewed; in some cases I have spoken or written to Matthew about my reactions to his work. These were not invariably favourable, and some of my published reviews contained a degree of adverse criticism.

I have always thought it a good idea for artists not to read reviews of themselves, and a better idea not to comment on them. An interesting exception to this rule arose, however, in early 1995, when I wrote a review of *Highland Fling* (then a year old) in the *Financial Times*. Matthew wrote to me to thank me – curiously, more for my particular reservations about the piece than for my general enthusiasm. He says in this book that this review helped to strengthen his resolve about the line he was going to take with his next work, *Swan Lake*.

My opinions occasionally emerge in this book, but they are not the point here. Indeed, there are several areas in which I have deliberately omitted them. The point has been to allow Matthew to speak about his career and work, and sometimes to provide supplementary information. Matthew and I have always conversed easily, and I have tried to preserve the manner in which we talk.

It was Walter Donohue at Faber and Faber who, after seeing *Swan Lake* in the West End and noticing how wide-ranging an audience it had, had the idea for this book; and it was Matthew who suggested that I collaborate on it with him. I am very grateful to both men. At every stage it has been interesting to find how much I did not actually know of Matthew's work, and to see more clearly how it connects with many other developments in the arts.

Matthew and I taped most of the interviews between May and July 1998. The versions assembled in this book are by no means straightforward transcripts. We began by talking through Matthew's process of work on his four 'classics' – *Nutcracker, Highland Fling, Swan Lake,*

Cinderella – over three days. Next we spent time on earlier work, and on AMP today. We returned to the four 'classics' in further detail; then to larger creative issues emerging from or apparent in Matthew's work; finally back to the four 'classics', in some cases going through Matthew's notebooks and in one case (Act Two of *Swan Lake*) watching the video together. Even after many relaxed days or half-days of interview and/or conversation, new points emerged. From the mass of often disordered talk, I have assembled this book.

Matthew is remarkably undefensive and unguarded in talking about his work, but his memory is often faulty or weak. Mine, by contrast, is detailed and fussy, and during the course of the book I found I had to remind Matthew of important things he had completely forgotten. He has often said in public that the first ballet he ever saw was Peter Darrell's production of *Swan Lake* for Scottish Ballet, as performed at Sadler's Wells in 1979, and it was a delicate moment when I had to point out to him that he had seen at least one other ballet (another *Swan Lake*) before that. Another delicate moment arose when, after more than two months of hard work on the book, I found, from a chance conversation over coffee with Etta Murfitt, that Matthew had omitted to tell me that, before choreographing *Swan Lake*, he had made a Dying Swan solo on Adam Cooper. 'There's something you've forgotten to tell me,' I said; Matthew listened, grinned and said, 'Oh, yes. You weren't asking the right questions.' If this book contains any other signs of my having omitted to ask the right questions, I apologize.

I was greatly assisted by being able to interview important members of Adventures in Motion Pictures: the producer and co-director Katharine Doré, whose crucial work for the company is not properly recognized in these pages; the designer Lez Brotherston; the dancers and assistant directors Etta Murfitt and Scott Ambler; and the dancers Adam Cooper, Will (William) Kemp and Ben Wright. Their generosity and thoughtfulness affected the book more than is apparent.

Katharine Doré has said that she feels her greatest achievement for AMP has been in enabling Matthew to conceive, rehearse and stage *Swan Lake*, and then to bring it to the West End without his being distracted by financial considerations. Those, she said, were her concern. Generously, she allowed me to prepare much of this book in the AMP office. It is a happy place in which to work, and I cannot sufficiently thank Philip Belfield, Katharine and Matthew's assistant, and Richard

McDermott, the company administrator, for the friendly assistance they gave me on innumerable occasions there. Thanks to them (thanks also to Martin Nielsen at the *Financial Times*), I am now less computer-illiterate than I was. There are many kindnesses for which I am indebted to other members of staff at AMP – especially Jonathan Stott and Simon Lacey – as I am to Mandy Bentley at the *Financial Times*.

The original interview tapes were transcribed for us by Lesley Howard. Various parts of the book have been read and corrected by June Bourne, Simon Carter, Emma Gladstone, Etta Murfitt, Martin Duncan and Elizabeth Marshall. Scott Ambler and Katharine Doré read, corrected and advised upon the text. Matthew Bourne and I have revised at every stage, and would cheerfully go on revising if time allowed. Walter Donohue has been a patient and thorough editor. To all of these people, my thanks.

A. M.

June 1999

I

Early Life
1960–82

MATTHEW BOURNE: When I was young, I believed that you could be cured by music; that when I was ill, if I put on my favourite music, it would make me better. Not just make me happier; I actually thought it would cure me. And I still feel that music is therapeutic. I remember my mum telling me that I would pick up songs before I could put sentences together. And today I can still recite hundreds of song lyrics. Later, I used to sing along with records a lot – really loudly, not just humming away. I used to perform in the same way as years later I did in ballet classes: all feeling and no technique! But I used to feel it so much.

I think all those things contributed to what I'm doing now. It's about feeling music, which is the basis of what I do.

ALASTAIR MACAULAY: *What were your schooldays like?*
MB: I think I was leading some kind of double life. I just had no interest in what was going on at school at all. I wasn't made to enjoy literature, or art, or anything that I came to love later on.

My interests were very different from everyone else's there. I wasn't into the current trends, or the current music. I already had my own interests. At school my best friend was Simon Carter; he remains my closest friend. I got to know him when I was eleven. It was quite a rough comprehensive school, in Walthamstow. We were very much a pair there, quite gossipy. That probably made getting through the whole thing tolerable.

What we were doing – especially between the ages of fourteen and sixteen – was autograph-collecting. We would come straight from school on a 38 bus to first nights and hotels, stage doors and all that.

1 Bourne, aged about fifteen, in an amateur piece *Mr Bojangles* (c. 1974).

That, I feel, was my education. Sometimes we'd get someone's autograph without really being aware of whose it was, but once we had it in our collection, we would look up who they were and would find out everything about them. If there was a playwright we'd not heard of, we'd find out who he was and what he'd done, and we'd follow his work from that point onwards.

AM: *I have a friend who, aged forty-three, admits that she still does Oscar acceptance speeches to the bathroom mirror. Were you that kind of child?*

MB: Yes. Not exactly Oscar acceptance speeches, but the first time I ever did an acceptance speech for an award – even though you feel very naff and pretentious in saying the things you say on those occasions – it felt strangely like something that I'd always wanted to do; and I think the same now if someone asks me for my autograph. It's very strange to be on the other side of things.

AM: *Do you ever now get the urge to ask somebody for their autograph?*

MB: Yes, I do. In a roundabout way, though. When Adventures in Motion Pictures took *Swan Lake* to Los Angeles, we found that the celebrities there very much expected to come round and congratulate us after the show. So I kept a visitors' book in my dressing-room and asked if people would write in it before they left. That, in a sense, was still keeping up the old thing, but now at a more personal level. It's one of the lovely things that have happened to me. When someone's seen something you've done and admired it, then there is dialogue instantly; and often the admiration is mutual.

AM: *Your boyhood was in Greater London – in Walthamstow. How much of your childhood, and how much of your very gradual process of becoming a creative artist, was connected with being a Londoner?*
MB: A lot. I've recently seen documentaries on TV of Kenneth Williams and Noël Coward. In both cases it was mentioned that they spent an enormous part of their childhood or early teenage years on buses around London, taking in a whole variety of people and life. Well, I was like that. So was my mother, funnily enough. In her teenage years she was all over London, in queues for theatres and seeing various performers at the Palladium, and so on. She was always there in the queue, on her own. I think access to all that influenced me a lot.

I think now that I was very into self-education, without knowing it. In 1979, when I was nineteen, I saw my first ballet, *Swan Lake*. I wonder now: what made me go to Covent Garden, then to Sadler's Wells? I know that I went on my own. I think that I thought it was about time I saw a ballet, to see if I liked it; and the 38 bus went past Sadler's Wells and through the West End. Later I did the same with opera, which, to a lesser degree, I followed up for a while. Opera hasn't become the big thing for me that dance became, but I went because I felt that this was something to be discovered. With most things, no one encouraged me to do it; I did it myself. And I read books because I felt, 'I've not read that author – and I should do.'

AM: *Your parents obviously gave you terrific freedom to go out by yourself to the West End.*
MB: They did, but maybe because my mum knew that's what she had done. I don't think they had any idea of what I should be doing with my life. I don't even remember a conversation about 'what I was going to do.' I did A levels, and then I'd had enough of education, because I didn't feel I was gaining anything from it – even to the point where I

did English Literature A level without actually reading the set books. I read Brodie's Notes; I just had so little interest in it.

So I applied for a job at the BBC. In a completely naive way, I thought that it would have some connection with entertainment. Quite soon afterwards I was offered a job in an office there, and I would get to watch all the radio shows. But it was an extremely naive approach; I can't even imagine what was going on in my head at the time.

AM: *Did the world seem either a frightening place or a strange place to you, the larger world beyond home?*
MB: I don't think it felt frightening. I had a happy home life with my parents and my brother Dan. I wasn't pressurized too much by them to be or do anything; and I was doing amateur theatricals all through those years.

AM: *I know you began to make shows for your own amateur company. How old were you when you started this?*
MB: The first production I staged was when I was five or six, I think. I did some fairy story that I've forgotten, something about the king's gold shoes. I remember the actual shoes – but not much about the rest of it.

But I was allowed to put on productions at school. Nothing with a script, but probably with music. I used to do productions of films that I'd seen, purely from memory, and I'd put them on with people in my class. Then it got to the point where I was allowed to pick from anyone in the school to do my shows. I did *Lady and the Tramp* and *Mary Poppins*, even *Cinderella*. I cast my brother as Cinderella; I was an ugly sister. All the men were women, all the women were men. It's very odd thinking that that's what I was doing then! I was probably about eight or nine at the time.

AM: *How much of these shows would have been dance? How much would have been speaking or singing?*
MB: It's difficult to remember completely, but I think it was a combination of songs and, certainly, some dancing and an improvised script of scenes. I don't remember writing anything or people having to learn words. I don't know what they were like, but they must have been reasonable, otherwise the authorities wouldn't have allowed me to do them. This wasn't part of what was going on at school; it was done outside of school. Then the school all piled in to watch.

4

So, at that point, I was seen to be someone who obviously wanted to act or work on stage; but then, when puberty hit, I became very introverted and quiet. At school, I never let that side come out again. I went on doing all my amateur shows, but only on the outskirts of school, not within school.

AM: *Using school friends?*

MB: Very rarely. I was almost embarrassed about it. At our school the girls were extremely rough, much more so than the boys. They used to beat you up. The fact that you liked to dance or sing wasn't the sort of thing you'd want known about yourself. So it was done with other people unconnected with school. My parents ran youth clubs, were youth workers for many years, and so had access to halls where I was able to have space to rehearse in the evenings. So it would be people who lived down the street, and friends of theirs – people at the youth clubs maybe – anyone interested who would be prepared to give up two evenings a week.

And I belonged to a Methodist church. One of the reasons I liked it so much was that there was a choir attached to it. We used to sing in the church every Sunday, rehearsing on a Tuesday evening; we also did shows, twice a year, of songs. I contributed numbers to those which involved dancing; and from that I formed another company, which was allowed to put on shows at the church hall and used guests from the choir. All this was when I was about fourteen or fifteen.

Then I had another company called Pumps when I was in my late teens – about seventeen, eighteen – which rehearsed and performed at youth clubs.

AM: *Would the numbers in these shows involve singing as well? Or would they be all dance?*

MB: The choir shows and the earlier shows had singing in, but that element gradually disappeared. By the time of the Pumps company, it was much more about dancing – and putting on a show.

I wasn't thinking in terms of myself as a choreographer, but I used to watch shows and films, and would want to imitate what I saw. People now would say I was inspired by what I saw; but I used to think purely in terms of: 'Let's steal that movement', and 'Let's try and do that thing that I remember'. I had no qualms about stealing, because I didn't feel I was in any kind of professional atmosphere.

AM: *During your childhood and adolescence, were you ever keen on the pop music of the day?*
MB: Not especially at the time, no. As an eighteen-year-old I started to go out and visit discos, around the time when disco was very big; but I wasn't buying a lot of the music. I enjoyed it, but I was listening to other things at home.

I was always into things from the past, really. The earliest things I was listening to were mostly shows, musicals.

AM: *Did you go endless times to* The Sound of Music?
MB: Yes, many times! You see, it was the first film that I saw at the cinema. I think I was taken to see it on my fifth birthday.

AM: *From that it was a mere skip to* Mary Poppins?
MB: Yes, very soon afterwards. After that, anything with Julie Andrews in it: *Star, Thoroughly Modern Millie . . .* But I was also very into *Funny Girl*. And plenty of other musicals, adaptations of stage shows that were made into films around that time. I remember seeing a lot of things on TV as well, a lot of MGM musicals – *Singin' in the Rain, The Band Wagon, Seven Brides for Seven Brothers, Kiss Me Kate*, all those things.

AM: *Were you a child of* West Side Story?
MB: Yes, very much. I regularly saw it at the cinema. It used to be on quite a lot then.

AM: *So now, having grown up through all of that, you find that, for pleasure, your musical taste is generally from Gershwin and Irving Berlin through to Rodgers and Hammerstein?*
MB: Yes. The sort of golden age of songwriters. I love the melody, and the wit of the lyrics. I love the way the words go into your memory without your having made any effort to learn them.

When I was using taped music for a lot of the pieces we were performing, I quite often incorporated these songs into what I was doing; and I could relate the movement to the lyrics – which is a very enjoyable way of working. You've got something to go on all the time; you can have fun with the way you go with or against the words. But ultimately I wouldn't be challenged in a theatrical way by that music, in the way I am by a score of Prokofiev or Tchaikovsky, where I feel the music's been designed to tell stories with movement.

AM: *Did your taste go back as far as ragtime?*

MB: Yes. In the 1970s Scott Joplin became popular with the film *The Sting*; and I liked that very much. That's how I got introduced to him, and that's why one of the first ballets I ever saw was Kenneth MacMillan's *Elite Syncopations* – because it was set to Joplin music, and had been on TV.

AM: *In your mid-teens you came across two shows that were a revelation to you. One was* Gypsy, *the other was* A Chorus Line. *What was it about them that so impressed you?*

MB: *Gypsy* gave me a love of live theatre. I wanted to be in it; I wanted to be part of that world. It is the ultimate theatre piece in many ways. It was at the Piccadilly Theatre – where we've performed *Swan Lake* and *Cinderella*, over twenty years later! – and Angela Lansbury played Mama Rose.

The amazing thing about Mama Rose is that, if it's played by the right person, she is an ordinary woman with an ambition for living through her daughters; and whether or not it's true that she could have been a star herself, that is what she has eating away at her.

AM: *Does this dichotomy express anything of what you were talking about in yourself? You're an ordinary chap who's happy to be a Londoner – but would you say you had a driving ambition to make it in showbiz?*

MB: I've never thought about it before, but now you've said it, I suppose there is something there, yes. Because the autograph-collecting was a way of being involved on the sidelines. It's meeting people in a very superficial way, but it's a way of being close to that world; and I suppose Mama Rose is the same. The closest she can get is to make her children, who aren't actually very talented, into something. But she's got the drive to make them do it, even though they don't particularly want it.

I've always said that I haven't got drive or ambition. Other people say that I have, but I don't see it. Other people say that I'm a workaholic, but I feel as though I'm lazy. I do spend all my time doing work-related things, I suppose.

AM: *So it is ambition of a kind; and you've lived with it for so long.*

MB: Yes. I was desperately jealous of child stars when I was a child myself, desperately jealous. I absolutely hated Mark Lester, who was Oliver in the film; I really wanted to be him. And the children in *Chitty*

Chitty Bang Bang . . . I remember thinking, 'How do you get to do that? How did they get those parts?'

AM: *Then you saw* A Chorus Line.

MB: I was sixteen. The difference is that it was more of a personal revelation to me. I saw it eleven times.

To hear people talking honestly about themselves – those monologues – revealing things about themselves and talking about their sexuality and family problems. Not that I was a problem person, but I did have my sexuality to deal with. I didn't come out to myself as gay until I was eighteen, but certainly I began to acknowledge that after seeing *A Chorus Line.* I think it was a great piece to have seen at that age. It was the beginning of me looking into myself, of being able to see who I was: turning the tables, and asking myself, 'What am I? What are my feelings and ambitions?'

AM: *Had you at any point found yourself in a milieu where you thought, 'This panics me. This is more than I can handle,' or just 'This is alien to me'?*

MB: Certainly there was one experience like that. I did try acting at one point, when I was fifteen, at Mountview theatre school. It was only an evening course that was supposed to lead to other things. I thought, because I was so into young film actors, such as Mark Lester and Jack Wild, that that was what I wanted to do. So I went there – and absolutely hated it. I didn't feel that I could be inventive in any way as an actor. There were acting games, which were like torture to me. I didn't enjoy the creative aspect of what I was being taught there at all; I hated speaking and felt that I was terrible at it. It didn't feel like the right form of expression for me.

AM: *Obviously you watched all kinds of musicals and popular entertainment. You've often spoken of your admiration of Fred Astaire. When did you first watch his films?*

MB: I used to watch Fred Astaire on TV as a child. I'm pretty convinced my parents used to make me watch his films, and that they told me he was a good thing. When I was five, six, seven – I don't remember a time when I wasn't aware of him or his films. Then I gradually singled him out as the one I liked the most.

AM: *Was there any particular point when you started to think, 'This isn't just adorable, it's also great choreography'?*

MB: I don't think I thought in terms of choreography in those days, even into my teens. I just got enormous pleasure from Astaire's dancing.

It was consistently interesting in a way that Gene Kelly wasn't. Not that I was consciously critical at the time. I always found the modesty of Astaire's personality more appealing, as well. I didn't go for the brashness and ego of Gene Kelly. The Fred and Ginger movies I had a particular love for – and then they disappeared for years. There was a whole period of time when they weren't shown on television. Then at the Everyman cinema in Hampstead, probably in the late 1970s, they showed all the Fred and Ginger numbers edited together from all the movies, in one day – something they've never done since. That had a big effect on me. It was so glorious to see all those numbers that I'd maybe only seen once before when I was seven or eight.

From that day onwards, I was absolutely convinced that this was what I wanted to do. I was so surprised at the variety and the seriousness of the work in the films. It was so rich.

AM: *Frederick Ashton often said that seeing Anna Pavlova for the first time, in his teens, was the revelation that changed his life. For you it was this Fred-and-Ginger-fest at Hampstead. How old were you at the time?*

MB: Maybe nineteen. I wanted at once to put something like those numbers into my shows. I've got videos of some of what I did then, which I've never shown. They're just cringe-making! One was a whole little fifteen-minute version of *On the Town*. I did a whole tango number; I can't remember what that was inspired by. We did an Adam and Eve ballet, which was based on the long Adam and Eve sequence that Shirley MacLaine does in the Cole Porter *Can Can* film.

AM: *When you did a can can or a tango, did you just pick up your idea of those dances from the films? Or did you make any formal study of what, for example, comprised a tango?*

MB: By the late 1970s, we had a video at home, and we used to tape everything musical from the TV. Some of these things I watched again and again, and knew them inside out. So I tended to borrow ideas or just copy them.

Inevitably, though, if you do try to use something you've seen, it turns into something else; and this, I suppose, was the beginning of me making choices as a choreographer.

AM: *Did you have any panic about the lack of direction in your life after leaving school? Was one part of you longing to get free of your humdrum existence?*

MB: I don't remember being panicked. I remember enjoying my life at that time so much – my social life, my theatre-going, lots of pubs and clubs. I was having a really good time. The jobs that I was doing were a bit boring; but when I worked for a while for the Keith Prowse theatre agency, I would get to go to the theatre every night for free. That was the reason for doing the job.

AM: *Did you leave home at this time?*

MB: No. I lived at home until I started my dance education at the Laban Centre, when I was twenty-two.

AM: *Did you have any particular feeling of freedom with all these pubs and clubs, the theatre life?*

MB: Yes. I felt very much that London was my playground; and I knew it very, very well. I spent a lot of time on the streets of London, and couldn't imagine myself anywhere else. I had no ambition to leave. Maybe that's what propels some people to go to university, or into career choices, more quickly than I did: they want to get away. I didn't have that sort of drive.

AM: *How important was sexual feeling to you from early boyhood until* A Chorus Line?

MB: I didn't have even a kiss till I was eighteen. At that age, I suppose, I realized it was time I did something.

It wasn't a very pressing thing, I must say; I was very involved in all the other things I was doing. In my teens, I never saw myself as physically involved in anything sexual. That's why I still have that distance in other aspects of my life. If I feel there's going to be any kind of contact, I'm off. I'm basically quite shy.

When I did have my first kiss with a man, and when I first had sex, I had no problems at all. It just seemed completely natural.

AM: *At the age of nineteen, you saw ballet for the first time. We'll talk about individual ballets and ballet choreographers in due course. But you recently mentioned that ballet itself, in general, you then found erotic.*

MB: I did. I don't mean it was the only appeal, or even the main appeal. What impressed me most was its seriousness as dance. I'd seen

Fred and Ginger handling serious emotion in dance, I'd heard serious music in musicals too; but, until ballet, I hadn't encountered a whole genre that seemed to make dance, and dancing to music, something serious as a matter of course. It was the impact of that which gave it an erotic quality, because it was seriously sexual and sensual. I had never found that kind of appeal in the stars and musicals and showbiz I'd been following up to that time.

AM: *To what degree was your erotic, or sensual, interest in ballet connected with the male performers? Or did you find that in the female performers too?*
MB: I definitely was sexually, or sensually, excited by a lot of male dancers. There's something about a male moving with feeling and beauty that I find very appealing. Dance movement can make someone appealing who wouldn't necessarily be appealing when just walking down the street.

On the other hand, I absolutely loved many of the women I saw dance – not in a desiring kind of way, but for the sexiness and the beauty of their dancing. So in some ways the appeal was the same, though I can't see it as a form of sexual desire. It's more a sense of eroticism coming out of the dancers' performance; it's an excitement in what they convey.

AM: *You're on record as saying that the two choreographers you most admire are the two Freds: Astaire and Ashton. Is that true?*
MB: Yes, it still is true.

AM: *I remember that you made a formal study of Astaire when you were a third-year BA student. But looking back now, can you see whether, or how, Astaire's style percolated into your work?*
MB: For one thing, I often incline towards a ballroomy style of partnering. One of the most important models for a great deal of what I do is the Astaire–Rogers format of starting a dance very simply, that then becomes more elaborate as it goes along. Likewise the device, in Astaire's own solos, of dancing on or around the furniture: the point being that dance can arise spontaneously in ordinary circumstances. With Astaire you so often see how he performs ordinary action, ordinary movement, and how that eventually flowers into dance. I've always tried to emulate that, but it's actually so difficult to do; and if you try to capture something of Astaire and Rogers themselves, it's virtually

impossible, because their dances are so much about their own personalities.

Still, I often find that to take an Astaire idea and to elaborate on it is
a good starting point for choreographic ideas of my own. Musically
it's always so wonderful, and rhythmically it's so inspiring, to see how
he plays with, or against, the music – quite amazingly off the music at
times – then gets back on to it. Astaire isn't easy to watch for someone
who's used to watching Gene Kelly, who's so on the music all the time
and so easy to watch. Particularly in tap solos, what Astaire does at
times is madness. Then, the more you see it, the more enjoyable it
becomes. Repeat viewings seem to give completeness to things that you
thought were unconnected before.

AM: *And the dance leads you deeper into the music somehow.*
MB: Yes. I'm not saying that I myself have got to that level of complexity in working with music; but I feel that Astaire's example is always
there, nudging you on, to stop you being so simple, or so on the music
– which is often the thing you have to remember most. When something's looking a bit boring, you think, 'Let's try to break it up a bit;
let's work against or around the music.'

AM: *Fred Ashton put one obvious Astaire quotation – the 'Oompah
Trot', which he had seen Fred Astaire doing on stage with his sister
Adele, and which Astaire does with Gracie Allen in the movie* Damsel
in Distress – *into his own 1948 ballet* Cinderella. *He and Robert Helpmann did it, as the two Ugly Sisters, in their duet with the oranges,
hilariously; and it remains in the choreography for the two Ugly Sisters
today. Do you find yourself consciously quoting Astaire movies when
you choreograph?*
MB: Yes, many times! The pas de deux in Act Two of my *Cinderella*
starts, absolutely, with the Astaire–Rogers idea I've been talking about:
they just walk, they elaborate on the walk, and then that builds into a
dance. The sort of things I tend to notice in Astaire, for possible use of
my own, are certainly not his tap numbers: certainly not in terms of
their steps; but I do take definite ideas from the duets. Not just Fred
and Ginger actually, but also Fred with, for example, Cyd Charisse.
'Dancing in the Dark' from *The Band Wagon* is one that I watch again
and again to remind me of something that's very simple but beautiful.
It reminds you that you don't have to be complex and try working

with lots of difficult lifts. If it's musical, and if it's felt, you can get by with something that's much simpler.

I've used Astaire exits a few times. I particularly love the exit at the end of *Let's Face the Music and Dance* – but, though I've tried more than once to put it into my work, it doesn't really work on stage! They arch right back while they're each on one leg; they each keep the other leg arched out in front; they start to fall forwards while still keeping that leg pointing forwards and while arching back. So you're left with this lovely image of them still in the air, in a sense. But in the film a curtain then comes across just as they're doing it. On stage, if you try to make dancers exit like that into the wings, half the audience can't see them properly anyway – because they're on the wrong side of the stage – and the other half is eventually going to see them plonking down on to the other leg. I know – I was still trying to bring that off at the end of the Spanish dance in *Swan Lake*! But in rehearsal it didn't work. So we changed it.

AM: *When did you first see Ashton choreography?*
MB: It must have been about 1980, when I was twenty. I think it was *La Fille mal gardée*. I just loved it. I suppose in some ways it was very close to the musicals I had been enjoying: it's got comedy, romance – a bit of everything. I saw it again and again; I took my mum to see it, and she loved it too. I also adored the pantomime aspect of it – the Widow Simone played by a man in such an un-drag way – and the sheer daring of having those dancing chickens at the very beginning. It all seemed very odd to me at the time; but I liked that. And it is also full of good choreography; it has dance interest throughout, even though it is a light piece. It's full of distinct characters, different kinds of dancing. I think that's why it's so rewarding.

After that, I just started to catch every Ashton I could. I still do. Naturally my Ashton knowledge is very dependent on what has been in repertory during the time I've been following it. Several of the other story ballets – *Cinderella, The Dream, A Month in the Country* – I've seen many, many times. But I had to wait years until I first saw *Symphonic Variations*.

I also began to watch the whole Royal Ballet repertory at that time: the classics, the MacMillan ballets, everything. Not just the Royal Ballet at Covent Garden: the Sadler's Wells Royal Ballet (now the Birmingham Royal Ballet) too. I saw a lot of new MacMillan ballets. One of the earliest pieces I saw, in 1980, made one of the strongest impressions: *Playground*. What I remember most is the way that he had adults within an institution playing children and children's games; and I liked the costumes that they wore in that piece. That was in my mind twelve years later when I did *Nutcracker*. I saw these evacuee *Nutcracker* children as being in shorts and little dresses, the way the dancers were in *Playground*.

AM: *I know that you're steeped in Walt Disney movies. Do you ever find that Disney is a natural influence on you?*
MB: It certainly is in terms of the way I work with stories. What Disney has done, very interestingly, and what I do, is to take old stories and retell them. You're taking a simple fairy story or a myth, and creating a version that will work for the modern audience. Most Disney films have now become the versions of those stories that we know. *Snow White and the Seven Dwarfs*: the Disney version is the most famous version of that story, even though it's quite different from the original. The same with all their works. That's an interesting phenomenon they've created.

I think in some ways that's the way I approach stories: How can I make this palatable? How can I make this work for a much bigger audience than it's already reaching? So that's what I have got from Disney. And the Disney people are quite daring at times, in how far they will go to tell a story.

AM: *Does Disney affect your movement?*
MB: No. I think it's all to do with story-telling.

AM: *Do you have in your video collection the* Silly Symphonies *or any early Mickey Mouse films?*
MB: They're very hard to get hold of, but I love watching them when I have the chance. They are very music-led; it's story-telling through music.

AM: *The subject of dancing to music leads me to the man I think of as the greatest of all choreographers: George Balanchine. New York City Ballet, which he founded in 1948, came here in 1979, when he was still very much its ballet-master-in-chief, and again in 1983, just months after his death, but still dancing a largely Balanchine repertory. How much of Balanchine did you see in those days? And to what degree were you interested in his work?*

MB: Well, I saw New York City Ballet in 1979. I went initially, mind you, more to see Baryshnikov than anything else. I thought of him as a film star, because he'd been in *The Turning Point*. I queued up to see him.

Balanchine choreography was a whole new world. A whole new world of choreography that seemed alien to me then. I probably enjoyed the music and the musicality of it.

Balanchine has never become my favourite choreographer. My body doesn't really respond to that style of ballet; and some of his pieces – such as his *Nutcracker* – I really don't buy; but I'd always try to see anything by him I hadn't seen before, and he can still surprise. On my last visit to New York, for example, I saw his *Walpurgisnacht* for the first time, where the girls all let down their hair halfway through. I really liked that. Just recently, I watched *Serenade* and *Western Symphony* on TV. I loved them both, and I realized how many ideas I've lifted from *Serenade* over the years – in pieces of mine from *Spitfire* (1988) to *Cinderella* (1997). I do see that he's a master. But in 1979, and again in 1983, the main impact was of a whole new bunch of exciting dancers I was seeing for the first time; and I was completely enamoured of ballet in general at that point as well: so I remember really having a great time.

AM: *Meanwhile you were also going to West End theatre. 1980 was the year of the Royal Shakespeare Company's epic production of* Nicholas Nickleby: *I presume you saw that?*
MB: Well, the way that piece told a story was very influential, not just for me, but for many other people. And later I worked twice with John Caird, who had co-directed *Nicholas Nickleby* with Trevor Nunn; I choreographed his productions of *As You Like It* (for the RSC, in 1989) and the West End musical *Children of Eden* (in 1991). I've always felt I learnt a lot from working with him. In particular, his open-mindedness towards ways of staging a story. Had I not had those experiences, I might not have done the sequence in Act Three of *Cinderella* with the screens; I just thought, 'I'll ask Lez Brotherston, the designer, for twelve screens, and I can do a whole series of scenes man-oeuvring those around to make different worlds.' There was a bit in *Children of Eden* that I always loved, when the dove flew from the ark. John Caird pursued this idea – and in rehearsal I thought, 'I just can't see this working at all' – where all the cast would hold up a simple

dove made of white tissue paper: they would turn around with it, it would disappear, they would pass it along, it would reappear; they were dotted all over the set, so that you saw stages of its flight. Frances Ruffelle, the girl who was singing the song at the time, just made a simple gesture as if to release the dove from her hands; and as she did, the first tissue came, and then you saw all these white flashes appear round the set. It really was brilliant. Such a lovely idea, and so simple. I thought, 'This is really great – you can create theatre from nothing, not just from spending a lot of money on big sets and special effects.' *Nicholas Nickleby* taught me that anything's up for grabs. You could build a carriage or a dormitory out of bits of set lying around, and create something out of nothing. The audience always loves pieces that manipulate simple means to make something wonderfully theatrical. I thought that we in AMP did that at times with *Deadly Serious* – we had a simple set that became lots of different things. We had a box that became a coffin, that became a table, that became a wardrobe. By turning it up on different ends, moving it around, we made it become different things. Audiences always respond to that.

I saw a lot of other West End productions then; I still do. I can see now that some of the ones I saw in the 1970s or 1980s have influenced my work with AMP. For example, the idea of Peter Shaffer's *Equus* was in my mind when I started to conceive *Swan Lake*. Probably there were others, whose influence I won't recognize until I find myself using them.

AM: *Up to these years, you'd been looking at theatre, films, ballet. Had you looked at any modern dance before the course?*
MB: Virtually at the same time that I started to go to ballet, I also started to see everything I could of all the bigger modern-dance companies. The first must have been Martha Graham, in 1979, in the season she did at Covent Garden with Liza Minnelli. That was actually just before I saw my first *Swan Lake*. Minnelli – who was playing the Narrator in Graham's *The Owl and the Pussycat* – was my reason for going; and my main memories now are of her and of Graham herself, who just spoke, at the side of the stage, with a microphone. I was nineteen, and I was fascinated to see Graham: she was a legendary figure, and she spoke for about half an hour. I don't remember not liking it, but I don't think it left any great impression.

In those days, there were very few small British modern-dance companies, whereas today there seem to be dozens. I started to go and see most of the dance companies that visited Sadler's Wells Theatre: the two leading British companies, Ballet Rambert (which later became Rambert Dance Company, but was already a modern-dance rather than a ballet troupe) and the much-missed London Contemporary Dance Theatre, and any that came from abroad.

One of the first modern-dance things I saw was Twyla Tharp's company, when it came for a fortnight to Sadler's Wells in 1981. I really took to that straightaway. I found it exciting because I felt that here was someone who was virtually doing whatever she wanted to do, expressing completely what she wanted to express at that time. I know now how formal her work really was, but that wasn't how it felt. It seemed so free. Having seen a fair bit of ballet by that point, I found it very unusual; but I was excited by it.

Her style as a whole made a big impact on me. I remember being at the bus stop afterwards – I'd just seen *Eight Jelly Rolls*, her 1971 piece to jazz music by Jell Roll Morton – and I remember still moving around, imitating the amazingly fluid, slouchy, Tharp style of that era as I stood there, waiting for the bus.

AM: *One of my enduring memories of that season is of coming out of Sadler's Wells after one performance and seeing people still moving at the bus stop. It seemed absolutely the most natural response at the time; Tharp in those days had the strongest kinaesthetic effect on people that I have ever known in dance. Long after the show it made all of us just wriggle happily, as if it was still going on inside us; but I didn't know you were one of the wrigglers at the bus stop!*

MB: That's the main thing I can remember about it now: me at the bus stop afterwards, still moving.

2

Training
1982–86

ALASTAIR MACAULAY: *What made you change your life and take a three-year dance course?*
MATTHEW BOURNE: I had begun working as an usher at the National Theatre in 1980, and one of the ushers there, Dan O'Neill, was studying at the London Contemporary Dance School at The Place. (He later danced – as did I – for Lea Anderson as one of her Featherstonehaughs.) He told me about dance training, and about the Laban Centre, which had then started its BA course in Dance Theatre – the only British BA in dance in those days.

AM: *What degree of training of any kind did you have before you auditioned for the Laban Centre?*
MB: I had no formal training at all. I belonged to a dance group that was based at a church that I went to. This was called Mathews Dance Workshop: no relation! It was run by a woman called Hilda Rodl. It's been going for over fifty years. It was a performance group, basically around dance, that was available for anyone who had an interest. They used to do ballet classes, warm-ups and so forth, but I felt that was not what I wanted to be doing, which was probably a sort of paranoia about people thinking I was doing something a bit sissy. So I just turned up and did my stuff after the class.

So I hadn't done a dance class of any kind when I went to audition for Laban. I was self-taught until that point: watching performances, copying from videos, from other people. I never thought in terms of technique or even warming up: I just observed and did it.

Frankly, I wouldn't have got into anywhere except the Laban Centre in those days. It's interesting: I remember that three of the Laban Centre

2 Bourne and Emma Gladstone performing for Transitions Dance Company in 1986 in Ashley Page's *The Organizing Principle.*

students who went on to bigger things, Lea Anderson, Catherine White (now Catherine Malone), and John Heath (later Jacob Marley), had all been rejected by The Place, if not also by other dance centres. We all knew, or came to know, that the technical standards at Laban auditions were lower; and yet we wanted to prove ourselves. Later on, curiously, things changed so much that, in the mid-1990s, the positions were almost exactly reversed. The Laban Centre reached the stage of only accepting girls with perfect bodies, while it was The Place who started to let in people with less than perfect techniques who had some basic enthusiasm driving them. Things have changed again since then; audition criteria never remain fixed for long.

AM: *You passed the audition. Were you advised to do training before you began the course?*
MB: No, nothing like that was said! There were only a few months between doing the audition and starting the course. David Massingham and I were the first people in our borough – Waltham Forest – to get a grant to do dance: probably the last as well, I should imagine;

but one of the reasons I got it was that, at that time, I was still putting on shows. The council got whoever was the most prominent in the borough in dance to adjudicate – she was a dancing teacher, and she'd come along to see one of my shows – and that's what I was judged on, and how I got the grant.

Particularly because it was Laban, I expressed a lot of interest in choreography when I auditioned. In the interview, I was asked what I'd seen most recently that I'd liked. Well, I just reeled off tons of things. So I think they were probably quite impressed by my interest. I don't think it was my marvellous dancing that got me in there! I can't imagine what I looked like.

AM: *The Laban Centre for Movement and Dance had moved to New Cross, in South East London, late in the 1970s, and has steadily expanded its premises and its scope since then. Certain crucial aspects of the work of its founder, Rudolf Laban, were maintained on all courses, but Dr Marion North, who had become its director during the 1970s, had developed the Centre in several new directions, and has continued to do so. There are former Laban students today who are still shocked by the fact that, under Marion North, the Centre began, in the 1970s, to embrace any teaching of dance technique or formal choreographic disciplines.*

Another new direction was North's establishment of the first British BA course in dance. It was, to be precise, a BA (Hons) course in Dance Theatre. I began to teach dance history there in 1980, a term before the first intake of BA students graduated. You began your course in September 1982, and yours was the fifth year of students to take it.

After graduating, you spent one further year in Transitions, the Centre's course for dance graduates preparing to become professional dancers. This, too, was a young course; yours was the third year of Transitions.

This was four years of intense study – yet you say that, hitherto, you'd never enjoyed schoolwork. What had changed?

MB: I enjoyed the course, first of all, because it was my choice to go there. I didn't feel any more that I was doing something I was obliged to do. And secondly, the subject – dance – just inspired me. Even when some of the teachers weren't inspiring, I was enthusiastic. I remember enjoying lectures: the guest lecturers, too. Do you remember Svetlana

Beriosova coming down to coach parts of *Swan Lake*? That was a major thrill.

AM: *Throughout that time, you were developing your technique as a choreographer. Looking back, to what degree do you now think that choreography can be taught? What do you think you learnt from a formal study of choreography? What do you wish you had learnt? What else do you wish might be taught to choreographers that might have been useful?*

MB: There are certain things I feel I did learn. Some just sparked off the imagination a bit; and I was fascinated by certain ideas we studied that other choreographers had formed, like Doris Humphrey's ideas about space and important areas of the stage. I still remember some of those things: where the strong points of the stage were, where the focal points were, and the travelling pathways that were the most prominent and registered the most. And the actual setting of choreographic tasks to do: obviously, I'd never done that before. To try to get to the essence of one idea by having a task set for you to do – you know, a solo that was purely using one idea – would concentrate my ideas and imagination. I think now that all those things help a student to find things that maybe are already there. What you can't teach is ideas; or imagination.

I don't think that you can teach choreography, but you can teach structures, and ideas, and ways of making movement: all the sorts of processes that you can go through to build the phrase. To me, all those kinds of things were very useful, and I still find myself using them. For example, reversing movement. Or, for another example, limiting what the body can do. Something I still use now is to isolate the upper and lower halves of the body; make one person work on the top half, another on the legs; then try to put those two separate products together, and see what happens. These processes sometimes come up with interesting results.

What is most valuable, I suppose, is enquiring about and developing movement. Of course, at Laban that went hand in hand with a lot of other things – ballet classes, modern-dance classes, movement study, history, music and other courses – but purely in terms of studying choreography, those are some of the things that I derived from it.

There was no one choreography teacher that influenced me in particular. The whole ethos was very much influenced by Bonnie Bird, and I do remember – indeed, have used during the 1990s – some of the things she'd say. Since she had danced with Martha Graham in the early 1930s and then had been Merce Cunningham's first 'proper' teacher in the late 1930s, it was exciting to come across her. But in my time she was moving into semi-retirement; she only spent six months of the year in Britain. No doubt as a result of her influence almost all my other choreography teachers at Laban were American; I would say that I learnt from all of them, or just from the whole discipline as it was being developed there. But I was hungry to learn. I liked the whole idea of studying choreography – of studying dance – just fascinated me.

Still, I've always thought that I learned more from watching choreography than from taking choreography classes. Studying choreography did lead me towards a certain amount of information; but I think that the more you watch great choreography, the more you learn from it. Even subconsciously: in fact, I always try to watch pieces for pleasure, rather than try to analyse them in any way.

I was lucky enough then to be seeing a fair number of works regularly in the theatre, seeing things again and again. And that's how they sink in. When I first see a piece, I tend to watch purely for enjoyment; even now. I'm not looking for things within; the first time I watch a dance, I just come away with an impression. But of course, the more you see a piece, the more you get from it. I wish I did that more now – watch a piece repeatedly – because I don't see works often enough for information or ideas to go in. It's always on second viewing that you really start to see; or so it is for me.

AM: *What about the degree to which you were required to keep notebooks on your own choreography and all that? Was that useful? Was that instructive?*

MB: Not always: because you felt sometimes that you couldn't – shouldn't – put a dance idea into words. That was the problem: trying to put into words something in movement. Sometimes it would spoil your idea: putting in black and white what you were trying to say in movement. It made it seem less interesting. At other times, however, that same requirement helped you really get to the essence of what it was you were doing.

But academically the Laban BA was an extremely taxing course at that time. Gruelling, too. I'm sure it's changed a lot now. When I hear of what other people have done at other colleges now to get a degree!

. . . For us, the combination of practical and academic work was enormous, especially as we were rehearsing things as well. Often all of us would be up all night writing one essay assignment or another. We'd be just sitting there in our kitchen in Tanners Hill, with coffees, trying to finish these essays, because we'd been rehearsing till nine in the evening and we still had written work to do for some deadline in the morning. We would do it together, to try to help each other get through it. But that was very bonding; we were in the same boat.

Still, those were fairly early days for degree-course dance studies. There was a great deal of emphasis on the academic and written side – to justify dance as an academic subject, and to justify ours as an academic course.

AM: *Are there academic – non-practical – subjects that you think are useful in such a course? I don't mean ones that you enjoyed; I mean ones that are useful to a choreographer.*
MB: In theory, most of what we did could be useful. Certainly we had drama classes, which was good, because very few places will do that. I think the notation is not of great interest or use to a choreographer. No choreographer I know uses a formal notation system, either Laban's or any other. That's a specialist area that I think we could have done without.

Movement analysis – movement study, it was called – obviously can help you see what you've done. That was a core subject at Laban, because it was central to Rudolf Laban's own work with dance and movement. I regarded it as an extension of choreography, really. But I don't have much to say about it now; I'm not aware of applying it.

Music we studied, in a very small way really: about once a week during the first half of the course. But that certainly helped me to do what I do now in terms of counts: in terms of the little notation that I make – my own system! – when I'm working on a piece. I remember once having to set a rhythmic pattern from *The Rite of Spring*, having to choreograph to that series of counts: that made you listen to music in a different way. Very important.

AM: *Did you learn to read a musical score?*
MB: No. That was taught up to a point, but it didn't really go in. Certain things I've remembered from it and have used in my own little notation; but I've borrowed things from that – stresses and accelerations – so I did learn something there that I've gone on to use.

AM: *You were taught choreography; and you were taught music. But how important was dancing to music as a part of your choreographic course? I ask, because in the world of modern dance – certainly at that time – there has been such a strong tradition of dancing without music.*

MB: A lot of what we did early on in the course was entirely without music. Most of the 'studies' that we had to do were in silence. They were, I suppose, trying to get to the essence of movement; trying not to bring in any musical aspect until later on. I do remember doing some short solos to music, but I don't remember any serious discussion about musical values in choreography or about whether a dance worked for the music it was set to. And I still feel that a lot of the choreography I see is set to music that – it feels – you could do virtually anything to. Either the music has a steady rhythm that never changes; or it's atmosphere music that feels as if you could dance right over it perfectly easily.

I don't remember being taught how to fit movement to music.

AM: *Was that something you learned for yourself?*

MB: Yes. Dance for me is – more and more – about the relationship between movement and music. I don't mind that modern-dance students are taught how to dance and choreograph without music; I do mind that they are taught little, if anything, about the connections between dance and music, between choreography and music. There are so many subtleties to be learnt, so many issues to be discussed: What music can or can't be choreographed to? What style of movement can suit which music? What sort of dance phrasing or dynamics will complement this or that musical phrasing or dynamics? Almost everyone in professional dance talks about this a great deal, and almost every choreographer concerns himself or herself with it all the time. But we weren't encouraged to think analytically about that at college; and I suspect that many – modern and ballet – students still aren't.

You know this already; but it's true that the most important thing, for me, was my interest in dance history. Learning more about that was very important to me. I feel that I've always involved dance history to some greater or lesser extent in what I've done on stage.

AM: *Were you interested in dance history before the course?*

MB: Yes. I'd started to be interested about two years before. I'd begun to read a lot of dance biographies: Buckle's *Nijinsky* and *Diaghilev*,

Taper's *Balanchine* . . . And books about the early Royal Ballet – the Vic-Wells Ballet, then the Sadler's Wells Ballet – and about Robert Helpmann and Margot Fonteyn. You see, whatever dance I'd be watching at the time would trigger me on to reading anything about it I could lay my hands on.

I also think that my musical education started when I started watching ballet. I had no knowledge of, or interest in, classical music before that point. I don't think I owned any recordings. I was into film music and into certain singers of jazz, swing, musicals: always a bit retro, never very current, just people I particularly liked – like Ella Fitzgerald. When I started to see ballets, I would grow to love the music, and I would go out and buy recordings of it. Then that would sometimes lead me to try listening to more works by the same composer. But most of my musical interest is led by ballet: not just music written for ballet, but concert music that ballet choreographers have used too. That's why I still don't have a great knowledge of some major composers that are not often used for dance – Bach, Haydn, Mozart, Beethoven – because not even Balanchine has choreographed much to their music.

So my musical taste is mostly formed by the Royal Ballet repertory, and by what has derived from that. Obviously my taste has gone on growing since that first exposure to the Royal; but that was my way into classical music. I do think that my interest in the past has always fed the work that I've done.

AM: *Do you think, though, that dance history is generally of use to a would-be choreographer? Would you recommend it?*
MB: I would think that some study of dance history is a necessity for a choreographer of classical ballet: in that genre, with such a tradition, such a legacy and such a repertory, to know where you're coming from is particularly important. But I also think that any choreographer should be interested in what's gone before. Plenty of modern-dance people feel that there's no point in learning about the long-distant past and, in particular, about the ballet past. No doubt dance history could be made to seem irrelevant to current dance practice. But to me it seemed very relevant.

I found that a formal study of history gave me a wider sense of dance practice. Even learning about long-dead ballerinas and long-extinct ballets interested me – because I was learning more about how dances and dancers had worked. As a choreographer, that knowledge can widen your options. It liberates you to hear how famous dances were made; to look at the great choreographers not as icons but as artists-in-the-making, and at the great masterpieces not as shrines but as works-in-progress; to get deeper into their methods.

People are so busy being contemporary and being innovative that they don't see how the past can be useful. Yet it can be a revelation. It allows you to develop your own way.

AM: *Was dance history the only area where you were encouraged to consider narrative seriously? Particularly in modern dance, particularly in the early 1980s, narrative was very unfashionable. It was regarded as impure, outmoded.*

MB: In general, yes. I do remember that once, in our choreography course, we were asked to make short solos in the character of some historical figure or other. Of course, most of the women chose to be Joan of Arc! I chose to be Nijinsky in the asylum; it was a memory dance in which I worked in images from his dance past. All very short; it must have been a two-minute solo. But otherwise we were strongly encouraged to avoid narrative, and, while at Laban, I tried to proceed along the approved lines more or less. I realize now that I was always drawn to narrative, but it needed time. I needed to accept what were my own strengths.

Even so, I was always thinking along some historical lines or other. The group piece I choreographed in my second year – the first you saw of mine – was pure 1930s. Then, in the third year, our Christmas entertainment, 'BA IIIs on Broadway', which was largely but not entirely my work, came out of Busby Berkeley movies – I used his music – and took choreographic ideas from the repertory I knew, like the Chosen Maiden being passed along the heads of everyone in MacMillan's *Rite of Spring*.

Dance history would have been the only place in which I was encouraged to analyse narrative seriously. Probably that helped what I do now, but I wasn't thinking of using narrative then. History for me was just a very good way of learning more about dance qualities and about choreography.

AM: *One part of your course was also aesthetics. Was that in the least use to a choreographer?*

MB: We did dance aesthetics throughout the three years; and a sub-section of that course was the two-term course in dance criticism – which

Choreography   1   Matthew Bourne BA
         5   June 1984
          FOR Dale and Bonnie

STIMULUS

I have long been fascinated by the few remaining photographs and drawings of Nijinsky's ballet "Jeux" (1913). I thought that I could use these groupings as a starting point for a choreographic study. The scenario of the original ballet is also a source of inspiration and could after certain changes be followed quite closely to its original form. It should be understood that I do not want to attempt to recreate the choreography of Nijinsky which has been completely lost, but to take the situation described in the scenario, and develop it in my own way, taking ideas from the few photographs that exist of the work and the six pastels by Valentine Gross, drawn at the time.

great

RESEARCH

The scenario, as described in Richard Buckle's book NIJINSKY, is very simple:-

3 From Bourne's BA course; choreographic coursework, 1984. The photograph, by Gerschel, is of Vaslav Nijinsky's ballet *Jeux* (1913). Nijinsky (centre) partners Tamara Karsavina and Ludmila Schollar.

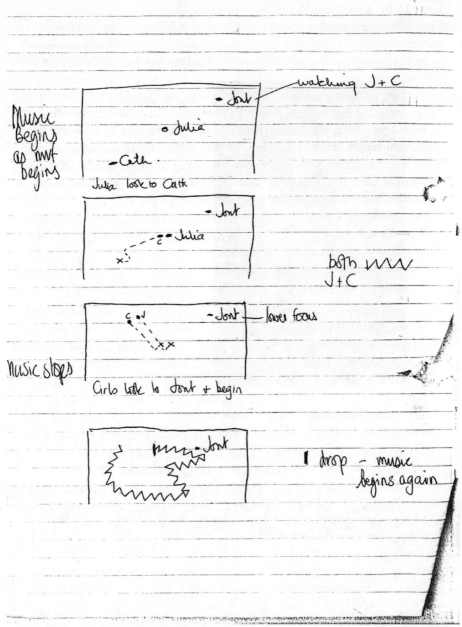

4 From Bourne's choreographic notebooks, 1984/85. *Ears to the Ground*, developed as an idea from Nijinsky's *Jeux*, was made for fellow BA students Catherine White, Julia Clarke and Jonathan Thrift.

you taught. And I would say, looking back now, that that was the first time I began to think critically about why a dance might be good or bad: to think about criteria. Until then, my instinct had been just to go to as many shows as possible, hoping that I would love most of them. That course encouraged us to look for pure-dance values in narrative works, for narrative values in plotless works, and to become more formally aware of our values. In my case, it did help me, in the long run, to look at my own work analytically. Also you showed us a variety of important dance works on video, as you did in history, and some of those made a lasting impression. So, for example, when I made *Spitfire* in 1988, I used one grouping idea from Balanchine's *Serenade*. Now that was a work I had only seen because you showed it to us.

Otherwise, no, I don't specially remember anything coming from all that aesthetics now. Yet I do remember at the time being interested in most of the things I was doing. I was just very interested in a subject – dance – that was so new to me, and that was taken so seriously. At the time I lapped it all up.

AM: *There was no particular area where you thought, 'This is a waste of my time'?*
MB: I never really took to 'Improv' – dance improvisation. There was a certain pretentious edge to the way we were encouraged to approach improvisatory movement that I didn't like. We would be set a task around which to improvise with movement. It could stem from a painting, for example; and I would find it futile to express this painting in movement. At the time I was watching a lot of very structured choreography in the theatre, so I just found this aimless.

I like intentional presentation of work. I've never been keen on chance things. That's why I've never been keen – as a general idea for dance theatre – on the Cunningham–Cage practice of making music and movement so independent of each other that they are only thrown together at the last minute. I recognize, of course, that sometimes, with Merce Cunningham himself, it has, in the event, worked beautifully. But by no means always; and I certainly think it's a very dodgy method for any other choreographer to use. Also I like an audience to be where it should be; I like the performance to be totally rehearsed, and nothing improvised. But the dance-theatre experiments of the 1960s and subsequent decades – all the experimental use of improvisation, of non-collaboration, of non-theatrical performance space, of making an audience move around or making a dance work impossible for the whole audience to see entirely – were held up in the early 1980s as exciting in modern-dance circles. And you know what? They still are. People still think it's so wonderful, and quite original, to work that way. A friend told me how exciting it had been the other night to see a piece that had been put on at King's Cross Station. You know: 'It's so much fun watching the public react to these dancers falling on the floor in the railway station.' But that kind of thing's been done a million times! Anyway, I just thought, 'Well, I can't think of anything worse.' I really do like to know the audience is there to watch, that there's a proscenium or some division between stage and audience, that this is the performance that has been rehearsed, and that this is what we intend to show the audience.

Obviously, you do use improvisation when you choreograph. You're improvising all the time when you're trying to come up with movement. You're trying to find things. But there's a specific goal there: you're aiming to end up with something concrete. That's why you're improvising. But in 'Improv' – as an area of study in itself – I felt that everything that had been created was lost straightaway. I didn't take to that.

AM: *What about dance vocabulary: how did your formal study at the Laban Centre enlarge, or change, your choice of movement?*
MB: I was studying lots of different techniques. That must have helped. The modern-dance techniques we studied included those developed by leading American choreographers: (Martha) Graham, (Merce) Cunningham, (Lester) Horton, (José) Limòn, (Alwin) Nikolais. Others, too. There was such a turnover of different teachers at Laban, that we had a lot of different dance styles going into our education. That was one of the very good things about the course. We never got to be great at any one particular technique; but at least we learnt to be adaptable and versatile. So, when you finally left the Centre, you could choose the technique that you knew felt best for you.

The ballet staff were varied as well. We were never really stuck with one ballet teacher for any long stretch. That, too, was a good thing.

AM: *Were there any particular styles that you found useful or congenial to your body?*
MB: I certainly didn't take to the Graham technique. It involves a particular amount of work on the floor. When I started it, I was twenty-

two, and my body just couldn't handle those extremes – in particular, the second positions on the floor. My weight was always too far back. I could never get my weight forwards on to my legs in the second position on the floor – which a lot of the movement required. So I was in a constant state of agony, trying to keep my weight forwards. And I think that that did permanent damage to my back. I've always had lower back problems since then.

I liked the drama of the Graham technique: the feeling. I admired its structure, too. But I couldn't do a lot of it successfully, and I really think it did me no good at all.

The one that I really enjoyed was the Cunningham technique. Partly because it had elements of ballet in it. Also because it had a formal structure – but one that I could do. I felt that I enjoyed both the look and the feel of it as well. I enjoyed its use of the back. The fact that it was upright, standing most of the time, was something that always appealed to me – because the fact that I wasn't very loose gave me problems on the floor. The Cunningham technique made me feel that I was a dancer. I liked what I saw in the mirror, when I was doing it. And it was a strong – strengthening – technique, whereas some other techniques felt a bit experimental, without building up any strength in you.

I also enjoyed the Limòn style. It gave you a greater sense of physical freedom, while also being grounded in a strong basis of technique.

What I now hate are classes where the movement is all about rolling around on the floor and getting in touch with your sacrum and all that waffle. There's a worrying stream of teachers and dancers, at the moment particularly, that have made all that very popular; and yet it's so wishy-washy. It's all about how it feels rather than how it looks. Nice to do – but dull to watch. I value those techniques – Cunningham, Limòn and Graham (if only it was better for my body) – where you can see the design, the form, in the movement. Where, in terms of pure movement, you can feel choreographic interest.

AM: *Twenty-two is pretty late to do your first ballet class. How did you find ballet suited your body?*
MB: I always felt that I had all the feeling but none of the technique! I used to enjoy doing it because I loved it musically; I responded to it. But I wasn't that brilliant at it, obviously, coming to it so late. I was always very disappointed in my assessments for it, the low marks I was

given, because I always felt that I did have a feeling for it; but not, I recognize, enough technique. I also enjoyed it, of course, because I was watching a lot of it on stage. So I knew what I was aiming for.

AM: *Did you ever feel you were trying to be something you weren't?*
MB: At college, definitely; particularly on the choreography course. I suppose, on any course, you try to please; and maybe I learnt from that. Still, at times I would try to do something for myself, and I was aware that some of my choices were frowned upon by certain choreography teachers. They wanted me to get more contemporary. That kind of reaction continued into the first years of Adventures in Motion Pictures. People – not least my former teachers – would say, 'Oh, when are you going to do something really new? When are you going to have something set in the present? When are you going to use new music?'

AM: *Now, your years at Laban were among the early years of Dance Umbrella. This festival of experimental dance, modern dance, post-modern dance, new dance, had had its first season in 1978; your first term at Laban coincided with the fourth Dance Umbrella. It's hard to explain now just how each Umbrella – occurring in such spaces as Riverside Studios, the ICA and The Place – opened British eyes in those years to new ideas of dance: to both the most radical local ideas and the most striking new work from abroad.*

But I very well remember that, for many Laban students, as for many other dance-goers, taking in some of the more way-out dance work was a difficult and sometimes infuriating part of their dance training. What are your memories?
MB: We used to have 'educational visits', as they were called; and I used to be our year's rep for them, which involved organizing the trips. I remember people creating such a fuss when we went to see Steve Paxton and Kei Takei. Certainly it made for a lot of discussion as to why we didn't like it, and whether this was dance. People were very angry and worked up about it.

AM: *What dance made you angry?*
MB: Steve Paxton I would still get angry about now. No, I don't get angry, but I just really have no interest in that kind of work. It may have involved some contact improvisation – that's what he was famous for – but what I remember is him working with a plank and a plastic carrier bag. No dance movement that I recall. That was the worst one,

the one where half our group wanted to walk out; and some of them did, in the middle of it, in a very obvious way. Kei Takei had something going for her; but her work involved a lot of props – stones and pine cones and things – and that's all that I remember now. Those are the main two that I remember being a big problem for everyone.

It takes you a long time to identify satisfactorily the kind of work that you don't like, and the reasons why. Most people in our group found that – by their third year – they were enjoying work they would have loathed in their first year. For some of them, that included ballet at the one extreme, as well as radical work at the other.

For me, I came to realize that the reason for like or dislike in dance has mostly to do with music and the use of music.

AM: *Two important small British companies at that time – promoted by Dance Umbrella but also performing in London at other points during the year – were Extemporary Dance Theatre and Second Stride. I mention them with particular pieces in mind.*

Extemporary had been founded in the 1970s; it closed at the end of the 1980s. But in 1983 it enjoyed a certain peak, during which one of the pieces it performed was Fergus Early's Naples. *This was an ironic update of August Bournonville's nineteenth-century Romantic ballet* Napoli *– using much of its music and some of its choreography, while also comically giving us aspects of the scruffy Naples of today. I wonder if that example of taking material from a period repertory ballet and looking at it from a modern ironic perspective made any impression upon you?*

MB: I'd forgotten that piece completely, but, now that you mention it, I remember enjoying it very much. I don't remember it being a version of *Napoli*. But the modernity of it seemed quite daring; and it was funny. It was costumed, it had a set, and the performers were all very much individuals with their own personalities. All that really stuck.

Extemporary was, for me at the time, the most exciting British company – along with Second Stride, which I think I discovered a little bit later on. I think that's the kind of company that we wanted to be when we started AMP in 1986. Extemporary was a model.

I remember them doing a residency at Laban, and creating solos that we were involved in watching and that they talked about. One of their dancers, Annelies Stoffel, had graduated from the Laban BA course in 1981, which was inspiring for all of us. In those days, nobody was sure if a BA graduate could make it as a professional dancer in Britain. Also, at that time, it was the whole idea of a rep company that we liked the idea of.

AM: *Second Stride had begun as a dance group in 1982 as another contemporary-dance repertory company, combining work by Richard Alston, Siobhan ('Sue') Davies, and Ian Spink. Since 1986, it has been entirely a group that reassembles for new projects by Spink.[1] But you began watching it in the period when Davies was still choreographing for it.*

There are two Second Stride pieces of that era that I would connect to your work, and one of them is her Carnival. *She made this first in 1982 to Saint-Saens's* Carnival of the Animals; *and its most successful dance, to the music we always know now as the Dying Swan music, was a solo for a male swan – although it was a multi-layered solo, in which he also gestured at playing the cello (as in the music) and at being a human making 'swan' silhouettes with his hand and arm.*

MB: *Carnival* was quite influential for me. Simply in its use of a piece of mainstream classical music, and in just being animals but in a very inventive, witty and simple way.

I also remember her *Plainsong* from that time, a very pure piece to Satie music. I really enjoyed the purity of that. Sue was dancing in it as well, which made a powerful impression. Her work then had a sort of peaceful quality; and that work had almost the simplicity and peaceful beauty of Ashton's *Symphonic Variations*. There was a wonderful feeling of community in it, I felt, even though it wasn't really about anything. I've still got it on video, as I have *Carnival*, so I remember them both better than some other pieces that I may also have loved at the time but have since forgotten.

AM: *I also want to ask you about one piece by Ian Spink, which I remember you watching:* Further and Further into Night, *which was – I think it's safe to say – a deconstruction of the Hitchcock film* Notorious. *It didn't retell the story of* Notorious; *it just took incidents, atmosphere and values, from that film, and put them together in a highly ironic, non-narrative, very imaginative way. Nobody at that time had ever made a dance based on a film – certainly not on a thriller. But in 1992 you made your own non-narrative Hitchcock piece,* Deadly Serious. *I presume there's a connection.*

1 Late in 1998, Second Stride folded. A.M.

MB: I actually went to a performance in 1985 at the ICA where they showed *Further and Further* and then *Notorious*. But I think I'd already seen the piece once before, during Dance Umbrella 1984. I very much liked it; and I can't pretend that our own Hitchcock piece wasn't partly triggered by it, by wanting to do something like that.

I also think some of Spink's methods of choreography have influenced me. In that piece and others he used both repetition (repetition of individual movements, of short sub-phrases) and a particular way of working with character.

Second Stride was a great model for us as a company, because it too felt like a company of strong people: strongly individual, characterful dancers.

AM: *The mid-1980s was a period when you could see the work of certain British choreographers in the repertories of more than one British company. Sue Davies was choreographing not just for Second Stride (then later for her own dance company), but also for London Contemporary Dance Theatre. And Richard Alston, who'd been one of the founders of Second Stride, was the resident choreographer of the Rambert. The Rambert had three 'house' choreographers: Christopher Bruce, Robert North and Alston. There was also a wonderful period, in 1983, when it staged two pieces by Frederick Ashton: a revival of his 1930 'Capriol Suite' and a staging of his 1975–6 Five Brahms Waltzes in the Manner of Isadora Duncan.*

MB: I loved all that period at Rambert. It felt that it was nodding to history. To see the mixture of very early Ashton work with Alston's current work was very exciting. You wished that there could be more companies like that, doing that variety of rep. And I just enjoyed a lot of the work that the Rambert was doing around that time.

AM: *What seemed more interesting to you about the Rambert than about London Contemporary Dance Theatre at that time?*

MB: Design. Variety of work. And the Rambert felt modern; London Contemporary somehow felt a little bit behind it, very conventionally 'modern-dance'.

AM: *At the Rambert in the early 1980s, were you interested in the work of Christopher Bruce? In 1993, he took charge of the Rambert again, whereas Alston and Davies now choreograph almost entirely for their own companies.*

MB: I did like Christopher Bruce at one point. I was into pieces like *Ghost Dances*, *Berlin Requiem* and *Cruel Garden*, because they're very theatrical. But then there's a folksy side to him that I don't like much.

Richard Alston's work I used to admire a lot. It felt like modern ballet to me. It felt like the future of the ballet – although it wasn't on pointe or anything – but it had a classical feeling to it. It also felt as if he was trying to emulate something that had been going on in early ballet, early British ballet anyway. That's why the Ashton–Alston connection was so interesting to observe, especially when Alston made a ballet in late 1983 for the Royal Ballet at Covent Garden too. His work also felt in the Diaghilev spirit too, because he commissioned designs from painters a lot and because he used new music. For me, admittedly, new music was a bit of a problem from time to time; but I understood that that was a great passion for him. I also thought, 'Someone's got to do it; to use new music', and he always showed that he was the one.

I was talking to friends the other night about this, saying that what you always saw with Alston, Davies and Bruce was that they really knew how to make dance, how to make phrases of movement that work; and you wholly admired the dance-making aspect of what they did. Nobody else has come along in Britain since then who has made pure dance with that kind of authority. They themselves are still working that way. In a way, their work has stayed where it was.

AM: *So when you see their work now, does it seem old-fashioned? Or does it seem a tonic?*
MB: Well, I wish I was more like that. You know, for Richard and for Sue, ultimately their love is movement; and movement invention; and creating movement. But I'm coming from somewhere else. The first thing that I have is all the other stuff – the ideas – and the last thing is the movement.

For Richard in particular, the movement just comes out of the movement of the music. I wish I could work that way – but put my ideas with it. Finding the movement is more of a struggle for me, whereas it seems to flow out of those people. And Sue has done interesting things with design in recent years. There's always interest in the way her works are staged. The lighting and the originality of the design, a lot of the time, have helped to keep her work looking very up-to-date. I also feel that she seems to have moved with something that is going on in dance at the moment. Whether you like it or not is another matter, but she has moved somewhere; I don't always feel that with Richard's work in the 1990s, although I've missed some of it. Sue's certainly does strike a chord with the way people enjoy moving now.

AM: *Another person who made a big impact on the British dance world in the 1980s was Michael Clark. Did you look at his work?*
MB: We were all very interested in Michael Clark, because he was big news at the time. He was a big dance star, and young. He was a discussion point for everyone. You either loved him or hated him.

AM: *Why would you have loved him or hated him?*
MB: Well, everyone loved his dancing and the look of him. His dancing was incredibly beautiful. I only started to watch him about 1983 or so, when he was an independent dancer, after his training with the Royal Ballet School and after his time with Ballet Rambert. And – the same has been said many times, I know – the reason to go to see his own choreography was to see the sections when he was dancing. I can't say all the stuff that surrounded it appealed to me at all: the punkish music, the dildos and bare bottoms, swallowing a goldfish – the shock values. I've never actually been into shock tactics in any way. I don't like being in an uncomfortable audience very much; I like the audience to be happy with what they're watching. And it didn't feel particularly shocking to me. It felt juvenile. I mean, I was older than other people at college. I know that I make use of some juvenile humour at times myself, but Clark's didn't really interest me. I found his work sexy, daring and exciting. But it didn't have any effect on me – and I hated the music.

AM: *During this period you carried on looking at the Royal Ballet.*
MB: Yes, and this was when I first saw Ashton's *Scènes de ballet*; and later, *Symphonic Variations*. I absolutely adored them. I think any young British choreographer would love looking at *Scènes de ballet* again and again: it's brilliantly made, and it's full of really surprising movement, even though it's a perfectly classical pure-dance ballet. I wished I could choreograph like that. But it shows such odd things! I love the entrance of the female corps de ballet when they come in, on pointe, but leaning right forwards from the waist, with their arms stretched behind them and upwards. They're in profile to the audience

and the way they lean forwards – like chickens! – is so strange. If you
see that when you're first learning to choreograph, as I was, it makes
you want to try something that isn't the first thing that comes into
your head, to go against the norm. It seemed a really daring piece to
me, and very exciting. Not something that I could ever do myself, but
something that I could take ideas from.

And *Symphonic* I loved as soon as I first saw it. I remember how
David Massingham and other people that I was around at the time all
had pictures of it on their walls. It was so perfect. The whole work has
a wonderful tranquillity and peace about it. And there's a section of it,
in the middle, that's so dreamlike: it's performed to a piano section,
and it feels as if everyone's floating on air. Certainly I can't think of
another piece that has the same sort of hold-your-breath perfection
about it – where you feel you haven't taken a breath the whole way
through it. Again, I can't see that it has had a direct influence on me,
but I think there's something there that you want to try to emulate.
Just the thought of it is inspiring.

Ashton was already in semi-retirement then, but there were a number of important revivals of his work. At the time it seemed like too
few, though by current standards it seems as if we were seeing Ashton
revivals all the time. I was very excited and interested in anything of
his I could see in those days. The revival of his *Romeo* in 1985; later
on, in 1988, the revival of his *Ondine*. And he was still making a few
new pieces in those days: just small pieces, but I'd always rush along to
see them. I particularly remember *Varii Capricci* in 1983, with Antoinette Sibley and Anthony Dowell dancing the leads, and with designs by
David Hockney. I was in love with those two dancers at the time, and I
liked the fact that it was a star vehicle for them. It was interesting that
it was set in the modern world, although I remember thinking it was a
little bit like an old man's view of a young world. The character Dowell played was a bit clichéd, with Elvis Presley hair and dark glasses.
Maybe that would have worked better with younger dancers, but at
that time they were both near the end of their careers.

AM: *Meanwhile, throughout this period, we were getting a fairly regular supply of ballets by Kenneth MacMillan, who was, I suppose, the
dominant British choreographer of that time. And against whom a lot
of people were reacting, because he was the storytelling, psychological,
expressionist choreographer of the period. Many people found that*

there was just too little dance content in his work. Other people were excited by the fact that he was, at any rate, still trying to shake up the conventional ballet audience. How did all of that affect you? And which ballets made an impression?

MB: Michael Clark was trying to shock through his dildos and things, whereas I thought Kenneth MacMillan's *Valley of Shadows* actually very shocking, but in the right way – because of its subject matter: depicting a concentration camp, and the gradual elimination of the Jews from their previously idyllic pre-war world. It was based on *The Garden of the Finzi Continis*. The ballet zigzagged between the garden and the concentration camp, with alternating music. Someone would be taken away from the garden, then you saw him or her in the concentration camp, and gradually the whole family ended up there. It was the destruction of a family. Well, when that was new, in 1982, it did show that MacMillan was still alive and kicking in no uncertain terms. I thought it was very powerful.

AM: *Did you see his full-length ballet* Isadora?

MB: *Isadora* was very, very influential for me. I must have seen it first around the time of its premiere in 1981, and I saw several performances of it. As soon as it was broadcast, I had it on video. What impressed me was that it felt like an original way of telling a story on the ballet stage – using words, which I've never done. I applauded MacMillan's right to do that. I loved certain sections of it; the sexiness of it really appealed to me then.

It was the first time I had ever seen Isadora Duncan depicted on stage. At that time, I hadn't seen the Isadora dances that Ashton had made, originally with Lynn Seymour. So I enjoyed the style of MacMillan's recreation of Isadora's movement very much. That way of moving to music, expressing music, which was the basis of her style of free dance . . . I've always found the idea of it – the idea of Isadora – exciting, and inspiring, and that was my first exposure to it.

AM: *Were you ever bothered by what people called the faults of these MacMillan ballets, their deficiencies?*

MB: Which were . . . ?

AM: *The thin movement. The constant, expressionistic effort to communicate a psychological or sociological point without giving you much to go by in terms of dance.*

MB: It's true that those pieces don't bear many viewings, but I don't think their weaknesses concerned me enormously at the time. I was very impressed by them as pieces of theatre. I can't fault MacMillan's desire to do what he was doing in choreography, and to look for psychological interest. What he was trying to do was very valid.

AM: *Now, towards the end of your BA course at Laban, I introduced you – at a Fred-and-Ginger film actually – to Ashley Page, who was moving also in an experimental direction. He was then a young Royal Ballet dancer who'd just started to grow up in a new way. He'd always danced in almost everybody else's new ballet, so he'd obviously been a very willing volunteer for everybody else's choreographic experiments there. Suddenly, like you, he was discovering all the other dance that was going in London. One would always see him in audiences – at Dance Umbrella, the Rambert, everywhere – at a time when it was extremely unusual to see any British ballet dancer at a non-ballet performance. Then, in 1984, he started to choreograph the Royal Ballet for the first time.*

When you two met, early in 1985, you straightaway became friends; and later that year he became interested in the work you and your colleagues were doing with Transitions. In fact, he choreographed for Transitions, which suddenly raised the national/international profile of that group.

MB: Actually, I got him that job. When we joined Transitions, one of the things we were asked was 'Who would you like to choreograph for you?' I said that I thought Ashley Page might be interested, if we asked him; and he was, because he hadn't done many professional pieces, and he was looking for more opportunities to choreograph. So we got the chance to work with him, which I was thrilled about. Emma Gladstone and I were the duet couple in his piece. He made a typically Ashley Page piece called *The Organizing Principle*. It was very mathematical – and organized in the way that only he can do. It also had within it many of the things that – when I look at it on video now – he's been doing ever since: taking classical movement and positions and putting them off on angles, for example. And the way he has the men manipulate the women in his pieces was, in essence, there, though in a very much simpler form. It's obviously gone through many stages of development and complexity now; but it was all there then, his way of wanting to present movement, and present women in particular. Mind you, in that piece he wanted Emma and me to resemble each other – we had to have the same boyish haircut, with gelled side parting!

AM: *Now, the two of you developed quite different choreographic styles and paths. He now choreographs maybe one piece per year for the Royal Ballet, usually a pure-dance non-narrative work in neo-classic style with some modern-dance elements. But you were good chums at that time, and took great interest in each other's work. Was that important for you?*

MB: Yes, it was. He was someone I'd liked very much as a dancer. I'd always found him very different from everyone else. He didn't smile, ever. And the Royal was a very smiley company, as most ballet companies are. He seemed like the odd one out. So when he started to choreograph for the Royal in 1984, I was already very interested in what he might do. And those first pieces he made I found very exciting. In his very first piece, *A Broken Set of Rules*, he used Michael Nyman music – which was very new and different at the time. Unfortunately, we've never stopped hearing it since! But at that time, to hear that sort of music at the Opera House, and to know that the orchestra were not happy about it – I thought it was exciting and bold on his part to do at all.

It was also exciting that he chose the younger members of the company to be in his work. So his work felt like the youth of the company expressing itself. And I did enjoy the piece very much. There was a purity about it, and it was obvious that he was doing something different with classical form.

Obviously we were doing very different things. But we were very supportive of each other's work – and still are to a certain degree. I don't see him a lot now, but fairly recently I watched a rehearsal for his new piece for an hour or so, and we talked about it a bit afterwards. And he enjoyed my *Cinderella*. I think that in some ways it's easy to have a friendly relationship with another choreographer who's doing very different work from yours, because there's no sense of any kind of competition – which does seem to affect a lot of people when they become successful in any way. Each of us can still appreciate what the other one's doing. He's quite provocative at times in what he says, quite funny.

AM: *While you were on the BA course for those three years, you were part of a large group of dance students who all got to know each other*

*extremely well. Quite a number of them have stayed with dancing in
one capacity or another. Some of them have gone on to be professional
dancers, some of them professional choreographers, some of them
dance teachers. How important was that group to you and to your
own development?*

MB: Very important – partly just because we were helping each other
to get through something so arduous. But also we were talking constantly about dance, about choreography, about the work we'd seen. It
was easier, in some ways, to talk to your fellow-students about what
you felt than it was to express yourself to members of staff in an essay
– because you didn't want to appear stupid in writing about what you
felt. With the other students, you could suss things out, talk things
through.

Particularly after the BA course, when we got into Transitions, that
was very important. We were making work with other choreographers,
like Ashley, and also on each other – which our group particularly
made part of the course. So to talk about each other's work, and our
own work, and the work that was being made on us, and all the
dances that we were seeing elsewhere – that mattered a lot, and I have
very happy memories of how intent and absorbed we all were.

It may have happened once or twice since then that Transitions dancers choreographed themselves. But we presented a whole show of our
own work as well. We insisted that we did a programme of our own
work, as well as the one we'd been given. I don't think that's ever happened since.

The Transitions course was the first time that I felt people had faith
in me as a performer, that the Laban Centre thought I had some kind
of stage talent. Until then, I would never have dared think that way.

Even now, I still have doubts about whether I can actually do the
next thing; whether I can achieve what people think I should be doing.
I have the same doubts about where to go next that I've always had –
until I get the idea for the next piece. Once I get that, I take off with it.

3

First Adventures in Motion Pictures,
1987–1990

ALASTAIR MACAULAY: *How did you come to name your company Adventures in Motion Pictures?*

MATTHEW BOURNE: It's pure fluke that the name Adventures in Motion Pictures has become particularly attached to my work. People often say that it's a good name for the company's style and for what I do; and there's truth in that. Of all the people who founded AMP, I was the one with the greatest interest in films. But that is all coincidence.

The last date of our Transitions year was in Hong Kong. We had been dancing in a festival of dance academies from around the world, and were flying back home on China Airways. So this was the end of our course, we were about to form our own company, we were looking for a name, and the plastic bag that the headsets came in had written on them: 'Adventures in Motion Pictures'. It was some sort of translation that the airline thought made sense, but didn't quite; and Emma Gladstone said, 'Oh, let's call it that.'

'Adventures' was quite a nice word. It felt like *The Famous Five*; each new piece was an Adventure. And Motion Pictures: moving pictures, dance . . . People have put a lot of emphasis on the film connotation in recent years, but certainly we didn't set out to have any kind of filmic connection when we started.

Because Transitions toured a lot, some of us had begun to have the idea of forming a company together. We liked performing together, and we wanted to perform our own work; and the particular personalities in the group at that time were what helped to form AMP. From that start, Emma Gladstone was the one that got us thinking in a business way straightaway – which was very important. She really was the administrator of the company when we began, and was named as a fellow director.

There were seven of us in the original AMP: Catherine White (now Malone), Emma Gladstone, Susan Lewis, Carrollynne Antoun, David Massingham, Keith Brazil and I. Catherine, David and I had known each other for four years, having been on the BA course and then Transitions. Emma Gladstone and Susan Lewis had also joined Transitions after doing other courses at the Laban Centre. Then there were two other dancers who hadn't been with Transitions, but who had been students at Laban: Keith Brazil, who'd just finished the BA course the year after us, and Carrollynne Antoun, who'd done the three-year Dance Theatre course there. So we'd all known each other for some time.

AM: *You were following a year or two after the formation of the Cholmondeleys, a similarly Laban-originated company. Its founder-choreographer, Lea Anderson, had been a BA student a year ahead of you. Did you decide on any parameters to the company?*

5 Bourne as the Rt Hon Remnant Blight in Jacob Marley's *Does Your Crimplene Go All Crusty When You Rub?* (1987).

MB: We all felt at the time that there wasn't a lot of work around for either dancers or choreographers. The example of the Cholmondeleys gave us some courage and inspiration to continue doing our own work. Until then, we in Transitions had all been thinking, 'Well, what are the companies we can audition for?' Forming a company didn't occur to us for a long time – whereas nowadays it would occur quite quickly to people who are at college. The scene has changed so much in the last few years, thanks to the seasons at The Place and elsewhere. But in those days there wasn't that outlet, that hope.

We had a desire not just to work with ourselves, but with other choreographers as well. Basically it was a rep company that we were forming. There wasn't only one choreographer within the company. At least three of us wanted to choreograph: myself, David, Catherine expressed an interest in choreographing. Keith eventually choreographed; and both Emma and Susan did pieces during a workshop period we set up. Being a rep company would give us all the chance to make work if we wanted to, and also give us the chance to commission work from other choreographers. So the first AMP programme was made up of pieces by me, David, Julia Clarke (who'd been on our BA course, but hadn't joined Transitions) and John Heath (who performed under the name of Jacob Marley, and who had been a Laban student).

We formed the group in 1986, but the first performance was in July 1987. It began as an entirely Laban-originated group – more by accident than design – but that changed. Jo Chandler was the first dancer we took from elsewhere; and we started to use choreographers from elsewhere too. I remember approaching Russell Maliphant to ask him to consider making a piece on us. We did a piece by the French choreographer Brigitte Farges, chiefly memorable for the fact that Clement Crisp wrote in the *Financial Times* that we looked like 'the rugby team from Lesbos'. We also did a piece by Ben Craft, who had danced with the Rambert and was working as an independent.

AM: *How did you keep body and soul together in those days?*
MB: I had a part-time job at the National Theatre, where I'd worked for two years full-time before I started at Laban, and where I'd continued to work part-time while I was on the course – the odd evening – ushering and on the bookshop. Most of us were on something called the Enterprise Allowance Scheme, which was a government scheme by which, if you were working towards forming your own company, for a

year you'd be paid £40 a week, as well as your rent and some money to live on. That helped you achieve what you were aiming at, as long as you didn't earn a fortune during that time.

AM: *How did the company progress, in terms of success, between 1987 and 1990?*
MB: We were very lucky very early on, because we were involved in a couple of evenings which gave us great exposure to a lot of people in the dance world.

We had a piece by Jacob Marley called *Does Your Crimplene Go All Crusty When You Rub?*, which was extremely successful. It was actually the work that got us noticed as a company. A very odd piece, very much of his mind. All of us played characters based on people from his childhood, people he knew in the village where he grew up. He was an orphan, adopted, a black boy living in a West Country village; and we were all characters in the awful village-hall disco. It was misinterpreted quite a lot. Some people thought that we were making fun of old people with Parkinson's disease, and others thought it was about a mental institution; but there was never any intention that it should be like an old people's home. We were just all very odd characters – dancing to Mantovani, Abba and traditional Scottish music. It was very, very different from anything else around at that time.

We were all playing characters – for virtually the first time in any of the work any of us had ever danced. I loved doing that. I absolutely took to 'being' someone. You see, I had got to a point in dancing with Transitions where I never quite knew how to perform the pieces facially, because I was never given any indication as to what the mood was, or what I was supposed to be doing. I ended up being a version of myself, naturally, but I just felt uncomfortable, not really knowing how I was supposed to be projecting these pieces. So after I had to be a person in *Crimplene*, I never really wanted to do anything else!

The Laban Centre very kindly gave us the use of its studio theatre for our opening performance; they didn't charge us. For the first performance of this new company, we did a programme of rep. One was a piece by me called *Overlap Lovers*: a tango piece in three sections. One was a David Massingham piece – *Worlds Apart* I think it was called. One was a piece by Julia Clarke called *Grecian 2000* – Butoh-inspired, a quite odd, theatrical piece.

The *Crimplene* piece was noticed by a couple of people. As a result, we were asked to be in a one-off Dance Umbrella cabaret-style evening in October. The year before, Dance Umbrella had started a programme where they were able to show shorter works by several different performers or companies in a cabaret setting. That particular year, it was going to be the opening-night gala of Dance Umbrella 1987, a money-raising event. So, luckily for us, the audience was full of everybody in the British modern-dance world at the time. John Ashford, who ran seasons at The Place, a lot of the promoters from around the country, a lot of critics, a lot of dance bigwigs were there; and we went down very well. We were reviewed, briefly but quite favourably, by about three critics; and several promoters expressed interest in presenting us. So there we were! Very, very soon after starting our new company, we had people asking us to perform, rather than us trying to get dates – though we did that too, thanks largely to Emma.

Then, quite soon after that, in January 1988, we were asked again to do my *Overlap Lovers* piece in a gala at Sadler's Wells to mark ten years of Dance Umbrella – something to raise money for the next autumn's festival. It was very high-profile, and very nerve-wracking for me. I remember standing at the back of Sadler's Wells stalls, next to Richard Alston, who was also standing there because his piece for the Rambert was on before mine. I remember being so nervous that, just before it started, I thought I was about to pass out through nerves: my legs were completely gone – Alston standing there, and this full house . . .

AM: *How did it go?*
MB: It went through without any disasters – that's all I knew at the time. But again, we got noticed. John Ashford expressed interest in presenting us at The Place, for example; and Clement Crisp gave me almost the only glowing review he's ever given me in the *Financial Times*: 'Very promising' – that sort of thing.

And so from then on we were reacting to offers, rather than trying to get dates – which, for so young a company, was a very enviable position to be in.

Lea Anderson had founded the Cholmondeleys (pronounced 'Chumleys'), her all-female group, a few years before. For one piece, she brought in a group of men as a chorus in one number; and she called them the Featherstonehaughs (pronounced 'Fanshaws'). Then she started to develop them as an independent group with a repertory of their own. Lea had never spoken to me while we'd overlapped as students at Laban; but in 1987 she came up to me, complimented me on my dancing, and asked me to be in this new group. So I became a founder Featherstonehaugh – all of which gives you some idea of the flexibility of the way that AMP worked at the time: the fact that I could be in two companies. The first two pieces she made for them – us, rather – were called *Clump* and *Slump*.

It may have been John Ashford who – maybe because I was in both groups at this time – had the idea of putting the Featherstonehaughs and AMP on together at the ICA for a two-week season in summer 1988. For AMP, the season was a landmark.

There were six pieces on this ICA programme. The Featherstonehaughs performed Lea's *Clump* and *Slump*. It was *Slump*'s première. And AMP did *Crimplene* again, a piece by David Massingham called *Mathematical Park*, and the first performances of my *Spitfire* (which was for four men, myself included), and *Buck and Wing*, a tap duet I'd made for Emma and Catherine. The whole programme was quite odd, quite different, but it went down very well. The season was sold out, and it got good reviews.

AM: *So how many performances per annum would AMP have been giving in that era?*
MB: In 1987, we probably hadn't performed more than about fifteen times; we gave almost that many performances at the ICA alone.

Still, I would think that, in the whole of the calendar year 1988, we can't have given more than thirty or forty performances – some in London, some on tour in England, maybe a date in Scotland. It's hard to explain to people outside that world, but, for a small modern-dance company, thirty performances per year is a lot! Then, it was amazing. Most modern-dance pieces are rehearsed for weeks on end – and then performed just once or twice. If you're lucky enough, you get a whole week of performances somewhere. Very few modern-dance pieces receive more than twelve performances, I would say. It may actually be harder now to get a tour together than it was then. Because we were lucky, my *Overlap Lovers* – which we didn't keep in rep very long – was probably performed about twenty times. My next piece, *Spitfire* – which I made for that ICA season that AMP shared with the Featherstonehaughs, and which has been revived over several years – has been done about forty times. And *Crimplene* had more performances than either.

That ICA season was the first in which we met Katharine Doré – no, not literally, because, the year before, when she'd been at Waterman's Arts Centre in Middlesex, she'd booked us to perform there. But now she had been to the Arts Council with a view to becoming a dance company administrator. So with this in mind, no doubt, she came along to one of those ICA performances; and, just a few weeks afterwards, she became AMP's administrator. She was assigned to us as part of a scheme from the Arts Council to give young companies administrative help. The Arts Council's idea was that small companies or solo performers would share an administrator. It was a good idea, actually, and several companies still work that way. She had a certain amount of choice in who she worked with; and so she also began administrating Rosemary Lee, who was working as a dance soloist (another Laban BA graduate, actually, though from just before my time there), and Pushkala Gopal, a British-based Indian dancer. We were lucky, because Katharine soon chose to concentrate full-time on us, and did so as soon as we were in a position to give her the work.

AM: *Was there any point where you felt any unpleasant resentment in the modern-dance world about the commercial appeal or comic emphasis of your work?*

MB: There were certainly some promoters who thought we were very lightweight – and possibly a little juvenile. Ours wasn't considered to be serious work. We certainly wouldn't have gone down very well at the Bagnolet New Choreography Festival – where all the other new British choreographers of that time were presenting work – or anything like that. We did try one tiny European tour once, late in 1988 I think, appearing in Amsterdam and Ghent. We did *Crimplene, Mathematical Park, Buck and Wing, Overlap Lovers* and *Spitfire*. It was a disaster. They just didn't find it funny. One review said, 'They performed five pieces, three of them unfortunately by Matthew Bourne'. I remember having to get that translated from the Dutch!

AM: Buck and Wing *I never saw.*

MB: I had been going through a Jessie Matthews phase just then, watching all her dance movies from the 1930s and listening to her songs. *Buck and Wing* was a female tap duet somewhat in her style. That was the idea, anyway. The problem for me was the music, which was commissioned from one of Lea Anderson's composers, Steve Blake; but, even though it was only six or seven minutes long, the music arrived late.

Jessie Matthews
'Head Over Heels'
(fast)
Turn Turn - end with back to audience
Crossedwalks hands above head   (Ondine style)
1,2,3.   4

Turn - chasing leg round in front
end

✓ Steps 1, 2, turn   Kick (head back, other
                                    arm pushes forward,

Tap   Jumping onto spot (overbalancing)
✓   fall back on heels

                Cross legs to turn a corner
                Then to turn on spot (false one to start)

6 *Buck and Wing*. From Bourne's notes. The diagrams refer to the 1930s dance films of Jessie Matthews and Eleanor Powell (to both of whom this work was dedicated) and to Frederick Ashton's 1958 ballet *Ondine*.

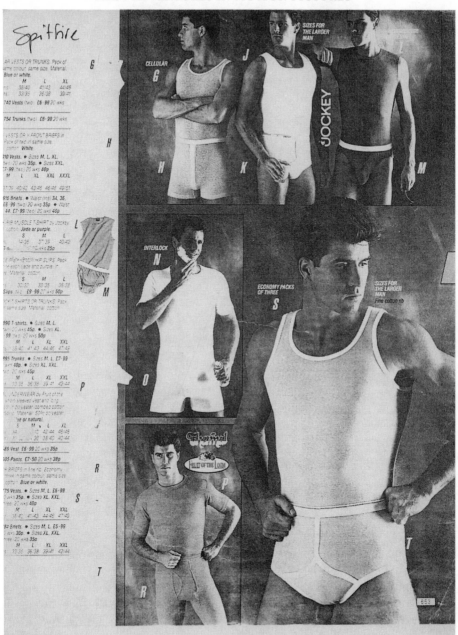

7 One of the pages of advertisements for male underwear used by Bourne as source material for *Spitfire* (1988).

8 *Spitfire* (1988). From Bourne's notebook. The first diagram refers to George Balanchine's ballet *Serenade* (1934).

9 *Spitfire*. From Bourne's notebook. The first diagram refers to George Balanchine's ballet *Apollo* (1928).

10 *Spitfire*. Left to right: David Waring, Keith Brazil (kneeling), Joachim Chandler, Matthew Bourne (supported). This quadruple image of posing virility is a deliberate gender-reversal of all-female groupings in such historic ballets as Jules Perrot's *Pas de Quatre* (1845) and Balanchine's *Serenade*. Multiple images of virility would remain important, but would become less ironic, in Bourne's later choreography.

That put me off working with composers, I must admit. I need the music to inspire me from the beginning.

AM: Spitfire, *however, was the most popular piece you had made.*
MB: It was based on the idea of men posing. Partly it was about the poses men do in underwear adverts. When I was young, looking at those ads was about as near to an erotic experience as I was likely to get! Of course, they also look silly; I've still got some of them in my *Spitfire* folder. And it was also about the way dancers, especially male dancers, strike poses in ballet: sometimes they're poses at the end of a solo, but sometimes they're poses right in the middle of a dance. And they're audience-oriented in the way that the underwear ads are camera-oriented.

Then, because I had had the idea of making a dance like this for four men posing in underwear, I thought of the most famous dance for four women in nineteenth-century ballet, the 1845 *Pas de Quatre*. So the four men do groupings from the famous lithographs. But there are ideas taken from all kinds of other sources, too. One of the first groupings they do is taken straight out of Balanchine's *Serenade*. Balanchine had four groups of four women doing it, near the opening of the ballet; it just amused me to try it with four men. And I set the whole thing to standard nineteenth-century music for virtuoso classical ballet: solo variations by Minkus and Glazounov from *Don Quixote*, *La Bayadère* and *The Four Seasons* [or *Birthday Offering*] (some of it originally music written for female dancers).

There were separate ideas for each dance: one was a man rubbing himself in oil; one was a sort of striptease, undressing; one was sleeping . . .

Spitfire – like the pieces that followed – felt and, in fact, still feels to me like the great marriage of two things: what I had always been interested in, and what I'd learnt at Laban. Now I was able to take the craft I'd learnt and apply it to the interests I'd had all along.

Spitfire has stood up quite well over the years. We last did it at a fund-raising gala in 1995; Adam Cooper was one of the dancers, in the first performance he ever did with AMP.

AM: *AMP went on commissioning pieces from Jacob Marley during this era.*
MB: Yes, there were two others after *Crimplene*. One was *My Little Peasant Dance*, to traditional Slavic music; the other was *I Surrender, Dear*.

AM: *I remember that you were already fond of the Bing Crosby recording of 'I Surrender, Dear': so, as soon as I heard that recording accompanying Marley's piece, I presumed you had had some influence on it.*

MB: John (Jacob Marley) usually needed to be helped with ideas for music. As well as the Crosby, he used the Mozart clarinet quintet! But his imagination was absolutely his own, and somehow he always made his eventual choice of music work. *I Surrender, Dear* was a really strange piece, funny and haunting.

AM: *Your next piece was* The Infernal Galop. *This was inspired by Paris, and was designed by David Manners. David had been your partner for two years; and it was he who first took you to Paris.*

MB: David Manners influenced a lot of AMP work throughout those years, because he had so many interests. In 1992, he designed *Deadly Serious* and *The Percys of Fitzrovia*. He also wrote a piece of music for *Deadly Serious*. He gave me the idea to do *The Percys of Fitzrovia*, for example, because he was already interested in the Bloomsbury set. He was someone that I could definitely develop ideas with, that I could talk to about what I should do next. The relationship we had is the longest of my life to date: we were together six years.

I think I can live with someone. I've got friends who find it's not something that suits them, but I'm very adaptable. If I've been somewhere for a week, it's home. I'm adaptable with people as well. And I very much enjoy having someone there to share things with. I think any relationship I've had has influenced my work, to a certain extent, because, if you're very involved with your work, you're discussing it constantly. Certainly David was an important influence throughout those years.

AM: *In* The Infernal Galop, *the mood, and even the subject-matter, of the dance changes from one item to the next. Was this a new format for you? And what put it into your head?*

MB: I find it very difficult to pin down exactly what it is that I do, and where I might have been influenced. Once you make a piece that's successful, it's its own piece. It has an inner life that's more important than its sources.

But yes: *The Infernal Galop* was the first revue type of piece that I did. I thought that I could do a piece around one idea, and here the idea was Paris; but in the event *The Infernal Galop* had several things within it. I would say that the revue format – a series of separate sketches adding up to a whole piece – was something I had recently noticed Lea Anderson doing very well; but I also brought to it my own interest in musicals, vaudeville and all those other areas. Actually, I think that's why *The Infernal Galop* and some of the pieces that followed have – to me, at least – something of the feeling of some of Ashton's early pieces, like his *Capriol Suite* and *Façade*. When Ashton made those, he was working a lot in the West End, and that gives them their flavour.

When I brought what I'd learnt about popular entertainment to my AMP choreography, I started to realize that I didn't fit very comfortably into the world of British contemporary dance. A lot of the people I was surrounded by were interested in more contemporary issues, art and music. I always had a fear that everyone thought I was commercial because my interests had come from other areas; and my instincts were always historical, never very contemporary. For *The Infernal Galop*, my starting point was Charles Trenet's recording of *La Mer*; and then other old songs and recordings of popular music, all as French as possible.

AM: *The solo to* La Mer *is the most enduring image. This was for Keith Brazil, in a dressing-gown. He lay down with his back to the audience, and his heels together; and, as soon as the song started, he waggled his flexed feet like flippers. And the way he raised his head made you suddenly see a seal, or a sea-lion. The whole audience would recognize the illusion in the same moments, and laugh. It was an adorable dance.*
MB: I can't think what put it in my head to do that to that music.

AM: *I would say now – though I never made the connection then – that that* La Mer *solo was connected to the male Swan solo that Sue Davies had made in* Carnival: *the use of bits of animal and human mime on a lyrical dance current, in both cases for a male dancer.*

This sets off quite a train. The idea of feet as flippers you used more overtly in the film Late Flowering Lust; *and the idea of dancers lying on their sides with their feet seemingly bound together recurs for the sylphs in* Highland Fling.
MB: Yes, but where did I get the basic concept for *La Mer*? With him in a dressing-gown, green socks, shirt and tie!

11 *The Infernal Galop*: Keith Brazil as the Merman in 'Fruits de Mer'. The
'flipper' feet recurred in Bourne's choreography for *Late-Flowering Lust* (1993),
and the entire human/animal nexus is a precursor of Bourne's swans in
Swan Lake (1995).

AM: *Well, there's a connection to* Carnival – *where the dancers are in
shirts and trousers, and where it's very clear that they're human beings
representing animals.*

MB: Well, what I loved in *Carnival* was the very simple means whereby
it created its images. I do remember Matthew Hawkins, for example,
being a chicken or cockerel. He had red gloves, which he put in his
mouth at one point. Things like that I enjoyed very much.

Elsewhere in *The Infernal Galop*, I was taking ideas directly from
the famous Brassai photographs of Paris in the 1920s; and, because I
was using a Trenet recording, I also took an idea from a picture of
Trenet by Jean Cocteau. The picture was on the cover of my Trenet
album, and it showed Trenet with wings sprouting from his back. We
used that in the finale of *The Infernal Galop*: the dancers leant forwards, one hand placed in the small of their back, fingers splayed like
spreading wings. Now that led to all kinds of other things later on, by
the way. There are winged images in *Highland Fling* and *Cinderella*,

12 One of Brassaï's classic photographs of Paris used as source material for *The Infernal Galop*. Bourne reproduced this pose exactly in his choreography, with Brazil in the bare-chested role (left) and himself as the bare-legged man (right).

13 *The Infernal Galop* (1992 revival). Left to right: Scott Ambler, Ally Fitzpatrick, Matthew Bourne, Etta Murfitt, Andrew George, Simon Murphy. The splayed-hands motif was taken from Jean Cocteau's picture of the singer Charles Trenet: Bourne later recycled it in his swan choreography in *Swan Lake*.

but I particularly returned to the Cocteau/Trenet image when I was making *Swan Lake*. The swans splay their fingers behind their backs that same way; it becomes their basic stationary position.

AM: *There's also a connection to Balanchine's* Apollo, *where the title character stands with one arm raised and one behind his back. In alternation, one hand makes a fist, the other splays its fingers. The alternation occurs like a metronome. But nothing's original: Balanchine said he was inspired for that by the neon lights flashing on and off in Piccadilly Circus.*

MB: Well, I'd certainly seen *Apollo*. But the connection wasn't in my mind.

It was *The Infernal Galop*, by the way, that introduced me to John

Caird. He and the composer Stephen Schwartz came to see it at a 1989 performance at Watermans. The place was half-empty, but those two men just adored it; as it happens, we've got a video of this performance, and throughout you just hear them laughing their heads off. When I met them afterwards, I was so thrilled, because Schwartz had written *Pippin*, which was a show I'd loved in the 1970s; and Caird had co-directed *Nicholas Nickleby*, of which I was a huge fan. This led to the two productions I mentioned earlier: the RSC *As You Like It*, and *Children of Eden*, the West End musical.

AM: *Soon after this, in spring 1990, you went to Brussels to look at the American choreographer Mark Morris's work. He and his dance company were then resident at the Monnaie Theatre in Brussels.*

MB: Katharine Doré and I went over together and saw a programme of six pieces, some of them new; the whole programme was called *Loud Music*. One was a big piece, danced in silence, called *Behemoth*; but what I remember best was a lovely duet, to Bach music with bells in it, called *Beautiful Day*.

I'd seen Mark Morris on his first visits to London in 1984 and 1985, when he'd been performing with only a very few dancers. So it was very impressive to see how his work had grown. And he was always musical.

Around that time, I also saw a wonderful British TV documentary on his work, *The Hidden Soul of Harmony*, which was largely about his full-evening Handel work *L'Allegro, il Penseroso, ed il Moderato*.

Later that year Katharine went to New York to see the Morris company dance *L'Allegro*. I've never seen it live, unfortunately.

AM: *Katharine has said to me that Mark Morris gave her the courage of her convictions, that she saw that you can build a company around one person's vision. Was that so for you?*

MB: I think that she, in particular, felt that inspiration – especially after speaking to Barry Alterman, who was her counterpart in the Morris company. Obviously we weren't at the level that Mark and Barry were at that time; and Mark was achieving great things in different areas. But, after spending time watching their work, Katharine felt she could do the same for me. This happened just at the time, 1990, when we began to see that AMP would probably be re-formed as a vehicle for my work alone.

AM: *Yes, but, before AMP became the Matthew Bourne company it now is, you were hoping to have a Mark Morris piece.*

MB: That's right. We actually have a fax that says, 'You will be the first company in Britain to have a Mark Morris piece in your rep, never fear.' We thought it was a great idea at the time, because we felt that there was a similarity between our dancers and his; that his dancers were all very individual, and had a spirit that was similar to ours. And we felt, having seen what we'd seen of him – and he wasn't being seen here at the time – that it would be a great coup to get someone like him to work here with us.

In the event, none of that happened. I started to make all the choreography for AMP soon after that; and the first British company – still the only British company, I think – to dance a Mark Morris piece was London Contemporary Dance Theatre, a season or two later.

AM: *Later in 1990, you made a pastoral piece called* Greenfingers. *There are passages of that which strongly remind me of Morris's* L'Allegro.

MB: The spark of *Greenfingers* really – as with a lot of those early pieces – was a particular piece of music that I felt I wanted to work with. Somebody had given me a tape of Percy Grainger music. We were rehearsing somewhere out of town – we were working on workshop pieces – and I was playing a lot of this music as we were driving through the countryside. It seemed to go so perfectly hand in hand: the country and this music. I particularly liked *Handel in the Strand*, although I didn't actually choreograph any dance to it – just used it later as a musical introduction. But I also love *Country Garden* and the other more famous pieces of Grainger that were on this tape. At the time, this tape was virtually the only recording of any Grainger music that you could get. It's become very voguish since, and there are very many more Grainger pieces available now. At the time, he was someone to whom I really responded – and I certainly wanted to work with that music. I felt it was very cheeky and quirky, oddly and delightfully orchestrated, and moving. Very similar, I found, to the kind of work that I was trying to do at the time.

The TV documentary about Mark Morris's *L'Allegro* made a great impression. What was shown, and what I remember reading about it, was scenes of people forming landscapes: becoming trees and whatever was necessary for the piece. I loved that idea. So I used that idea in

Greenfingers: those bits where people are trees, where they've got blossom and branches and bits and pieces like that.

The title of *Greenfingers*, and the whole approach, also felt very Lea Anderson to me – the use of the body, the gestural fingers, the short and sweet structure. I don't work that way any more, and nor does Lea, but I was happy to take some influence from her at that time. Again, there was plenty of early Ashton in my head while I made it.

Greenfingers was full of very quick, sharp images. It was the beginning of a style of choreography that I began to use a lot at the time: to have a blanket idea, list all the images that I could think of around that idea, cram as many of those images as I could into one piece of music, then go from one representational image to another, and try to create dance around all that.

AM: *Who were your dancers for* Greenfingers?

MB: Catherine White, Keith Brazil, Bill Eldridge, Susan Lewis. There is a bit where two of them become topiary, and the arms of the other two look like garden shears. The first two hit positions – like cherubs on one leg – and the others cut up their backs. It's a literal image, but the theory was always that, if you just show it very quickly and sharply, it's almost gone in a blink. It's all in the timing.

Another image is catching things in nets. There is also some tea-drinking. In the *Country Garden* music, the women hold their teacups and the men pour the tea. Actually, the women mime holding cups, very daintily; but the men actually mime being teapots, one hand on hip like a teapot handle, the other arm extended like the spout, and they tip sideways as if to pour tea. 'Teapot' became an AMP motif: we used it again in *Highland Fling*!

AM: *That's there deliberately as a comic reflection of domesticity?*

MB: Yes.

AM: *And you saw all this as being about England?*

MB: Yes. I'm very much a town person, I suppose. But driving through the country with this music made me love the idea of doing a piece about the English countryside. The combination of music with idea worked so well.

AM: *I want to ask you about dynamics. Today, when you talk about the dynamics you're looking for in dancers, you often emphasize in conversation the quality of flow, of legato. And you're always trying to get ballet-trained dancers to go for connections between positions rather than just holding static positions, as many of them are inclined to do. That makes sense to me from what I see of your work. Yet it also seems to me that quite a lot of your style actually has a hefty mixture of staccato. It goes from position to position to position. And it seems to me that this staccato quality – which you mix with legato – became very marked around the time of* Greenfingers. *Is that accidental? Or were you very definitely wanting that?*

MB: I was sometimes conscious that what we were doing was somewhere between dance and gesture, between dance and mime. But I thought that it needed to be sharper and cleaner to come across well. I've been watching myself in a couple of old AMP videos lately – and I'm so sharp and spot on! I was quite impressed by myself. Not in a dance way, I hasten to add, but just in the precision of timing and attack. Well, I think that was part of our general desire to get things across: to be very clear and clean on what we were trying to show, which becomes a dynamic interest as well.

AM: *I never saw* Greenfingers *on stage. But you wrote to me at that time to tell me that you were dedicating it to me. Is there any particular reason why you dedicated that piece to me?*

MB: I felt that, within it, there were lots of nods to dance history, and to things that you'd drawn my attention to, and to discussions we'd had when we were watching pieces. I felt it showed a lot of the lessons I'd learnt. Also you were a farmer's son who became a dance critic, so I thought the country subject would appeal to you. You adore Ashton choreography, and I felt that *Greenfingers* was a very Fred type of piece.

AM: *At what stage of your career do you think you learnt most?*

MB: I'm still feeding off things I got excited about a long time ago. In those early AMP years, I felt both that I was learning a great deal and that I was putting to good use everything I'd already learnt.

I'll tell you what was very interesting to me: the other day, when we were looking through old photos of nineteenth-century and early twentieth-century dance history for this book, I thought, 'I must look at these more again now.' I remember being so inspired by mere pictures of older works, by seeing how highly designed a lot of the choreography seems to have been, in both ballet and contemporary work. I think that, earlier on, I was using many of those images in my mind. I could do with an influx of that again – to go back to looking at pieces that I loved and watched years ago. I feel that I learnt the most about choreography and theatre in those years when I was regularly watching a lot of other people's work, a lot of good and great choreography.

I've learnt other things along the way. Everything has fed into what I've done. I feel more experienced now and able to tackle more mature subject matter. But in choreographic terms, that period of watching, learning and discussing work was very inspiring to me.

AM: *That stage of Adventures in Motion Pictures finally ended when the other founder members got work that took them in other directions. Were there hard feelings involved? Or was it just natural?*

MB: I remember Emma very tearfully telling me that she was going to join the Cholmondeleys. There was no hard feeling. It was just a hard decision to make. But she felt that's where her future lay. She had become quite bogged down with AMP administration. Until Katharine Doré took over, Emma had been doing all that, with my help to a certain extent; and she was very tempted by the chance to work with Lea Anderson as one of the Cholmondeleys. David Massingham felt the company was moving in a direction that wasn't very him – that is, the humorous aspect of what we were doing with Jacob Marley and me at times. We were known as 'the funny company', and that certainly didn't suit David. He was much more into pure dance, structure and movement invention. There were some painful conversations with him at that time; and eventually he formed his own company. Catherine White got an offer she couldn't refuse to go and tour with the Pet Shop Boys, choreographed by Jacob Marley, all around the world. And Keith was doing his own work. Carrollynne had already left. Emma and David were gone before I made *Greenfingers*.

AMP nearly folded. I wasn't sure I could keep it going as a Matthew Bourne company, or start over again with new dancers.

AM: *But you did.*

MB: Yes, and *Greensleeves*, the last piece I made on the old AMP, led directly to *Town and Country*, the first piece I made on the new AMP. And *Town and Country* is still, to me, one of the most important pieces I've ever made.

4

Further Adventures in Motion Pictures, 1991–1994

MATTHEW BOURNE: A lot of the Adventures in Motion Pictures dancers today find themselves in tears at the end of *Swan Lake*, when they see it from out front rather than actually dancing in it themselves. During the West End run, when we had more dancers, the first time they were able to go out and watch a performance they would always come backstage afterwards in floods of tears, saying, 'I never thought it was like that; I never believed when I was doing it that it looked like that.' This was lovely, and I've always wanted to react to it that way myself. But you know, I never have. (I felt with *Swan Lake* that I'm much more mature as a person; I knew what I was doing with it, and found the rehearsal process quite easy. I enjoyed it very much, and am very proud of the result. But I didn't feel that I was on a mission.) I'm always conscious of the effects that I was trying to create in *Swan Lake*, so I find it difficult to be moved by it.

Whereas, when I watch *Town & Country* – although it's very frivolous at times and I was much less mature when I made it – by the end I am much more moved. I feel very, very connected to all the things in that piece. I'm like that now when I watch it on video, and I was like that in 1991 when I was dancing in it. I wasn't on in the last section, and I would stand in the wings, and always shed a little tear. I love the music so much, as well.

Part of my emotion about *Town & Country* is about the time and the people and the making of it. But not all. I always felt that it was an affecting piece, but, because much of it was also light and humorous, often it was not taken very seriously. We were the company that people – even some critics – enjoyed watching, but didn't like to talk about in too serious a light. Only some critics, mind you; three critics wrote

14 *Town & Country* (1991): Matthew Bourne and Scott Ambler in 'Dearest Love' in the 'Town' section.

first-rate reviews of *Town & Country*, actually. You would see some senior British critics coming to the show and seemingly having a great night out and laughing away; and you would think, 'Oh, they're really enjoying this.' Then they would write awful things in the next day's newspaper. Yet you could tell, from the way they'd obviously enjoyed writing the reviews, that they'd responded to the elements within the piece more than they admitted. There is a peculiar embarrassment that affects some people who want to be taken as authoritative observers when they're faced with light, frivolous material: they don't want to take it seriously as art.

Anyway, to me *Town & Country* is very important. It has a special innocence about it; it's probably that that makes me cry at the end. And I'm proud of it because it was my first full-evening piece. I probably respond to it because it was made partly on my own body, when I was still one of the company's dancers. But I also value it – and this matters a lot – because I'd just discovered a new bunch of AMP dancers, whom I loved working with, and three of whom are still with me.

As I said about *Greenfingers*, it contains a lot of what I'd learnt from all kinds of different sources. With it, I'd begun a new way of working, which I still use. I love its music, and the whole English world it creates. People now talk of me as a recycler – as a choreographer who can only handle new-look versions of traditional full-length ballets. In any case, I don't think of *Swan Lake* or *Cinderella* as recycling; but when I look at *Town & Country*, it feels as if it unquestionably has a world of its own on stage.

ALASTAIR MACAULAY: *Yes, but it's a world we've known all our lives. We take one look at these English characters and English settings and we recognize them. That's a real gift – Ashton had it – but it's the kind of gift most critics undervalue. Tell me how you expanded* Greenfingers *into* Town & Country.

MB: To be honest, I can't exactly remember – apart from the fact that I lived down the road from the Town & Country Club. I passed that every day, so maybe that sparked off an idea.

Obviously, the original short piece, *Greenfingers*, had been very much to do with England and Englishness, the rural side. So now I thought, 'Let's show the two sides – town life and country life.' They do go hand in hand pretty much, the two sets of characteristics. I thought that the contrast would be nice for a full evening work.

AM: Town *comes first. Much of this is a portrait of old upstairs-downstairs class values, yes? The housemaid, the toffs who dump their coats on her in a vast pile, the idea of arriving for a weekend party . . .*

MB: I always stated in the publicity that *Town & Country* was about an England that everyone supposedly remembers but probably never existed. It was very much about class. I think that, if I did it again, I'd go a lot further into all that. I'd probably do a whole evening of *Town* and a whole evening of *Country*. It was such a rich area for me to delve into that all the ideas came very easily. We could have done another complete show with other ideas of Englishness too.

At the time, we felt we were being quite daring in terms of structure. We started off with a group of people arriving in what looks like a hotel foyer, with coats and bags and sports equipment; and then we went into a sequence of people being washed – in the foyer! – in bath tubs and being dressed by their maid and their manservant. I was trying to set up a framework that I could then be very subversive with and eccentric about. Within this setting, anything was possible. It had a surreal feeling about it. Scott sits there quietly in the foyer – a privileged young English gentleman – and suddenly the maid and valet do a George Formby number to him, complete with ukulele. All this to Elgar's *Pomp and Circumstance*! Then, equally suddenly, when left alone, he produces some needlework. It's all utterly English, but utterly illogical.

AM: *And, amid this, you also suddenly had two men – Scott Ambler and yourself – dance together to Noël Coward's 'Dearest Love'. Was that the most clearly gay dance that you had yet made?*
MB: Definitely, yes.

AM: *How did that come about? And how would you describe the element of gayness in your choreography?*
MB: This is something that I've often spoken about in conjunction with *Swan Lake*. But the 'Dearest Love' duet – even more than *Swan Lake* – was a reaction against a lot of physical theatre that was around at the time. DV8, to be specific, had just been showing some very violent male duets. Well, I wanted to do something that was very simple and romantic. 'Dearest Love' is basically a Fred-and-Ginger number for two men – apart from the fact that they have trouble looking each other in the eyes and are obviously a slightly repressed pair. But they do end up pretty close, pretty much together.

AM: *Because of the initial repression, the ending is very touching. It's also the most serious emotion in the whole* Town *section.*
MB: Yes. One of the choreographic ideas was that we never looked at each other, but that all these little signals were going on. We may be putting our hands on each other, but are never actually making eye contact. When one of us even begins to look at the other, the other turns away quite quickly. But that was very much a representation of Coward himself. He seemed someone who hid his sexuality from the world.

Then we go into a whole, pocket-sized version of *Brief Encounter* in this same setting – which becomes a railway station. So the piece is also about changing a simple set into other things as well. We did have a lot of fun with that also in *Deadly Serious*, this idea of making many things out of simple sets, turning them into other things by lighting or by moving them around. In *Town & Country*, what we do is almost a précis of the *Brief Encounter* film: Celia Johnson getting something in

15 *Town & Country*. Left to right (Ally Fitzpatrick, Matthew Bourne, Ben Wright, Etta Murfitt, Scott Ambler, Jamie Watton). The choreography here provides a doubled version of David Lean's *Brief Encounter* film: Bourne would quote this same episode, although for peripheral characters, in Act Three of his *Cinderella* (1997).

her eye and Trevor Howard helping her, their second meeting in the park, their visit to the cinema, their bumping into his friend, back at the railway station.

AM: *The* Brief Encounter *scene is duplicated, with the same railway café episode happening at the same time on both right and left sides of the stage, quite close to each other in fact. Why the duplication? And what do you think the result is?*
MB: We had a theory at the time that if you were doing movement that was pretty naturalistic – mime or even just simple acting – it wouldn't look like choreography unless it was duetted in some way, that you wouldn't necessarily know that this was a thing set to counts – and all those moves, eye gestures: everything was on counts. So, because they weren't dance movements, having them doubled drew your attention to them as movements. It also enabled us to comment at the end – by having one end one way and the other another. With

one couple, he comes back to her; with the other, he comes back just for a handkerchief that he's forgotten. It allows for a little punch-line gag at the end.

AM: *To me this recalls what Ian Spink had done in* Further and Further into Night *– taking sequences of movement from Hitchcock's film* Notorious, *duplicating them, repeating them. But we've spoken of that piece. This theory about duplication: is it one you've now dropped?*

MB: No, I still use it. In the underground station sequences in *Cinderella*, most of those people are in twos. You've got two male prostitutes, two female prostitutes. They're doing unison work, because what they're doing is not actually dance material, it's danced gesture and a certain amount of physical movement. If it was done individually, it would look less choreographed. So the duplication is to show that there is a choreographic form to it; and by showing that form, you are actually drawing attention to the specifics of the movement more than if only one person did it.

AM: *But, by making it look more choreographed, the danger is that you make it look less spontaneous. Two prostitutes don't do ordinary movements at precisely the same time. You're happy with taking that risk?*

MB: As long as there's enough combination of things going on at the same time, yes. I think that if you were doing a duet for two men alone on an underground station, you wouldn't want the whole thing to be a double solo in unison. You could develop the idea – to come in and out of unison maybe; but, in *Town & Country*, if we'd just had one couple (and one waiter) doing the café scene from *Brief Encounter*, audiences would wonder what's the point of just doing a mime version of the film. By giving them a split-focus doubling of the same episode, we're showing them a variation on the film.

Obviously, the film is a classic image of Englishness, so the duplication gives you some kind of 'There'll always be an England' idea – an idea that in England *Brief Encounter* is forever being repeated and relived. And it makes it funnier. In the railway café scene, Scott and I wait at the two tables simultaneously; and at one point, when the Noël Coward recording goes into a passage where Coward himself speaks sentimentally ('We may meet again . . .'), we lip-synch him. We were really playing waitresses, by the way, though we never had time to put on special waitresses' costumes! At the end, when the two girls playing Celia Johnson left their hats behind – what Clement Crisp in his review called 'that unforgivable hat' she wears in the film – both Scott and I took the hats and put them on our own heads.

AM: *The danger with that kind of choreographic device, when you're not going for comedy, is that movement can look contrived. This brings us on to general aspects of choreographic theory and practice. Duplication is one technique of bringing a gesture home. Repetition is another: not doing it twice at the same time, but twice in succession. Do you believe in using repetition as a device?*
MB: Yes.

AM: *But repetition is a very curious form of emphasis. You repeat in choreography a gesture that in life might well only be done once.*
MB: Sometimes you feel you may have hammered something home enough by doing it once, but I think that often for an audience it is not enough. An audience wants the chance to see and to take in what it is you're trying to get across. By repeating something a second or third time, you make an audience notice it. The first time people will have seen it, but won't necessarily remember it. The repetition is for the untrained eye. I think that something only becomes significant if it's done more than once or if it's held for a long period of time, so that you have time to take it in.

AM: *This kind of repetition and duplication of gesture often charac-terizes what ballet people, in lighter works, call* demi-caractère *choreo-graphy. It also marks the heavier kind of dance works – both ballet and modern-dance – that are often labelled as expressionistic. It's there in Leonide Massine's comedy ballets, in Kurt Jooss's The Green Table, in Ninette de Valois's story ballets – all mid-war choreography – and it carries through to some post-war choreography such as certain ballets by John Cranko and Kenneth MacMillan. The danger in most of these cases is that gestures are done twice to the left and twice to the right; and the emphasis is heavy. The audience isn't just being made to see the point, it's being bludgeoned. In The Rake's Progress – one of those famous ballets by de Valois that are actually a trial on the nerves to see more than once a year – the mother of the Betrayed Girl comes on doing the same sequence of bourrée, bourrée, stamp, shake the fist at the Rake; bourrée, bourrée, stamp, shake the fist at the Rake – eight*

16 *Town & Country*. Left to right: Scott Ambler, Ben Wright (bending),
Matthew Bourne, Ally Fitzpatrick. The 'milking' image is a deliberate quotation
from the Milkmaid dance in Frederick Ashton's 1931 ballet *Façade*.

*times as she moves slowly across the stage. We got the point the first
time; twice might just be all right. But eight times is insulting.*
MB: This repetition of gesture happens quite a lot in ballet, particularly
in narrative ballet. If you're going to repeat something, you should put
something else in between, so that the repetition doesn't immediately
follow. If, within several different movements, you repeat the same one
movement, it draws more attention to it. Just use the one movement as
a motif. But there are many options. Sometimes the cumulative effect
of something that builds and builds can, obviously, have a big emotional impact.

AM: *For the* Country *part, you now expanded beyond what you'd
already choreographed in* Greenfingers.
MB: Yes. Because I delved further into Grainger, I tried to find more
music than had been on my original tape. The only other tape of
Grainger music available at the time was an album of songs put
together by Benjamin Britten and Peter Pears. A lot of pieces were sung

by Peter Pears; there was some choral singing too, and one piece was 'Shallow Brown', sung by John Shirley-Quirk. It's been re-recorded now several times – once by a woman, last year – but I still think that's the best version, the most moving. I found it an overwhelming piece of music that just made me cry – not really knowing why. Obviously, there's something going on in the lyrics that is very moving, but it's not specific. It's about someone leaving someone. And it's got such a strange and haunting orchestration as well.

AM: *'Shallow Brown' makes me cry too. To me, your staging of it looks like an erotic nightmare – but very powerful and poetic. The change of mood is really extraordinary.*

The idea of the erotic dream, the vision in which the protagonist suddenly sees the full sensual allure of the other main person in her or his mind, this – I believe – from now on becomes an important theme in your works. It takes the dream, or vision, to overwhelm the hero or heroine and show them how smitten they are by the beauty, or the spell, of the other person.

MB: It's certainly a dream. The solo begins with Jamie Watton on the ground. It's like someone who's having a tormented dream. There are sections where he's feeling the ground next to him, like a person in bed who's missing something, like you might when you wake up in the morning. That was one of the ideas: that there was a missing person. Then struggling with the dream, and this dream becoming more of a reality. The dream is happening in the distance behind him.

It's got that idea of covering the eyes in it as well – which I later used in *Cinderella*. A sleepwalking idea: dream walking, dream dancing. And you know what? I've only recently realized that I took this idea from Balanchine's *Serenade*. With Balanchine, of course, the fateful figure who shields the hero's eyes is female. With me, at least in *Shallow Brown* and in *Cinderella*, it's male. At the end, there is a figure taken across the landscape at the back. It's actually Etta Murfitt on my shoulders, but the light is just on her face; it's a person in Jamie's mind. But it was my first attempt to do something that was a bit more serious in tone.

There's a bit where the chorus group come shuffling on with their hands wrapped over their heads. For me, this connects to the pictures of Nijinsky in *Narcisse* and *Spectre*; I like having the hands very relaxed, just hanging, and I like the hands and arms in contact with the face. But here it's part of tree imagery: blossom on trees.

Then there's a section which begins with the funeral of a hedgehog. We do a little walk across the back; and Scott holds the dead hedgehog. We take it very, very seriously: that's the thing. Then we do a dance at the end, which is another beautiful Grainger piece, called 'The Sussex Mummers' Christmas Carol'. It has a connection with the land; it's to do with Thanksgiving – we kiss the soil at one point. We were cringing a little to ourselves when we were first doing it! But that whole section became very important and meaningful; and it ends with us all just looking up into the sky. There was some special quality it had which came about through us making it and working as a team for the first time. You really remember those things, especially as a performer: those moments when you have the chance just to stop and feel something.

AM: Greenfingers *was already School of Ashton* – Fille mal gardée, *but also the young Ashton of* Capriol Suite *and* Façade. Country *is more so.*
MB: As I've said, I liked those early revue pieces because they seemed so open in structure and such a wonderful way of doing lots of short, sweet little numbers. I miss that way of working now, and, whenever I can use that format within a bigger piece, I try to do it.

You mentioned mood changes within *Town & Country*. It was wonderful to realize that you don't have to do a piece that's all along the same lines; and that, if you are using different ideas within it, they don't all have to be funny. The clog dance in the *Country* section used to go down like wildfire with audiences – gales of laughter. But the emotion of 'Shallow Brown' hit home too.

AM: *In* Town & Country, *the change of mood is drastic – and beautiful. Did you learn that from Ashton?*
MB: I think so. I always feel that, if you're laughing one minute and you're moved the next, you experience it more because of the difference in the way you felt. I've experimented in some pieces with trying to do it very quickly. We've had people laughing and suddenly taken aback by something, or moved by something.

That's just one method. The cumulative approach is also very effective: building steadily to one emotional climax, even when the audience can half-feel it coming.

AM: *You were still dancing in* Town & Country. *What would you say the difference has been between the works that you've danced in and the more recent works in which you haven't?*

MB: The positive thing about dancing in a piece yourself, when you actually have to create the movement for yourself as well as for everyone else, is that the movement tends to be more personal and works for your body. You know you're going to be doing it, and you approach movement in a different way. That's inevitable.

It also makes the pieces very personal to you. When I watch *Town & Country*, I see that a lot of the movement is very much from my own body, and is movement that I was happy doing. It would be nice to take a piece like that, now that I'm not going to dance in it any more, and develop it.

I also see that those pieces suffer from a lack of attention from me as a choreographer or a director. There's a point where they tend to stop – where I have to go into them, become one of the dancers, have a performance relationship with the people I'm doing it with and remember what I'm doing dance-wise.

AM: *You mean you would like to be giving more coaching to the others on the way they perform?*
MB: Certainly that, but also, more importantly, I can see the weaknesses choreographically. In fact, in the circumstances of my performing, I'm sometimes surprised the pieces are as interesting as they are. They've had virtually no attention from an outside eye for so long by the time they're put on stage, yet they are quite tightly choreographed in many ways. I suppose I left less to chance then. I was aware that I would be in the pieces and so wouldn't be watching them. I suppose we did use video then in rehearsal, but it's not the same.

AM: *The modern AMP really began with* Town & Country *in 1991, with the new nucleus of six dancers. Had any of them been with you before?*
MB: No. I found myself in the position of not having a company and wondering whether to continue. I said to Katharine, 'I'll try one more show and see if I can make it work with other people.' So I literally auditioned a new company.

A couple of people were highly recommended: they were Scott Ambler and Etta Murfitt. The people who'd recommended them thought they were right for the sort of thing I was doing. I don't think they came with any great sense of what we were doing at that time. We had just had a couple of successes with small works. There wasn't an AMP style. We had been working with different choreographers. This was the first attempt at a full evening of my work, and it was the point where it became solely my company as well. The other dancers I took on were Ally Fitzpatrick, Jamie Watton, and Ben Wright.

AM: *Ben Wright has gone and come back again since?*
MB: Yes. *Town & Country* was his very first job. Then he got offered a contract with London Contemporary Dance Theatre and went to join them. We always kept in touch, and he came back for *Swan Lake*, since then he's been in everything we've done.

Jamie Watton only did the one show with us. He went on to form his own company, and is now doing very well with it. Ally Fitzpatrick was with us until the rehearsals for *Highland Fling* in 1994. She doesn't dance any more, but she made a lasting impression on us all. We still refer to her a lot – very affectionately.

AM: *Scott Ambler and Etta Murfitt are the most important of this nucleus to you, I guess?*
MB: Yes. I think they definitely helped to develop the AMP style.

AM: *From now on, AMP becomes larger and tackles bigger pieces, narrative pieces, and then becomes a big West End company. But did the style itself, the movement, and the attitude to work, change?*
MB: I think it did, because I was very much the boss straightaway and wasn't answering to other choreographers in the company. All the people in the old AMP, don't forget, had been college friends, and there had been a lot of history between us. It had very much had a sort of co-op feeling. Now, because I was the only original member left, it established me as much more of a leader. I'd given these new dancers jobs, and there was no history. That was good, actually.

It was a strange situation to be in, but it was a fresh start. I began to form what I felt I wanted to do. And what made me love it was how quickly humour emerged between us. We had such fun making it. I remember laughing such a lot in rehearsals. We used to be hysterical, laughing. It's such a happy memory for all of us.

AM: *And it was now that you began the collaborative method, which has remained your formula.*
MB: One of the things that made the pieces so collaborative was that we premièred them out of London. We had an agreement with South West Arts that we premièred our shows in that region. And so most of those shows for the next few years – *Town & Country, Deadly Serious, High-*

land Fling, *The Percys of Fitzrovia* – were made in Bristol for three months each. We would be away from home all that time, spending the whole time together, evenings as well a lot of the time. There was twenty-four-hour involvement with people. You'd go out for a meal in the evening; inevitably, you'd talk about what you'd done during the day; and ideas would come up from that. And because we were away from home and all our other concerns, both the dancers and I tended to concentrate on the work a lot more.

I was trying things out a bit with people on *Town & Country*. Initially, I felt it was my job to lead. I wasn't asking much of them; and I had already made the *Greenfingers* section of the work. But, as it went along, we realized we were thinking along the same lines and laughing at the same things. So I asked them to contribute; and using dancers' contributions has been the way I've worked ever since.

AM: *Tradition has it that Balanchine told his dancers, 'Don't think, dear, just do.' This is often misinterpreted to imply that he wanted his dancers to be mindless robots. What Balanchine wanted was spontaneity rather than calculation: for dancers to be coolly stepping over the brink rather than dramatically signalling that they were stepping over the brink. When dancers show that they know their motivation, it can be a simply terrible spectacle.*

MB: Still, 'Don't think, just do' is something I'd never say.

AM: *There was a cartoon in a recent* New Yorker *of a dog being filmed by a whole camera set, sitting on a lawn with a bone. The dog is saying, 'OK, so I dig a hole, and put the bone in the hole. But what's my motivation for burying it?'*

MB: I am, I think, instinctive enough to know when a dancer should just get on and dance. And that's a good thing. But I think the reason I've had loyalty from people for a long time – and also the reason why a lot of people like working for me – is that I've never said 'Don't think' to anyone. I always listen – and I will always listen – to their ideas and to what they have to say. Sometimes I'll say, 'No, I don't think that's a good idea.'

AM: *Is that still true when you're working on coaching a later cast to do a show you've already made and had success with?*

MB: Yes, quite often. Again, there are things that I know I want within it: things that have been established as the choreography; but if they can't do some of it, or there's a problem with some of it, I'm happy to change it. I'm always considering revisions anyway. No piece is ever finished. I have pushed people quite hard sometimes because of that.

AM: *I do remember going to one West End performance of your* Swan Lake *and Iain Webb, one of your rehearsal directors, turning up in the interval to tell you, 'Lynn Seymour has got another idea about her role!' – and you rolled your eyes.*

MB: Yes, but I'd always try to make time to listen to any new ideas Lynn or anyone else had about their role, even in the middle of a West End run. In fact, the role of the Queen is a nice example of how much I can adjust a role for a dancer. Fiona Chadwick was the original, and I still think she gave – gives – the definitive performance. Isabel Mortimer then did it, very well indeed, along lines very similar to Fiona's. But when Lynn joined the cast, she was an older dancer and several movements just didn't suit her at all. So it had to be rechoreographed. And Lynn was so intelligent and instinctive and canny that she then thought – couldn't help thinking – of all kinds of different accentuations. We'd discuss them, of course. Not every idea was perfect. But it was wonderful to work with someone who was so keen to put her own very original stamp on a role within a framework that had already been established.

AM: *Another example is that of Gelsey Kirkland. Her second book, all about dancing MacMillan's Juliet and Petipa's Sleeping Beauty with the Royal Ballet and finding the motivation for every little movement, becomes ludicrous; and, when she coached one English National Ballet dancer as Giselle, she took whole rehearsals before they even made the first entrance through the cottage door.*

MB: It's a delicate thing. Part of what gets these people on stage and doing what they do is that kind of enquiring mind, and that kind of involvement in their characters. You can't quash that; you mustn't. You have to give them their chance to go somewhere with it and bring it back.

AM: *You're right. When Bob Gottlieb was editing Margot Fonteyn's* Autobiography, *he asked her to expand on her roles. What, for example, did she feel about Giselle? 'Well, Bob,' she said, 'I just wait behind the cottage door until it's my cue, and when it is, I come out.' She was an intelligent woman, but she spoke as if 'Don't think, just do' was her motto too. In private, though, she would say to people, 'I have to have a reason for doing this step. I can't do this step unless I see its purpose.' But naming that purpose in words was something she avoided at all costs.*

There are so many ways of working with dancers. I'm sure you're always inspired by the famous stories of Ashton walking into rehearsals and saying, 'Oh, I don't know what I'm going to do today. But last night I had a dream of a fountain. Hop around, become a fountain somehow.'

Would you ever do this to your dancers, though? Ashton walked into rehearsal without actually telling the young Anthony Dowell and Antoinette Sibley that they were dancing Oberon and Titania. All they knew was that they were being summoned for a pas de deux. Is that conceivable to you?

MB: I can't see me doing that at the moment. He certainly didn't always work that way, did he? I wonder why he did in that case. Perhaps he was waiting to see what they would be like to work with. You can't always be dealing with character. There are times when we experiment with the idea of flying, for example, and there are certainly no characters involved. It's a concept, or an image, or a feeling that's more abstract.

AM: *What collaboration, if any, had you done before* Town & Country?

MB: I had recently worked with the theatre director John Caird. I always say I learnt a lot about the working process from him. He has a way of making every member of the company feel very important, and of involving them on the level of character development. This is the way I work now, to get each ensemble dancer to give his or her role a character that they've worked on – a character that's not necessarily relevant to the plot, but which gives the show an interior life – and I learnt that from him. So I began to see myself more as a director, so that I could actually initiate some involvement from the performers, rather than me having to do everything.

AM: *A director isn't actually creating a play or a musical, he's simply shaping the production. But you are creating a new dance text. Therefore what you're doing also resembles the methods of a writer/director. Like Mike Leigh. It reminds me also of the dance group Second Stride.*

Did you know about that process? Or are these resemblances mere accident?

MB: I didn't know about Second Stride's process, but they seemed to be a group of very intelligent individuals who – it would appear from watching the productions – had a great involvement in the conception of what they were doing.

I do think that the Mike Leigh connection is very interesting, because, having admired him for a long time before his talent was recognized, I found it an inspiration to hear then how he worked: how he made his actors become those characters before they even worked on the play as such. They would even go out as those characters into supermarkets and 'be' them, and improvise in that way. That inspired me to develop dancers' characters and their knowledge of the people that they were playing before we entered into any kind of movement.

The other thing about Mike Leigh is that people have said that his work is a caricature, an exaggeration, of people. And now people have said the same of mine. But I've never found his work exaggerated at all. I think you meet people like that all the time! You just don't notice how strange people are.

AM: *People say about Dickens that he's full of caricatures. But actually, when you meet certain people, you say, 'How Dickensian!'*
MB: I noticed that on holiday, just last week, watching people on beaches and thinking of Jacques Tati. People are just so funny, the way they walk into the sea and the way their bodies are. If you actually put a camera on that, it looks exaggerated. It looks as though you've taken it too far. But people are very, very strange!

AM: *The Adventures in Motion Pictures acting style: you've mentioned an emphasis on precise counts and timing, and there's a very precise focus that people on stage have to each other; but it also includes a large element of addressing things to the audience. Was that conscious or accidental? Where does it come from?*
MB: We've always likened our acting style to silent movies, especially in a larger theatre. We're trying to get something across.

AM: *You say 'always'. But you never thought of silent movies when you named your company Adventures in Motion Pictures. Nor would I say that the acting style involved in the Jacob Marley pieces was like silent movies. So at what point did your acting style become conscious?*

MB: *Town & Country*, and then *Deadly Serious*. *Spitfire* was certainly very frontal, but that's because it's about ballet performance.

The acting style is obviously to do with getting an idea across. Rather than playing it to each other, you have to be able to stage it, so that the audience can see it. In that respect, our style is very frontal. I've often had a problem with contemporary dancers, for most of whom it doesn't come very naturally to take in the audience, whereas I like to make a connection with the audience. Our mission is to be clear, and to engage. To me, the face and eyes, in particular, are very important.

AM: *You've been talking of* Town & Country *as if it was a major landmark for you. But was it for your audience?*
MB: It was something that some people fell in love with. We had a week at the Royal Court that autumn, as part of its Barclays New Stages season in 1991. Jasper Conran, for example, came five times. He saw it on the first night and then came back every night afterwards to see it again.

Nicholas Payne and Martin Duncan came to see it then, which led to *Nutcracker* the following year. Yes, *Town & Country* was a real turning point for me and for AMP.

AM: *When had you begun work on it?*
MB: The very beginning of 1991. It premièred around March, April. We danced it maybe thirty times at most. The Royal Court must have been one of the last times we did it. You didn't revive a piece after its first year in those days, because all of us wanted to make new pieces, and there simply weren't enough performances yet to keep both old and new full-length pieces in repertory. I think the most performances we ever did of any piece prior to *Swan Lake* was *Deadly Serious*. That we did about forty-five times. We thought that was a very good tour: quite an achievement. Now we think an eight-week season of eight shows a week is a nice short season. It's odd.

AM: *You opened* Deadly Serious *in April 1992?*
MB: Yes. 1992 was a terrible year for me – a great year in some ways, but very hard – with three new pieces made in one year, two of them full-length. We made *Deadly Serious*, we opened in Bristol, toured it, did it in London. We went straight into *Nutcracker* rehearsals for five weeks, to première at the Edinburgh Festival in August.

Everything went wrong at the dress rehearsal – chaotic, a nightmare, the set wasn't working – and we had all the pressure of all the national and international press coming to the first night, without any previews. I'd never do that now! Directly following that, we went into a three-month rehearsal period for *The Percys of Fitzrovia*. During the first three weeks of rehearsal, nothing happened; we still had nothing to show. It was the nearest that I've ever come to feeling that I was going mad. I remember coming in one morning and saying to Ally at breakfast, 'I think I'm going mad, I think I'm having a breakdown.' We premièred *The Percys* for a week in Bristol, but then didn't tour it at that point. Instead, we went straight back into rehearsals for *Nutcracker* for the Opera North tour, which happened over Christmas, going into January 1993. Then we had to revive *The Percys* in two weeks, to open at the Lyric Hammersmith for a three-week season and tour it. Since *The Percys* wasn't a full-length work, we also revived *The Infernal Galop* as the other half of that programme. For a small company, this was colossal. We were all completely exhausted. There are parts of *The Percys* where we were all sitting down on chairs: that's because we were all shattered. I didn't dance in our original *Nutcracker* production (though I did later on), but I was dancing in *Deadly Serious* and *The Percys* and *The Infernal Galop*. My darkest time came when *The Percys* had its London opening at the Lyric Hammersmith. It was the day Nureyev died. A lot of people came quite depressed by that, so they weren't really in the mood for this Bloomsbury piece we had made. I think also that it was not rehearsed well enough. It needed confidence and full characterization to make it work. The reviews were terrible. You were the only critic who said anything nice about it – in a personal letter, at the end of the season, not in print.

Fortunately, *Deadly Serious* and *Nutcracker* were big successes, and a lot of 1993 was taken up by further performances of them. In Christmas 1993, we did *Nutcracker* as an independent production as the Christmas show at Sadler's Wells. That was a success, so we did it again there at Christmas 1994.

AM: Deadly Serious *was a Hitchcock piece, in two sections: black and white, then colour.*
MB: It was billed as a double feature; and it was presented like two films. Part One – based loosely on the black and white era of Hitchcock – is mainly ideas from *Rebecca*. Part Two – based on Hitchcock's

colour movies – is partly *North by Northwest*, but quite a few other Hitchcocks thrown in. They had titles as well. The first half was called *Overwrought*, which is a word Mrs Danvers says in *Rebecca*: 'You're feeling overwrought, Madam.' The second half was called *Rear Entry*. These titles were in the programme. We billed it like two movie posters: 'Rear Entry, danced in glorious technicolor and not starring . . .' and then we'd list all the names of the Hitchcock stars we were, in effect, playing: Cary Grant, Doris Day . . . And it had a year: 1958. The first half was 1939.

AM: *We've already talked about Ian Spink's Second Stride piece about Hitchcock's* Notorious: Further and Further into Night *(1984). But why your own interest in Hitchcock?*
MB: Well, I'm always satisfied at the end of one of his films that I've had a complete piece of entertainment which has done everything I wanted it to. It's been exciting, it's usually been funny, it has star performances. It has a good story, and is very cinematic. Often the story is told through long sequences without dialogue, with strong set pieces of imagery that you remember long afterwards.

Hitchcock had quite a varied output as well. There are changing interests, over a very long career. And there are a lot of interestingly perverse sexual tensions and subcurrents going on in his films. Quite often there's a gay subtext, and strong characters.

And often, strangely, people give the best performances they've ever given in his films, although he didn't claim to direct anyone much. There must have been something about the atmosphere of the way he worked which made people give these great performances: people you didn't expect to give good performances, like Kim Novak, Doris Day. James Stewart revealed very different things about himself in Hitchcock's films. I think it was what Hitchcock could see in people that would make them work in a different way in his films.

AM: *Did you find you not only needed to see the movies but also to read around them?*
MB: Yes. Certainly we watched lots of Hitchcock movies at the start of rehearsals; the dancers just loved that! And I had read a lot around Hitchcock's ideas of movie-making. That was interesting for me, because I felt it was very visual. It's about the camera moving. Each shot was planned before, and story-boarded. I think that helped me to think about developing the plot of a dance piece. Previous to that, I

would probably have thought everything would need to be developed in a studio with movement.

AM: *What sense do you think* Deadly Serious *made to people who don't know their Hitchcock? Did you intend the result to be comic, poetic, crazy – what?*

MB: We always thought that, even if you didn't specifically know those films, you would certainly know the general type of film we were dealing with. It was obviously more fun if you knew the films. But the intention in tone was similar to *Town & Country*: we were trying to go in and out of humour, and to change the mood quite rapidly from time to time.

I think most of it comes across as fairly comic. But there are some chilling moments. It ends that way in the second half, where we finish off with duets. That part is based on *Rear Window*, the section about voyeurism. The duets could be love duets. But it's the difference between violence and love-making, and how close they can be. It ends up with one partner in each duet dead at the end and one person walking away. So it's actually a murder you're watching and not a love duet – and you see the closeness of those things. The very end is a light bulb being hit, swinging from side to side across the stage. Quite chilling.

AM: *By calling it* Deadly Serious, *you make sure that everybody goes to it thinking, 'Oh good, I'm going to laugh at this one'. Especially with a company already known as the funny company of British modern dance.*

MB: We did have lots of little sub-titles or selling points: phrases like 'It's No Joke'. We were still well known for *Crimplene* and *Spitfire* and certain funny sections of *Town & Country*. The audience liked the humour of *Deadly Serious*, even if the serious ending also made its impact. It was a very popular piece, actually. We were asked to do it more than any other piece we'd done up to that point. I think it was because the idea was very clean and simple. The inspiration for it was clearer to many people than *Town & Country* probably was. It was specifically about one thing. On tour, a lot of people thought they were coming to see a film, because of the name of the company and because the poster is very much like a film poster. But we didn't get any complaints.

However, I was always worried about it as a piece. I felt there wasn't enough dancing in it. That didn't concern the company, mind you – just me.

AM: *What did your preparation for* Deadly Serious *involve?*
MB: Before rehearsals, there was already a great deal of involvement with David Manners on the design and ideas and the music.

AM: *You've mentioned that he wrote a bit of the score. But there's a lot of different music in this piece.*
MB: We used a few vocalists within it. There's Marlene Dietrich singing 'You Do Something to Me', which is the hypnosis dance – partly for the quality of her voice, which has a hypnotic quality. We had a bit of Dinah Washington at the end: a recording of the time, the late 1950s. Also Peggy Lee's 'Mr Wonderful', which we make into a song about Cary Grant; and Etta Murfitt sang 'Che Serà Serà' live on stage. That was there as a joke. It's around someone who's supposedly been killed, but she goes on singing 'Whatever will be, will be' to it.

And two pieces of Sibelius. We used a very old recording of him conducting that lovely 'Valse Triste', from about 1907. It's ancient and slightly off-key at times, and it's got a weird crackly quality, which gives it the creepiness that works for the scene when Mrs Danvers comes down the staircase with her candle. The other Sibelius is a piece of incidental music from *The Tempest*, during a section we call 'Corridors', where Mrs Danvers is showing the second Mrs de Wynter round the house, with all the portraits and things, and she keeps coming across odd things in the house. It's a lovely piece of music.

The piece we use for the nightmare sequence at the end of the first half is Grofé, *Grand Canyon Suite*, again a historic recording, which gives it atmosphere. We used some actual Hitchcock music, some Bernard Herrmann, and the Hitchcock theme from his television series. It's the *Funeral Dance of the Marionettes*, by Gounod. We used it for a dinner party sequence: we eat dinner, then play charades, and all the charades we perform are the titles of Hitchcock films. That was quite a choreographic task! Mine was *Marnie*. 'Sounds like car'; and then 'knee'. You weren't supposed to get any of the charades really, and the second Mrs de Wynter has a terrible time too. They're all so into it, so good at playing charades and guessing them at top speed – and the second Mrs de Wynter is so out of her depth. Mrs Danvers' one is the easiest; she does *Rope*.

AM: *You don't get dafter than that.*

MB: But that was fun! It was just another way of coming up with movement. We all made up our own charade, developed it a bit, and fitted it into the time that we needed. Then we choreographed all the reactions. So that was a nice little process, because each person had a solo, and everyone's reactions to it were also choreographed to counts. Very difficult to remember, I must say – quite complicated.

AM: *I know that Scott Ambler insists that the action or mime bits of his roles – of all AMP roles – must be very precisely counted.*

MB: It annoys the hell out of me when people don't do that, and Scott more so. He feels that's AMP's style, the style we worked on a lot as a small company. He thinks that our comic or dramatic timing is very much to do with how we organize the acting in terms of counts – where we all look at the same time, how we draw the audience's focus to things with group physicality. And he's right; but it's just more difficult nowadays with a larger group. At the time of *Deadly Serious*, we were very tightly choreographed indeed. There was nothing at all left to chance in it.

AM: *I think my favourite piece is the first part, the* Rebecca *part. But you're always taking each situation off into the daffiest dimensions, so that the second Mrs de Wynter is forever blithely going around her new fabulous ancestral home – and she's terribly, terribly in love – and meanwhile, whenever she's not looking, her husband is up to God knows what with the boy in the tennis shorts. Who is the boy in tennis shorts, by the way?*

MB: He's Guy Haines, from *Strangers on a Train*. That was a film that has always had quite strong gay connotations, with the relationship between Guy and Bruno, who obviously fancies this tennis hero. So I thought Guy the tennis hero was quite a good character to put in.

AM: *How far would you say the relationship between the second Mrs de Wynter and Mrs Danvers goes?*

MB: We try to bring that out a bit as well, but certainly no more than in the film. There is a lesbian angle there; just a suggestion. I have such affection for Ally Fitzpatrick, who played Mrs Danvers. She was always wonderful to perform with, so *into* her roles. She used to sit for at least half an hour before a performance just smoking, really getting into character. And she was great to be on stage with, because you

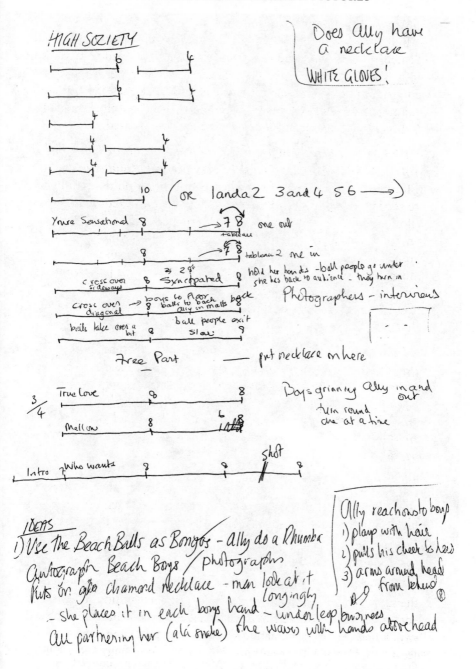

17 *Deadly Serious*. From Bourne's notes for the second half.

87

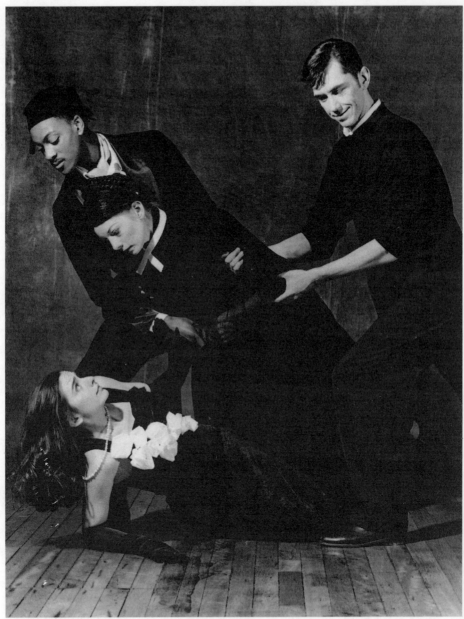

18 *Deadly Serious*. Left to right: Matthew Thomas (standing), Etta Murfitt (on floor) as the second Mrs de Wynter, Ally Fitzpatrick as Mrs Danvers, Scott Ambler as Norman Bates. From the work's first half. In the event, Matthew Thomas did not perform in *Deadly Serious*.

19 *Deadly Serious*. Matthew Bourne as Max de Wynter.

completely believed her all the time. But the moment when she starts combing Mrs de Wynter's hair and suddenly starts unbuttoning her own long dress – to reveal a shorter dress underneath – always used to make me laugh.

Also we have Norman Bates in there, from *Psycho*, as played by Scott. He's Mrs Danvers' son, supposedly, and he's into women's clothes and dressing up. The whole household is into kinky things. He's very jealous of Mrs de Wynter's dress. He's also aware of what his mother is up to. There's a bit where she starts to take her gloves off – she's always taking bits of her clothes off – and he looks disapprovingly at her. It was fun to create our own story around familiar stories, to put separate Hitchcock stories together.

AM: *Describe* The Percys of Fitzrovia.
MB: It was suggested by David Manners. He was very into the Bloomsbury set and the different arts and characters involved. This seemed another chance to do something with an English side to it. And full of character.

Because we were doing it alongside *The Infernal Galop*, we felt we

could do something a little bit more experimental. Rather than doing a
dozen quick changes and playing lots of different characters and lots
of different ideas, we were going to be the same characters and work
purely through character, with different sections that featured each
character in turn. So we had a section about listening to music; a section about a political activist (or someone who was trying to get his
point across with a political pamphlet of some kind); a section about a
poet having writer's block and trying to get ideas – which was very
appropriate! There was a section about beauty – the thing of beauty –
in which we had flowers. We cast Simon Murphy as an androgynous
figure with a bit of Carrington in him: his role was called the Exquisite.
Another section was artist-and-model: I was the artist, Duncan Grant;
Ally Fitzpatrick was Vanessa Bell, the Mother Earth figure and sculp-
tress, baking inedible buns all the time for everyone – which we actually
included in the piece! Scott was a Lytton Strachey type of character. Etta
was a more flamboyant character, like Nina Hamnett.

AM: *Am I right in thinking I saw an image from the famous Fokine/
Diaghilev ballet* Schéhérazade? *Somebody gets down on their knees
before Etta; she's got egret's feathers erupting from her headdress; and
she arches back glamorously with her arms in the air above her. Now,
that's the classic pose for Nijinsky as the Golden Slave and Ida Ruben-
stein as Zobeide. Is that not conscious?*
MB: I don't think so. You see, you're full of these precedents I'm not
aware of!

AM: *But, in the flower section for the Exquisite, you do put in a quote
from the Rose Adagio of* The Sleeping Beauty, *yes?*
MB: Yes, that's there.

AM: *And the music was what?*
MB: There's a bit of Tchaikovsky in it, *Piano Concerto No. 1*. We
mimed playing the famous chords at the beginning. There's a lot of
salon music in it, actually: pieces that I found on a salon recording
which I really liked.

I liked the piece very much. After three nightmare weeks in which
we came up with no movement at all, we toned things down a bit, and
got very specific about each section. The first piece that worked was all
about reading a book; it was such a limiting, simple idea that it suddenly took off.

AM: *Then, in summer 1993, you made a TV film,* Late-Flowering Lust, *a Betjeman piece with the actor Nigel Hawthorne.*

MB: Yes. The only other one we've done for TV – also in 1993 – is a short film called *Drip*. That was a dance for the camera, character-based and set in a theatrical boarding house. It was around the theme of narcissism. We were all actors or singers or various fans or ballroom dancers. But it didn't quite work.

Late Flowering Lust is a very happy memory for all of us, though, and was a very good experience for me. It's about fifty minutes long. Because it had a quite reasonably sized budget, was filmed on location, and planned to last a reasonable length of time – to fill an hour slot on TV – it had a lot of possibilities for different kinds of ideas. Usually, when you get any TV opportunity, it's only for something brief. But this was a major piece. For me, it was a different way of choreographing, because it had to be arranged in terms of shots. It was like choreographing loads of little vignettes that were then put together in different places to complete the music. But when you see it put together, it's exciting.

It was Nicholas Hytner, the director, who set this project up. He had liked my work, and had worked with the actor Nigel Hawthorne on *The Madness of King George*. He was involved in the initial planning stages, then left us to get on with it. The director who made the film was David Hinton; and he, Nigel and I collaborated closely to plan the whole piece. The music is by Jim Parker. He had written it about twenty years before, to go with Betjeman reading a number of his own poems. I'm very fond of those recordings, but I have to say that our recording is better, because Betjeman himself wasn't musically very precise, whereas Nigel's timing is just wonderful. The three of us spent a lot of time choosing which Betjemania we would use, and the dramatic idea of the whole piece. We chose twelve poems – out of about fifty of the Parker recordings – and created a small story of some English country weekend, in which Nigel played a Betjemanesque figure: an older man who came, hopefully, for a quiet weekend away with friends in the country, and turned up to find that the daughter of the house had returned from finishing school and had invited a lot of her young friends over. It was about him observing these young people, particularly the women; and remembering; and feeling old – and trying to be young again. These women remind him of various women he used to like: the sporty girl; the schoolgirl . . . Different sorts of characters, all very Betjemanesque.

Basically, he is ignored by them. They never actually acknowledge his existence throughout the whole thing. He is very much on the sidelines. Even at the end, when he drives off and waves them goodbye, there's a 'Who's that?' feeling to their reaction. 'Who was he?' It's very poignant.

This was the piece, for the record, that converted Cameron Mackintosh to my work. He hadn't liked the musical *Children of Eden*, and that had put him off using me in any of his productions. But when he saw *Late Flowering Lust* in 1994, he adored it; gave copies of it to lots of people; and hired me to do the dances for the Palladium production of *Oliver!* later that year.

Making it was certainly difficult. We had five weeks in which to rehearse and then two weeks to film twelve poems. On the Friday of each of those weeks, we went to the location – a place in Stevenage called Bennington Lordship, which is absolutely beautiful. So that we could see where we were going to be dancing certain sections, we used the actual layout of the place: there were some steps, and two mounds in the grass, which we used for choreographic sequences. We used the location to create the movement; the movement wasn't just casually imposed on the location. But the difficult thing was to rehearse all twelve poems and then to record them on film individually. It was a twelve-day shoot. Day One was Poem One, and so forth . . . Well, by the time you got to Poem Twelve on Day Twelve, you hadn't rehearsed it for two weeks. Yet there was all the crew waiting to do it. Remembering all that work was very difficult. Still, we did it. And the whole thing is a very happy memory. When you see the film, it's very beautiful to look at. We all look gorgeous in it. We were so pampered! We would get in, and have our hair and make-up done; and the beautiful costumes . . . And it was lovely weather. Simon Murphy – our dancer who died three years ago – was in it, and so it's a lovely memory of him too.

I also found *Late Flowering Lust* very exciting in terms of discovering what you can do for film. It's rare that you can really work on something that's an hour long in dance for the screen.

AM: *During these years, the personnel and size of the company kept changing. For* Nutcracker, *in 1992, you took on twelve other trained dancers in addition to your current six; you also took on four non-dancing actors. Were any of these to be of lasting importance to AMP?*

MB: Some of the people that came then are still there now. Maxine Fone, for example, Sara Cook (Saranne Curtin, as she later became) and Barry Atkinson, who plays the Private Secretary in *Swan Lake* and the Father in *Cinderella*. There are some other people who have come and gone a bit, but several of them have come back. Teresa Barker was in *Nutcracker* originally. She'd been a founder Cholmondeley, and had been on the BA course at Laban the year ahead of me. She stayed with us for six years.

So AMP began with a nucleus of dancers, but *Nutcracker* gave us this wider pool of dancers that we could use or not use as well. So, although we went on still doing small works afterwards, when we did *Late Flowering Lust*, Maxine came and did it. With each show we've done, the possibilities of what dancers we might use have become wider.

AM: *Your next new stage show was* Highland Fling, *your full-length version of the Romantic ballet* La Sylphide, *in 1994. We're discussing that in a separate chapter. But fill me in now on the AMP chronology from then (1994) till now.*
MB: Yes. *Highland Fling* we premièred in Bristol, in the spring of the year, and then toured it. That production stayed around quite a long time. We first showed it in London at the Lilian Baylis Theatre; the next year, 1995, we brought it back to the Donmar Warehouse. In between, we took it to Italy. We revived *Nutcracker* a second time at Sadler's Wells for Christmas 1994.

The last half of 1995, most of 1996, and the beginning of 1997 were taken up by *Swan Lake*: first at Sadler's Wells, then on tour, then in the West End, then in Los Angeles. But in between the West End and LA seasons, to fulfil Arts Council funding requirements, we revived *Highland Fling* in London again, just for a week, this time at The Place. We even did a royal gala of it, to raise funds for The Place.

Then the last half of 1997 and the start of 1998 were taken up with *Cinderella*, the only show we've ever opened in the West End itself. Right now – summer 1998 – we're preparing to take *Swan Lake* to Broadway this autumn and *Cinderella* to Los Angeles early in 1999.

AM: *You have great love of – and pride in – this early work. But to what degree, if any, do you think there was any justification in the 'juvenile' tag that was sometimes applied to you? Would you adjust any of these pieces now if you were reviving them?*

MB: It is justified up to a point. But it's also something that certainly a large number of the audience really enjoyed about the company. People enjoyed the fact that they were laughing, that this was a form of entertainment that they didn't often get in a dance performance, and that the company was, in a way, quite charming.

Sometimes, you know, the old things are the best. And if you dare to be a bit obvious or frivolous or old-fashioned – and I do mean 'dare' when you bear in mind the highbrow tone so often adopted in the modern-dance world – then your more original and serious touches can be that much more effective.

Probably I would revise these pieces now, because I would be in the position of directing them without performing in them too. Maybe I would cut some ideas. Some I simply wouldn't revive: *Deadly Serious*, for instance. Certainly, however, I've thought about doing *Town & Country* with young dancers, so as to make the innocence of that piece still work.

AM: *I think now that some people felt uneasy and unsure how to take your early work because, while the dancers were often showing innocence, youthfulness, lightness, they were also often looking out front at the same time. The mixture of calculation, or knowingness, in address with the innocent lightness of what was going on on stage left some people in the audience thinking, 'Is this serious? Is this light? What is it?'*

MB: Good point. My view now, with humorous things, is that, if you look as though you think you're funny, it's not funny. If you look to the audience as though you're asking for a response, it doesn't work. My lesson to performers is: Show what it is that you're trying to show, but don't be too obvious about it, and don't ask for laughs.

AM: *The 'juvenile' tag carried on into* The Nutcracker *somewhat and certainly into* Highland Fling. *Do you think it's fair there?*

MB: I certainly see it in *Nutcracker*; I see it to a lesser degree in *Highland Fling*. You yourself felt that there was some schoolboy humour in *Highland Fling* when you saw that.

AM: *Well, obviously* Highland Fling *starts with some schoolboy humour, but I enjoy that too. A larger reaction I have, though, to both* Nutcracker *and* Highland Fling *is the odd feeling that you might be embarrassed by the prospect of handling serious emotion: that you'd*

rather get through emotion by giving it an entirely comic emphasis. In
Swan Lake, you refuted that totally. But I'm not sure that you ever did
a complete refutation until Swan Lake.

MB: Well, you wrote a basically complimentary review of *Highland
Fling* when it came back to the Donmar Warehouse in 1995, but that
was your chief adverse criticism. And reading your review probably
went some way towards making me stick to my guns with *Swan Lake*.

AM: *What guns?*

MB: I always go into a piece with serious intent. And I certainly did
with *Highland Fling*. But I get very pulled in the direction of humour,
either by ideas of my own that make me laugh or by hilarious suggestions made by people within the company. Whenever that came up
with *Swan Lake*, I pulled back and said, 'No, this isn't the place to do
that. We're not going to do that here.' Often I would get quite a lot of
opposition. People would say, 'Look, this is going to be really funny.
This is really going to work.' Obviously *Swan Lake* does have its
funny moments; but I was far more rigorous than before in deciding
where humour could and couldn't occur.

5

Nutcracker
1992

Idea

MATTHEW BOURNE: I was initially shocked to be asked to do *Nutcracker*. It was something that I would never have considered. We had six dancers, myself included. For music like that you need a big production, more dancers, more money, more everything.

ALASTAIR MACAULAY: *Who came to you with the idea?*
MB: We were performing *Town & Country* at the Royal Court for a week, in 1991, because we were one of the Barclays New Stages award winners that year, and the Royal Court staged a season of the winners' work. A lot of work for us came out of that one week, no doubt because it was the first time we'd performed in a London performance space that wasn't specifically known as a dance venue. For that reason, we later looked into other spaces not specifically associated with dance, like the Lyric Hammersmith and the Donmar Warehouse.

One of the people who came to see us was Nicholas Payne, who was then artistic director of Opera North; I think he brought Martin Duncan with him. Martin had directed an opera or two for Opera North at that point, and the idea he had at first was to produce Offenbach's *Orpheus in the Underworld*, using Adventures in Motion Pictures. I didn't take to that idea at the time – I can't remember why – and later he produced it with another choreographer. But next Nicholas and he told me that they were planning to mount a centenary production of the 1892 St Petersburg Tchaikovsky double-bill of the opera *Yolanta* and the ballet *Nutcracker* – to recreate the original programme, but with new productions of both pieces. They had had the idea from the conductor David Lloyd-Jones, who is a great Tchaikovsky buff.

20 *Nutcracker* (1992): pre-production photograph. Above, left to right: orphanage children played by Matthew Bourne, Etta Murfitt as Clara, Simon Murphy. Kneeling: Scott Ambler and Ally Fitzpatrick as the Dross children Fritz and Sugar. In the eventual production, Bourne did not play an orphan until the 1993 revival.

Nobody had put these two Tchaikovsky pieces on together since the première at the Maryinsky. Because there were so many classical versions of *Nutcracker* around, they thought, 'Well, if we're going to spend money on this, we'd like to do something different.' I think they had cast around quite a bit, even talking to the Rambert; and I believe that noses were put out of joint at Northern Ballet, who, naturally, felt that they were the rightful people to do a co-production with Opera North. Certainly I remember there was surprise when they offered it to us.

I can see now what they saw in us: the humour, the ironic acting style, the story-telling, the accessibility, the use of more traditional music. I think they thought those things would suit *The Nutcracker*, which is famously quite a light piece – but, once delved into, is not so light. But at the time we were such a small company! In addition to us six dancers, we had Katharine our administrator and one technician, Petrus Bertschinger. So the idea came as a shock. Then, very quickly, I thought, 'What a fantastic idea! That's what I'd love to do' – not that I saw it as a career move into the classics at the time. *The Nutcracker* seemed the right piece to do at the point we were at at that stage; I could see how it suited the sort of performers we had and the kind of work we were doing; and it was an exciting next step into doing full-length works of more substance. So I was happy to take it on at the time, and I consciously gave all the leading roles to people already in the AMP company. That may not have been the best idea in every case, but in most cases it worked really well.

By the way, whereas most productions are called *The Nutcracker*, we removed the definite article: so it's just *Nutcracker*.

AM: *Though* The Nutcracker *is staged all over the world, especially at Christmas time, most productions in the last forty years have had different choreography. Only a few keep sections of the original 1892 choreography by Lev Ivanov, and almost all of them have scenarios somewhat different from that. What previous* Nutcrackers *had you experienced? In London, it has, for almost five decades, been an annual institution with London Festival Ballet – or, as that company became in 1987, English National Ballet.*

MB: I may have seen one – the one staged by Ronald Hynd – at Festival Ballet. If so, it made virtually no impression.

The first one I really took in was Peter Wright's production for the

Royal Ballet in 1984 – the one that the Royal still do (not to be confused with his later one for the Birmingham Royal Ballet, which is different in many ways). I remember that it hadn't been danced until then at Covent Garden for several years. I enjoyed the music so much, some of it familiar and all of it memorable. And the whole shape of the piece was a completely new experience for me. People often talk of *The Nutcracker* as a bore, but for me it was completely fresh. In those days, it still seemed that if the Royal Ballet did it, that was a seal of approval; this was the best version that you were going to get.

On the whole, that production was, I believe, the most complete return to the 1892 original I've ever encountered. It felt – mainly – very faithful.

AM: *That traditional* Nutcracker *tells the story of Clara Stahlbaum – an unusual heroine for a nineteenth-century ballet both because she's a child and because she's from a middle-class family – and of the Christmas family party where her present from the magician Drosselmayer is a Nutcracker. At night, the room changes size, the toys and Christmas tree attain huge proportions, and Clara and the Nutcracker and the toy soldiers fight a battle against human-size mice. They win, and he takes her on a journey, through the Kingdom of Snow, to the Kingdom of Sweets.*

There are several dichotomies in the traditional Nutcracker. *Act One is virtually all story and only occasional dance, Act Two is virtually all dance and only occasional story. Although Drosselmayer is the magician who has effected all the transformations in Act One – his nephew is the human Nutcracker who has been imprisoned in the toy Nutcracker – he never himself goes on the magic journey. By contrast, the ballerina of the piece, the Sugar Plum Fairy, is only seen in Act Two: she is the monarch of the Kingdom of Sweets, and the pas de deux she dances with her cavalier is the ultimate climax of the whole dance display that the Sweets put on for Clara and the Nutcracker. Clara and the Nutcracker are the heroine and hero of the story, but they scarcely dance at all.*

Peter Wright's staging makes a few changes – you see Drosselmayer and his nephew reunited at the end of the ballet, for example – but the basic gist of that original scenario is honoured in his Royal Ballet production. (His other production, for the Birmingham Royal Ballet, takes more liberties, as do most Nutcrackers.*)*

MB: Sometimes the Wright staging at Covent Garden went too far. There were bits that were probably very impressive if you were a historian, but that don't work any more. There's that silly bit when the Sugar Plum Fairy has to jump on a gossamer cloak – a butterfly's wing or something – and her cavalier pulls the cloak along the floor, with her on it. It's sort of fun, but only if you're aware that they're trying to do something as authentic as possible.

It's easy to say what I went against when I came to do *Nutcracker*. Often I enjoy a ballet in the theatre, but when I come to tackle it myself, I delve into it deeper and ask myself a lot of questions about it that I wouldn't ask if I was 'just watching' the ballet.

AM: *Had you any other* Nutcrackers *under your belt between the Royal Ballet one and your own?*
MB: I'd seen, on TV, *The Hard Nut* – Mark Morris's 1990 version in Brussels – which I was only partly happy with. It wasted some of the music. The fact that there was a new version around wasn't intimidating.

AM: *Your* Nutcracker *was your first story ballet?*
MB: First full-length story ballet, yes. The first half of *Deadly Serious* had a story; and there were individual sections of other pieces that told little stories. But this was our first to sustain one story across a whole evening.

AM: *So what non-*Nutcracker *works did you have in mind as models of how to make a dance story work over a full evening?*
MB: As in pieces I'd made before, I tended to take inspiration from other ballets for different sections of what I was doing. I wouldn't really use one previous ballet as an overall model for a whole piece of my own. I'd seen – was familiar with – most of the Frederick Ashton and Kenneth MacMillan full-length ballets, most of the surviving nineteenth-century ballets. I don't remember using any of those consciously as a model, though I'm sure they went into what I did.

AM: The Nutcracker *is usually done as a full-length evening by itself, albeit a short one. The same goes for* Yolanta, *which I've seen two Russian companies do as the only work of the evening. So – I well remember – the prospect of having both pieces on one programme seemed extremely daunting. But in fact the whole evening lasted three-and-a-half hours (which is less than, say, the four hours that* The Sleeping Beauty *still takes when danced without cuts at its home theatre). This was partly because you performed Nutcracker without an interval between its two acts, and partly because Yolanta has no interval anyway. The evening's sole interval occurred between the two works.*

And the evening worked very well as a tribute to Tchaikovsky himself, because the music and the stories of Yolanta and Nutcracker are so very different. His sheer diversity really hit home.

MB: Yes. In *Nutcracker* we didn't even bring down a curtain between the two acts. Later, when we did present it as an independent full-length work at Sadler's Wells, we changed that, and restored an interval.

AM: *With Nutcracker, you suddenly had a company of twenty-two dancers. What funding did you have?*

MB: I think the initial production was mainly funded by Opera North and the Kobler Trust. We may even have put a little money into it. Some money came from the Arts Council.

AM: *How long did it run with Opera North?*

MB: Just during the *Yolanta/Nutcracker* centenary year. First at the Edinburgh Festival in August. Then in Leeds, at Opera North's home theatre. Then a tour of about four venues. About fifteen performances at most, which is not very many for a new full-length work. We didn't get the chance to get into it really.

AM: *Then, when you realized that Nutcracker worked, you decided to present it as a separate project?*

MB: Yes. At Sadler's Wells Theatre, first for Christmas 1993, then again for Christmas 1994.

AM: *Did you look at the original Hoffmann story of* The Nutcracker *and/or the original scenario for the 1892 ballet?*

MB: The starting point would always be to do all those things, to read as much around the subject as possible, to read any source material for the original that you can get your hands on, so you know what you're going against or going with, so that you're knowledgeable about the piece as a whole. Often an idea from the original story or scenario will trigger you off to a parallel idea, and that re-states for you what the essence of the piece is about. Even if you don't use anything from the original, it will often have made its impression somewhere.

The Nutcracker, as a ballet, I felt to be quite confusing, actually. The story never made complete sense to me in any version that I read or saw. A lot was explained by pure magic, and I always found that rather annoying. Even in very detailed scenarios, important patches of the story would pass in a blur of magic, without explaining anything. It's always: 'Well, this man Drosselmayer is magic, so everything he does is fine, and it's the magical hour of midnight . . .' and so on. I wanted to make it more logical than that, if I could; but not take away from the fact that there are magical characters and magical occurrences in it. An important part of the story has to remain fantasy.

AM: *Is there any Hoffmann left in your* Nutcracker?
MB: I think there was a spirit of Hoffmann we tried to capture; Martin Duncan was particularly keen on that, and it's something I'd like to make yet more of, if and when I rework *Nutcracker*. The nastiness of the orphanage, and the way that its governors turn into rat-people: I think those show the spirit of Hoffmann without lifting anything specific from the Hoffmann story.

AM: *Why did you decide to set* Nutcracker – *at least its first scene and its ending – in an orphanage?*
MB: There were several things I knew I wanted to do at once. This is the same with most pieces I do: I need immediately to find a few particular things that I know I'm going to do, and then I can relax for a while before starting all the detailed work. As soon as I think, 'I'm going to do *Swan Lake* with male swans,' that's fine. With *The Nutcracker*, several things came to mind.

The orphanage setting came about for practical reasons. We still had a small company: twenty-two performers, of whom four were non-dancers. So I thought, if we were going to involve children as characters at all – which you have to in *The Nutcracker* – we didn't have enough dancers to convey both parents and children at the same time. Therefore I thought, 'Why don't we have everyone as children? Make it all about children; about children without parents?' I also decided that the Christmas party in most traditional ballet versions was too sumptuous. For most children who are coming to see *The Nutcracker* – for anyone, for that matter – the party sections are almost as much a fantasy as the fantasy sections that come later. If you already start with this big fantasy Victorian Christmas with an enormous tree and presents, it doesn't seem serious if you go anywhere else fantastic after that. So I thought it would be good to have a real contrast. That's where the idea of the orphanage came in – to make it a very grim, really pathetic Christmas. For instance, a little twig for the Christmas tree.

AM: *Were you thinking of Dickens at all? The sadness of* A Christmas Carol?
MB: Absolutely – and the orphanage in *Oliver Twist* and Dotheboys Hall in *Nicholas Nickleby*. We wanted sadness, and, as well, a sort of bitter-sweet humour. The way the children were all dressed up for Christmas to impress the governors of the orphanage – and then it was all snatched away from them; all the presents were taken away. Having the two rich kids as well – the Drosses as we called them, the children of Dr and Mrs Dross – that was very nice to play with.

AM: *Had you used the idea of children in any previous choreography?*
MB: I think we'd been quite innocent in a way, innocent in approach, especially in parts of *Town and Country*. But we hadn't been children.

21 *Nutcracker*: pre-production photograph. Andrew George (left), Simon Murphy, and Leslie the dummy. Though George played the Nutcracker in the production, here he seems to take on the role of the magician Drosselmayer, the Nutcracker's uncle in E.T.A. Hoffmann's story.

I had devised a sketch, years ago, using Joyce Grenfell's nursery-school sketches.

A second decision I made was that the Nutcracker doll itself would be a ventriloquist's dummy, because I've always found those dummies frightening and creepy. They do have a life of their own. A dummy has a mouth that moves, like a Nutcracker doll – and it has a sinister quality, too. I still have our dummy upstairs – the one we rehearsed with, not the one we ended up using on stage. He's called Leslie.

AM: *Did you buy Leslie as preparation for* Nutcracker, *or did you happen to have him anyway?*
MB: No, I had him anyway. I bought him in the theatrical shop in Cecil Court.

AM: *So, having him anyway, you knew you'd got to work him into the show!*
MB: I think they probably designed those faces to look as though they had an indeterminate expression. In rehearsals, we used to think that his face changed. We used to come in each day, and we'd look at him, and we really felt that some days he looked happier than others.

AM: *It's like the masks worn by the* commedia dell'arte: *they're expressive, but what they express seems to change according to how they're worn and how they catch the light.*
MB: I think the dummy did bring a sinister edge with it. I love the film *Dead of Night*, which contains (along with several other short stories) the story with Michael Redgrave about a 'vent' taken over by his dummy. Also there's an Anthony Hopkins film called *Magic* with the same theme. I'm fascinated by the dummy/vent relationship – breathing life (and personality) into a piece of wood. It's an idea I'd like to investigate again.

AM: *Well, there is a whole lineage of doll and statue ballets:* Pygmalion, Coppélia, La Boutique Fantasque, The Steadfast Tin Soldier . . . *You're in good company. But how did you fit this dummy into the* Nutcracker *story?*
MB: We decided that the governors of the orphanage – who visit once a year to check on conditions and things – come there on Christmas Eve. The people who run the orphanage, Dr and Mrs Dross, have organized a display for them of dances and physical fitness and so forth. These governors bring presents for the children, which are basically second-

hand toys. These are given to the children, one at a time. And one of the toys is this old ventriloquist's dummy. Then, once the governors have left, the presents – including the dummy – are snatched back and thrown into a big box. But whereas the Nutcracker doll really is something magic in the usual scenario, this dummy is only magic in Clara's imagination. Once the nightmare sequence starts, there are lights flashing from the box, and it eventually comes to life – but in a much larger form. The toy she loves comes to life; but only because it's in her dream.

Another initial idea I had for *Nutcracker* was that the snowflake scene was going to be on ice. I'd been watching lots of Sonja Henie films; and I just thought she was so perfect for the Sugar Plum Fairy – or Sugar, as she was in our version (Princess Sugar, as she becomes in Act Two). That sort of sickly sweet personality. I showed photos of Sonja Henie to Anthony Ward as my idea for the designs, because I wanted everyone to look like her.

AM: *Sonja Henie! Sometimes I blush when I talk to you.*
MB: Everyone thinks, of course, that I took the ice-skating idea from *Les Patineurs*, the Ashton ballet. Well, that was in my head as well – but only as an idea. I hadn't seen *Patineurs* for five years; I'd never watched it often, and I had almost no specific memories from it. All I consciously took from it was the basic fact that you could give the illusion of ice-skating on a dry stage. Of course, *Patineurs* brings that off better than we could hope to do.

AM: *Were there any important ideas you originally had for your* Nutcracker *that you then discarded?*
MB: Yes. The most important thing was about Dr Dross – which was, at the time, too nasty to deal with, I think. I had this idea – which Martin dissuaded me from – of Clara being Dr Dross's favourite. Drosselmayer is, after all, attracted to her in the original story and in the original ballet. I thought that Clara's whole fantasy could be triggered off by suggesting a child-abuse story. I had seen a documentary recently about child abuse; and I also knew someone who'd been abused as a child, who described the situation to me and what he felt and how sometimes the mind would completely block out the situation, would fix on to something else, and then would even forget that it had happened. I felt that we could suggest this sort of situation with Dr Dross.

One early version of our scenario says that he comes in at midnight, creeps into the dormitory, makes his way to Clara's bed, and tucks her in tenderly. I put it like that because I didn't want it to be too obvious what was happening. Then, in a later scenario, we wrote that, as Dross tucked her in, they sort of sunk into the bed together, that the bed swallowed them both up, and that then she emerged into this fantasy world. So no specific abuse was shown – but the idea was planted.

I think it was too strong an idea for Martin; and too strong, he may have thought, for Opera North.

AM: *Do you think he was right? Or would you reconsider it now?*
MB: I would reconsider it now, because I do still like it as an idea. And I think I have developed enough skill in presenting things so that they can be taken in different ways by different viewers. I think I could do it in a way subtle enough for those people who wanted to see that aspect, while not making it too frightening or off-putting for a family audience. And I think it gives some explanation as to why she goes off into a fantasy – the whole idea of her blocking out Dr Dross would be good.

AM: *I'm curious about several original details in your first published scenario, not all of which you used on stage. For example, you planned that the pillow feathers should become the snow. Where did that idea come from?*
MB: That was inspired by the Jean Vigo film *Zéro de Conduite*, where there's an enormous pillow fight in a school and the fight actually fills the screen with feathers. I thought that would be a great way for going into the snow; it would create a snow world. We didn't do it in the end because feathers are an absolute nightmare to deal with. But the idea was still there: the orphanage dormitory has its white pillows and sheets, and there is a pillow fight, though not with feathers. A lot of pillows are thrown around.

AM: Zéro de Conduite *is one of the classic screen treatments of childhood. Did you look at any other films about children?*
MB: Not that I remember. I do recall looking at lots of Victorian photographic portraits of children: books which contained pictures of very serious-looking children. We decided to use this in our development of the children's characters – quite disturbed, serious-minded kids, who have had difficult lives. Our research also took us to the Museum of Childhood and to a reproduction of a Victorian schoolroom in London's East End.

22 From Jean Vigo's film *Zéro de Conduite* (1933). The snowstorm of flying feathers in this dormitory pillowfight scene was one of Bourne's initial inspirations for *Nutcracker*, connecting the orphanage dormitory scene to the later snow scene, even though the feathers/snow connection proved impossible to show in the theatre.

Preparation

ALASTAIR MACAULAY: *How did you start on this* Nutcracker? *Did you begin by working with Martin Duncan on the scenario?*

MATTHEW BOURNE: Yes. For me, that was the most successful aspect of our collaboration, the most rewarding. He was a director, he was also a composer, and he had been involved in writing scenarios for several successful anarchic pantomimes – such as *Cinderella and her Naughty, Naughty Sisters*, which had run at the Lyric Hammersmith. So in coming to *The Nutcracker*, his mind was quite subversive.

A lot of his original ideas we didn't end up using – the same goes for many of my own ideas – but the collaboration with him was very good inasmuch as it made me concentrate my mind at the story meetings that we had to develop the plot. This was the first time I'd had to do that. The production was so large that the set needed to be built prior to rehearsals. Therefore the whole piece had to be structured and designed before rehearsals began – and that is the pattern for work I've used ever since. At the time, though, this was a different discipline. In a small production, major things could change during rehearsals; you could be creating along the way and come up with new ideas at short notice. Whereas with this, you had to have at least your basic ideas ready for each scene; you had to fit your action into a set and costumes that had been already designed – which didn't allow for you to change very much beyond the details. So the basic idea had to be formed.

AM: *You worked on the scenario with him over a period of weeks? Months? How long did it take?*
MB: We had meetings regularly for several months. But not every week. He was busy. And I was making *Deadly Serious*.

AM: *During that period, I imagine you're having sessions alone with the music? Or do you go over the score with friends?*
MB: I usually work with the music on my own. I listen to it a lot on a Walkman, when I'm just walking down the street or on the tube and the music's playing, and suddenly it just strikes me in a different way. When I get an idea, I get so excited by it, because I know that that's another thing solved. Or I get excited because I just know it's going to work theatrically and I want people to see it.

Like many other directors that I've worked with, Martin helped me to learn how to become a director myself. I really wasn't a director at that point; but he was. And he helped me gain a different viewpoint on things, because, although I'm still a choreographer, I realize – the way I work – that I'm now a director too.

The problem for Martin was that, later, when we actually came to choreograph the piece, he was also directing the companion-piece opera, which took up a great deal of his time. Inevitably, decisions had to be made, and I couldn't keep passing them through him. So once we got going, his involvement wasn't as great as he may have wanted. There wasn't a lot he could do, because in essence the whole thing is choreographed, so he may have felt redundant at times, not having enough to do. He was certainly useful and helpful with the direction of individual performers.

AM: *When I spoke to him recently, he said that he entered into the entire* Nutcracker *project because he wanted to find what it would be* like, as a theatre/opera director, to work with dancers, and I think he found it very exciting from that point of view. He very much enjoyed working on the character backgrounds with the dancers, especially for the orphanage, so that the orphans all had names and interior lives. He remembers asking each 'orphan' basic questions such as: 'How long have you been in this home? How did you arrive here?' Also he remembers working with them on how to react: showing them that some reactions can be very small on stage but can still make an impact.

MB: All that's true. Even so, my impression is that it wasn't satisfying for him as a whole, though I think he was right to be pleased with all his considerable contributions to it. Really, I don't think it works when a director has to make a piece with a choreographer – simply because, in essence, if you're a choreographer, you need to direct also; you need to have that overall control.

AM: *What specific ideas did he bring to it?*
MB: When first we came up with our original scenario, he pushed it towards the fantastical direction that he liked. So the whole idea of Sweetie Land, and of Prince Bonbon, Queen Candy, King Sherbert and all those things – that was very him. I tend to like more realistic characters; my way wouldn't naturally have been to go so fantastical; and, inevitably, I found that quite difficult in terms of choreography, especially in the effect that that had on the costume designs for group dances. The shape of the costumes was such that you just couldn't see any form to a group dance. There were too many big pink blobs, or too many men with heavy boots on. It was all right when they were doing their individual dances.

But it was successful in many ways, and that's due to Martin. People love the look of those characters, and you gained as well as lost by having them. If it were redesigned now, I would like to make some of the costumes more danceable, but I would bear in mind how well the fantastical side went down.

Something we both wanted was to make all the characters that we saw in the orphanage turn into characters in Sweetie Land, as we called the fantasy land of Act Two. (The Kingdom of Sweets, it's usually called in the ballet. Or, originally, Confiturembourg.) Everyone reappears in a different guise, and everyone is recognizably a version of what they were as an orphan. That worked well for a piece with fewer dancers.

The audience seemed to enjoy that process of recognition: that the child with glasses in the orphanage became the Gobstopper with the glasses in Act Two, and so forth. The twins in stripy pyjamas who were good to Clara in Act One became her attendant Cupids later on.

AM: *But were you also intending to make a point about the nature of dreams? That Clara populated her fantasy with people she knew from the orphanage – the orphanage being the only world she knew?*
MB: Yes, absolutely, because dreams have to develop out of some lived experience. This device also enabled us to have a narrative through-line with a childish love-story, without having to introduce characters halfway through – whereas in the ballet you only meet the Sugar Plum Fairy and all her realm for the first time in Act Two, all out of the blue.

AM: *How did you think of handling the love issue in* The Nutcracker?
MB: Because our *Nutcracker* was all about kids, it had to be a sort of schoolgirl crush on another boy in the class: the tallest boy, probably the most mature boy. That was Andrew George, who's very tall.

AM: *Like Julian in the* Famous Five *books, who's the most 'mature' and the most heroic of the children.*
MB: Yes. Clara has a crush on him in the orphanage, and has dreams about him. But he's also quite fancied by Sugar, the daughter of the Drosses who run the orphanage; she's the rich girl. So the competition is set up there: a conflict between the children being continued. Our *Nutcracker* is therefore also about a girl reaching maturity, and about that sort of love becoming more real as it goes along – at least in her dream.

AM: *And how do you introduce it into your story?*
MB: At one point during her dream, she's left alone, holding the coat that the giant Nutcracker has had on. He reappears – without the Nutcracker mask – as a man: basically as the grown-up boy she fancied in the orphanage; but now he's shirtless. They have this 'getting to know you' kind of duet. She tests his mouth with her finger to see if he's still the Nutcracker and if she can open his mouth; and he bites her. Basically, he's a big, sexy young man – and she's still a little girl looking at him in wonder. The whole scene is sexy, and it ends with him being joined by other similarly dressed men in a *Spitfire*-like dance that is all about maleness and its overpowering effect on this little girl. I wanted some kind of sexual awakening there, in her dream, her private thoughts.

23 *Nutcracker*, Act One. Clara (Etta Murfitt) suddenly sees the Nutcracker (Andrew George) transformed as the leader of a group of 'beefcake' young men. Images of virile beauty as multiple objects of desire are important to Bourne's work, spanning from *Spitfire* (1988) to *Swan Lake* (1995).

AM: *And the gesture of putting her fingers in the Nutcracker man's mouth is, of course, sexual.*

MB: Yes. What they do there, especially the way she touches him, is all very tentative. It's about discovering somebody else's body.

AM: *What are his feelings for her?*

MB: It being her dream, he's a problematic character. He's a bit flighty in it, because, though at this point he's happy with her, he soon just as easily goes off with someone else. However, her dream could also turn into a nightmare, and it does when he goes off with Sugar during the skating sequence. Sugar flirts with him, she's very beautiful, she pretends to get an injury, he saves her. Basically he's gullible. He falls for the charms of Sonja Henie. But, when reality returns at the very end, he does go off with Clara – and that's all fine, and as it should be.

AM: *You make it sound like a Bette Davis movie, with Miriam Hopkins as her rival.*

MB: It is! Well, Sugar becomes a sort of spoilt brat character. We were looking for conflict; I remember that we talked a lot about that, and I still do. When I come up with any idea, I always say, 'What's going on here? Where's the drama? Where's the conflict?'

We tried to keep the plot going through the snowflake scene. In most versions, Clara has just been journeying – you're never sure why – and then the snow scene happens and you're satisfied by the fact that this is the first decent bit of dancing, but that's all. I think it's nice to have a bit of a story left there, a 'What's going to happen next?' feeling. Ours is a skating party, but there's also a definite situation going on. Sugar now reappears as Princess Sugar; she entraps the Nutcracker and runs off with him. So the end of Act One has a cliff-hanger feel. He's gone off with another woman, with the rival; and Clara's left on her own once again.

AM: *How much of a pause was there in your original production between Acts One and Two?*
MB: None. It ended with her on stage, and then it kept going. The curtain didn't come down. Part of the initial challenge of this production was the continuation of the story and the sets. She stayed on stage at the end and was still distraught at the beginning of the Act Two music: which is when we introduced the two Cupid characters. They were the twins who'd helped her mend the Nutcracker doll in the first act, when it got broken by Sugar and Fritz.

When we redid the production, we did put an interval in, and we added a set change.

AM: *Are the Cupids the first people to introduce you to the fact that the characters are transformed in Act Two?*
MB: Yes. I'm not quite sure how the idea of them came about. They're still wearing the glasses that they were wearing previously, and they've now got wings – but I think we put them in the pyjamas because one of the original ideas we had had for the second half of the snow scene was that it was to do with sleep, sheets and bedding: she was dreaming, and the thing that suggested snow at the back of the stage was like a wavy sheet that was held in space. So the Cupids were part of that whole thing. They give her her dress, which came from above, from heaven, brought down by two doves. (That scene is called 'Help From Above'.) And the Cupids give her the courage to carry on, to go and fight to get her man back. They take her off in a Cupid-mobile!

AM: *There's definitely an angelic feeling to Tchaikovsky's music there.*
MB: I suppose I'm always drawn to things like that. I like angels and Cupidy, winged characters.

Another element is that Fritz becomes a character in the second half, called Prince Bonbon. He's still Sugar's brother, obviously working for her. So there's a constant battle all the way through: two girls fighting for the same man, one with a brother, one without. *The Nutcracker* is a light piece, and we weren't making it any great tragedy. We just gave it a bit more feeling, a bit more of an on-going plot; and we decided to make all those national dances in Act Two continue the plot in some way, however small. So the Spanish Dance, the Chinese Dance, all those dances became about guests getting into a wedding party and about Clara not being able to get in.

AM: *And you kept that plot tension going longer than in any other* Nutcracker, *because your hero is with the wrong woman from just before the end of Act One through to just before the end of Act Two. Usually, the story of* Nutcracker *has arrived at happy-ever-after – at Eden, as W.H. Auden once wrote in an essay about the Balanchine production – around the start of Act Two.*
MB: It's true, ours never really resolves until the very end. I always used to feel an enormous sense of relief on the audience's part at the end. When they finally got together, it used to get a round of applause, because by that point everyone so wanted it to happen.

AM: *Did you realize during the planning stage that there might be a problem between your narrative and the music? There isn't really any conflict in the music in Act Two, and virtually no narrative.*
MB: It was certainly harder to create 'drama' in Act Two. Where a problem arose, for many reasons, was in the Sugar Plum grand pas de deux. In our version, it ends up being danced by the Nutcracker and Sugar: which doesn't completely work, because she's not the person you want to see him dancing that music with. However, if we were going to go with that story, that was the only way we could do it, because it was the Sugar–Nutcracker wedding that Clara was gate-crashing. And this did work very well about two-thirds of the way through the music, when a certain amount of sadness can be heard in the orchestration. At that point, we had Clara appear at the top of the huge Busby Berkeley wedding cake; she looks down on to the dancers,

the Nutcracker and Sugar, and the tragic tone in the music suddenly expresses her plight, her yearning, and her despair.

I must admit it was hard work to make a narrative from Act Two, both in planning and in rehearsal. That was the real challenge. Some plot points – trying to find reasons for these dances – were only solved in rehearsal, like the Mirlitons and the Sugar Plum Fairy variation. The score for Act One's no problem at all; it's all story-telling, with great scenes and with dances very clearly defined. Act Two's a series of dances, with very little music to go on that actually tells any story. We found reasons for all the dances in the end, but I remember it being an enormous struggle. When you get a simple idea – like the Mirlitons music occurring in Princess Sugar's bedroom, with a mirror and all her friends getting her ready for the wedding – it helps a lot, because then you've got something to work with. It doesn't have to be an idea with any great depth, just something that builds up some sense of continuity, without that feeling of just bringing on one dance after another in a parade.

AM: *Have you ever been able to get all the story of a piece fixed before you entered rehearsals?*
MB: No, no, definitely not.

AM: *You're still adjusting – determining – the story all the time.*
MB: Some pretty major solutions come about quite late on, through the sheer chemistry of rehearsals. In fact, I've never felt that I've solved every problem by the time of the first night.

I've just found the draft of an AMP announcement that was written some time before we choreographed *Nutcracker* that shows how the show was at an early stage of conception.[1] We wrote it to try to raise some money for the Opera North double bill. The statement about our intentions reads:

'As AMP's choreographer, I was instantly thrilled at the prospect of radically re-interpreting this ballet classic, using a contemporary dance idiom, but more specifically AMP's particular style of dance theatre. Nicholas Payne has brought together an exciting team to collaborate on this project, including the internationally renowned artist, Howard Hodgkin'

– who, as we know, eventually didn't design it –

1 Document in Bourne's own collection.

'and the director Martin Duncan, who will be devising the new Nutcracker scenario with me and also directing the opera. Howard, Martin and I have shared initial ideas and have found much common ground and a mutual excitement about the project. We are writing a narrative which can be understood whilst watching the production, rather than one that needs extensive programme notes explaining who has put a spell on whom before the ballet began.'

Bit of a nasty sentence there!

'Having researched into many previous and current productions of *Nutcracker*, we have decided to keep the basic structure, as dictated by the music, and indeed some of the characters, Clara, Fritz, Sugar Plum and Herr Drosselmeyer, who becomes Dr Dross. But to rethink many of the scenes and to give the piece a narrative that extends beyond the first act – where the plot normally ends and we get a series of divertissements.

'Artistic Treatment. At this stage, the treatment is not yet fully conceived, but initial ideas place Act 1 in a grim orphanage, run in rather Dickensian fashion by Dr Dross. Preparations are afoot for the annual Christmas visit by the school's Board of Governors. A play and a dance are being rehearsed by the children, all played by AMP dancers. Decorations are being put up to cover the usually dirty bare walls of the dormitory and the children are dressed up in party clothes. The Board arrives, the entertainment compèred by Dr Dross, is presented, and gifts are handed to the children. Clara, Dr Dross's favourite, receives a Nutcracker doll'

– which changed. Actually, I think I already wanted to use Leslie, but didn't feel the need to explain our 'take' on the doll at this stage.

'Knowing that the gifts and Christmas finery are generally snatched away once the governors have left, Clara hides the doll behind the Christmas tree. After the party, later that night, when all the children have been put into their beds (several into each bed), Clara creeps out and retrieves her Nutcracker, bringing him back to her bed to sleep by her side. At midnight, Dr Dross, batlike, creeps into the dormitory and makes his way to Clara's bed, he tucks her in tenderly.'

This whole thing went.

'From this point, we enter into Clara's nightmare dream world and the scenario will evolve from ideas of a young girl's adolescent fantasies. The Nutcracker doll, having defended Clara from various horrors in the dormitory, such as rat people and flying children, turns into a handsome and gorgeous hunk, with whom Clara instantly falls in love. An enormous pillow fight turns the dormitory into a feather (snow) strewn landscape, where we find the glamorous and vain Sugar Plum Fairy, who enchants the gorgeous Nutcracker hunk and steals him away to the Land of Sweeties. Clara, now alone, decides to go off and search for her man. She journeys through many lands (various national dances) before arriving in the Kingdom of Sweeties to confront Sugar Plum and her attendants.'

You see, that was the original idea.

AM: *Why and when did Howard Hodgkin fall out of the production?*
MB: Howard started work on it, but I think ultimately had problems with the technical side of creating a narrative piece. He had worked quite successfully with Richard Alston at the Rambert on two or three pieces, especially *Pulcinella,* and also with Ashley Page. Very beautiful designs for those pieces. But I think my style – of wanting beds and props and all those things – was something that Howard had never had to achieve. It needed a simpler idea for Howard to come up with something. But very happily he agreed to become a patron of the company. So it wasn't a fall-out of any kind; it just wasn't something that we felt together was going to work. He's a big admirer of the company, and I'm certainly a great admirer of his work.

It was then that Anthony Ward was brought in. We gave him certain specific design ideas, and he brought others. We wanted all those beds for Act One, because they were quite important for giving the orphanage the right sense of place. We knew we were going to need quite a few props, and in rehearsal at AMP we always try to work with as many props as possible, to get a sense of the place and situation.

One big design idea we had had was that the Nutcracker kind of creates an earthquake or explosion in Act One. He magically cracks open the back wall of the orphanage – but at the same time this tree is growing at the back as well. It's the little twiggy tree the orphanage used by way of a Christmas tree; it's been thrown out the window, but now you can see it growing up behind the window.

AM: *Where did that idea come from?*
MB: We wanted to have a tree growing. We felt that it was one of the main things you have to deliver with *Nutcracker.* But, for the purposes of the plot, the Christmas tree we'd had in the first place was a little black twig virtually, with a little bit of tinsel on it. When it grew, it had a more evil, oppressive feel to it; and there's a big hand-like branch that crashes into the room at one point. So the growth of the tree creates the

break-up of the orphanage walls. It's like roots growing into the building, uprooting the foundations.

Anthony Ward also helped us to solve Act Two. That first scenario still says that Clara travels through various lands, with various national dances. We hadn't found what to do with them. All our ideas were centred around the action up to the snow, and everything seemed to work up to that point. Then the rest of it was something that had to be solved. When Anthony came in as the designer, many of his ideas went into creating that second act. He said, for example, 'Wouldn't it be fun to do some Marshmallow people? And some Liquorice people?' So then we tried to mix the feel of the music, like the Spanish music, to a Sweetie idea, which was Liquorice Allsorts. So their hair was made of liquorice.

But we were also trying to give a reason for the dances, and I honestly can't remember whose idea it was to have Clara trying to get in without an invitation.

AM: *Well, it's a way of keeping the plot's suspense.*
MB: Yes. We were very keen for that to happen.

AM: *It was a centenary production. Did you decide to use every scrap of music?*
MB: We didn't use the dance in Act Two that's often cut: 'Mère Gigogne', 'Mother Ginger'. We just didn't feel it was relevant. I sometimes thought, when we revived it, 'Should we find a way of putting it in?'

AM: *What's your musical expertise? Do you go back to the score itself? Can you read a score to any degree?*
MB: No, nothing at all. I have no musical training.

AM: *Do you have one recording? Do you find you buy more recordings than one to give yourself different ideas of tempi when you're preparing?*
MB: Yes. I usually get as many as I can.

AM: *Does that make a big difference, the difference between Bonynge and Lanchbery and Rozhdestvensky?*
MB: Yes, quite a lot. It definitely affects the story, because some recordings feel more dramatic. But also some recordings give you a different dance feeling when you start moving to them.

AM: *In a score like* Nutcracker, *do you have a clear idea which bits of music are dance music and which bits are action music?*
MB: Definitely.

AM: *There are some sections of* Nutcracker *where it's questionable whether the music is meant to support dance or action. For example, all the music after the battle in Act One before the snow scene Tchaikovsky wrote, following Petipa's guidelines, as action music; but quite a few choreographers have set a dance to it. You do too.*
MB: Well, I think that's dance music. There's a point where it goes into dance music. And it has so much feeling as well. It doesn't feel just like it's journeying music to me; it feel as if it's saying something. Then we move on.

It's usually quite clear to me – even when it's the other way round: when something is supposedly dance music and I don't feel it is. Like the end of *Cinderella*: I never felt that was dance music. As I say, I think it's very clear that most of *Nutcracker* Act One is story-telling music really. It does have these few dances within it – the children's march, the grandfather's dance – but relatively little dance music over-all. Some music in the original is meant to accompany toy dances; in our version, Martin and I decided early on to have a school display. So we had an Isadora-Duncan-type dance and then a keep-fit dance. I remembered how, at the Laban Centre, Bonnie Bird told us how, in the 1930s, some American colleges required their girls to bring 'twelve yards of chiffon for self-expression'! And that gave me the idea of an institutionalized Isadorable dance. The keep-fit dance was an easy decision: we gave it skipping-ropes and dumb-bells and all that.

AM: *Do you have any ideas for specific actions or dance movements before you begin rehearsals?*
MB: As far as action goes, I'll usually have listened to the music quite a lot and will have imagined what will happen to it. There are certain bits where I know that people enter and that the music would be good for certain events to occur. Or there'll be music where I think, 'Oh God, there's something obviously happening here – what is it?' I've usually got those things pinpointed along the way.

In the days of doing *Nutcracker*, I used to choreograph a lot more before rehearsals. I wasn't as confident about doing things then. I always started off with a lot of ideas for steps – but never enough, because I can never store that much in my head! I don't worry about that so much now; I tend to do it on the spot much more. Or I'll work it out the night before with Scott and Etta or some other people that I pick. With *Nutcracker*, because we were out on tour with *Deadly Serious*, when we had a free day, we did some rehearsal preparation for *Nutcracker*. That was when we worked out some of the school display dances and a lot of material for the skating sequence. Not much more than that, actually.

AM: *Have you already got an idea of the counts for each stretch of music before you come to rehearsals?*
MB: Yes. I'll have worked out all the counts for myself before we ever rehearse anything.

Development

MATTHEW BOURNE: Here are a few little notes I wrote for Act One. It's quite interesting to see what details changed or never got pursued:

'Preparations, First Section: paper chains, Christmas tree, party clothes, checked for nits and dirty hands, visit of Board.

'Inspections and Rehearsals: Board of Governors inspect kids and watch them dance, give them presents.

'Nutcracker doll. Sugar wants it, Fritz breaks it. Bandage. Hides it under tree.

'Performance of musical chairs.' In the event, we didn't do the musical chairs.

'Dr Dross compère. Matron does a turn. Play. Different dances. To bed.

'Presents taken away. Night clothes. Crowd into beds. Small rats are seen. Put out stockings for Christmas. Clara gets out of bed, gets Nutcracker, puts him to bed.

'Dr Dross enters. Adolescent fantasies. Bat-like. Tampers with Clara. They sink into the bed. Tree shakes.' So, you see, it was still a very frightening idea at that stage.

'Christmas tree grows. Kids shake in beds. Nutcracker grows full size, still has bandages.' I think we imagine him quite frightening as well at this point. 'Comes out of bed.' So he was originally going to be in the bed with her and then appear somehow.

'The Battle. Flying kids in nightshirts.' Well, we obviously couldn't do that, because we couldn't fly anybody. 'Pillow fight. Feathers. Rat people.' I think the family were going to become rat versions of themselves. They were going to have snouts and be exaggerations of themselves. 'Nutcracker is knocked out defending Clara. After battle: is he dead? Turns into hunk. They walk through the Christmas tree into snow. Iced-over pond (*Les Patineurs*).'

ALASTAIR MACAULAY: *So you see, you were thinking of* Patineurs *somewhat at that stage.*

MB: Yes, I'd forgotten that. Now Act Two.

'Clara is left alone.

'Vision. Two Cupids show her vision of Bohemian life in Sweetie Land, (debauched). The Governors are there' – which they weren't.

'Journey. Each time Clara and the Cupids appear, they are more bedraggled.

'Land of the Sweeties. Waltz of the Flowers. Confrontation. Back in the dorm. She throws doll across room. The real Prince is in her bed.'

AM: *Are these ideas that you would have put down after initial discussions with Martin?*

MB: They may be the notes I was taking from our discussions. I think we may have been talking, and I was just writing down these quick ideas for things that we came up with, for each section.

AM: *What about your breakdown of the score?*

MB: It's just counts, more or less. It has some things written on it: 'Clara's solo, Etta enters.' 'The Isadora Dance.'

AM: *Let's look at these titles. You've got 'Overture'. What happens in the Overture?*

MB: The orphans enter during the Overture. They introduce themselves in front of a front cloth, and they stare at the audience – as children might, if they were pushed on to a stage.

AM: *Etta – as Clara – is the first. Then the others come on. Then we have the Orphanage Preparations.*

MB: This is the cleaning and the putting up of decorations, and the bringing in of the small Christmas tree in preparation for the Governors' visit. Then they are drilled.

AM: *Then you've got 'Clara's solo'. What kind of solo?*

MB: She does a very childlike, jumpy little solo for the boy in the orphanage that she fancies – who later becomes the Nutcracker character. Then she's made fun of by the others, and laughed at.

AM: *'Mrs Dross re-enters. Line up. Dr Dross enters.'*
MB: And he inspects them. They line up for him.

AM: *'Prepare for dance.'*
MB: They've rehearsed this dance to show to the Governors. The funny thing is they don't actually ever show it to them. But that's the idea: that they do the dance as a rehearsal. The 'Children's March' is very much made up of mock ballet partnering. Not classical, more like folksy ballet movements and childlike stampings. That goes into a 'Fritz and Sugar's Dance', which is a display from those two, who are supposedly trained dancers, because they've had classes and they do a little tap section in their dance. So they're showing how it's done. Then there's a scene where the kids rebel, once the Drosses have left, and they mess up Fritz's and Sugar's dance for them.

Next the Governors arrive. They're presented with bouquets by Sugar and Fritz, and there are various displays that the orphans put on for the Governors. They do a little bow and curtsey to them, then there's a 'Medical Dance', which was basically four eights, very fast inspections of each other. They were inspecting for nits, and in each other's ears – and that thing they used to do in schools, where you used to have to go behind a screen and lower your underpants and cough – those kind of things.

Then the Governors present two very big parcels. They pick two children to bring in these parcels, and the two think the presents are for them; but they're actually for Fritz and Sugar, who then open these presents, with everyone looking on rather jealously. Fritz gets a toy gun and some sweets. Sugar gets some sweets and a beautiful Victorian doll.

AM: *Sugar and Fritz: are these two based on the two dreadful Squeers children in* Nicholas Nickleby – *Fanny and Wackford Junior?*
MB: They are a bit, yes. They're the worst kind of spoilt brats. Great characters to play. They go away to eat all their sweets and make themselves sick. They used to have – inside their sweets boxes – some Nutella, so that it looked as though as they were eating the sweets, because they got chocolate all over their faces.

Meanwhile the kids do their exhibition dances. The Isadora Dance is

24 *Nutcracker*, Act One. Dr Dross (Barry Atkinson, centre) directing one of the orphans' display dances. Andrew George, playing the orphan who later becomes the Nutcracker, is seated on the extreme left.

basically a free-expression display with lengths of chiffon, which the girls and boys do. It's all based on Grecian-type dancing. Even at my school, I remember, we did this – when we went into the hall one afternoon a week, there was something on the radio, and you were asked to be a tree or something to the music, and pranced around in your plimsolls. At Laban it was always a joke. This little Isadora Dance is led by Mrs Dross. It's her little party piece, and she's very proud of herself. This is her way of showing herself off. She was once a dancer – a very long time ago.

Then we did the Eurhythmics, as it's called here. This again is something I got from Laban. There were several students who had studied Eurhythmics, and we learnt how it went back to Dalcroze. Here it's basically a keep-fit dance, and it's packed with lots of things: dumbbells, skipping ropes. It's a highly designed little number. The end position of the Eurhythmics Dance is very complex: it's all skipping ropes; they intertwine, and open them out – like the ribbons in Ashton's *Fille mal Gardée*.

The Governors bring in a basketful of presents. One at a time, the kids come forward and get their gifts. They can pick which one they want. This is where the sissy boy picks a doll. Mrs Dross snatches it back and gives him a football – which always got a very big laugh. The Nutcracker is the last one to be picked. It's hidden away in the basket somewhere. Clara picks him and dances a solo with him.

Then Fritz and Sugar re-enter, covered in chocolate, with the dolls. Sugar comes over to Clara, who shows off her doll – that his mouth moves. Sugar presses her doll's face and its mouth doesn't move. So she dumps her doll, gets Fritz to try to take the Nutcracker dummy, and both the Nutcracker's arms get pulled off as they pull him apart. Then we have a little Doctors and Nurses section, where the twins in the orphanage, who both wear glasses, help Clara. They play doctors and nurses, put on mock hospital masks and pass the instruments. They put him together again, and give him back to her. She thanks them; and thereafter they're her helpers.

The Governors have gone off into another room, by the way, while all this stuff's going on, for a drink. Now they re-enter and prepare for the Governors' Dance. The Dross couple are now a bit drunk and having quite a good time. There's a bit of flirting going on between Dr Dross and one of the Governors' wives. They do a dance. The kids snigger at it, and think the adults are ridiculous.

AM: *In the traditional ballet, you then get the departure of the guests, the beginning of the magic, the arrival of the mice, then the vast growth of the Christmas tree. But in your version?*
MB: An enormous amount happens in a short piece of music. The governors of the orphanage, who are quite well-meaning people, leave – duly impressed by the way the orphans are treated, although we see that it is all a sham. The presents are snatched back – which happens just as the music goes rather sad. The orphans all undress for bed; all the presents and all the decorations are pulled down; the poor old Christmas tree is thrown out of the window of the orphanage. By the end of that piece of music, the orphans are all in bed, the lights are turned off, there's silence. It's the end of the day.

Then, to the change in the music where in most *Nutcrackers* you generally get the first mouse coming on, Sugar re-enters. (In my first plan, this is when Dr Dross was to come back and tuck Clara tenderly into bed. It's very furtive music.) Sugar is looking for the Nutcracker doll, the ventriloquist's dummy, which she quite likes the look of. She's jealous of it, because it can do things her doll can't: i.e. move its mouth and speak. So she comes to try and find it in the darkness of the dormitory, and hunts around all the beds. Eventually, she sees a flashing light coming from a big chest, in which all the presents and things have been put. He's been put in there.

But, halfway through that search, we get the midnight chime. At that point, Clara has seen her coming; she's hiding from Sugar behind the beds – and now you feel as though you've gone into another world. Actually, I feel it's really the least clever aspect of our plot, that we just go off into the dream world at that time. But it's hard to fight that in *Nutcracker*. The other world starts with the flashing light. Sugar opens up the box. A giant Nutcracker doll appears, like Frankenstein's monster. She runs off screaming to her family. Then we get the Christmas-tree music. The children are fearful of the Nutcracker, to begin with. He's a frightening figure – big and lumbering: scary. And he creates the earthquake or explosion I was just talking about before, magically cracking open the back wall of the orphanage, so that we can see the tree growing huge at the back. That music, with all its rising scales, is tremendous, and we made it a really alarming experience for the children: they're scared of what's happening to the tree, and they're quite frightened of the Nutcracker as well. Lots of sound effects were added to the Christmas-tree music, by the way: big explosions and thunder-cracks. They looked as if they were activated by the Nutcracker's arm movements; visually they were on specific parts of the score. But then, when the music reaches its climax – what I call the Philip Glass bit of music! – the orphans realize that the Nutcracker is there to help them and that, basically, he is giving them the means of escape from the orphanage. So suddenly they all look at him in a new light. They've got a new friend.

They hide him away just before the Drosses re-enter with Sugar. She's pointing to the box where he's been, and saying, 'There's a monster in there' or something similar. Dr Dross tries to shoot him, but he's not in there. All this goes on as the music starts for the battle with the mice; but our battle is between the family and the orphans.

It's just a big fight – and quite funny as well. The orphans tie Mrs Dross on to a bed. Someone gets the gun from Dr Dross. It's all about chasing – and a way of getting rid of the beds in the dormitory. Each of the Drosses gets dumped on to a bed, and hit with pillows, or shoved into a sack. Then that family are carted off on beds. Eventually the set is cleared of beds, there's great joy, all the orphans escape through a big crack in the wall to a better land, and Clara is left alone.

She's wondering where the Nutcracker's gone. After all, he's triumphed and saved the orphans from the Drosses and has finished off Dr Dross, as it were. So where is he now? She goes off stage, looking for him, and returns, carrying the coat he was wearing. He's disappeared; but suddenly now she is confronted by him – or rather, by the now handsome, hunky Nutcracker man he has become. The top half of his costume has been taken away and the head he had on – he had a sort of plastic head, which looked like a ventriloquist's dummy – has gone too. The reason you know it's him is that the socks he's wearing are quite significant, stripy socks, which are quite clearly visible because he's got quite high-cut trousers.

The first thing that he does is try to open his mouth and he bites her finger; we know she's making the same gesture she did with it earlier on. They do a duet, when she discovers his body and awakening sexual feelings. That vision is multiplied by all the other men in the company coming in bare-chested, giving an image of masculinity and sexuality. She almost passes out with glee. It does have quite an effect in the theatre.

He then directs her towards this new land, which is the Land of Snow – or 'The Frozen Lake', as we called it – and they encounter, first of all, the twins, who are now in beautiful Sonja Henie skating outfits. The women here are in little fur-edged skirts and the men in bobble hats and scarves and big winter jumpers. They all skate past them. It's a lovely, friendly world. Clara is cheering up slightly – but she then encounters the Drosses, who she runs away from. They wave at her in a friendly way – also in skating outfits. It's a world where everyone smiles and is happy to see each other. Eventually, all the orphans re-enter, now happily enjoying themselves.

'The Skating Party.' We tried to keep the drama going through even this big dance sequence, with the introduction of Princess Sugar – as she is now. She is Sugar Dross, and she is now the Sonja Henie figure, the Princess of Snow Land, of the Frozen Lake; and she obviously takes a liking to the Nutcracker character. She does a mock fall to the ground. He saves her, she thanks him, and thereafter she pretends to have an injured ankle. So she's a scheming little minx! And her brother, Fritz, is involved in this – Prince Bonbon, as he has become. He's her partner in crime. He enables Sugar to run off with the Nutcracker,

25 *Nutcracker*, Act One. Princess Sugar (Ally Fitzpatrick), lifted during the skating scene. This momentary lift, as frozen in this photograph, accidentally evokes a travelling tableau in Frederick Ashton's 'skating' ballet *Les Patineurs* (1937). This image became a poster and logo for Bourne's *Nutcracker*.

who is enticed by her beauty. Clara, to be honest, does look a little drab next to Princess Sugar, because she's just in her nightdress and her bunches. Sugar is all beautiful, with fur and so forth. So that's how Act One finishes, with Clara left alone in the middle of the Frozen Pond, pretty distraught, obviously.

AM: *In the original Opera North production, you then carried straight on into Act Two.*

MB: This starts with a section called 'Help From Above'. Two Cupid characters enter – they're the twins from the orphanage who helped her put the Nutcracker together again! They say that she's not looking great; she needs to tart herself up a bit, win back her man. So they present her magically with a new dress. She looks a lot better now, and they take her off to the Land of the Sweeties.

Now we get the re-entry of Sugar with the Nutcracker. She's got her skating boots over her shoulder – real skating boots, with the blades on. They're followed by Fritz, who's sort of pissed off with them for being so lovey-dovey together. Then there are the mime scenes where we arrive at Sweetie Land. And the door to the castle has a sort of sexual look to it

26 *Nutcracker*, Act Two. The two pyjama-clad Cupids:
Maxine Fone, left, and Phil Hill, right.

also. It's like a big mouth, but it has been likened to a vagina also. (I think that may have been intentional on Anthony's part.) Princess Sugar introduces the Nutcracker to the world of Sweetie Land, which is a delicious one, in that you can eat and taste the buildings and the people . . .

AM: *You make it sound very* Hansel and Gretel.

MB: Definitely. I know Martin was certainly into that aspect of fairy stories. But the point was also about values. In Sweetie Land everyone is judged on how they taste: surface values only.

Sugar shows the Nutcracker that you can lick the set, which he does. Then she introduces him to her parents – who are the alter egos of Dr and Mrs Dross. They are the monarchs here – King Sherbert and Queen Candy – and they spend a bit of time judging whether he's appropriate or not. (Sugar wastes no time in explaining that she means to marry him.) The Queen tastes him quite a lot to see if he's up to scratch. They decide that he is, and that they shall be married. Then, just as they're entering the castle gates, Clara re-enters with the Cupids. She's just in time to see the Nutcracker go in with Sugar and the

Drosses. She tries to follow, and the Cupids encourage her; but a Security Doorman comes out, and stops her.

Clara wonders how to get in. This keeps her on tenterhooks for a large part of Act Two. You need an invitation to enter; and so all the dances that follow are about people who turn up with their invitations to enter the castle – invitations to the wedding of Princess Sugar and the Nutcracker. Just as Clara explains to the Security Doorman that she hasn't got an invitation, the Spanish Liquorice dancer arrives – she's got her invitation between her teeth, and she presents it – and then her two male Liquorice Allsorts (they've got shiny black hair) join her. They dance the Spanish Dance; Clara tries to copy the movement to try and get sexier. The Spaniard sweeties pass on into the castle.

The next person Clara encounters is the Knickerbocker Glory. He enters in a puff of smoke – he's smoking some sort of dope, he's very druggy. That's in the music: the Arabian Dance, with all that hypnotic feeling. The original idea was that he was dripping. He has ice-cream hair with the cherry on top, and it's all dripping down him – that greasy sort of feeling: slimy, yugh! Now, he happens to have two invitations, his own and a spare; and Clara is slightly taken in by what is coming from his cigarette, almost hypnotized, nearly enticed by him. But she doesn't like what she might have to do to get that invitation – he actually offers it to her and she declines – because he's a nasty bit of work. He enters the castle without her – in another puff of smoke.

Then you have the Marshmallow girls – which is the Chinese Dance. They're just flighty, Marilyn Monroe dumb-blonde-type girly-girly characters, pink and fluffy and chatty, all with their invites in their handbags. They all come in as a gossipy group. Clara tries to weave her way in amongst them, but she's found out at the last minute.

AM: *You mention Marilyn. Do you often have a movie idea behind your characters?*
MB: Quite often, really.

AM: *Is there one in the Arabian Dance?*
MB: Funnily enough, not originally. But later on, yes. Later on, I did it myself just for one season at Sadler's Wells; and I must admit I felt like Terry Thomas – because of the cigarette all the time between my teeth. I felt very slimy. I know Terry Thomas isn't really like that, but I did have him in mind a lot.

The last one was the Gobstoppers Dance – to the Cossack music.

27 *Nutcracker*, Act Two. Two Gobstoppers: Phil Hill and Jason Lewis.

They're very rough, skinhead types, rude and lewd. They end up fighting each other at the end of their dance – and while the Doorman comes forward to break up the fight, Clara manages to creep into the castle behind him. This is the dance that people usually like the most, because the basic idea obviously feels as if it's taking liberties; it strikes people as outrageous to have these head-banging, punky types to Tchaikovsky. I've achieved that effect a couple of times, where the reaction from the audience initially shows you that they feel it's wrong and then it feels right quite quickly afterwards. I think the same thing happens in *Swan Lake* in the Soho scene: at first it seems to have gone a bit too far – but then you realize that it's in the music somewhere, and that it works.

AM: *And you go straight from the Gobstoppers into the Mirlitons?*
MB: Yes, but that's a new scene.

AM: *So you have little silent passages in between dances to cover this action?*
MB: Not silence – we had applause!

AM: *And, instead of acknowledging applause, you fitted action to it?*
MB: Yes. After a while, you work out ways of getting applause. You can find ways of winning it without bowing after each dance. You just give each dance a finish that requires applause – and it generally happens.

AM: *But you yourselves, in* The Nutcracker, *just carry on.*
MB: Yes. It was aimed to be continuous.

AM: *So now you change scenes, you get into the castle . . .*
MB: All that happens is that a mirror comes down behind the doorway, so we're now in a room with a big mirror in it. Princess Sugar enters; it's her room. Then her friends – who are the Marshmallow girls, and are dressed in a similar colour to her – enter. It shows a sort of bitchiness between women: they do her hair, say how beautiful she looks, but also gossip about her behind her back.

AM: *It's a dance about conventional feminine vanity?*
MB: Yes, that kind of thing. Then, halfway through the Mirlitons, Clara manages to barge her way into the room. Sugar dismisses all the other girls, has a showdown with Clara, then calls in her brother Fritz to help get rid of Clara.

He manages to, and then leaves Sugar once again alone – she's already admiring herself in the mirror. At the end of the dance, Fritz rejoins her and pops a sweet into her mouth. She spins to the floor, and they both end up chewing, looking at each other in a self-satisfied manner. So, again, I'd decided to keep telling a story at that point.

Next is the long musical introduction to the Waltz of the Flowers, the harp solo, which was a transition into the wedding party. A huge invitation descends, quite far down stage, on an angle: 'You are invited to the wedding of Sugar and the Nutcracker.' The light goes on to it – and goes off the rest of the stage. Clara comes in, sees the invitation, reads it, and then runs off.

The invitation flies back up, and we reveal vast multi-tiered wedding cake, dripping with multi-coloured icing and candles, with all the Sweetie characters we've seen entering the castle all stuck to its various tiers like edible decorations! It's a real applause moment. This cake was Anthony Ward's idea, actually. It was one of the first things he said: 'I want a big cake and what can you do with that?' I liked the idea. It seemed relevant, in a nice way. This is Sweetie Land, and we've just been introduced to all its various characters – liquorice and marsh-mallows and things. Then to re-establish them all together – as though they were part of this huge delicious cake – was a really good idea. When the curtain goes up on the cake, it feels as if these characters are part of it, because they're still. If you screw your eyes a little bit, they almost look as if they're stuck on to it. All that was Anthony's idea, very much along Busby Berkeley lines.

Then we're into the Waltz of the Flowers, a long dance, which is all about tasting each other in a debauched way, referred to by the company as the 'Licking Dance', a big 'getting to know each other' company number. At the end of this, Sugar and the Nutcracker enter with long veils or capes attached to them, which are used in the choreography as a device for creating shapes and lines and arches. They're very long – about twelve, fifteen feet long – and made of silk. They're for people to jump over; or they billow up and people go under them. I

28 *Nutcracker*, Act Two. Princess Sugar (Ally Fitzpatrick) and the Nutcracker (Andrew George), with Clara (Etta Murfitt) above. During the climactic pas de deux for Sugar and the Nutcracker, Clara suddenly appears at the top of the Sweetie Land wedding-cake, adding a new tragic note to the nuptial jubilance. The cake, inspired by Busby Berkeley films, is designed by Anthony Ward.

think it's similar to the last act of Ashton's *Cinderella*, but taken further.

When the capes are removed and the stage is cleared, Sugar and the Nutcracker go into their duet. It has a certain amount of floor work, which was our way of making it not just your average pas de deux adagio. Still, this is the bit that, in some ways, made least sense. With everyone leaving the stage, the whole thing looks so set up. But one particular point worked very well: the cake behind them lights up again, and at its top, you see Clara, looking down. It happens to a tragic piece of music, and it catches the idea that she's lost her man for ever. Then, as that adagio ends, there's a wedding ceremony. This is held with everybody else present, and King Sherbert proclaims them man and wife.

They all form in a social, ballroom-type setting around the stage for the Nutcracker's solo. This is basically a very brief, throwaway, bump-and-grind number. He just rolls his hips a bit. We were thinking of him as some Take That! boy-band idol. I'd certainly do something a bit different now, I think; but it was the right thing at that time for Andrew (George).

Next, the Sugar Plum solo starts off as a solo for Princess Sugar. This involves gestures of popping cherries into her mouth; she is obviously showing off, just as she did in the orphanage. But then, during the same musical item, Clara makes her way into the ballroom. Part of the reason for this is that it's a very long number, and – at least the way the AMP company was at the time – it didn't feel right to sustain a solo for that length of time. I wanted the story to come in again. So once again, Clara interrupts this scene; and to avoid the social embarrassment of this confrontation, the Nutcracker and Sugar's brother, Prince Fritz, come in and interrupt by dancing with them, so as to create a quartet. There are bits within the quartet where the partners swap. This involves various dramatic looks across to each other – a very similar device to what we do in *Swan Lake*, in the czardas, where the Prince and the Swan dance with different women, but look across to each other. The reason I've done this a couple of times is that it keeps some sort of story alive by having the central characters participate in a social dance in which other things are going on. So it's all dramatic, but it is still basically a dance; and it ends with Clara being carted off again by Fritz.

The coda music is the culmination of the wedding. Everyone dances with everyone, and, at the end, everyone chucks confetti in the air. There's a big wedding-photo-group finish. Clara has been chucked out for good! And then we go into the final celebratory waltz, which is a little history of social dance. This includes lots of social dance steps, including head-banging, pogo-ing, little Spanish movements, fashion-model moves, sixties dance, seventies dance . . .

At the end, when it's at its maddest, Clara re-enters. She's done a quick change; she's back in the night-dress that she fell asleep in. It's as if she's sleep-walking now: she walks across the front, very slowly, holding the Nutcracker dummy. Sugar and Nutcracker come toward her. As they pass her, she falls to the ground, just behind them. The stage clears. The palace turns into the orphanage. Then the dawn. She's asleep on the floor of the dormitory, back in the orphanage, alone. She wakes up, finds she's holding the Nutcracker dummy, and kicks him across the floor, because he's been a bastard to her, he's betrayed her. She makes to get back into bed, pulls the bed covers back – and he's there in her bed, the Nutcracker boy, without a shirt again, quite sexy. And it's not her dream any more.

AM: *Are they alone in the dormitory? Or are the other children asleep in their beds too?*
MB: We would have liked to have the full dormitory, actually. But there was no time. We could only get one bed on stage again. So – to suggest the rest of the dormitory – we put the bed in the middle.

When it turns out that he liked Clara all along, they plan, and decide to escape together from the orphanage. He opens the back window (they've tied sheets together from the beds); they climb down the sheets, and exit. The show ends with the twins running on in their nightclothes just as Clara's about to escape out of the window after him. They wave her on her way, wishing her good luck and goodbye. And that's the curtain.

Then we dance a sort of jolly musical bow, using the coda music again, which always got a great reaction. Years later, I tried to do the same musical bow again in *Cinderella*. It's OK in terms of a show like that, especially in a West End situation. Obviously with an ending like *Swan Lake* you couldn't do that.

Rehearsal

MATTHEW BOURNE: The fact that, for *Nutcracker*, we would have a sixty- or seventy-piece orchestra was already incredible; but also our conductor, David Lloyd-Jones, was so enthusiastic about the whole project. To have his seal of approval meant a great deal – basically because he absolutely adores Tchaikovsky; he conducts in Russia; he speaks Russian. And he was very encouraging. I remember him coming into a rehearsal and I was counting. Now I always count the way I hear rather than the way a musician would count. I count in melodic phrases, and I pinpoint certain sounds in the score and orchestration. The way I count the snowflakes is just ridiculous! David is quite imposing – he looks like a great man; he's very tall and actually very Russian-looking – and I said, 'Oh, I'm so embarrassed. I know this isn't the right way to count this music, but it's just the way I hear it.' I showed him the graphs that I do to counts, and he said, 'Absolutely, absolutely. Perfect way of doing it, because that's what the audience sees and hears. You're hitting all the right points in it; you're going with the flow of the music.' That made me feel good; I had been feeling vulnerable.

ALASTAIR MACAULAY: *You had your AMP nucleus of six dancers already. When you were auditioning the other twelve new performers, what were you looking for?*
MB: We were looking for a cross-section of looks. You know how kids in a group always look so odd and different? Some have shot up before the others and are much taller; they're like little adults. We wanted to catch that look. So at that point we were looking for a company of characters – and we ended up with some quite odd shapes and sizes. We didn't want them to look like a dance company. We were looking for people who had the potential to act a bit and show personality.

AM: *How do you test that in an audition?*
MB: We used to do things that showed us a bit of acting. In particular we used the 'Brief Encounter' sequence from *Town and Country*, where they go to the cinema, watch a film and change the mood according to counts. There were four counts of them laughing at something, four counts of them getting all upset, four counts for tears. It all helped to see if they had any potential for silent acting. You tend to be

able to see whether people have an intelligence in the way they dance, the intelligence to develop an acting performance.

AM: *How do you judge this kind of intelligence?*
MB: It's to do with a naturalness in the way that they present move-ment – and a sincerity about the way the movement is done. It involves the entire person; it's not superficial, not bodily only. Some people draw you to them in that way. Also how they react when they're not dancing in the audition, what sort of questions they ask, how they are with people, whether they're comfortable with themselves: all those things I look at.

AM: *How did you start the rehearsals?*
MB: We started *Nutcracker* with a sort of homework. We told every-one that they were playing a child at an orphanage. I wanted them to go away and bring in, the next day, their little life history – how they got to the orphanage; have they got a special friend in the orphanage – that sort of thing. The next day they were to tell everyone about their character.

AM: *How did you arrive at this method? From theatre directors?*
MB: In *Children of Eden*, I remember us doing workshops, in little groups of five or six, on floods and on things for the Ark, rather than: 'You are the ensemble – you will run around screaming now.' So they all came up with their own flood story, and they were all characters. Very memorable sessions. I saw how well that went down with perfor-mers. They got so involved in their characters.

So in *Nutcracker* the dancers came in the next day, and they told us how old they were, their names, how they got there, and anything they knew about their past.

AM: *Had they all known that they were going to be children in an orphanage before Day One?*
MB: Not the newcomers to the company, no.

AM: *Was it a problem for any of them, having to invent a life that way?*
MB: No. It's odd, but I never encountered any kind of resistance to act-ing from anyone in the company. I found that, somewhere inside, they're all performers. They all want to be on stage, and acting is just an extension of that. Sometimes people are not that hot, or are too over the top, or too obvious; but then you steer them.

It helps if they've got something close to home to deal with, something that they've developed themselves. The reason I get them to do it that way – and not just say to them: 'You are this character' – is that they inevitably choose something they know they can achieve. Especially when they've not really had the acting experience to develop something that's not themselves, it usually happens that, when they stand up and talk about their characters, they're really talking about themselves a lot of the time.

Sometimes this becomes very interesting! We had an instance with one dancer in *Cinderella*. He had to tell us all about his character, who was the boyfriend of one of the sisters. It went on for about three-quarters of an hour; it was like a novel. It became quite funny; we were all laughing away. But we all knew that it was really him, so that it became quite sad, to hear all the stuff that was coming out.

AM: *Did he realize how much?*
MB: I don't think so, no.

AM: *Is that part of the trick of it? That they don't realize that they're playing themselves?*
MB: I think so, yes, sometimes. They develop a character that is never totally themselves; but when they're playing something close to home, you get an honesty, a kind of truth from them as performers. It does work well; and, with *Nutcracker*, it was a new thing for everyone.

The next stage is to put the characters that they've described into a situation with the other characters. They don't have to relate to each other, but they can if they want. So they improvise around, with some sort of guidelines. Maybe – as children in the *Nutcracker* orphanage – they've all got a toy. Then you see what happens. They tell us who their best friend is, and which ones they hate. Or one of them says: 'I haven't got any friends' – that sort of thing. It helped us start the scenes off.

AM: *How are you directing or advising on all this?*
MB: There are some things you know you're aiming for. I told two of them they were twins, for example. It was Maxine Fone and Simon Murphy: they had a similar way of performing, and they looked slightly alike. But it was quite open for the majority of people. With the principal characters, who were all played by the AMP nucleus of dancers, we'd already talked about it in greater detail. They knew the

main story I wanted to construct; but a lot of the other stories were incidental to the main one, and could be flexible. And so, once I knew what their characters were, it enabled me to flesh out scenes I had only previously conceived in a general way. For example, I knew that there was a scene about children getting presents and what music it happens to; but I hadn't worked out precisely what happened in that scene. We would think, 'Which one did this? It's got to be that one, 'cos he doesn't like her.' Or, 'The little timid one, or the girly boy who picks the doll out of the bag – it would obviously be that one.'

It was great to have a room full of characters, rather than just a room full of people waiting to be told what to do. One thing led to another, especially as they thought of the wider situation – say, the matron coming in. Instantly, a lot of work's done for you. Each one knows how his or her character would probably react – whether he or she was the one that stood up to her, or the one who would hide. Some people get so involved with their character that they feel it's that character's show. They have a whole story going on that's not relevant, and you have to pull them back from it. But you don't want to destroy them too much. They've got to be allowed to feel fully about what they're doing – but maybe you position it in a corner somewhere.

When everyone is involved, they've had their own input into the production, and they can all tell you which bit was theirs and which section was their idea – which creates in them a loyalty and commitment to the performance every night.

AM: *At what point do you start connecting the characterizations to the story and to the music?*

MB: With something that's not a dance, what we tended to do (and still do) was to map out some action. Sometimes – as we found with the family in *Cinderella* – they're all doing different things all the time, and it's very difficult to keep track. So you make sure each one knows that he or she has got something to do, and is getting on with it. Then we play the music to find the points. The more we play it, the more we find those things within it. And we'll hear something in the music that will give us new ideas that relate to that section. Then we'll go backwards and forwards like that for a while. Action and music feed each other, until we've set something. It's quite laborious, because I, obviously, always want it to relate to the music completely; I'll have

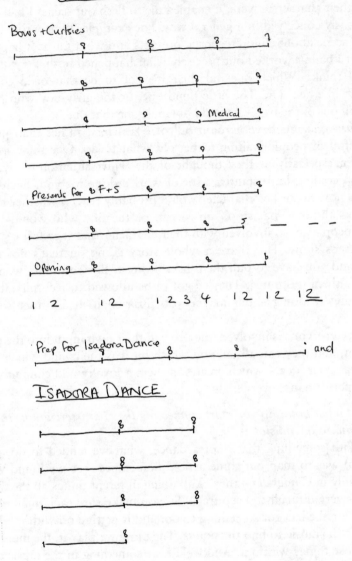

29 *Nutcracker*. From Bourne's notes on the music in the Christmas scene of Act One.

counts as well and, if the dancers can't quite hear cues in the music, then I'll give them their counts.

AM: *This process of becoming orphanage children: did that prepare them for what they were going to do in Act Two?*

MB: Yes, because something of their original characters was supposed to be visible later on as well. So the aggressive Gobstopper boys in Act Two had been the tough, rough ones in the orphanage – one of them with a plaster on his head.

AM: *Do you ask everybody to come to all rehearsals?*

MB: It's funny you should ask that. Early on, I do quite a lot of preparation work with everyone; I talk a lot; I show them pictures, videos – whatever I want them to see. I make sure they've got an overview of the whole thing. I want them to know what it is they're working towards and I want everyone to be clear on the plot.

But I hate wasting people's time! Some directors that I've worked with will have people hanging around watching, or sometimes even waiting in the corridors, just in case. I don't do that. Also, I can't quite handle a big group all the time. I need some times in a day when I'm just intimate with people. Sometimes I get more done if I just keep a couple of people behind – even if it is a group dance – and work on some stuff with them. Then, the next day, we just hand it over. It's easier than having everyone discuss everything.

I will say, 'Please, if you've got any ideas, I'd love to hear them.' Mind you, this can get out of hand. There are times when I just want everyone to stop. Some are more subtle than others, or more understanding. You don't want to rule out the fact that someone might have a great idea and that you might lose it. The good does outweigh the bad in this method of working. Still, at times, I've said, 'Right, I'm taking over now. This is what I want.' They take it quite well!

AM: *What kind of research into orphanages did you do?*

MB: We went to the Ragged School Museum of East End Life, which was a Victorian school for the poor. This suggested some of the ideas that we may have put into it.

AM: *The show starts with more or less three-dimensional orphans; and then you suddenly get this monster matron, Mrs Dross, a frightening cartoon. You really flesh out the cartoon. You understand her whole character, very vividly, the moment you see her.*

MB: I suppose I did conceive those two Drosses more as cartoony characters than the kids, because the kids are the ones that you need the sympathy for. Whereas she is symbolic in her nastiness. She's quite grotesque in a lot of ways.

AM: *Rosie Allen plays this role. How did you fix her whole performance style?*

MB: I can't remember basing her on anyone in particular. I suppose it comes very much from her, her manner, the way she holds herself. I knew that she should have a vanity about her, so that when she does her Isadora Dance, that's her chance to show off.

AM: *Somewhere between the rounded realism and pathos of the orphans and the cartoon grotesquerie of the Dross parents are Sugar and Fritz. How would you describe the mixture of caricature and realism in their characters?*

MB: A halfway house. They're quite caricatured brats to begin with. Spoilt. But I tried to give them moments of sympathy as well. There's a bit where no one wants to play with Fritz. His parents have gone off with the Governors, and the kids have all got their toys. He hasn't got anyone to show off to, or anyone to play with. He goes to a couple of the children, puts his arm round their shoulders – and they run away. He's more or less alone.

The same with Sugar, really. She's so spoilt, but in her way she does want the friendship of the other children. She quite fancies the boy that Clara fancies and she tries to impress him. But when she doesn't get her way, she resorts to violence.

AM: *What is also uncanny in Sugar is that she is terribly demure much of the time and, of course, hideously perfect. Although she does become a much nastier character, she's not an instant brat.*

MB: No. She's not that caricatured really, is she? She's not like Violet-Elizabeth in the *William* books; she's not stamping her feet and screaming all the time. She is quite demure, yes, but Ally was good at suggesting that she was very two-faced. I remember there was one point in rehearsal where, just before the dance where the orphans are sitting around and she and Fritz are doing a little display, she had to circle round and look at everyone; and the whole company all reacted as one to her face: they all gasped, she had such a superior, evil look in her eye as she went round. That was Ally's big talent: a complete immersion in character, even in rehearsals, so that you were almost frightened by her at times.

AM: *She left AMP in 1994; Sugar was the last role she created. Andrew George, your Nutcracker, was in your next production,* Highland Fling, *but left before* Swan Lake.
MB: He choreographed a lot for operas – that was why he left – and he'd been the Nutcracker and didn't want to be merely a big swan in *Swan Lake*. The Nutcracker role had been geared closely for his talents.

If and when I stage *Nutcracker* again, I will adjust it for the technical level we have now achieved with our more recent dancers, but only to some degree. Etta, who was our Clara, was and is a beautiful dancer. She has great charm and a wonderful spirit when she dances. Ally had enormous acting talent, incredible preparation and great feeling for her characters. But – as she would probably admit herself – her technical level wouldn't work now in today's company.

There is now a danger, in doing pieces like this, of losing character when working with technically better-trained dancers. The odd characters that we had within the show originally helped to make it what it was. To try to hit that fine line is something I'm still concerned about. I often worry, 'Have I lost a lot of my characterful dancers?' I know that I've got some very good technical dancers, but I need those others to bring the scenes alive when necessary. *Nutcracker* was made up of a lot of interesting people. And I will be conscious of that when I do it again, to make sure it still has that element, which is an important part of the show.

AM: *Act One of Tchaikovsky's* Nutcracker *was, I think, unprecedented in ballet music, in the way that it has almost no breaks for applause. Three or four dances during the opening party can win just brief applause, but thereafter the music is absolutely continuous. And it keeps changing in the most astonishing way, from diminutive detail to colossal romance.*
MB: That's why it's a shame that Act Two is not similar. I always feel – if you're thinking of it as a piece for kids – that what kids most like is being told a story. But it's hard to tell a story in Act Two, and unless you find a way of doing so, then – despite what ballet people say – I really don't think *Nutcracker* is a great piece for kids. You can't just get by on lots of colour. The famous Balanchine version for New York

City Ballet is not great for kids. After setting up some sort of story and an array of characters, it becomes just a series of dances. It stops making any attempt to make sense; and I think that, in some ways, it puts any child with intelligence off ballet. Children must wonder, 'What on earth is going on?'

AM: *In the dance when Clara discovers her hero Nutcracker bare-chested and then the whole of the male sex behind him, she actually walks down a male staircase. How did you suddenly dream up that?*
MB: I've often used that idea of using people as objects. I don't know whether I've seen it somewhere, but I like it. I used it again in Act One of *Swan Lake*, when the Young Prince walks down a human staircase from his bed.

AM: *Mark Morris has two women walking up parallel human stair-cases in* L'Allegro, *which you may have seen in the 1990 TV documentary on him. I think he, in turn, had lifted the idea from a Paul Taylor dance.*
MB: Actually, I think I must have taken it from something I'd seen earlier. But I can't remember what.

AM: *The Snow Dance: which bits come from Sonja Henie?*
MB: Quite a lot, actually; more than is necessary, in some ways. Sometimes, when we're making movement, we get very attached to one idea – as we still were with *Cinderella* at times – and then stick with it, where we could actually relax, open it out, and make more of possibly larger movement. That's probably what I would go back and consider revising now.

We watched a lot of Sonja Henie films; it was great fun. She had a very odd style. We used a lot of her affectation, and her personality as well, for the whole company: that sense of delight and wonder at everything we were doing. She has this way of running on her toes which I've never seen anyone do before or since. We used that for Sugar's first entrance. But it only looks strange when it's on ice; so it's actually a bit of a red herring on stage. If you're trying to create an ice effect on a stage without ice, it's slightly confusing to see someone running on tiptoes. However, we used it!

AM: *When you were a student in the early 1980s, Torvill and Dean were enjoying their great days: did the memory of that linger in your mind?*

MB: I suppose so. We did watch some Torvill and Dean, but the sort of invention that they did didn't work very well on stage.

We tried to do some death spirals, but they're very difficult to pull off, unless you are on ice. You want the stage to be more slippery than you would for other dancing, so that you can slide on it, to make the idea work.

AM: *You have a wonderful device of making people just strike a pose and then hold it on stage, as if they were sailing forwards on ice.*
MB: We tried to do some movement which had a sense of travelling but was actually on the spot. So we did it with our focus travelling somewhere. Or we had them balancing on the spot and shaking their own skirts, giving an effect of the wind on them. That used to work very well.

AM: *Another marvellous bit is when their male partners shake their skirts for them. Then there's also a wonderful moment where you really get the notion of the girls pushing off in the way that people do on ice. First you get Sugar, then another pair of girls, then another pair, each coming forwards and just holding the pose as if they're rid-ing for yards. You get the sense of the push-off, and then – though they don't move – the sailing momentum on ice. They're virtually still. Just the stillness somehow gives you the feeling of momentum, although in fact there is no momentum.*
MB: That's quite a hard thing to pull off. It can become a bit static. You have to find a way of making it work. Later on, we divided it up more, so that there were some people doing it and some people moving – so we got a sense of movement as well through that.

Another sequence, with the men and the women together, is where you get the woman pushed away by the man: i.e. she's the one who's supposed to be sent travelling back along the ice, as he pushes her away. But what we do is: he pushes her away, but it's him who moves backwards and she stays on the spot. That's a good idea which we almost didn't make enough of. It's brief, and it's disguised.

The idea behind the whole scene was that these orphans have been now released into a beautiful world. There they all are, in their bobble hats and scarves, having a fantastic time. I told everyone that what I wanted was a look of wonder on their faces; we had to rehearse this look, because some people had enormous trouble with trying to smile that way. So we tried looking upwards in wonder, and even opening our mouths when jumping – things like that. It made everybody laugh so much that we had to talk at length about those things – the smile, the open mouth – but it actually has an effect. It gets the idea across; and that idea, basically, was sheer joy and pleasure and fun and escapism. Because we'd seen the orphans all so regimented beforehand, this Snow scene had an extra feeling of happiness. They had escaped into a beautiful new world.

AM: *Your Act Two, in the theatre, has a complicated series of sets. How did you rehearse these scenes?*
MB: In this or other shows, we always try to get a sense of the physical aspect of the set by using larger props. The one thing we never had, when rehearsing *Nutcracker*, was the huge cake for the Waltz of the Flowers.

AM: *Act Two, musically, is almost all separate dances. On the one hand, you have to work up the applause that they require. On the other hand, you have to establish that there's a continuum that will make you want to see the next dance and the continuation of the story.*
MB: Yes. But no one takes a bow at any point in our *Nutcracker.*

AM: *And there are never any dances just for dance's sake alone. Everything's always plainly part of the story.*
MB: Yes.

AM: *Where did you do your homework for the Spanish Dance? You've now choreographed several; there's another in* Swan Lake.
MB: I feel as though that's not something I do have to do a lot of homework for. I've got books on Spanish dance forms; and sometimes we've brought a book in, and looked at arm positions and maybe used those. But Spanish dance is a style that I really like and I feel happy playing around with it.

AM: *The Spanish Dance in* Nutcracker *is for one woman (Teresa Barker, later Isabel Mortimer) and two men. The Spanish Dance in* Swan Lake *is also for a single woman and a clutch of men. The other national dances in Act Three of* Swan Lake *are also each for one woman and multiple men. Is that idea – one girl with two or more men partnering her – a format you're fond of for these divertissements?*

MB: Yes. In *Swan Lake*, the task is to feature each woman, each Princess, in a different way. It's very MGM musicals: the female star with her chorus. I enjoy that.

But the other national dances in *Nutcracker* have different formats. I like them; they're all funny, light. Again, there's a juvenile side coming out in me here, but, in *Nutcracker* – which is about children – that works fine. The Gobstoppers used the idea of skate-boarding bovver boys: BMX-type thugs.

AM: *The next dance, the 'Mirlitons', has probably the most famous, or notorious, music in* Nutcracker – *at least, to those of us in Britain who remember the old Cadbury's Fruit and Nut(case) advert that used to employ it. What's it like, tackling that?*

MB: I'm always slightly nervous of tackling very famous pieces of music. At that point, using Sugar and her flighty friends in her room, I was thinking: 'We'll do a gestural dance with this.' It became too intimate a dance for a big stage, I felt, because there were a lot of tiny little ideas in it. If I was to do it again now, I would find more dancing in it.

AM: Nutcracker *has two big waltzes. We've spoken of the Waltz of the Snowflakes at the end of Act One. Now, over halfway through Act Two, you have the Waltz of the Flowers. I can't help feeling that this is the much harder to choreograph of the two. Is that true?*

MB: It shouldn't be; but yes. The Snowflakes Dance has dynamic changes within the music. There's a point where the storm picks up, which is great: it gives you another idea to work with. Then it goes back to something beautiful for a wonderful ending. That helps you a lot. The Waltz of the Flowers just goes on and on along the same vein. It just builds as it goes along, but without any strong variation. Therefore, trying to sustain one idea throughout it – it's a long dance – is quite difficult.

It actually took us a long time to determine what that dance was about. They're all Sweet characters, so the idea we came up with in the end was that it was all to do with taste. Because in Sweetie Land you are judged on how you taste, rather than how you look, this is a whole dance about people tasting each other, licking each other. And this helped to add a sexual connotation. But it was fun as well. Earlier in Act Two, when Sugar introduces the Nutcracker to her parents, the King and Queen of Sweetie Land, they almost take a bite to see what he tastes like. That's in the music, where there's traditionally the Nutcracker's long mime passage, telling the Sugar Plum Fairy on his arrival in the Kingdom of Sweets about his fight with the mice and Clara's help. When David Lloyd-Jones arrived, he was a bit thrown by it to begin with; but afterwards he was forever telling the orchestras we played with: 'You know why they're doing this, don't you? It's because that's how they judge each other in Sweetie Land.'

AM: *But wasn't it hard to sustain a licking idea throughout five minutes of waltz music?*
MB: Yes. Maybe I'd find other things to do with it now. There was too much repetition – not just of the basic idea, but of the steps as well. Some of it was really good, I think, but I don't think I made it all fully visible enough. And the dance level of the company, in a big dance number like this, was patchy at the time. This is the sort of number we would be able to sustain far better with the overall level of dancers we have today. Still, the charm of it certainly made it work for audiences, most of whom don't notice technical things much – or choreography as such. They just know whether they're enjoying it or not.

We finished it off with the ceremonial entrance of Sugar and the Nutcracker wearing long capes. I'm sure I took this from something I'd seen, but I can't remember what. Partly, I think, from the final scene of Ashton's ballet *Cinderella*, where Cinderella and the Prince come on with those very long trains behind them. We used the trains, with a lot of elaborate manoeuvring around: people running under them, people holding them up, people dancing under and around them.

AM: *Then the music for the big Sugar Plum pas de deux, opening with its colossal – sublime, virtually tragic – adagio.*
MB: Here, too, I would try to create more interesting duet work. This was always the low point of our *Nutcracker* for a lot of people. It's one of the most overpowering pieces of music to dance to; it keeps climaxing again and again. It isn't possible to cut it, and you need the right two people to sustain so huge a number. At that point, it would have been wiser, with those dancers, not to build them up and expose them so much. We left the stage empty for them, as if they were going to deliver a virtuosic pas de deux. It was my fault, not theirs. In those days, I felt that that's what you were supposed to do – what *Nutcracker* called for.

I quite like some of it, but now I feel it just doesn't go far enough. It wasn't until *Swan Lake*, when I worked with Adam Cooper and Fiona

Chadwick, and *Cinderella*, when I worked with Sarah Wildor and Adam, that I really attempted to develop partnering much further. Scott and Etta have also been a great help in the development of that aspect of my choreography.

At the time, though, this show was very much appreciated precisely because people felt relieved to see a *Nutcracker* that had a through line, was a lot of fun, and had very charming performers. A lot of its weaknesses were forgiven; people were won over in other ways. And we were still telling a story. We turned the very end of that adagio into their wedding – Sugar's and Nutcracker's – brought on the father to oversee it and to pronounce them married, with everyone else present. That helped; and the whole number improved each time we did it.

AM: *After the solo dances for the Nutcracker and Sugar, you then have a coda that is, as you've said, a medley of twentieth-century social dance. What actual kinds of dance?*

MB: There's the twist, there's punk pogo-ing, various sixties and seventies types of dance – all through the century actually. There's the tango, for example; there's some ballroomy, partnered stuff, which a couple of times goes down to the floor as well. It's all very modelly and posey.

We also tried to give it the whirlwind, falling-back-to-earth feeling of coming out of a dream. In particular, we thought of the whole pack of cards in *Alice* flying down through the air and back to reality.

There are points all along the way where – in *Nutcracker* or with other shows – we were still fixing details of the story as we went along in rehearsals. But at least in *Nutcracker* I knew what the end was going to be, and that it would work. That's always comforting. What was worrying in *Swan Lake* was that, for a very long time, I really didn't know how it was going to end.

However, endings give you different problems. I always get to a stage in rehearsals where there's what feels like an undo-able amount of music left to choreograph before the first night. In *Highland Fling*, there was a good eight-and-a-half minutes of music, with just one day left to choreograph it. I knew how it would end, but the problem, as often for me, was how to fill that music to get there. Curiously, the last act of *Swan Lake* just fell into place at short notice and gave me no grief, whereas the stress of finishing *Nutcracker*, *Highland Fling* and *Cinderella* was tremendous. *Swan Lake* was the only one where I felt I wasn't going mad. With *Cinderella*, I was waking up in the middle of the night with cold sweats, hearing all the music that I hadn't yet worked out how to solve.

Production

ALASTAIR MACAULAY: *Was* Nutcracker *the first time you worked with live music?*
MATTHEW BOURNE: Basically, yes. We had done one performance of *Town and Country* at the Queen Elizabeth Hall to mostly live music, which was great. But *Nutcracker* was the first production that was always accompanied by live music, and that's such a pleasure.

AM: *Did you have the offstage children's choir that Tchaikovsky asks for during the* Waltz of the Snowflakes?
MB: Maybe for the Edinburgh première, but never on tour or at Sadler's Wells. We just couldn't quite stretch to that expense. But it would have been nice; and very relevant.

AM: *You performed* Nutcracker *in the centenary double bill with* Yolanta *for Opera North, throughout August and September 1992. Then what?*
MB: After the initial success at Edinburgh, in August 1992, Opera North revived the double bill in Leeds on the actual centenary, on December 18. That led to a tour – Nottingham, Birmingham, Manchester – that lasted up to early 1993. While that was going on, we decided to do *Nutcracker* by itself at Sadler's Wells, for Christmas 1993. I think we did it with sponsorship. Kobler Trust put money into both runs.

AM: *This meant that you were beginning to see some future for an enlarged AMP. Did that lead to extra AMP administration?*
MB: Yes. The company's steadily grown. By that point, we probably had an administrator as well as Katharine.

AM: *Once the original* Yolanta/Nutcracker *run ended in 1992, how large did the company remain? Were people just under contract for individual seasons or tours?*
MB: Yes. After the Opera North tour, we had no intention of continuing with a big company. We had talked about doing another full-length Tchaikovsky, i.e. *Swan Lake*. And Katharine got to work on that in

advance. She talked to the Arts Council about what we wanted to do. So the plan was there to do it, if we could. But there was no plan to employ all those extra people again until we did *Nutcracker* the following Christmas. In the meantime, during 1993, we did a second tour of *Deadly Serious*. There was a lot of demand for that show. Then, in summer 1993, we made the TV film of the Betjeman *Late Flowering Lust*. We had been planning originally to do that as a stage production with Nigel Hawthorne, but it changed when the offer for the film came through from the BBC.

We then did *Nutcracker* at Sadler's Wells in Christmas 1993 and again Christmas 1994. But we had to deliver a new stage show quite quickly for 1994, because we had prior funding for that financial year. And, because I had enjoyed working with a theatrical score, *Highland Fling* came about, early in 1994. I hadn't intended to do those classics in a row like that, and yet I had already begun to plan *Swan Lake* (even though that took more than another year to come to fruition), and now I decided to re-do *La Sylphide* as *Highland Fling*.

Next, I worked on the West End production of *Oliver!*, which occupied me for most of the second half of 1994.

AM: *Was it with* Nutcracker *that the Friends of AMP started?*
MB: Yes, at first in a very small way. It's grown since then, especially with *Swan Lake*, and has about 700 members now. They're very loyal and generous, and we do events for them. They are just one of several big new dimensions to AMP's work that began with *Nutcracker*.

AM: *What changes did you make between the première of the production in August 1992 and its three revivals – the first with Opera North in winter 1992–3, the others at Sadler's Wells over Christmas 1993 and 1994?*
MB: A lot of work was done to make the choreography clearer. The thing about doing any new productions, especially with less experienced dancers, is that it actually takes a while for the choreography to reveal itself – because it's not got into their bodies yet in a good way, and it's not been analysed well enough. Once you've seen something in performance on stage, it becomes very easy to see where the problems, or the weaknesses, lie.

I anyway tend to try to improve any piece choreographically each time it's revived: I try to make it richer. If I see a weakness anywhere, or a lack of something, or something I can improve, then I work on that. Often it's just a detail of steps, but it's then that you can open yourself up more to working on the steps and the movement. It doesn't matter whether the piece is already a success. *Swan Lake* has been a very big success, but I'm still looking at small revisions.

AM: *It's interesting that you've constantly been mentioning ways in which you would consider revising your original* Nutcracker *if and when you do it again.*

MB: Well, I do want to do *Nutcracker* again, and whenever I revive a piece, I consider every way, small or large, in which we might improve it. There are elements within *Nutcracker* that I think I could make stronger. There are moments in Act Two within the Clara–Sugar relationship and within the relationship with Fritz, where I think it would be good to make it more of an adult drama, to show that Clara is on the point of becoming a woman. At the moment, it still feels as if they're children playing these roles.

We could certainly make it nastier at times. Even in the earlier scenes, I could probably think of a few more nasty things to happen to the children, before they got released into a wonderful world. I feel it is there in the music. The people of Sweetie Land could be more decadent characters in a decadent world. We did conceive it that way, but the costumes took it in a more sugary direction.

AM: *To do* Nutcracker *again, would you have it redesigned?*

MB: Only certain aspects. But yes. A lot of costumes would need to be redesigned.

AM: *What do you think you achieved with* Nutcracker *that you hadn't achieved before?*

MB: A completeness. A piece that felt like a whole, rather than an assembly of separate items. One of the interesting things about our full-length 'ballet' pieces – *Nutcracker, Highland Fling, Swan Lake* and *Cinderella* – is that there is very little you can lift from them as a set piece. When we're asked to do a gala or a TV appearance, there's very little that will work on its own. You would need an explanation to show why these things are happening this way – which tells you how relevant the story is all the time. Whereas, before that, *The Infernal Galop, Town and Country, Deadly Serious* and others were all made up of short numbers, little set pieces, vignettes, that could be lifted out and performed on their own.

What I enjoyed doing most about *Nutcracker* was telling a complete story. And I was very proud to have worked with Tchaikovsky, quite honoured. Having worked with directors by that point, and found how rewarding it was to tell a story with sustained characters to a great score – it was the beginnings of feeling that there was something that we could do as a company that nobody else was doing. And this was accompanied by a certain amount of acceptance and wide encouragement from establishment people and press for what we were doing. Working with a complete piece of great music was perhaps the greatest pleasure of all.

AM: *I hate to say it, but I don't think you'll ever have the chance to work again with a score like Act One of* Nutcracker.
MB: No, there's nothing much else like it.

6

Highland Fling
1994

Idea

ALASTAIR MACAULAY: *You yourself nickname these four last full-length works 'classics'* – Nutcracker, Highland Fling, Swan Lake, Cinderella – *because they use the scores and (to some extent) the scenarios of ballet 'classics'. And I always feel that I should declare an interest here because, when teaching dance history to you and other students in the early 1980s, I paid considerable emphasis to these ballets, an emphasis unusual perhaps in modern-dance academe. In fact, in your very first term at the Laban Centre, we concentrated on Romanticism and the nineteenth-century ballet repertory.* La Sylphide *(the basis for your* Highland Fling*),* Swan Lake *and* The Nutcracker *were all discussed in some detail. The whole idea of Romanticism, in its full political and social context, was a wonderful way in which to make dance students see the excitement of history; and it was good to make them see how much there is to say about each of these old ballet warhorses when they're taken seriously.*

La Sylphide is, in most ways, the prototypical Romantic ballet; it was the first ballet that I used to ask students to consider, particularly its story.

MATTHEW BOURNE: Yes, and, in 1982, that was probably my first exposure to *La Sylphide*. The story really is a good one. That was what appealed to me when I was looking for the next full-length piece to make after *Nutcracker*. I had seen it on stage a few times, and I must admit I'd never found it very impressive. You know, I loved going to see *The Nutcracker* and *Swan Lake* and *Cinderella* before I ever thought of doing my own versions of them. But all that drew me to *La*

30 *Highland Fling* (1994). Publicity handout. The two images of the Sylphide and James are of late nineteenth-century and early twentieth-century photographs of dancers in August Bournonville's version of *La Sylphide* (1836) above a Scottish tartan.

31 *La Sylphide* (1832): opening image. Marie Taglioni (kneeling) as the Sylphide in the original Paris Opera production, with her brother Paul as the sleeping James. The sylphide is appearing in James's dream. This production of *La Sylphide* (choreographed by Filippo Taglioni, father to Marie and Paul, to a scenario by the tenor Adolphe Nourrit) became the archetype of Romantic ballet throughout the nineteenth century – as well as the basis of Bourne's *Highland Fling*.

Sylphide was its story. I re-read the scenario, I read a little bit about how the piece was the essence of Romanticism, I reminded myself – again, by reading – of what Romanticism was, and then I went out to buy a CD of the music.

AM: *So let's reconsider* La Sylphide. *Its première in 1832 changed the course of ballet history. It is about the love between a Scots farmer, James, and a winged female sprite from the glens, the Sylphide. It has all kinds of archetypal Romantic dualism. Act One is set in a Scottish farm-house, in which only one character – the Sylphide herself – is supernatural: she alone shows the full language of classical ballet, dancing on pointe and in a soft romantic tutu. Act Two is set in the supernatural*

32 *Highland Fling*. Maxine Fone as the Sylph and Scott Ambler as James. In Bourne's variant of *La Sylphide*, James is stoned and the Sylph is a zombie-like drug-induced hallucination.

33 *Highland Fling*. Maxine Fone as the Sylph. The use of unpointed bare feet and angled knees is inspired here by accounts and pictures of the dancing of Isadora Duncan.

world of a Scottish forest, in which she is one of many sylphides, all female and all dancing classical ballet; James is the only human – and the only male – in their scenes there.

MB: The idea of two worlds is very appealing: two different worlds with the interval in between. It was a nice, neat contrast and structure, and it was a good length. I could see quite a lot of potential. But also a big challenge, because, after all, this was to be a small-scale touring show with only seven people in it. It was quite a decision to do a piece like this, to see if a small-scale full-length piece could work as well as a large-scale ballet. Very little change of set would be possible; this was a production made to tour to quite intimate venues.

AM: *The ballet's scenario is itself perfect Romanticism. James leaves his fiancée, Effie, to pursue the Sylphide – even though she is literally unattainable. He is impetuous, and offends the old witch Madge. How-ever, when he later encounters Madge in the forest, he is tantalized by the fact that he can never hold the Sylphide. Madge offers him a magic scarf with which he can bind the Sylphide to him. He takes it, but it is poisoned, and causes the Sylphide's death. (The moral about trying to hold the unattainable is clear.) As he is grieving, Madge draws his attention to a wedding procession in the distance. Effie is now getting married to another man, Gurn, who has loved her all along; and James has nothing left, either in the real world or the supernatural one.*

Were there other particular features that appealed to you in this?

MB: As I said before, I remember having to make a decision very quickly as to what to do. I looked for a complete score, as I had done with *Nutcracker*, to find one that I thought would work. I don't remember looking at any other one ballet. As you know, *Swan Lake* was a project we wanted to do, but later. And what took my fancy straightaway was the idea of putting *Sylphide* into modern-day Scotland. Virtually everything I'd done had been set in the past, and people were always saying to me, 'When are you going to do something that's set in the present?' So it was fun to take what is virtually the oldest ballet in the repertory, with its romantically Walter Scott notion of Scotland, and transfer it to the present day.

AM: *Were you thinking of what Fergus Early had done, in* Naples *(1983) to Bournonville's* Napoli *by transposing it to modern-day Naples? Or of the* I, Giselle *he and Jackie Lansley had made (1980) as a feminist version of* Giselle?

MB: I'd seen and liked *Naples*, but – my memory being what it is – I'd forgotten it. It may have influenced me, but subconsciously.

AM: *After* La Sylphide, Romantic *dualism – with the hero from the real world, the heroine from the supernatural one – became a standard recipe for many ballet scenarios throughout the nineteenth century. Ballet became largely a drama about the ethereal or exotic ballerina, whose element was the air, and the mortal and earthbound hero, whose love for her is doomed and tragic. And ballet dancing became something essentially feminine. I'm generalizing, of course; there are important and honourable exceptions to this rule.*

The 1832 Paris version became world-famous, in particular, because it was the perfect vehicle for the Romantic ballerina Marie Taglioni, the dance sensation of the era. The music is by Schneitzhoeffer, and this version – its original choreography was by Filippo Taglioni, Marie's father and teacher – has been reconstructed a few times.

However, the version we usually see derives from 1836 and Copenhagen. The Danish choreographer August Bournonville used the original scenario, but changed its emphasis in certain ways. In particular, he gave much more dancing to the role of James. He commissioned a new score by the Danish composer Løvensjkold – it is his Opus 1. Particularly since the Second World War, it is this version that has gained international currency.

MB: I didn't know *La Sylphide* terribly well on stage. I'd seen Peter Schaufuss's version for London Festival Ballet several years before, and wasn't mad about it. I appreciated it on one level as a piece of history, but I never got excited about it as a theatre piece.

Seeing it again recently, first with the Australian Ballet and then with American Ballet Theatre, I have to say the Bournonville choreography doesn't interest me very much. It also seems unmusical. It's not my favourite piece in terms of dance, whereas *Giselle* completely works for me still. In particular, I can't bear Madge the witch.

It took me time, curiously, to find much in the *Sylphide* music. Perhaps Løvenskjold sounded small fry after Tchaikovsky. I remember that I went out and bought the CD with the idea of staging it already in my mind as a possibility; and when I listened to it, I was slightly disappointed at first. It all sounded the same, I thought, and dated. I blush to say that now, because actually it is a wonderful score, and bit by bit I came to realize how theatrical it is.

AM: *What were your first ideas for the Sylph?*
MB: We decided that she should be not as pure as in the original; that she should have a kind of evil side to her as well. That comes out in a sort of naughtiness, a kind of daring to be different, daring him to be different as well.

AM: *Well, Bournonville talks about her that way in his memoirs. He calls her a 'dark angel' and talks of her 'poisonous breath'.*
You say, 'We decided.' I'm curious what you yourself decided before it became 'we'.
MB: It's difficult to remember sometimes. But – this is interesting – originally the Sylph was going to be a man. Then, when I decided that that would be a better idea for *Swan Lake* – the two ideas were floating around in my head at the same time – I quickly changed it.

AM: *Who did you have in mind to dance this male sylph?*

MB: Me – would you believe! And then – I think partly because I knew that *Oliver!* would prevent me from dancing in the piece anyway, partly when I had the *Swan Lake* idea of male swans – I just ruled it out.

AM: *How funny – because* La Sylphide *was already a gender-reversal. When Adolphe Nourrit created the scenario for* La Sylphide *in late 1831, he based it on Charles Nodier's story* Trilby, *which has a male spirit haunting and luring a female Scottish ferrywoman. But Nourrit, a tenor who had himself appeared on stage with Taglioni in certain operas, could see the potential in making the spirit a female role. Did you know about the* Trilby *original?*

MB: Again, if I did, I forgot. I was just interested in playing games with the conventional expectations of gender. *Spitfire* had been an all-male pas de quatre. In *Deadly Serious*, whenever we went into any kind of couplings, because there was a cast of four men and two women, there would always be one male couple, which sometimes had connotations and sometimes didn't. So we were always playing with sexual roles.

AM: *When did you think of putting drugs into it?*

MB: Very early on. That was the basis of doing the piece. It's the logic of why James sees her and why nobody else does. She's an hallucination. I knew that drugs occur in several later Romantic ballets – the most famous being in *La Bayadère*, where the whole scene of the Shades is an opium dream – and I wanted to connect that to the way people take drugs today. As *Trainspotting* shows, there's a big drug culture in Scotland, some of it very grim; but I also wanted plenty of comedy.

AM: *Your James is a junkie, and your version of the story makes it a 'Just Say No to Drugs' show. Did you know people who had taken too many drugs?*

MB: Not directly, no. I do now, actually, a few. But not then. I myself had had no personal experience whatsoever, and I don't think it's something I needed to have experienced to make this piece. But I certainly wasn't into making any great anti-drugs message. There seemed to be enough of that around. Drugs in general, however, just seemed very relevant.

The main message is that James is the kind of crass man who tries to impose his own possessive and destructive male desires upon his fantasies, as well as on his own disastrous real life. It is James's story.

AM: *Your Scotsmen are all lager louts?*
MB: Yes. I wanted them all to be rough and coarse. Then I thought, 'What's the most coarse? What's the worst place? What's the most we can make of this idea? What's the most unexpected beginning? Where would you find him?' Which is why it actually starts in a urinal – pretty startling for *La Sylphide* – with nasty graffiti on the walls. A urinal is a secret place, the place in clubs where people generally go to take drugs. So it would be the natural place for our James; and it's an unusual place for the Sylph to appear.

AM: *When we first see her, she comes up from the top of the urinal?*
MB: Yes.

AM: *I hate to say it, but isn't this the second urinal you've choreographed?*
MB: I'm afraid so, yes. There's history for you! Fame for no other reason: 'Incorporated two urinals into works, one French and one Scottish' – the other urinal being a cottaging scene in *Infernal Galop*.

AM: *Do the girls drink?*
MB: Yes. They're a pretty rough bunch, as a whole. So – as I was saying about the punk Gobstoppers in *Nutcracker* – the audience feels a kind of shock at the beginning of it, and then an added enjoyment when they realize that it will work. And the Sylph doesn't look the way you'd expect: not all beautiful. She looks a bit druggy herself, a sort of 'Say No to Drugs' victim.

Preparation

MATTHEW BOURNE: I purposely changed the title so as not to put off the kind of venues we were going to. We were performing in arts centres and the sort of venues that would normally have small contemporary dance companies. If we'd have been doing *La Sylphide*, it wouldn't necessarily have gone down as well.

ALASTAIR MACAULAY: *Do you remember where you did your homework?*
MB: I probably went through my old dance history notes! I tend to

look into the Balanchine Festival of Ballet book. In the old edition, the scenarios are really excellent as stories. I looked at other dance history books (my notebooks have a Xerox from Lincoln Kirstein's *Movement and Metaphor*), and other views of Romantic iconography. I bought a book on the Romantic movement in art, and read around the wildness and the passion of all that. At once I thought that that went very well with the cliché of the Scottish character: hot-tempered, violent, abusive with drugs and drink.

And the music just kept growing on me; I ended up loving it. It's full of energy, variety, melody. We consciously made decisions to play up to the melodrama of the music, and not make our production too realistic. To that music, it had to be a very heightened form of drama; so the means by which we were telling the story had to be heightened as well. We decided – unlike in *Nutcracker* and *Swan Lake*, where we tried to tell the story through acting and dance – to use gesture and our own more literal form of ballet mime, to add to the melodrama. The more I listened to the music, the more the melodrama within it seemed to suggest lots of arguments and tempers flying about. It did seem to suit the characters and the setting, and it helped the story quite a lot. In Act One, though, we didn't completely follow the original music. We actually added a couple of musical items: the sort of tampering I wouldn't do in a larger-scale work. Because we were using recorded music anyway, it just seemed perfect to have *Brigadoon* playing on the TV when you first go into the flat. *Brigadoon*'s a piece that everyone loves to hate, really. And we also put the Wedding March in, just after the wedding reel, to show that they had actually got married.

I really like *Highland Fling* as a piece, actually. Whenever I come back to look at it again after a while, I see how everything gets tied up very neatly. Everything has its place, and it's very clear. I particularly like Act Two. We had completely our own story going on there, and I was working quite independently of how Bournonville uses the same music. Virtually the whole of the second half is a dance drama; it's danced from beginning to end, virtually the whole time.

AM: *That's interesting because – even though it's modern dress –* Highland Fling *seems less radical than your other shows. Am I wrong?*
MB: Well, it was my first real attempt to do something with a tragic ending. There's a lot of humour, and then, suddenly, when the Sylph's wings get cut off, very suddenly it has a change of mood.

I think it says something about a certain type of man. He appears to want something different. He's got this homely girl, Effie, who does the ironing and all the housework and is sweet, pretty, and seems the perfect wife; but he's excited by the Sylph, who's naughty, and sexy, and alluring, and strange. Then he quickly gets bored with her being different, cuts her wings off, and – basically – tries to turn her into a woman like Effie. He doesn't want her to be as she is; he wants her to stay at home and do the housework.

At the end of Act One, which is set in a high-rise, he jumps out of the window to follow the Sylph. Act Two takes place, logically speaking, in his mind while he's falling to his death. It's all over then. The sylphs kill him.

AM: *So the problem with James is not that he takes drugs, but that he has the crassest kind of male mentality in the first place.*
MB: Yes. And that kind of maleness is shown very much in the first scene: the disco scene at the pub. This is to additional music – or, rather, to Løvenskjold's overture. We thought there weren't enough dance possibilities in Act One, so we wanted to have an opening that had more movement and dance, and would introduce the characters. Well, they do all sorts of crass things in that. They're swearing, belching, throwing up, snogging in the toilets, peeing. It's all very much introducing that world.

As we went along with it, we talked about it a lot. When AMP was a smaller company, we would often sit around talking for hours about what a piece was saying and where it was going; and the more we delved into it, the more reasons we found for things and the richer it seemed.

AM: *You knew from the first that you were going to have male and female sylphs?*
MB: Yes. Out of necessity, but also because we'd already been challenging sexual roles in our smaller shows in various ways.

AM: *There's no difference between a male and female sylph?*
MB: No. Well, here and there, there are some slight differences with things that they do, but only at one point do they dance separately. And they are slightly differently dressed. All the sylphs have a costume like the one for Scottish country dancing, but all in white. They all wear sashes; the women have simple dresses, the men have kilts and

belts and baggy shirts. (Clement Crisp wrote in the *Financial Times* that our sylphs looked 'like manic dirty laundry'.)

So they're like dead Scottish highland dancers. And they have these ties in their hair, which was inspired by Björk, who tied her hair in knots. I seem to remember that was my idea.

AM: *Do you think of your sylphs as having gender?*
MB: Yes.

AM: *And, having decided not to have a male Sylph, you decided to make the Sylph this rather wraith-like female.*
MB: Yes. What I didn't want was a conventional-feeling, romantic love-interest story. I didn't want it to be all pretty and dainty – that didn't feel right. I needed her to be touching at times, but she was more of an animal, a creature, dirtier, a bit more bedraggled, like someone that had lived in a forest, covered with grass stains. And she was destructive as well. Like Tinkerbell in *Peter Pan*. She's got a two-edged personality, which I like.

AM: *Your sylphs are barefoot. Taglioni danced in pointe-shoes; but, curiously, a number of the Romantic lithographs depict her – like a Grecian statue – with bare feet. Were you thinking of those pictures?*
MB: We certainly looked at a lot of those pictures, in books of the Romantic Ballet. And we also decided to use ideas, not just from *La Sylphide*, but from the whole of Romantic ballet that followed. Certainly aspects of *Giselle* (1841) went into our version. In Act Two, our sylphs are much more like the demonic dead spirits of *Giselle*, the wilis of its Act Two, than they are like the ethereal, harmless sylphs of *La Sylphide*. The way they enter is very much like the way they do in *Giselle*, and the inspiration for the structure of the whole thing was much more *Giselle* than *La Sylphide*. In the beginning, we even had a queen of the sylphs, like the queen of the wilis in *Giselle*, though we cut her out when she proved just one character too many. And our Sylph throws flowers to James, which is very *Giselle*. (Usually in *Giselle* he doesn't attempt to catch them, but I once saw Wayne Eagling catch them very effectively at Covent Garden, and so I put that into our version.)

The other big influence on all the sylphs is Isadora Duncan, or the feeling of Isadora. I love that kind of movement. Of course, I don't really know exactly how Isadora moved – I never saw her dance – and

yet I feel I know what this kind of movement is. It's a spiritual aban-
donment, a very centred kind of movement that spreads through the
limbs from the centre of the torso, a very free way of interpreting
music, and a floaty use of costumes. Our sylphs do a lot of jumping,
and their arms keep moving while they're travelling through the air –
not positional – because I wanted everything to come from some sort
of impetus somewhere; and I feel that's very Isadora-ish. As are their
bare feet.

I also had a book that's all about Fokine's *Les Sylphides*. It has
many pictures, and we looked at it to get ideas for gestures, such as a
'listen' phrase we used. Whereas the 1832/36 *La Sylphide* didn't much
inspire me in terms of its choreography – particularly in the dances for
the sylphs themselves – the plotless 1908/9 *Les Sylphides* was a perfect
thing to use.

AM: *When Fokine made it, he was probably more inspired by Isadora
(whom he had seen dancing just a few years before, and whom he
greatly admired) than he was by the Romantic ballet, which for him
was mainly an idea of the past – largely, as for you too, shaped by
Giselle – which he preferred to the more virtuoso ballet of more recent
decades. Isadora danced to Romantic music, and her dancing had the
simplicity and economy that he found poetic. So, even though she herself said she was the enemy of the ballet, she is not an inappropriate
inspiration to a latterday Romantic ballet.*

*At times in Act Two your sylphs become parts of the wood: trees,
brambles, landscape.*
MB: We felt that the sylphs were always watching, that they could be
within a tree, that they could become a tree, that they could be anything they wanted to be. We knew we had a virtually empty stage and
a backdrop. So our sylphs could become landscape. The stage becomes
designed with people.

AM: *There are times when they also seem very sculptural – and, interestingly, like sculpture from just the neo-classical era from which
Romanticism exploded. Is this accidental?*
MB: I certainly remember that we looked at lots of statues and paintings from the early nineteenth century.

AM: *I suspect that this connects to the way Taglioni danced; the classical and sculptural qualities of her dancing were especially praised, as*

well as the floating quality and lightness and pointe-work for which she is more renowned.

When did the subtitle A Romantic Ballet *become* A Romantic Wee Ballet?

MB: Obviously a bit later on. Likewise, it was later that James changed from being a Scottish crofter to an unemployed Scottish welder.

AM: *In the original, the witch Madge has an important function in both Acts One and Two.*

MB: Yes. She's there in our first act. She's the ex-girlfriend of James; she's into tarot reading, seeing into the future and those sorts of things; she's a New Age kind of woman. So she makes the predictions, like Madge in the traditional *Sylphide*. She also supplies him with drugs, so she's responsible for his downfall there. Because they're ex-lovers, they've got an antagonistic relationship anyway; but she's still in love with him as well. She's jealous, basically – that's why she makes the prediction. But also he needs her, because she's the supplier. Unlike the traditional Madge, she's there throughout Act One; she's a fixed member of his social circle.

AM: *But she doesn't come back as Madge in your Act Two at all. This is the main change you made in the scenario.*

MB: In Act Two she is not relevant. That's why Act Two feels more like *Giselle*, because it's just him and the sylphs.

AM: *By removing Madge from Act Two, you remove some degree of plot. So that left you with music to fill in another way.*

MB: The strange thing is people always think – I suppose it's one of the questions you were hinting at earlier – that everything comes from story, feeling, and character in my work; but really, one of the things I'm looking for when I enter into doing something is the dance possibilities. 'Where can we get more dancing into this?' That was why, in *Highland Fling*, we also used Løvenskjold's overture. It feels like dance music and it builds up a great atmosphere. Likewise, the witches' dance at the beginning of Act Two. We even extended Act Two to put more dancing in: we used the beginning of the overture again, so that each act begins in the same way.

AM: *Do you distinguish between dance and acting, or between dance and what I would call physical theatre?*

MB: I've always found those definitions difficult to deal with. I'm never conscious of saying, 'All right, now we just dance.' But I know when I enter into doing a piece, there have to be good reasons for dance within the story that we're telling. People are always suggesting different books and plays and saying, 'Why don't you do . . .?' I just think, 'But how does that turn into dance?'

By removing Madge from Act Two, we made it clear that the reason why the Sylph loses her wings is entirely to do with James's will. The whole show is based around him.

AM: *What about the music for her and other witches at the cauldron that opens Act Two?*
MB: It's such great music, the cauldron bit; it has that lovely witches'-brew, demonic feel to it. So it helps to introduce the world of the sylphs.

AM: *That makes it more* Giselle-*like, because you get the dark element?*
MB: Yes. And, as in *Giselle*, the beginning of the second act is about being introduced to the sylphs before the central characters re-enter. James only re-enters halfway into the music, and then we don't actually identify the Sylph. He's looking for her, but she's like all the others – until a particular point in the music, where they come face to face.

AM: *Later on, how does she lose her wings?*
MB: In one scene, the sylphs are all round him, and he's enjoying being in their world. They teach him how to fly, how to be a fairy; and it culminates in a big dance. Then they get too physical. They all want a piece of him, because he's a human. He brushes them all off and says, 'You have to choose between them or me. We're leaving together.' He's seen the way she is in the forest; he wants her to stop being what she is; he wants to turn her into a real woman. So she gets her little sylph bag and goes off with him. He takes her to another place in the woods, gets the shears out, and cuts her wings off – with garden shears. It's all very bloody – not pretty, but a real shock. It makes complete sense.

AM: *Then she dies?*
MB: She's around a bit longer. He's shocked at the whole thing that's happened. She comes back on and acts like someone who's had an arm cut off. She's shaking, and she does a version of some movement they've done earlier on. It's like the mad scene in *Giselle*, where she half does the steps she used to do but now in a broken way. The

Sylphide music's lovely at this point as well. James begs forgiveness from her: he tries to get her to move again and to dance again; he helps her around the stage. She's nearly dead; she keeps on drooping and coming to life again.

It builds up again to the climax where she finally does die. Then the sylphs pick her up and take her away. It's done so that, as he lifts her up and they take her from him, it's as if she's disappeared. She's not there any more. And he's alone. He does a regretful solo. Her wings are left behind, and he puts them in the little bag that she's left, so that he's got them as a souvenir. It's ridiculous and very moving at the same time.

AM: *Did you know that Alicia Markova used to have a little bag for the wings she wore as Giselle? She wrote that she knew she had made* Giselle *famous when she left the bag in a taxi once and the driver said, 'Excuse me, madam, you've left your wings'!*
MB: And I thought we'd invented the wing-bag! I didn't know that story. Anyway, then the sylphs come back and have their revenge on him. They attack and kill him; but we don't see them actually do that. They do the death symbol; and then we have this little scene at the end to suggest his death, where Gurn and Effie are at home in front of the fire, drinking coffee. James appears at the window. He's now a sylph; he's got wings: he's haunting them.

AM: *This was your first collaboration with the designer Lez Brotherston.*
MB: We're much on the same wavelength in terms of the ideas that he comes up with. He listens; he'll talk things through; he'll get an idea of what we think we're going for, and then he will visualize them – very well, actually – in fully realized, painted drawings. When I first worked with him, I was always slightly embarrassed to say when I didn't like something, because it looked as if he'd put so much work into it. I said to him once, 'I don't know what to say sometimes.' He just said, 'Really, this is the best way to do it. I work very quickly like this, and this is the way I like to show you what the idea is. This is the best way.' So from that point onwards, it's always been fine. He does churn out beautifully realized drawings very quickly, and he works quickly in general with the sets later on. There's never any break, pondering on things for weeks on end; and he happily scraps ideas very quickly, which is great.

AM: *Diaghilev sent Picasso back six times to re-do the sketches for the set for* The Three-Cornered Hat. *So you're in good company.*

MB: It's a good working relationship Lez and I have. I think he particularly enjoys working for this company. We give him more freedom and the chance to have his own say in what goes on. He's very good at adapting costumes for dance, and very aware of what you can dance in and what you can't – aware of the way things should be cut, etc. He had already worked with Northern Ballet a lot, so he's used to dance floors and dancers' problems, and all those things you need to know about when working with a dance company. He's also very clever at making something look as if an enormous amount of money's been spent on it when it hasn't.

Rehearsals

MATTHEW BOURNE: Before the rehearsals began, I worked out all the counts for the music. I can do it quite quickly if the music's not too difficult. I can virtually do it while I'm listening to it one time through; but it would be something I'd come back to. I would do the counts first; then, once I'd got the counts sorted out, I'd listen to the music again, looking at my counts, which are in graph form; then I'd stop the tape where I thought something particular might happen and make a note above the particular column; and then I'd come back to it again and maybe write notes.

ALASTAIR MACAULAY: *When would you first have started doing this?*
MB: About a month before rehearsals; I would know the music very well by that time, and would already have an idea of what I'd do to it.

Having done just *Nutcracker*, I was very involved by this new way of working. It's because I could actually work with the score in advance in that way; and, having all this, I was very excited at entering the rehearsal period. Looking through my notes here, I can see all kinds of initial ideas: Cathy from *Wuthering Heights*, James as a crack addict, James having a seizure at the Highland Games. Then 'Madge injects him'. Oh yes, and everybody was going to bring toasters as wedding presents. These are some of my first thoughts.

Then, opposite, I've written counts: not how many beats there are in each bar, but the groups of counts I feel that the music falls into for my purposes. Very often I'm looking – if the music has two, four or eight beats in the bar – for counts of eight. If it's in three/four tempo, I'll adjust. But it's hard for me to know now which notes I wrote before rehearsal or during rehearsals. There are plenty of notes here that show ideas we had but never used. Some of them are ideas I brought to the first rehearsals; some of them are ideas we all came up with during rehearsals. Quite often the ideas that we never wrote down are the ideas that we ended up using.

A few things happened around the time of *Highland Fling* that connected with the piece. My friend James McCloskey – who had designed the first piece I did for AMP, *Overlap Lovers*, and all my amateur shows before I went to Laban – died from Aids two weeks before it premièred. Even the fact that his name was James seemed relevant. And within the show we had, as Gurn, Simon Murphy, who was also suffering from Aids at the time. There came a point where he couldn't continue with it; and although it was a humorous piece in many ways, that always made the end more touching in a way for those of us who were involved in it.

Highland Fling was also the first small-scale show I wasn't dancing in myself.

AM: *Does that change the physical style of a piece?*
MB: Yes, very much. I think that, when I was in the first performances of pieces, I got more physically involved, obviously, because I had to learn and develop the material and actually dance it as well. Sometimes that can lead you to develop material in a different way, to physically find more details and connections, which you don't do so much when you're not in it: you rely on other people a bit more to develop the movement. When you're not dancing, you watch more. The good thing is that, if you're working with good people, you get a lot of ideas you wouldn't have necessarily found it you relied only on your own physical or imaginative instincts. But it's wise to try to physicalize things if you still can, because otherwise you lose your own style of movement. Certainly I feel that there are particular things that I emphasize and that I like to do.

AM: *How long did you have to rehearse* Highland Fling?
MB: For small shows like that, we used to have eight weeks. For *Nutcracker*, we'd had five weeks, which was ridiculous – nothing. But we were all buoyed up by the success of *Nutcracker*, and we thought, 'This is what we're going to do – to retell these stories.' We felt we had

a seal of approval for that, we felt braver; and I was now very into everything making sense, into giving references for everything.

We did the same character homework with these characters, but we talked about the story more first, to make sure the relationships were already sorted out. So I told them the general storyline, who they were, and what their relationships were with each other. Then they'd come back with more of a character and how they saw it. That would then help with fleshing out the individual scenes.

So here's the list of characters I wrote out during rehearsals after we'd all talked about them: 'James, or Jimmy, unemployed welder. Glasgow. Drink and hard drugs. Sympathetic.' I thought that, as he was the hero, he needed to have some sympathetic quality. The performers all chose their own jobs. Scott Ambler played James: it's the most central role I've ever given him, even more than the Prince in *Swan Lake*.

AM: *You had to cast all the roles among this small nucleus of AMP dancers. Were there any problems?*
MB: Simon Murphy had problems initially with Gurn. I wanted him to be a drip, and he didn't take to that. He solved it by making Gurn a born-again Christian, simple and nice, with a smily T-shirt with a 'Jesus Loves Me' slogan. He used to carry around a Bible when he did it, too. It worked really well. The notes just say 'Gurn, supervisor in furniture warehouse. Everything in moderation. Sympathetic. Born again.'

When Phil Hill took over that part, in 1985, he didn't like the born-again Christian thing, and he did his little strong-man act, which worked as well.

'Effie, clothes shop. Day-release business management. Slightly prudish. Unimaginative.' This was Emily Piercy, who went on to do the Prince's girlfriend in *Swan Lake* so well.

'Madge MacPherson, bar maid who organizes discos. Drug dealer small time.' This was Etta Murfitt; she just loved having a role that was so different from Clara in *Nutcracker*!

'Dorty, beauty therapist. Tough, common, materialistic, trashy, and has a sexual relationship with Robbie.' This was Rosie (Rosemary) Allen; again, quite a change from her role as Mrs Dross.

'Robbie's a red-head, oil rigger. Laddish, loutish, sexist.' This was Andrew George, who'd been the Nutcracker.

AM: *None of you were Scottish?*

MB: No. And, because I was worried about it being too clichéd, quite late on in rehearsals I went to my friend the actor Alan Cumming. I'd known him since he played Silvius in the RSCs 1989 *As You Like It*, for which I choreographed the dances.[1] He's Scottish, and I brought him in to watch, and asked him, 'Do you think it's OK?' He liked it a lot, thought it was fine, and helped us with a lot of Scottish graffiti in our toilets! – words that we wouldn't otherwise have known. Here are some notes I made during a meal with him. 'Haud yer wheest' means shut up; 'I've got the painters in' means having a period; 'Getting off at Paisley' means withdrawing(!). 'Lena Zavaroni gives me the dry boke'; 'Fur coat, nae knickers'; 'Taggart is a faggot'; 'I love Isla St. Clair'. (Clement Crisp quoted some of these in his review and said, 'This is the level of humour in this piece.')

Then graffiti more related to the characters: 'Gurn is a dork. Madge is a les. James for Effie' (with a heart written round it). 'Dorty is a slag.' 'Jimmy is a fairy.'

As I've said elsewhere about any idea, I go for the most Scottish or the most French or the most whatever it is that you can do. The set was covered in any Scottish references we could find.

AM: *I remember laughing out loud at seeing those graffiti.*

MB: One of them was: 'Sit on my face, Jean Brodie.'

AM: *Your initial sketch for a poster says, 'Highland Fling – a romantic new ballet.' Then it adds in the corner, in your hand, 'As sweet as a Glasgow kiss.'*

MB: That's quite good, I should have used that. A 'Glasgow kiss' is a head butt, by the way. I learnt that from Alan.

Here are some notes I wrote, fairly early on, for the first scene: 'Smoochy dance. James corners Effie while Madge is in ladies. Four 8s, disco together, dance while talking. Then have a pee, go, freshen up.'

AM: *Is it clear what drugs James is taking?*

MB: I must have changed my mind about that. We had to decide whether he would inject or smoke or swallow. But I think we plumped

1 When Bourne won two Tony Awards for *Swan Lake* in New York in June 1999, one of them was presented to him by Alan Cumming – himself a Tony-winner the previous year for his performance on Broadway in *Cabaret*.

for Ecstasy, partly because it seemed very popular at the time, partly because we wanted to show him taking pills.

AM: *Later on for this scene in the toilets, you've written down character ideas: 'Use sinks, adjust clothes, pose, apply make-up, argue, gossip, laugh, take drugs, drink, have a pee, revive James, Robbie has a nose-bleed, 2 people lean against each other, Dorty feeling a bit sick.' For the fight at the end, you've written: 'Three 8s plus . . . James going wild, Effie and Madge fighting. Centre it around this' – so that's a note about spacing – 'Girl intervenes, Dorty and Robbie get involved, free for all.'*

In your notes for the next scene, you've got plenty of eights counted out, with bits of scenario written where appropriate. At one point you've written: 'Syncopated altercation about partners.'

MB: That means I knew the movement would look good if syncopated against the music.

AM: *The Sylph actually makes her first appearance in this toilet scene, rising up from the urinal wall. And it is the Sylph – later, the other sylphs also – that suddenly lend a whole new astonishing dimension of seriousness to Highland Fling. How did you start off with your idea of the Sylph?*

MB: As always, much depends on casting. I'd already imagined the Sylph being like Tinkerbell, and I cast Maxine Fone in the role. She was just perfect. She's got a naughty side to her, she can look very beautiful, and she's not a woman that will accept playing a little pretty, nothingy sort of female character. She has to have a bit more spunk. And, while everyone else was researching their human characters, she did lots of research into sylphs and fairies. It was very much her thing: she loves anything Gothic; she loves horror movies; she reads constantly around the areas of fairies and goblins. She already had a lot of material, went and bought a lot more, and told us a lot about what fairies do: all the types of fairies there are, bits of information which were quite useful for coming up with movement material as well. So a great deal of our conception of the sylphs came from her.

AM: *Therefore, for Maxine and perhaps for you, a sylph is somebody with a life of her (or his) own: she's not just a figment of James's imagination?*

MB: In any kind of dream or hallucination situation, you have to create characters that have their own life. You believe in them. You have to believe that James did fly out of the window and go somewhere – and that, though this did happen in fantasy, it really happened. If you say, 'All you are is a figment of his imagination', then you haven't got much to go on.

I think that Maxine's body type really helped the piece as well. She's so petite; she's got a lovely little body. When the wings get cut off at the end, she seems so tiny and frail; her little hands were so shaky, you felt for her. I think that, by the end, you like her as a character. Yet she's quite destructive in the first act; she just causes havoc and smashes things. But her mischievousness is very appealing.

AM: *I do think you're on to something that was in the original* Sylphide. *Bournonville writes about the ballet in his memoirs, as if he rather regrets having tampered with something so tragic and dark and dangerous. He says, 'For me, the Sylphide has been what she was for James, a dark angel who tempered everything with her poisonous breath.'*

MB: I do feel that it's there in the music. That's probably why I find the Bournonville ballet – at least, as it is produced today – annoying; and I don't find the witch frightening. Nothing really works for me in it well enough. It just seems pretty and period and harmless – unlike the score.

Here are some notes from research into sylphs: 'A middle nature between man and angels.' 'Known as sylphs in the highlands.' 'Evil fairies are strong and wicked in the highlands.' 'Fairies avenge wrongdoings with blights and illnesses or even death.' 'Especially handsome men are desired as lovers by fairies preparing princesses.'

AM: *One thing the sylphs have in common with the swans of* Swan Lake *is black-lined eyes, which gives a zombie impression. Is that the wrong word to use?*

MB: If 'zombie' means 'living dead', I think that's true. Less so in *Swan Lake*.

AM: *Now we're into your notes for the next scene. 'It is morning, James is asleep. TV on. 'Brigadoon'. Gurn turns it off. Hangover. Drug dance: Gurn and Robbie. They collapse or leave. Sylph enters (behind chair): solo. Sylph wakes up James . . . He sleepwalks. She leans on him. Balances her. Lifts her while he is asleep, tries to kiss her. She disappears, maybe later. He is shit scared.'*
Why the idea of sleepwalking?

MB: Because I wanted it to feel as if it was in stages, as if this was just the beginning of him being aware of her. I wanted to give the impression that he is actually asleep through all this. So that starts the scene. Then, suddenly, the development of the hallucination becomes a reality to him. I think sleepwalking does show a kind of sub-conscious need. It expresses something deeper within you.

AM: *From that we go back to trivial domestic matters. 'Effie enters with Madge and Dorty. They've been shopping for wedding things at Brides, wedding presents. The women clear up and do the housework: housework dance, feather duster dance, washing line, ironing. Men get in the way.'*
MB: Clichés abound!

AM: *'Effie, Gurn, Dorty emerge. Feather dusters. James gets in the way. Robbie hoovers.'*
MB: Robbie works on an oil rig and he's home for the weekend. So he's very randy. But they put a pinny on him and make him hoover.

AM: *'Gurn helps Effie with ironing. Lovesick.' It looks to me as if you've got an awful lot thoroughly conceived before you get to rehearsals. All this stuff about getting the performers to flesh out their roles is a fraud! You work out everything in advance.*
MB: But I'm prepared to change everything – and often do – during rehearsals.

AM: *Later, you have all Madge's predictions: 'Faster, strange rhythm, cards slower.' Then 'Robbie oil death.'*
MB: Death on his oil rig. We didn't mime that in the end. There's only enough music to do Dorty. You see, I also wrote, 'Gurn, he will sin,' because Gurn is a born-again Christian; but we never did it.

AM: *Next, after James has taken more drugs, he sees the Sylph again. 'She seduces him with her abandoned sexuality (She is a tease. Uses length of chiffon to entrap him.) Finds butterfly. (She is a butterfly.) Feeling her face/body. Puts his hand through her. She intoxicates him. He begins to move like her . . .' Tell me about the Sylph's 'abandoned sexuality'.*
MB: She's freer with her movement, obviously, than anyone else is so far. And she has a kind of freedom in the way she's dressed; she's bare-legged. She represents a sexuality to him that his prospective wife,

Effie, doesn't. We were actively going against the image that one usually has of the Sylph, to make her more of a sexual being, as an alternative to Effie.

AM: *The Sylphide is really an adultery fantasy. But you're right. Taglioni's father trained her so that 'Women and children should be able to watch you dance without blushing.' And Gautier called her 'a Christian dancer', as opposed to Fanny Elssler (his favourite), a 'pagan dancer'.*

MB: 'Uses length of chiffon to entrap him.' We didn't do that in the end, but the idea was to reverse the traditional *Sylphide*, where he uses chiffon to try to entrap her.

As for 'butterfly', we had the idea that she was a real butterfly, that there was some sort of logic to his hallucination. Later on, he does bring on a real butterfly, at the end of the act, and he looks at her in the same way.

'Feeling her face/body. Puts his hand through her.' There's a bit where she runs towards him, and passes through him, and she comes out the other side. That's the effect we tried to give.

AM: *There's one lift in Act One, where she's on his chest, but she slowly moves her legs through a kind of scissor shape. It's wonderful, because you feel her progress forwards through the air even while she's leaning down on his body like some huge force.*

MB: Maxine saw herself very much as a vampire.

AM: *Then she has a wonderful movement when she bourrées back on half-toe in first position, writhing her shoulders up and down alternately in a figure-of-eight roll. What gave you that idea?*

MB: Goodness knows. But I'm very fond of using the shoulders. It always suggests something sexual and abandoned to me, and that's what I wanted from her at that point. It's very Ashton, as well. There's a movement I love in *Marguerite and Armand*, though I only know that ballet from film, when she's being kissed on the chest and she goes backwards, with her back to you; and the shoulders just give.

AM: *Am I right in thinking that there always has to be an impetus in or through the torso in your work?*

MB: Yes. I'm always looking for where the movement starts. Often dancers don't pick up on it. Like ripples through the arms, which we used a lot in *Swan Lake*. People start it around the biceps somehow. I

34 *Highland Fling.* Scott Ambler as James, Maxine Fone as the Sylph. In this lift – inspired by Ashton choreography – the Sylph walks forwards through the air while pressing down upon James and pushing him backwards.

always want it to start at the shoulder or in the back, but they're afraid of doing that, because it doesn't feel right. I say, 'Don't be afraid, because it's much more creature-like to do that, if you're a swan or whatever.' I always think of Ginger Rogers with her shoulders often so up; it's very interesting. And Lynn Seymour is actually rather like that. She completely distorts the upper torso and neckline when she wants; she'll hoist the whole of the shoulders up and around and put them into everything. Really inspiring.

AM: *And she ends up having immense repose around the shoulders too.*

MB: I've always enjoyed the use of the back in everything. That's what I always loved about watching Ashton's work. So whenever I see a possibility for that, I always get people to emphasize, or overemphasize, that.

AM: *Well, Ashton's two favourite words in rehearsal were 'Bend' and 'More'.*

MB: Right. You can see why; that's what dancing's all about. People who move that way – you just love watching them so much more than someone who's all prim and precise. It comes much more naturally to dancers with a contemporary background. They don't feel tied down by classical training; that freedom comes more easily.

AM: *At the end of this episode for the Sylph and James, you've written 'Soothes him. Faster. And she throws washing in the air.'*

MB: As he begins to want her, she shows the other side of her personality, which is naughty, wild. She wrecks the room: all the stuff that's just been tidied up, and the ironing that's just been done. She pulls pictures off the wall, and dumps the washing everywhere; so that when she disappears and he's left, it looks to all intents and purposes as if he's wrecked the room, when the others come in.

AM: *At one point here – so unlike a Romantic ballerina – she even walks on her heels around the room.*

MB: Yes, she stomps a bit. She becomes more like a naughty child.

AM: *Also here she sends up the whole Taglioni image. She's in a temper and she sarcastically does the classic Taglioni pose of resting her chin on the fingertip of one hand (with that elbow resting in turn on her other fingertip).*

MB: Yes, that's part of her naughty period. She starts off more serene and sexual, then she switches.

AM: *During the scene that follows, you wrote at one point, 'Bournonville phrase.'*
MB: We did allude to some Bournonville movement, in some jumps and some uses of the head. We also decided here to show that there was some sort of reality to the Sylph. Gurn returns to the house, alone, and hears the Sylph in the kitchen. He goes in – and comes out holding a white butterfly, stroking it. The idea is that that really is the Sylph. She may be an illusion in James's mind, but this butterfly is what he has projected the illusion on to.

AM: *Then we come to the reel. You've written, 'Bigger, swords.'*
MB: We did a dance with the men's legs being swords and the women dancing over them, crossing legs, and jumping.

AM: *Now it says 'teapot'. Is that the same 'teapot' dance idea of domesticity you used in* Town and Country?
MB: Yes. For the men. The left hand's on your hip, the right hand is the spout, and you tip from the waist like a teapot. The girls are like teacups, and the men 'pour tea' into them. The music just seemed to have a little pretty feel about it here, which put the idea into my head.

AM: *When the curtain goes up on Act Two, we see the sylphs looking like so much nightmare scenery. They hold their arms like broken wings over their heads.*
MB: It's to create a sense of mystery. I wanted the idea that they were peering from behind things: that they were within the forest all the time, so that they were looking behind trees, between twigs. So rather than being wings, those arms are more like branches in our minds.

AM: *How do men feel being sylphs?*
MB: Quite happy. And there was a lot of nice dance material to do, which they enjoyed.

AM: *So how did your fairy research turn into movement in Act Two?*
MB: We began with various improvs. (The sylphs had names, by the way: Oona, Nuala, Taboo, Ethna, Mab and Nymphibia are the ones in my notes, but we came up with others for the men later.) One improv was using Romantic gestures. We had looked at the old lithographs and paintings of the Romantic ballet, looking particularly at the

gesture of the position of the arms, and we used some of those gestures to develop movement, making phrases where you worked through these positions and made them transitional. A lot of the arm positions we studied and used – sometimes in a way that's ended up being quite disguised.

Another was about hunting and eating and killing. It was Maxine's idea that the sylphs should kill little animals, bring them on stage, and eat them. What did they eat? Worms, for example; mice. Fairies have to survive! So there is quite a savage feel to them.

Likewise we did one improv – it never really went into the piece, or a little bit maybe – where we experimented with flying. We tried lifts in which you lift a person as if they're in flight, for example.

From these various improvs and ideas, people came up with phrases. One example is the moon phrase, which the sylphs do when they first appear at the beginning of the act, when they're all opening towards the moon. They're moon worshippers, and it's a full moon. It's a directional phrase of movement. We had a big light that was like the moon as well.

We decided that the sylphs were all part of the Sylph. They felt what she felt. When she was in pain, they were in pain. When she was in love, they were in love. We also wanted the sylphs to be able to use the floor. Their wings had to be rubberized, so that, if they rolled on their wings, they would come back into place. Above, all we wanted to be very free and wild. We took this from the meaning of Romanticism.

AM: *So, with your dancers, you develop all these phrases. You're using the music, and you're using ideas of character. Do you carry on until you've got enough phrases to fill the music? Or do you think 'Maybe seven different phrases is all I need for Act Two'? How do you get from individual phrases to the whole of a dance?*

MB: It is surprising how few you need to make a dance, because you can do so many variations on a phrase. You can divide it up, you can use separate elements of it – especially when it comes to working with a group – you can do variations on one movement in the phrase. So I do manipulate phrases a lot.

AM: *You say 'I' rather than 'we' for once. Is the manipulation of phrases your particular business?*

MB: That's mine.

AM: *Do you enjoy that aspect of it?*

MB: I do. The making of the phrase is less enjoyable for me, because it's finding something from nowhere, whereas, once you've got something to work with, it's much more fun. And I am always the one who sets it musically, who fits it to the counts.

AM: *Does all this make you see yourself as a craftsman?*

MB: In some respects, yes. If I'm given a phrase, the thing I will quite often do is change the counts. I will look at the movement, but then count it in a different way, re-emphasizing certain aspects.

AM: *By changing the counts, you're really trying to re-emphasize the dynamics?*

MB: Yes. I find that, when most dancers give you movement, the dynamic interest is the thing that's missing. They're more into trying to find some interesting movement, than making that movement interesting to watch. It's usually very even; dynamically flat.

AM: *When you put in a step like pas de chat, how strict are you about its execution? What quality are you looking for? Do you want the feet to meet in the air?*

MB: I personally like it when the legs are quite spread, so that it's not too neat.

AM: *And when they open out beyond the shoulder line.*

MB: Yes. I like the openness of Balanchine pas de chat, rather than the contained British ballet way of doing the step. In fact, in *Swan Lake* we call our *pas de chat* 'Merrill Ashley', because she used to do that step so brilliantly in Balanchine's choreography in New York City Ballet.

AM: *Did you get Lez to design around the dancers? Did they have any say in what they wore?*

MB: Yes: the women generally! I don't know why – it may be sexist to say this – but the women always have more to say about their costumes. There's a way of being seen, a way that they're happy looking. I'm not so sure that it's ever to do with the character they're playing. Some of the men, and perhaps some women, will say, 'I think my character should have this' and 'I need this to make this character work.' A lot of the women are quite particular about what they wear, how it's cut, and so on, but Lez won't be that pliable with them. If he's decided that this is what he wants, that's what he'll do.

AM: *Now, in Act Two, for the first scene between James and the Sylph, you've written, 'He wants to "have" her. He must become a sylph to do so. She feeds him with butterflies, etc.' Then, 'Animals? Birds'.*

MB: This was when we were working on how sylphs need to eat.

AM: *One thing I love in the* Highland Fling *choreography for all the sylphs – but especially for her – is the way that the line of the leg often continues straight up the angled line of the back.*

MB: I wanted that line through the body, but with the neck not continuing the line. Which is a very *Giselle* thing: with the head down, but with the arms in line with the body.

AM: *Particularly with Maxine Fone, there are moments where you give her a more fully outstretched ballet outline than you ever do with either the swans of* Swan Lake *or anyone in* Cinderella. *She really flies off into the wings with grands jetés like Giselle.*

MB: Yes. That's right for Maxine, and right for the Sylph – who's supernatural.

At the end of that first sequence, the sylphs become trees, like a landscape for James to walk through. By them passing him by – he comes from one direction, they're all going in the other – there's the illusion that there's a moving landscape. It feels like he's travelling somewhere through the forest, while he's looking for her.

AM: *You've written, 'Sylph diverts.' That presumably means divertissement dances by the sylphs. 'The sylphs (plural) seduce him. Initiation ceremony. They carry her around. "La Bayadère" type entrance.'*

MB: I was probably thinking of a zigzag entrance, with a phrase that repeated, as in the famous entrance of the corps de ballet of Shades in the ballet *La Bayadère*. We didn't do it in the end. Or, rather, they do move in a zigzag column, but from the front of the stage to the back, the opposite direction to that in *Bayadère*. And it's a much more complicated phrase; it's not a repetition. It's a phrase that two people start, and as they're coming along this way, the next two start it across the back. So the phrases overlap. In fact, here in the notes, I've already written 'Echo canon' for what they do.

AM: *The idea of an ensemble zigzag entrance – which you use in the more traditional direction for the entry of the Swans in* Swan Lake *is, you know perfectly well, a favourite device of the nineteenth-century*

choreographer Marius Petipa. In both cases, you're aware of that pre-cedent.
MB: Yes, absolutely.

AM: *Later: 'He is taught how to fly.'*
MB: Yes. There's a little mime sequence where he asks questions and they say, 'Well, you can't be a sylph, because you haven't got wings', or 'You're not a fairy.' We were making up mime gestures here, which was a lot of fun. James wants to learn to fly, so they teach him how. They do movement; he copies them. So, by the end of that 'sylph diverts' sequence, he has become an honorary sylph.

The notes say: 'Teaching how to be a sylph. Queen presents him with wings after initiation. He tries them. They laugh. She gives him the hand of a sylph in marriage. A sylph is rampant. Orgy. He is spent, exhausted.' A lot of the detail here we dropped: for example, we didn't have a sylph queen in the end. The marriage – by 'a sylph', I think we always meant 'the Sylph' – was to parallel the human wedding in Act One; and the orgy was to show how much more liberated and voluptuous sylphs are.

AM: *And you've written 'ecstasy'. Erotic ecstasy, fantasy ecstasy, drug ecstasy?*
MB: It means that he found what he's looking for – for a while. This is where we move into Love Land, as we used to call it. Everyone is just having a wonderful time. Because the sylphs are a reflection of the Sylph, they feel what she feels. Everyone takes up the feeling of James and the Sylph, who are in love, temporarily anyway.

AM: *'Slow motion': does that happen?*
MB: Not literally. I often have those ideas of playing with time, with one couple slow and the others all going at top speed, for example. It's a Fred Astaire thing from *Easter Parade*: he dances in slow motion in front of a chorus of people who are dancing at the right speed, as it were.

AM: *Now, in the scene when he has had enough of all this bliss, you've put, 'He puts her in a pinny and gives her a feather duster.' That is the clearest example so far that he is a male chauvinist pig.*
MB: We didn't do that. But that was the idea. A lot of details fell into place while we were doing it. For example, the bit about James cutting off the Sylph's wings. That, with all the social/gender issues that we

saw within it, occurred to us because we were always looking for answers and reasons.

AM: *On the right-hand page again, a particularly careful analysis of the counts here: '8, 9, 10, 8, 8, 8, 12'; then '1, 2 and 2 and 3 threatening. Corner him. She goes mad. She comes out. Blood on hands. Wings thrown out. They shake. They run when he runs out, avert their eyes. James blood on hands.' On the next left page, there's something you've written, then scrubbed out: 'Long death. She becomes ugly and distorted without her wings. They carry the dying body.'*

MB: We did all that.

AM: *In the right-hand column, you've written: 'She revives. Phrases 8s, tossing. 10s, tossing. 8s, first section. 8 moon phrase. Duet.' Then, beneath that, you've put: 'Blood appears. She is blind.' She does go blind in the original.*

On the left-hand page: 'The sylphs attack James in revenge for the Sylph's death.' This looks like a prototype idea for what happens in Act Four of your Swan Lake.

MB: The feeling was the same; but I didn't intend any connection.

AM: *Then, in the final scene: 'Effie and Gurn are snuggled in an armchair in front of the fire. The figure of James, now a lonely sylph, is seen at the window (à la* Wuthering Heights*). Effie walks across and draws the curtain. Gurn crushes a butterfly.'*

MB: In the event, she doesn't actually get up to draw the curtain. But James remains in the window. And Gurn crushing the sylph butterfly I really liked as an image; but it was one image too many at the end. So, to keep it simple, we cut it. But, on the armchair they are sitting on, there is a butterfly. He just picks it up when Effie goes to sleep with him. He looks at it, crushes it in his hand, drops it on the floor.

AM: *You have here some pages written during rehearsals.*

MB: Yes, to help keep track of what phrases we'd got. 'Clap, listen', for example, is a phrase we developed from *Les Sylphides*. 'Catching butterflies' is a jumpy phrase. 'Picking berries' involves a certain amount of mime. 'Teaching flying' is a dance they all do. The phrase starts with a sissonne – a jump in which the feet scissor outwards from two feet to one – which they teach James.

And here is a floor plan of the set. We had an adaptable set, with pieces that were moved by the performers. So one side was the toilets,

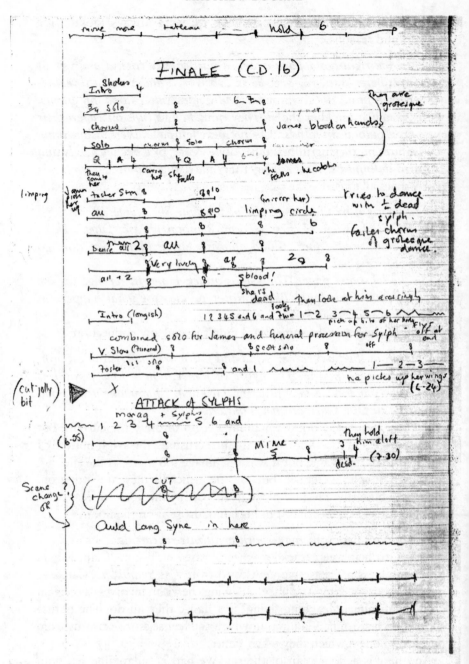

35 *Highland Fling*. Bourne's initial notes on the music for the end of Act Two,
supplemented by notes made in rehearsal.

in the opening scene; and when the set turned around, it became the walls of the living room.

AM: *Were there any points where the music proved tricky?*
MB: There was one long section in Act Two, just after she's had the wings cut off and does a little solo, where there was lots more music even though it felt that the story was at an end. We really struggled with that part. But we found some quite simple ideas which worked well, about him trying to make her alive again, picking her up, putting her arm in his, as if they were getting married and walking forwards. Then she was lifted by the two male sylphs away from him, as if they were taking her away. Then he would walk forwards, but she wasn't there. He would go looking for her again, but as if everything else was invisible. Then he would get her again, and again the male sylphs would take her off somewhere. But it was one of those times, towards the end of the rehearsal period, when I was going a bit mad. There's always a point when I go a bit mad.

AM: *Is that visible to others?*
MB: I think so, yes! It's horrible. Funnily enough, I really don't enjoy the aspect of actually getting a piece finished. I like all the build-up to it, and there are certain parts of rehearsal that I really enjoy. But my favourite thing is creating ideas beforehand, and then working on it once it's finished. I find that it's like getting blood out of a stone sometimes, especially towards the end of a rehearsal period. I always feel that I just haven't got a single idea left. Your mind has been so much within the piece for so many weeks and nights. Curiously, the easiest one that I've done is *Swan Lake*. I didn't have any problem; I just loved every minute of doing that and got on with it and wasn't worried about it. With *Cinderella*, largely because I was ill in the middle of the rehearsal period, I was so short of time by the end that I was waking up in cold sweats in the middle of the night, remembering bits of music that we hadn't done yet and thinking, 'There's absolutely no way we can get this done.' But the company has always recognized the point where I get like that. And they're always very supportive, all of them. They buoy me up, and make me do more; and they'll help. That's when Scott and Etta come into their own. They agree to stay late every night; they'll put the show first before their families. That's why I worry about doing work for other companies: I know that, if I don't have those people around me, I couldn't get it finished. Choreography

has to be made against the clock; and when you see the time ticking by, it's sometimes frightening.

Performance

MATTHEW BOURNE: We tended to rehearse and première everything in Bristol because we had funding from there. With *Highland Fling*, we did some touring, then we performed it in London at the Lilian Baylis Theatre, which was not ideal for it. But we've now done it at three different places in London: the others being the Donmar Warehouse in 1995 and the Place in 1997.

ALASTAIR MACAULAY: *What on earth was it like to do* Highland Fling *at the Donmar Warehouse with the audience on three sides?*
MB: I didn't feel it was the best, because of the limited stage space and the proximity of the audience. But the sort of audiences that were coming to it absolutely loved being that close to dancing. They had never seen anything like that so close up; and, because it was a theatre sort of audience, that was the comment I used to get: 'It was so great to see it so close up.' But also it helped the performers to get inside the characters a lot more. With no distance, you really felt involved and within the whole thing. It worked there – and it certainly increased our audience in a different direction. It helped us with that transition into the West End.

AM: *Did you ever do it in Scotland?*
MB: Yes, once. At the Edinburgh Festival, as part of a charity ball evening. There was a fashion show, and we did *Highland Fling*. It went down very well. I'd love to do it in Glasgow, of course, though that would be a bit nerve-wracking.

7

Oliver! (1994) and other Musicals

ALASTAIR MACAULAY: *Before* Swan Lake, *something important came along, which was Cameron Mackintosh's 1994 West End production of the Lionel Bart musical* Oliver! *This was revived at the London Palladium; Sam Mendes directed, and you choreographed. The show was a big success, running in that three-thousand-seat theatre for three years. While we've been doing these interviews in summer 1998, you've just been preparing and launching a touring version of the production, which may run for several more years. At what point had Cameron Mackintosh become aware of your work?*

MATTHEW BOURNE: He had seen *Children of Eden*, which he didn't like very much, and that put him off me for quite a long while. The thing that really made him interested was *Late Flowering Lust*, which he absolutely loved. I hadn't met him at all, but when I was invited to his house to talk about *Oliver!*, he suggested that I meet with Sam to see if we would get along. The only person on the production with whom I'd worked before was Anthony Ward, our designer for *Nutcracker*.

Once Cameron decides he likes you, he can be very loyal to you.

AM: *Among other things, I believe* Oliver! *gave you the most secure income you'd ever had.*

MB: The first effect, though, was that it stopped me from performing. I had been planning on being in *Highland Fling*, but when I got the job in *Oliver!*, I couldn't. The tour of *Highland Fling* had to go ahead, which was fine. Choreographically, it actually had big benefits for that and later shows, because it obliged me to get a whole picture of each production. Personally, however, it was quite a big thing at the time, because I love performing so much.

It created a different feeling in me as a director of a company. Suddenly, I had that distance from the performers: I wasn't one of them. So it was a new way of working. That's developed over the last three years or so, especially as the company's got bigger.

Financially, obviously, *Oliver!* has helped me enormously. Because it is a success, that brings me in a secure income throughout its run. Such shows – when they are successes – are like gifts for any director or choreographer. I'm better known for *Swan Lake* and other AMP productions, but those to date have not brought in regular income by any means.

AM: *Did* Oliver! *involve the biggest company you'd ever worked with?*
MB: No. The biggest company had been back in 1991, when I choreographed *Show Boat* in Sweden. That had been for a state company – the Malmö Stadtheater – which is made up of an acting company, an opera company and a ballet company, all sharing the same theatre. For any productions they did, they used people from all three companies; and the theatre's got the largest stage in Europe – the size of a football pitch! There must have been about eighty to eighty-five people in the production. About thirty of them were dancers.

That was a very odd production, because *Show Boat* is about blacks and whites in America, and there are no black performers in Sweden at all. So the Swedish performers were blacked up, like *The Black and White Minstrel Show*. Can you imagine that happening here? But it's somehow acceptable there. Still, I felt very uncomfortable about it, I must say.

I love *Show Boat* so much, and I enjoyed working on it. It was a good challenge at the time. A few of the principal dancers felt it was beneath them, and wouldn't appear. However, there was much more dancing in that production than there is in, say, the *Show Boat* that's just come to London from Broadway; and several numbers were on a very big scale. 'Can't Help Lovin' Dat Man' in the current production here feels quite minimal and naturalistic, whereas in our production it turned into a far more developed number.

AM: *Did you learn from doing it?*
MB: Yes, very much. Among other things, I had to deal with the estate of Oscar Hammerstein, which deals with *Show Boat*. There were arguments involved about which numbers you include or exclude – the entire text is on the John McGlinn EMI recording, but some

items have to be cut in live performance – and I was involved in giving reasons why I thought certain numbers were relevant to our production. Because ours wasn't what the Hammerstein estate saw as a first-class production – it wasn't in, say, New York or London, it was in Malmö – there was a lot of material that they weren't prepared to give me. So the negotiation, on a business level, and the subsequent change of plans meant that I learnt a lot about the adaptation of choreography to suit anyone other than myself: i.e. the composer's/lyricists's estate.

One of the director's ideas for the production – something that wouldn't happen in New York or London – was that Magnolia and Gay had dancing counterparts, principal dancers from the company. So when they sang 'Make Believe', it was also danced by this other couple; and so 'Make Believe' went off into a new direction. And the couple re-emerged at different times within the show.

AM: *How nice to have a director who's that dance-friendly.*
MB: Yes, he was, and he wanted a lot of dance in it. His name is Ronnie Danielson. He has an original approach, particularly with musicals – which he regularly did. He had seen my work in London – *Children of Eden* and some AMP stuff.

AM: *How many dancers did you use in* Oliver!*?*
MB: Two casts, each of twenty-four kids . . . and about another twenty-four or twenty-five adults. The majority of the dance work in *Oliver!*, though, is with the kids. (I put in some preparatory work on the 'Food' number and on 'Consider Yourself' with Etta Murfitt and Scott Ambler.)

Sam Mendes, who has since become a great friend, hadn't really worked with choreographers much before. And there was, from him and from Cameron, a certain amount of resistance to actually letting the show go off into anything experimental in terms of staging movement or dance. Cameron knew *Oliver!* inside out and was extremely proud of his association with it. (Lionel Bart was there as well, of course. He, actually, is quite open to experiment. He was always saying, 'Try it!')[1]

For example, 'Boy for Sale' is basically just a song for Mr Bumble on the street. With Geoff Garratt and Jonathan Butterell, who were my

1 Lionel Bart died, after this interview, in April 1999.

dance assistants on it, I worked out this whole number with the company, which was very stylized. We had people on the streets stopping and turning. It had an entire pattern to it, while the snow was coming down. Quite simple, but it looked very good, I thought. But that, at that stage, was just taking things too far for Sam and Cameron. They didn't want to be worried by something that looked like another style. But I felt, and still feel, that it would work.

I felt with *Oliver!* overall that I could have done more inventive things, if I could have done what I wanted to do. But I was dealing with Sam and Cameron and Lionel, all with very strong opinions. Often what would be put to me was: 'This doesn't look natural' or 'This doesn't look real.' (Dancing by its very nature is never a realistic or naturalistic way of telling a story, is it?) Or they'd say, 'This is too difficult' or 'The company can't do this.' But the people making the complaint didn't realize that dance – or any kind of movement – needs rehearsal. Performers don't just 'get' it instantly. This is especially true with people who aren't trained dancers. You need to give a company of performers the time to make something work; but when you're collaborating on a production, your colleagues are constantly asking you to simplify or cut sequences that could have been much more interesting, had there been time given to develop them. So you end up with something more conventional and predictable. That's a bit disappointing.

Working with the kids was great and a real pleasure. You either like working with kids or you don't. I had a great time with them. It was why I kept in contact with the show for quite a long time after it opened. I went in once a week or so to keep an eye on it; and I worked with each new cast, because it was always a pleasure to work with a new bunch of kids. Whatever you give them to do, it ends up looking charming. Kids do things in their own way, because they're not trained. You get an approximation of what you've given them, but, when it's done with enthusiasm and energy, it looks fantastic. And their characters come out through the way they move. That's such a joy; and each new cast kept it alive, because they were so different.

I think that, after a while of working on *Oliver!*, we realized you can't resist what it is. When Fagin comes in, it's like a musical turn. Fagin himself is a turn, a comic act, in the way that Lionel's structured the show. He comes in at a good point in the show, he does half an hour, and then he goes back to his dressing room. This allows for a certain amount of flexibility in the role – which can be awkward for choreography. We had five different men doing Fagin during the course of the run – Jonathan Pryce, Jim Dale, Robert Lindsay, Barry Humphries, Russ Abbott – and each one wanted to do something different from the last. But each one has to fit in with the kids, who have to be extremely drilled and to know exactly what they're doing. For the kids, everything's to counts. They know that they stand here; and, if they don't, they're told off. It's very much that kind of relationship. So there can be quite a conflict between the precision of the kids and the individuality of each Fagin.

It's funny with leading actors and actresses. As soon as you mention somebody else's name in their role, you have to be very careful about what you say. We would all say, 'That thing that Jim did' or 'That Jonathan thing.' But, as soon as you've said that, you've lost your current Fagin a bit. They don't want to know that they're being asked to do something that was someone else's idea. So we made changes, both with the Fagins and with what the kids did, but not always for the better. Ultimately, you should just be stronger and say, 'This version works best – we're doing this.' But it's not easy when they're star actors trying to put their individual stamp on the role.

Oliver! was the hardest job I've ever done. What I learnt most from it was the difference between how something feels in a studio and how it looks on stage, which has affected what I've done since. Apart from 'Food, Glorious Food', almost every number was completely changed when it reached the stage. A huge amount of rehearsal work was a complete waste of time; and the preview performances become more and more important. I wouldn't do a show now without a lot of previews. Preferably, I'd like to rehearse a show, get it on stage out of London for a couple of weeks, then have another two or three weeks' rehearsals before it opens in town and is reviewed. When you see a show on stage, you immediately see so many problems you've got to solve that you've never seen in a studio.

'Consider Yourself', for example. We did versions in the studio that were fantastic a lot of the time. So many ideas. We created waves of people, so that it felt as it you were walking down different streets and different pathways. In the studio it looked fantastic, because you could see everyone all the time. We had these hollow structures that represented part of the set, and they were like scaffolding. Even when people were in them, they were still visible, and the whole room looked busy. But on stage: 'Where is everyone?' Suddenly people seemed to be off stage as much as they were on, doing all these cross-overs, getting off to come to a new place, or climbing down ladders to get somewhere else. The effect in the studio was a lot of action, because you saw all these pathways and transitions; but on stage, you were wasting people a lot of the time. Some people who were at the top of a tower spent the whole middle of the number getting down a ladder and then coming on. You realized that you'd wasted them. So the whole thing was changed. And every number was changed. This involved working extremely quickly, at the last minute, on things that needed to go on stage that night: a nightmare to me and the cast.

Cameron was very demanding – quite kind to me; but if something doesn't work, though sometimes he hates to say it, he has to say it. And he's usually right as well. That was how I learnt to respect him as a producer. He doesn't always know how to solve a problem; he just says, 'It doesn't feel right, it doesn't make me feel the right things. I don't know what you need to do, but that's your job. I just know it doesn't work.' The other thing that I like about Cameron is that he is such an enthusiast. He has remained a fan with a childlike pleasure in his work. I can relate to that.

8

Swan Lake
1995

36 *Swan Lake*. Adam Cooper as the Swan: pre-production photograph. Dancers and choreographers often adopt different positions when modelling studio photographic images of their stage choreography. However, the pre-production images created by Bourne and his dancers in the photographer Hugo Glendinning's studio before actual rehearsals had begun are an important, perhaps unique, example of studio-created dance photographic images contributing to subsequent choreography. In particular, Bourne devised certain 'swan' motifs that later entered the choreography. The wreathing of arms above the head in this photograph is a motif inspired by Nijinsky photographs; and it came to characterise all the swans in Bourne's choreography. Another feature here, Cooper's direct stare under lowered brows into the camera, was later incorporated from this photograph as a central motif into publicity images for Bourne's production.

Idea

MATTHEW BOURNE: Like anyone, I saw swans in parks when I was a child. But had no special affinity with them. Actually, I rather disliked swans: found them frightening. It was only when I knew I wanted to do my own *Swan Lake* that I started to look at them a bit more and ask, 'What exactly are they? What exactly do they move like?' And my Swan was never just a swan. He was animal, pagan, in my mind. I was also thinking of *Equus*, you see; I'd seen both the West End production and the movie.

ALASTAIR MACAULAY: *There are large parts of your* Swan Lake *that aren't the Matthew Bourne story – but there are parts that are. I don't think any of its Oedipal mother–son anguish is your story; you yourself have a good relationship with both your parents. But there is something in the fascination with the beloved-dreamed Swan that comes out of you.*

MB: I don't need to have gone through things in my life to put them on the stage. But at that time, yes, this did seem a more personally 'felt' piece in some respects. When I was making it, I had had a lot of rejections; and I hadn't been in a relationship for a while – before which I'd gone through a difficult ending to a long-term relationship. So yes: I think all that must have affected it quite a lot. That may be what drove some of the Prince's emotional neediness in my mind – also the strange worship of a symbol, of a beautiful male creature-person. I suppose I have always had people like that in my life – people that you have a feeling for from a distance.

AM: *I've already pointed out, when we were talking of* Highland Fling, *that the 1832* La Sylphide – *the prototype for innumerable Romantic/ classical ballets that followed throughout the nineteenth and twentieth centuries – was itself a gender-reversal of Nodier's story* Trilby. *In the 1840s, the choreographer Jules Perrot made a ballet or two along* Trilby *rather than* La Sylphide *lines, in which he himself danced a male spirit who pursued or lured a mortal heroine.*

Another French Romantic, Théophile Gautier, wrote the poem 'Le Spectre de la Rose'. In this the more-or-less male spirit of the rose addresses the girl whose breast he/it had adorned at her first ball. In 1910, as you well know, Fokine made a short ballet of 'Le Spectre de

37 *L'Après-midi d'un faune:* Vaslav Nijinsky as the Faun, with his sister
Bronislava Nijinska as a Nymph, in 1912. The many photographs of Nijinsky
(1888–1950) dancing have been a longstanding inspiration to Bourne's
choreography. Those taken of him as the Faune in his own radical 1912 ballet
were a particular stimulus to Bourne's conception of the Swan.

*la Rose'. Its central idea was of the Girl – played by Tamara Karsavina
– asleep in her armchair and visited in her dreams by the spirit of the
rose, danced by Nijinsky: which is a diametric gender-reversal of the
premise of* La Sylphide, *which begins with James asleep in his armchair
and the dancing female Sylph visiting him in his dreams.*

*The idea of the male dream object: how conscious were you of that
from Nijinsky's role in* Spectre?
MB: I don't think I was. You see, I was also thinking of other Nijinsky
roles, especially the Faun, who isn't a dream object – although that
kind of image can certainly fill your dreams.

Unconsciously, though, perhaps there is a connection. When I first
thought of doing *Swan Lake*, I wasn't thinking of Adam Cooper or of
anyone from the ballet world; but in due course, one part of my idea
for the male Swan became absolutely related to my excitement in
working with Adam. I certainly used to glorify – though I don't now –

dancers in his field, ballet. I would see them as little gods or goddesses. I found that Adam had, certainly on stage, a mystery about him that could have appealed to me because of my early enjoyment of those Nijinsky pictures. Mind you, this emerged gradually.

Before Adam, I had thought that Ashley Page was like Nijinsky in personality. The fact that he didn't smile much, that he was never flirting with the audience, that he had strange eyes, I found appealing, and quite unlike anyone else at the Royal. Adam – even though in build and dance style he's actually very different from Ashley – I felt had a similar persona on stage.

AM: *I think you're imagining both Ashley Page and Adam Cooper dancing Nijinsky's Faun. But are you imagining either of them dancing other Nijinsky roles? For example,* Spectre?
MB: No, not really. They're both more mortal, more masculine I suppose, than Nijinsky probably was.

AM: *Did you straightaway think of a male protagonist in the double role of* Swan Lake *– as both 'the White Swan' Odette and 'the Black Swan' Odile, as the roles are known in most versions?*
MB: I don't think that came straight away, no. My immediate idea was of a corps of male swans.

AM: *And a male Prince. So straightaway it becomes a sexual drama to some degree in your mind?*
MB: Yes. That was something that probably interested me from the first: the sexual issues within it. Because our production was so big and so much of a gamble (financially), I probably have played that down to some extent, in terms of the way I talk about it.[1] Certainly, early on, there were people saying, 'Don't play that aspect up.' The fear of a lot

---

1 Certain points from a handwritten announcement of his *Swan Lake* production, dated June 1994, are of interest here. (AMP/Bourne archive)

Bourne wrote (fourth paragraph) '*Swan Lake* is a great classical ballet, when performed with imagination and style, and AMP's version will be born of a great love and respect for the beauty and power of the original staging . . .' (Sixth paragraph.) 'AMP's previous interpretations of classics such as *Nutcracker* and *La Sylphide (Highland Fling)* have been radically different and yet faithful to their source material. The company has attempted to retell these stories by applying a modern-day logic, but without losing the essence of magic which is essential to these pieces. We have tried to look for contemporary messages within these stories whilst retaining the more universal themes of love and betrayal, good and evil. The same maxims will apply to our treatment of *Swan Lake*.' (Seventh paragraph.) 'AMP is renowned for its witty approach to dance, and humour often plays an important part in the success of our work. However, as proved in the company's most recent show, *Highland Fling*,

of investors was that it would get labelled 'The Gay *Swan Lake*'. But, yes, I think my initial impetus to do it was that sexual drama would be a strong part of it.

Still, the more I went along, the more I found other things in it. The Swan is free, in my version, and he's beautiful. Everyone's interested in him; everyone wants him. The Prince projects on to him. I found that it could be seen, and interpreted, in different ways; and, when we were making it, I made it a little more open for interpretation.

AM: *You made your* Swan Lake *in 1995. Before you started rehearsals in August that year, you drew up the scenario. Did you collaborate with anyone on this?*

MB: No, the scenario for this one's very much mine. I didn't really discuss it with anyone much to begin with. Before rehearsals began, Lez Brotherston, the designer, was the next biggest contributor.

The idea of doing it came to me soon after we had opened *Nutcracker* in Edinburgh in 1992. I had also been toying with the idea of dancing the role of the Sylph myself in what later became *Highland Fling*. And, the moment I dropped that idea, I thought of *Swan Lake* with male swans.

AM: *Is there any conscious effort on your part to make the Prince's drama in* Swan Lake *a reflection of Tchaikovsky's own life?*

MB: No. It has been mentioned, particularly by Jann Parry in the *Observer*; and I can see the reason why: the fact that he was a repressed homosexual. It isn't what I had in mind; but it's a valid point. He wrote the music, and that feeling is somehow there in the music.

AM: *So what else, after male swans, did you have in mind at first?*

MB: The second idea that made me know that *Swan Lake* was worth doing – and that it would work – was the Royal aspect to it. I could see the male swan in my mind, I never at any point doubted that it would work; but, when I started to think about the Royal aspect, then

---

that lightness of touch can also be switched into sequences of shocking cruelty and bitter tragedy, made all the more powerful by their easy juxtaposition. These elements are particularly important to *Swan Lake*, which has at its heart a tragic love story of unattainable desire.'

Only in the eighth paragraph does Bourne – after naming Anthony Ward (designer) and David Lloyd-Jones (conductor) as his colleagues on this production – announce 'a full corps de ballet of *male* swans'.

38 *Swan Lake*: Stuart Dawes as the young Prince, Isabel Mortimer as the Queen, Scott Ambler as the adult Prince. Pre-publicity photograph. Although no such scene occurs in the production, the Prince's phobia of press cameras became an element in due course. Only at the very end are the adult Prince and his younger self seen onstage at the same time.

I saw how all the scandal surrounding the British Royal Family – and the introduction of young, new members of the Royal Family: Diana and Fergie and so on – could be applied to the story of *Swan Lake*. Because of the way a prince can be hounded and can't have a relationship without intrusion – basically can't be the person that he wants to be, e.g. Charles and Camilla – I thought it was so relevant to the plot of *Swan Lake*. I thought that this was something that would work for an audience. Admittedly, the initial intention wasn't for it to look as specific as it ended up being. It was going to be a world that we'd created – a kingdom somewhere in Europe: Ruritania, Marchovia, wherever – with no particular historical period. We never intended to represent the current Royal Family. Several of its members gave us some of our ideas – the corgi is the most obvious example – but that's all.

I always felt that there was a certain amount of satire to be had from the Queen figure in *Swan Lake*. The private-public life was what I wanted to play with quite a lot. I've always liked characters that have two sides to them: two things going on. You think you know them; and then you don't. You can surprise the audience with character development.

AM: *Very few people in the last hundred years have made serious dramas about royalty. This has been the era for plays and operas and even ballets about middle- and working-class people. Still, when the central character is royal, you know that on his/her fate the destinies of many other people hang; and therefore you respond not just to private trouble but also to public implications. So a tragic dimension emerges. That's what happens in your Swan Lake. You restored the tragedy.*

MB: It's funny, isn't it? As soon as you call someone a prince, it all becomes very heroic and symbolic. Speaking in dance terms, ballet lends itself very naturally to royal characters. That's why the role of the Queen in our production is sought after now by quite a number of ex-ballerinas. A ballerina has what appears to the public to be a royal bearing, which works instantly for that role very well.

Obviously, ballet is full of princes and princesses; but we're saying that there is more to them than the more formal side that ballet usually shows. We're saying that royalty has another side: that there are real people beneath that ballet-like exterior.

AM: *In 1950, Ashton made* Illuminations *for New York City Ballet. At one point, the protagonist knocks the crowns off a royal, or mock-royal, couple. When this was brought to London later in 1950, Princess Marina, the Duchess of Kent, would hardly address Ashton at a gala performance, she so strongly disapproved. In 1977, MacMillan created a scandal of sorts by choreographing some* Gloriana *dances in which Elizabeth I (Lynn Seymour) was shown cavorting more or less sexually with a number of lovers. Since MacMillan made it for the Covent Garden gala marking Queen Elizabeth II's silver jubilee, it didn't go down too well.*

Something in the climate has changed since those days. Alan Bennett had a great success when he put the current Queen on stage in A Question of Attribution *in 1988; and he did so with a good deal of comedy. Did you see that?*

MB: I saw it on TV. The shock was that Prunella Scales was actually playing the Queen; but apparently the Royals liked that. It was done with such charm and affection that he got away with it. Actually, I think that the British Royals are no problem in this respect. The trouble starts with other people, who choose to get offended on their behalf when Royals are represented.

I was expecting more fuss about that aspect in the press. We had a lot of national press coverage, but all about the male swan issue. Lots of 'corps-blimey!' jokey items – using pictures side by side of Margot Fonteyn as Odette and Adam as our Swan. Really silly, awful pieces.

The worst of them used a picture of Adam lifted on Scott's back; the caption read: 'Bum me up, Scotty'. Yet they didn't pick up on the Royal aspect at all – though the Prince's Girlfriend is so obviously like Fergie. That awful costume she wears: very much like a short version of those terrible outfits Fergie used to wear. We always referred to her as a Fergie type – though Emily, who plays her, changed that somewhat. Lez Brotherston, in particular, made her look a little bit like Fergie: the long hair and bubbly personality and awful dresses. She may be a bit of a Sloaney type, but she's probably just a fun-loving girl, oblivious to the faux pas that she is creating, especially in the Royal Box. That's like Fergie; and even like Diana. Those two were often caught doing things that would have been quite normal behaviour for most young women; but because they were royal now, it was deemed to be unsuitable and wrong. So that side of the girlfriend's personality worked for that character.

I have a feeling a lot of the Royals might have watched our production on TV; to have come to see it might have been a bit close to home. Still, I think they would have loved the Royal Box sequence – especially Princess Margaret. When she came to see our *Cinderella*, I said, 'You must see *Swan Lake*.' She said, 'I've seen it.' I said, 'Where?' She said, 'On the television.' I said to her, 'It's much better live. You must see it some time.' She didn't comment after that. But, when we did the Royal Variety Show, we were told that we were one of about three personal requests from the Queen for what she wanted to see in that year's line-up. More recently, I was one of the people invited to the big Windsor Castle reception for British artists. So I don't think there's any sense of them being offended by *Swan Lake* at all.

AM: *Was it clear to you in conception that your production was going to be Oedipal?*
MB: Yes. I thought that one very clear aspect of royalty is its coldness between parents and children; and the idea of making the Queen a younger woman, who had younger lovers who were of similar age to the Prince, was another factor.

My friend Alan Cumming did *Hamlet* at the Donmar Warehouse in 1993; and I'd seen that production twice. I'd also seen Mark Rylance play it with the Royal Shakespeare Company in 1989; and the Zeffirelli film with Mel Gibson as well. So it was in my mind quite a lot. All those versions were very different, but obviously that relationship

between Hamlet and his mother made a big impact in each of them –
especially Hamlet's jealousy of her having another lover, another husband. I wanted to bring out the Prince's jealousy along those lines.
Each time I saw *Hamlet*, I understood it more, and – because I was
working on my *Swan Lake* – I saw how that story could help mine.
Eleanor Bron as the queen was great in the Alan Cumming *Hamlet*;
they deepened the whole idea of the mother–son relationship for me.
And Alan made Hamlet so tortured as a character. All that fed my
Swan Lake, I can see that now.

AM: *Any inspiration from films in conceiving your* Swan Lake?
MB: I've learnt a lot from Hitchcock's films. Character structure; suspense; gradual revelation of surprising aspects of character. Even the
look of Hitchcock films comes into it. I can't be specific about this. I've
always loved Hitchcock, and we steeped ourselves in his movies when
we made *Deadly Serious* in 1992, but I didn't go back to look at any
of his movies when I was preparing *Swan Lake*. It's just that, in general, I feel there's a Hitchcock connection: in the character of the Prince
and his paranoia and jealousy, in the way Rick Fisher lights it and uses
shadow, in the strange mother–son relationship.

The one specific borrowing from Hitchcock in *Swan Lake* comes in
Act Four. It's from *The Birds*, of course. No doubt my own childhood
alarm about wild birds made me all the more attuned to that film. It
only came to my mind suddenly, when we were doing Act Four, late in
the rehearsal process. I didn't check out the film; I know it so well.
Basically, we do the scene from *The Birds* where Tippi Hedren is sitting
on a bench outside the school and there have already been several bird
attacks. She's in the foreground: one bird swoops down and lands on a
sort of playground climbing frame behind her; then another one
comes; then two come. She's getting more nervous about the whole
thing; she's lighting a cigarette, smoking it. She sees one bird flying
past; she follows its path, and then suddenly she sees that there are
hundreds of them there. You've seen a few arrive, and now suddenly
you get this shock – that the whole frame is full of them. Next, she
quietly tries to move away, to get the children away from the school,
before they attack.

AM: *Your equivalent in* Swan Lake *is to do what?*
MB: The swans come on to the bed. We have the Prince and the Swan
downstage – in a similar position to Tippi Hedren, in the foreground –

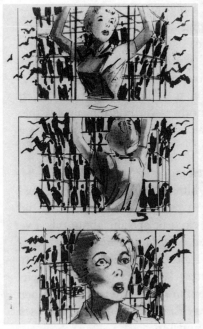

39 Sketches of Tippi Hedren and the children's climbing-frame in Alfred Hitchcock's 1963 film *The Birds*. Bourne took this sequence as a direct model for the passage when the swans climb on to the Prince's bed in Act Four of *Swan Lake*.
40 *Swan Lake*, Act Four. The swans on the Prince's bed.

and this build-up of swans. The bed is in centre-stage: they come on from the wings and jump on to it – some of them come from round it and hang on to it – they all have different ways of getting on to it. They jump, they slide across the bed. It's quite a powerful moment: a build-up of power and menace; the swans are obviously angry and about to attack – and I owe it to Hitchcock.

AM: *So what had* Swan Lake *been to you before you made your own? When was the first time you ever saw* Swan Lake *on stage?*
MB: The way I've remembered it for years is that I first saw the Scottish Ballet production, Peter Darrell's production. It was at Sadler's Wells in 1979, and I'm on record as saying it was not only my first *Swan Lake* but also the first ballet I ever saw. I've just discovered that it wasn't! But we'll come to that.

AM: *That Darrell production is a drug-dream retelling of* Swan Lake; *it has a fairly tormented, psychological drama. The swan scenes are opium-induced hallucinations in the Prince's mind.*

MB: Yes, but I thought this was *Swan Lake*; that all *Swan Lakes* would be along these lines. I didn't know then that Darrell's treatment of the story was something new.

AM: *Maybe it's also relevant that Darrell's production – unlike most* Swan Lakes – *uses the 1877 score that Tchaikovsky wrote for the original Moscow staging version. This 1877 score, in each of its four acts, is quite different from the version of the* Swan Lake *score we usually hear in the theatre; and even that 1877 score, as you now know, has its alternative options within Act Three.*[2]

Your own Swan Lake *is almost entirely drawn from the 1877 score. And although it has several musical re-orderings, it has fewer of them than most* Swan Lakes. *In particular, your Act Four uses only the music that Tchaikovsky wrote for it.*

MB: As you can imagine, I knew none of that then; and my memory is that, because I loved the piece so much – I'd never seen a full-length dance piece before – I very quickly followed it up by seeing it again that summer, at Covent Garden. This time it was the National Ballet of Canada doing the Erik Bruhn production with Karen Kain.

During these conversations with you, however, I've discovered that I must have seen the Canadian production first! It came to Covent Garden early in August that year. The Scottish production came to Sadler's Wells about a fortnight later. This tells you something about my memory.

AM: *Bruhn's Canadian version is also a psycho-drama.*

MB: I don't remember it well. I just remember the swans, which made a greater impression with a bigger ballet company on a bigger stage than in the Scottish production. I was surprised at how fast they moved; I wasn't expecting that! The Darrell one certainly left a deeper impression on my mind. So much so that, for years, I've assumed it was the first I saw. I remember thinking, after the second *Swan Lake* in

2 The Moscow production as a whole was choreographed by Julius Reisinger; but, when the second-cast Moscow ballerina tried to interpolate into Act III a new grand pas de deux that Marius Petipa had choreographed for her to music by Minkus, Tchaikovsky wrote music to fit it rather than have his score messed around further. So from the very beginning there were alternative versions, by Tchaikovsky himself, of the *Swan Lake* score.

a fortnight, 'This is really different!' I had thought it would be the same. I had thought *Swan Lake* was *Swan Lake*.

AM: *And now, almost twenty years later, someone is probably thinking that your* Swan Lake *is the one and only* Swan Lake.
MB: That's literally true, I've discovered! Especially with young audiences.

AM: *1979 was a busy dance summer by London standards. In July 1979, the month before those two first* Swan Lakes, *you yourself had seen Martha Graham's company at Covent Garden; in the month afterwards, September, you saw New York City Ballet.*
Later that year, the Royal Ballet staged a new/old production, very traditional in outline and drawn from its own previous productions, at Covent Garden. It was set in the mediaeval Age of Chivalry; which is – you'll forgive my saying this – where Tchaikovsky intended it. It was full of major classical choreography, albeit by five or more choreographers, some of them then still alive.
The main text was the one arranged by Lev Ivanov and Marius Petipa for the 1895 St Petersburg production (for which Tchaikovsky had probably planned to revise his score, but died in 1893). Because the Petipa–Ivanov choreography endured so well, the 1895 Swan Lake *has come down as 'the' traditional* Swan Lake *– though every production of it makes large or small departures from it. We'll come to some of those departures later.*
I know that you saw that Royal Ballet staging, produced by its then artistic director Norman Morrice, quite a number of times. How did it strike you, after your first two Swan Lakes?
MB: Ballet is so strange and exciting when you first see it that you remember few specific details afterwards. Yes, those first two productions I'd seen had been more psychological; yes, I do remember the Prince smoking opium in the Darrell production; and, yes, I was aware of differences between each production. But I think I may also have made connections between them that weren't intended. Because of the Darrell production, I think I always saw the Prince in the Royal Ballet's *Swan Lake* as a more complex figure than he actually was in that production. He always intrigued me. I know in that particular production there wasn't a lot to go on – I have the official 1980 video, with Makarova and Dowell in the lead roles, so I can

check out my memories – but, through the music, you can feel more. To me that character was quite complex.

AM: *Perhaps that's because that production used, in Act One, a 'moody' adagio solo that Nureyev had added in 1963, to show the Prince in pensive mood. As danced by Anthony Dowell and other Royal Ballet men of that era, it usually made a poetic effect, and gave the Prince a period of Romantic solitude early on in the drama.*

MB: My memory of that solo is one of the things I take most strongly from that production. I always liked that music; and even though I know Tchaikovsky probably didn't write it for the Prince (it's part of the pas de trois divertissement, I think), it sounds as if it's approaching the core of *Swan Lake*. Certainly I wanted to have that music, as a solo for the Prince, somewhere in my *Swan Lake*; and I use it just at the same point as Nureyev, just before he sees the swans at the end of Act One.

The Prince always interested me quite a lot in the traditional *Swan Lake* anyway. I suppose it was the possibilities of what was really going on. After all, he turns down one batch of women his mother puts before him in Act One; then he turns down another batch in Act Three, more emphatically. With some ballet dancers in the role, I couldn't help giggling.

I had no sense of disappointment in that production; I was excited by it. I may have projected on to it psychological ideas from the Darrell production; if so, they enriched it for me. I wasn't analysing things much; I just absorbed. And I was a balletomane: I saw virtually all the ballerinas at Covent Garden do it; I remember watching all the younger ones making their debuts as Odette-Odile. I used to like Bryony Brind in the role; and, of course, Fiona Chadwick – who later created the Queen in my production. I never saw Natalia Makarova on stage, but I watched the video of her performance a lot in those days.

AM: *Now, that Royal production, however traditional in appearance, had supplementary choreography by Frederick Ashton, by Ninette de Valois and by Nureyev. The whole fourth act was by Ashton.*

Then, in 1987, the Royal Ballet brought in a new production, which returned completely to the 1895 St Petersburg musical text and to a great degree to the 1895 choreographic text too – though there's always dispute about a great many details. On the other hand, this production – by the company's new artistic director Anthony Dowell and designed by Yolanda Sonnabend – updated the ballet to the nineteenth century.

MB: Yes; and, though it's interesting to see the original choreography, that production never made as strong an impression on me. The designs and the choreography aren't really in the same world as each other. So, by this time, I had learnt that *Swan Lake* was what a producer made it; that the structure is up there for grabs; and that the *Swan Lake* experience has to be as strong and poetic in drama as it is in dance.

There are ways of doing it well, and ways of messing it up. If you look at the video of the 1964 Nureyev production in Vienna, with Fonteyn dancing, it plays around with the music in a dreadful way. To me, that's unacceptable.

In the 1987 Royal Ballet *Swan Lake*, we lost a lot of the Ashton choreography, which I missed. I know that the music he used for Act Four includes one piece of music that Tchaikovsky had written for Act Three (in mine, I use it in Act One, for the Prince and the Queen); but it always felt like 'core' *Swan Lake* music – it felt right. Whereas I really didn't like the music for the swan dances in the 'traditional' Ivanov Act Four. Where does it come from?

AM: *Two of the pieces are actually Tchaikovsky piano music that he wrote in the last year of his life; he may have earmarked them for the St Petersburg* Swan Lake, *but it was Drigo who arranged them orchestrally and put them into the balle after Tchaikovsky's death.*

MB: They never felt appropriate to me at all; and, you know, Act Four never felt to me, in any production, so substantial that it merited an intermission before it – the second, or even sometimes the third interval of the evening – not even with Ashton. So when it came to my production, I always knew I wanted it to run straight on from Act Three. In fact, when you go back to the music Tchaikovsky wrote for Act Four, it's an extremely short act anyway.

I was very much aware when we began to plan our *Swan Lake* that it would coincide with the centenary of the 1895 production.

AM: *The traditional* Swan Lake *has Rothbart the sorcerer presiding, in the guise of an owl, as an evil genius over the Swan scenes. (Usually he looks more like a giant bat.) Odette, the Swan Queen, is under his spell; and, when she seems likely to break free from his power with the*

help of Prince Siegfried's love, Rothbart then goes so far as to intro-
duce Siegfried to his daughter Odile. Siegfried thinks that Odile is
Odette and swears love to her. Because he has thereby broken his vow
of love to her, Odette's doom is sealed – at least until, at the very end,
she decides to commit suicide, in which Siegfried joins her. That love-
death gesture at last breaks Rothbart's power.

  So Rothbart is very much at the core of the traditional Swan Lake.
The music's most famous theme is connected to his fateful power over
Odette. Yet you cut him out. I like Rothbart in the traditional version;
but the fact that you omit him strikes me as maybe the most brilliant
feature of your production, because the element of magic and of fate
that he represents, and the fatalism of that great theme in the music,
now become shifted entirely to the Prince's mind. The central drama of
the Swan scenes in the traditional version is about Odette being torn
between Rothbart and her hopes of freedom and love. The other scenes
are more about Siegfried. But in your version the drama is always
focused on the Prince; and it is the conflict in his own mind that the
story is all about. What led you to cut Rothbart out?
MB: I felt that he wasn't relevant to the story I was telling. I didn't want
anything to be explained by magic, and I feel that that's what he was
there for. So I decided simply to create the lesser role of the Private Secretary (originally he was the Press Secretary) as a sort of Rothbart substitute – someone manipulative at court who was just bad news for the
prince – but who didn't really affect the swan scenes in any way. Perhaps
you could argue that the Prince has been under his thumb since childhood and that even the dream of the Swan had been controlled by this
man. There is perhaps a connection; but not a magic one.

  Above all, I didn't want that three-way relationship – Prince, Swan,
Rothbart – in the Swan scenes. I just wanted the simplicity of the
Prince and the swans without something else controlling it. After all,
it's in his mind. So it didn't seem appropriate to have anyone else
involved.

AM: *So there is a romantic, unbridgeable gap between the Swan and the*
Prince in your Swan Lake as in the traditional one. But that gap isn't
created by Rothbart's power in your version, it's created by the block,
the repression, in the Prince's own mind. He can't fully grasp the Swan,
be at one with it, for reasons that are entirely in his own mind.
MB: Yes, that's right.

AM: *Do you remember any other* Swan Lakes *that made any impression, good or bad, before you set to work on your own?*

MB: I'd seen the Mats Ek one on video. I'd already seen his *Giselle*. The liberties that he took with those pieces must have given me a bit of a push as well to look at things – but, actually, his is a little too radical for me in some ways: the music is terribly cut and edited; and there are sounds within it, vocalizations, that I didn't like. Basically, though, I liked aspects of what he did; and I liked some of his movement style as well. He was the first new choreographer I'd seen for years whose work actually felt like something that I tuned into.

His *Swan Lake* is a very surreal world, for one thing, as opposed to the more literal world that I set it in. His is a world where everyone's got a bald head – but they seem to have a bun in there somewhere as well, I seem to remember! It's the Prince's story very much; but there is a strong mother-figure, a queen, and it's very nightmarish, I think. The White Swan-Black Swan is danced by Ana Laguna – who's an amazing dancer, but quite mannish in a way. She's got a great face, but it's like Georgia Brown or someone like that: she's got a sort of rough-edged look to her. So the way the Swan was portrayed was very confrontational; and the Prince, though it's his story, was a bit of a puppet figure.

I liked the fluidity of his movement. It's actually also very exact in terms of gesture – but also full of dance. He's managed to combine the two very well, managed to combine interesting upper-body gestural movement with some more rhythmic lower-body dance interest. And it's very flighty as well, which is nice.

I'll tell you what I think I was most inspired by, when watching it. To see contemporary movements to that traditional music – both in *Giselle* and *Swan Lake* – suddenly makes you see familiar, or great, music in an entirely new light. I think this is the strength of a lot of modern choreography: if it uses good music in a musical way, it feels much more like real choreography. Too many of the traditional ballets – I say this, even though I've loved watching several of them – don't feel like living choreography any more.

AM: *But is this solely a dance response on your part? Or had you seen any theatre or opera productions that updated classic texts?*

MB: In the 1980s, I saw a lot of opera productions at English National Opera, and, yes, I was inspired by the liberties that the producers took.

Some of them were updated, some were psychological, some were both: they seemed to be doing something very boldly which the ballet world wasn't. I remember reading the story of Dvořák's opera *Rusalka* beforehand and thinking, 'Well, this is the *Swan Lake* story' – but then, in that David Pountney staging at English National Opera, it became something quite different. The words told the more traditional story about a water-nymph and a prince; the production showed a very psychosexual, daughter-father-nursery interpretation of that story. That may have influenced my *Nutcracker* a little.

The famous Jonathan Miller *Rigoletto*, updated to gangster America, and – much more radically – the Pountney *Hansel and Gretel*, with its Freudian treatment of the Mother and Witch as the same person: all those were very exciting. And they were hits. Here were these producers changing the whole look and setting of a work, and people just loved it.

There are good reasons why these liberties aren't taken in the world of classical ballet: because it's the choreographic text, with all its stylistic tradition, which is being kept going as well as the music, whereas in opera only the music is being preserved from one production to the next. In ballet, if you try updating, it usually doesn't work. Look at Derek Deane's *Giselle* for English National Ballet. Why update it to the 1920s but keep the old choreography? They're wearing dresses they would do the charleston in, but they do the same ballet steps you see in other *Giselles*. It doesn't feel right.

I do think it's possible to make the traditional versions come alive in their original period settings, by the way; I really do. But that's for someone else to try; that isn't what I do.

AM: *As you know, you were by no means the first to choreograph a male Swan. I remember now – something I've tried to forget for years – a production by Roland Petit called* Ma Pavlova, *in which dozens of men all came on doing Pavlova's Dying Swan movements. Why they did, I neither understood nor cared.*

You had seen the Swan that Philippe Giraudeau (and, later, Jonathan Lunn) danced in Siobhan Davies's Carnival, *to the Saint-Saëns Swan music that, because of Anna Pavlova, everybody thinks of as the Dying Swan music. Was that an influence?*

MB: I had seen it – though really I remember it from watching it on video – and liked it very much as an idea. My vision of the Swan was different, because I saw it as more of an animal – even more than a bird, in some ways. I saw it as a pagan thing almost. As soon as I thought of doing *Swan Lake*, I thought of doing it with men; and it was always the wildness of swans that I wanted to show, that I felt would work – relating more to Act Four initially. Then the other thing that probably relates more to the Sue Davies Swan is that I also wanted to do something more lyrical for men – without emasculating them in any way. At the time there was a lot of violent male dancing around, European stuff – Eurotrash, Eurocrash, whatever it is – and all Lloyd Newson's physical theatre with his group DV8, with men hurling themselves against walls and on to the floor. I was reacting against that; I wanted to do something beautiful for men.

AM: *I wonder if – accidentally – your* Swan Lake *took ideas not only from* Hamlet *the play but also from Robert Helpmann's ballet* Hamlet. *That, too, is a psychodrama – Ophelia and the Queen become confused in the Prince's mind – set to Tchaikovsky. It had designs by Leslie Hurry, who was also responsible for the* Swan Lake *you often saw at Covent Garden. You saw that* Hamlet *in 1980, with Anthony Dowell and Antoinette Sibley in the lead roles, and you've often looked at the photographs of the original production, with Helpmann himself and Fonteyn. I even have a dim memory that 'Bobby' (after Helpmann) was your nickname among some of your friends on the BA course at the Laban Centre, though you may have originated it.*

MB: Because of the amount of make-up I wore on stage!

1980 is a long time ago. But I certainly loved that *Hamlet* at the time; and I've always seen Scott as a latterday Helpmann in terms of acting. You know what? I even used to toy with the idea – years ago – of calling the company 'The Helpmanns'.

AM: *There are resemblances between your* Swan Lake *and Kenneth MacMillan's ballet* Mayerling. *That, too, is about the private lives of royalty: in particular the protagonist, Crown Prince Rudolf. In particular, both* Mayerling *and your* Swan Lake *have an Oedipal scene between royal mother and son, in which he strives to communicate and she is guarded and embarrassed.*

Needless to say, the British ballet press have made much of the parallels between Mayerling *and your* Swan Lake. *(Ironically – though people have now forgotten this – when* Mayerling *was new in 1978, some of the same critics discussed its parallels to the traditional* Swan Lake: *which has its Oedipal tensions too.) The fact that your first-cast*

Prince and Queen were Adam Cooper and Fiona Chadwick heigh-
tened the connection: he had danced Rudolf, she had danced more
roles than one in Mayerling. *Later, Lynn Seymour, MacMillan's most*
famous muse and one of the dancers of the original cast in Mayerling,
played the role of the Queen in your production.

You've seen Mayerling. *At what point did you think of any resem-*
blance to that?

MB: To be quite honest, I didn't even remember the Prince–Queen section of *Mayerling*. It had been a long time since I'd seen it, I'd never
known it well, and I had grown confused – as *Mayerling* audiences
often are – about which character is which: especially which is his
mother, the Empress, and which is his ex-mistress, the Countess. What
I liked most was the idea of the central character: a prince who was
out of control, desperate. I think that aspects of that probably went
into the overall feeling of my production.

I have seen *Mayerling* again since; I do see that a resemblance is
there. It came out of the fact that the Queen shows so much affection
and love and sexual interest in all those other young men, but the one
person she should be showing it to, her son, she can't even touch –
probably because she was having this kind of relationship with other
men. I'm sure that the MacMillan productions in general encouraged
me to address different dramatic ideas; and I also think that, in the
back of my mind, I thought it would be great to create a male role that
was a great challenge for a male dancer – in the same way that Rudolf
in *Mayerling* has become almost the one role that all male Royal Ballet
dancers seem to want to play. In my case, of course, I was planning not
one big male role but two. In films, the women are always complaining
there aren't enough roles for women; but it's the opposite in ballet.

But that was only in the back of my mind. I didn't know if I could
create a big male role. What I was initially interested in was to push
male dancing. To show different kinds of male lyricism: that was what
was in the forefront of my mind.

AM: *Would you say that you have a message to pass on in your* Swan
Lake?

MB: When I'm asked to sum up what *Swan Lake* is all about, I say
that it's about a very simple thing. It's about somebody who needs
love: who needs, in the most basic and simple way, to be held.

I suppose you could say that *Cinderella* is the same story.

AM: *But it's not the story of* Highland Fling.

MB: No, it's not. It is of *Nutcracker*, though. *Highland Fling*, in some sense, is about wanting something but not knowing what you want. Which is what *Swan Lake*'s also about: not knowing what you want out of a person.

AM: *To what degree are all your shows about sexual longing? The 'Shallow Brown' dream in* Town and Country, *the emotion that Clara has for her Nutcracker hero, the adulterous desire that James has for one female after another (primarily the Sylph) in* Highland Fling, *the Prince's feeling for the Swan, and the longing that Cinderella and the Pilot have for each other: these are all striking stage visions of sexual desire.*

MB: I always see that as the basis of a good story. I'm very 'into' the dramatic structure of having sets of characters – as in the old-style traditions of drama: I like my central couple connected by love or desire, my comic character people on the sidelines, and a villain too. Very Disney; but also very *EastEnders*. A lot of directors I know watch *EastEnders* with great pleasure, because it has all the essence of drama in it: your villains, your nice people, your young lovers, your comics – it's all there somehow, everything's catered for. But I suppose that I particularly need to feel something for the central person, or for the central relationship.

AM: *But beyond having a central relationship, you make an unusual emphasis on the huge longing of one central character for another. And unusual emphasis, too, on the distance between them.*

MB: I think that, once they're together, the drama's finished. The longing is the interesting thing. That, and the journey of getting together or not.

AM: *I would say that, very often in your work, it is also a longing for beauty. At several points in your shows, there is a moment of either the shock of beauty or the shock of sexual allure: in fact, a moment when the recognition of beauty becomes the recognition of sexual desire. For example, when Clara suddenly sees the bare-torsoed Nutcracker along with – by implication – the whole of the male sex.*

MB: I think that's true.[3] I think those feelings are something that I feel a lot of people share, so I'm aware of the impact they will have on a

3 Bourne headed an earlier rough version of the announcement quoted in note 1 with this: '"There is a swan whose name is extasy . . ." Aleister Crowley.'

viewer. Yes, it's true; at that moment in *Nutcracker* and at the moment when the Swan first enters, I want the audience to feel the same impact as the character in the piece. I want them to be slightly overwhelmed by the beauty of what I'm showing, to feel its excitement.

AM: *Are you conscious that, along with all of that, jealousy is frequently an important element in your dance dramas?*
MB: I think it is, yes. Funnily enough, I myself am really not a jealous person; but I find it a very powerful emotion to play with, and the drama that ensues from it.

I like making my central character suffer quite a lot. Maybe they have a good ending, maybe they don't; but I like piling on the agony for the central character, and I've done it in several pieces. It started with all the things the second Mrs De Wynter goes through in *Deadly Serious*. And it happens to Clara in *Nutcracker*: lots of agony, lots of obstacles, before she gets what she wants. Likewise Cinderella.

AM: *Your works put me in mind – not in their physicality, but in their ideas – of some of the sexual psychodramas that Martha Graham put on stage between the 1940s and 1960s. Errand into the Maze (1947) is a particularly strong example, and it made a huge impact here in 1979. It shows a woman's terror and fascination with a bare-chested male, part-animal, brutally sexual Creature of Fear. He's a phallic symbol of sorts, and shows plenty of naked flesh; she is much more fully clothed, and the drama is about the change in her perception of him.*

You saw Errand into the Maze *at the Graham gala you attended in July 1979. Do you have any memory of it?*
MB: No. I do like seeing early modern-dance works, and the photographs are all so interesting; but I don't remember seeing that one. I look forward to seeing it again one day!

AM: *These four 'classics', as you nickname them, aren't they also about your love of eccentricity and variety? In each piece, you seem determined to show us that characters don't have to conform to one ideal type. Do you always want to have short and tall, stocky and skinny dancers?*
MB: Yes. When we had a smaller company, we had a mixture of sizes. It was an odd group of people – going right up in height to Andrew George, who's six foot four – with quite a range of shapes. When we first tried to cast a bigger show, *Nutcracker*, we decided to keep that

range of shapes and sizes. I know now that that's one of the reasons why our audiences are wider than a ballet audience. Sure, they love to see beautiful dancers; but they also love to see people with whom they feel they themselves have some connection. The same goes for the mixture of races in the company.

AM: *When you're casting the swans today, do you ever think, 'We haven't got a black dancer, we're running out of short boys'?*
MB: Ultimately, we always cast because of talent. We'd never cast anyone over someone else for any other reason. But, if we've got a choice between two people we're equally interested in, we'll go for the one who does most to widen the mix of people in the company.

Swan Lake divides itself up nicely that way. You have to have some small guys for cygnets, some big boys for big swans. When I talk to people at auditions, I tend to make a point of saying that. Sometimes they ask, 'Are you looking for one racial type? Are you looking for certain particular physical types?' 'No,' I say, 'we're looking for dancers.' And you see these tiny little dancers, or very tall dancers, looking so relieved that they're not going to be discriminated against.

I know that a lot of our regular audience have favourites within the company who aren't necessarily in principal roles, whom they follow and watch and like to see doing different roles. It's because the company has such a mixture of people that they enjoy that.

AM: *So when did you think, 'I want Adam Cooper as the Swan'? And when did Adam Cooper indicate an interest in your work?*
MB: About a year and a half before the production. It was the first time we did *Highland Fling* in London, at the small Lilian Baylis Theatre that was part of the old Sadler's Wells, in spring 1994. Iain Webb, who is now one of our rehearsal directors, came to see it with his wife, Margaret Barbieri. He was then a Royal Ballet dancer; she, of course, had been a leading ballerina with the Sadler's Wells Royal Ballet. She then invited me to choreograph a piece (*Boutique*) on her students at London Studio Centre; and Iain came back to see *Highland Fling* a second time, this time bringing Adam and Sarah Wildor. Adam and Sarah were both rising stars of the Royal at Covent Garden, and I met them both briefly afterwards, because they wanted to say how much they'd enjoyed it. Then, a week or so later, Iain told me that he thought that they had expressed interest in working with me.

At the time I was having a problem anyway with the idea of casting

41 *Swan Lake*. Adam Cooper as the Swan. Pre-publicity photograph. Here the entire body shape shows how far, in part, from traditional *Swan Lake* choreography Bourne was preparing to go.

42 *Swan Lake*. Adam Cooper as the Swan. Pre-publicity photograph. Although the swept-back 'wings' and bent-forward torso occur in some other productions of swan choreography, here the bare feet, bare calves, and bent knees show a new emphasis, while the Swan's direct stare into the camera shows the disturbing dream/nightmare psychological force with which Bourne was planning to invest the character.

this *Swan Lake*. I had mentioned the Swan role to one or two people, but I really hadn't decided. I certainly didn't feel then that I was in a position to approach just anyone in the whole dance world – which I do feel now. I would never have felt then that I had any kind of cachet to interest anyone from the Royal Ballet. So I was thinking, 'I'll find the right person from within our company,' or 'We'll audition to find someone to do it.'

AM: *Ben Wright remembers that at one point you mentioned the role to him; and that he couldn't imagine himself in it, and asked to be considered for the Prince instead.*

MB: I must say I've completely forgotten that. As you know, Ben helped to create the role of the Prince, and – after Scott – has been dancing it, extremely well, ever since the initial Sadler's Wells season.

Anyway, when Iain said that, I thought instantly: 'Wouldn't he – Adam – be perfect for that role?' I had seen him dance plenty of roles; he appealed to me as a dancer. He's very manly. And I think, above all, that it was the way he uses his arms that was the most appealing factor for this role. I could also see great intelligence in his work. Having met him briefly, I felt he was the sort of person that I could get on with – which is very important to me.

So I arranged to meet him, with Iain again. We went for a meal, and I said I had an idea for him. I didn't know anything about him at the time. I'd got an impression that he was an underdog Royal Ballet principal dancer, but someone who the Royal would mainly use for the more modern roles and in new choreography; which was good, I thought, for me. I think he'd danced some William Forsythe ballets with them by that point. Then, when I actually met him, I realized that he had a great love of the classics too: that, even though he wasn't doing the leading roles in them, he still loved the whole idea of them. That's why he enjoyed *Highland Fling*. And he loved the idea of working with those old scores and doing something different with them.

I think he was quite taken aback when I said it was the Swan that I wanted him to do. It obviously hadn't occurred to him that that would be the role he would be offered; and he probably pretended to be a little less shocked than he was. I think the whole experience of doing this role has changed him a lot; but at the time he would have been a bit worried. He's said to me since that, when he found that there was a Prince as well, he was taken aback; but you see, I never really talked to him in any depth about how we were going to approach it. I didn't say it was gay; I didn't say it wasn't. I just said, 'There's a Prince, and there's a Swan.' I told him the basic ideas for the story, and that the Swan was something in the Prince's imagination. That was all. I didn't really get specific with him about it.

AM: *Adam is heterosexual. But you didn't even tell him that his role was going to have – as the Stranger in Act Three – plenty of hetero activities?*
MB: Not at that stage, no. The next stage was to ask the artistic direc-tor of the Royal Ballet, Anthony Dowell, to give Adam leave of absence from the Royal Ballet. This was in summer 1994, about a year before we started rehearsals. Dowell talked to me about musicals quite a lot to begin with – they're his passion – but kept this very bemused approach to the whole project. The main thing I remember is just explaining what the part was and what we were doing, in wanting Adam to play the Swan. Then, when I said there would also be a male Prince, he just said 'Oh dear', with raised eyebrows.

Actually, I think Dowell found the idea of the project quite exciting. I'm sure the initial reason that he let Adam do it was that he knew that he himself would have wanted to do something like that at that point in his career. He knew how few opportunities there were for male dancers to do a big role in a full-length ballet, and I think that's the reason why he felt he couldn't say no. That was the dancer coming out in him.

Next, in spring 1995, when AMP did a fund-raising gala at the Don-mar Warehouse, I made a swan solo for Adam. This was an important 'do' for us. Nigel Hawthorne, who's become a patron of our company, spoke at the dinner afterwards, and we certainly felt the honour of that because it was his first public engagement here after the Oscar cere-mony and all the brouhaha he'd been through there.

The performance included items old and new. There was a section called 'On the Air', in which four numbers were danced to old music on the gramophone; that was an easy 'link', since all four of them had been made to old recordings (three of them, originally, on 78s). Two of these were revivals: the Lovers' Duet from *Infernal Galop* (Edith Piaf's 'Hymne à l'amour', and Scott Ambler and I danced 'Dearest Love' (Noel Coward singing) from *Town and Country*. Two of them were new, both to old recordings by Richard Tauber, whose recordings I had recently started to fall in love with. While Scott and I sat at the side in our *Town and Country* costumes, Etta Murfitt and Emily Piercy danced to his recording of 'Girls were Made to Love and Kiss'. Then, after we'd danced 'Dearest Love', Adam danced to Tauber's sung version of the Saint-Saëns 'Swan'. The *Infernal Galop* Lovers' Duet came last. Later, two dancers from London Studio Centre danced a duet from *Boutique*, the version of the Rossini-Respighi *Boutique Fantasque* I'd made for Margaret Barbieri's students there. Finally, Adam danced in a revival of *Spitfire*, alongside Ben Wright, Phil Hill and Scott.

I didn't know what Adam wanted at that stage; I choreographed all the solo, and took him through it movement by movement. Possibly he found that difficult. He'd say, 'Oh, you look better than I do.' Possibly I used a few movements from earlier work I'd made. But we got used to working together – it was made, for nothing, in a week – and so it was an invaluable preparation for work later that year on *Swan Lake*. But it wasn't a try-out for actual Swan movement. Ironically, the solo wasn't about a swan at all. It was about dying, or illness. There were little catches in Tauber's voice that gave me the idea of someone with ailments, of things going wrong. Adam wore simple black trousers, a black cut-off T-shirt, and bare feet.

AM: *Was it an Aids dance?*
MB: Not at all. Really not. Nor did Adam 'die' at the end. It was more about someone coping with something that had gone wrong with him. I'd love to do it again.

AM: *Did you always plan the Prince as a role for Scott Ambler?*
MB: Yes.

AM: *When did he and Adam Cooper meet?*
MB: Probably quite soon after Adam agreed to do it. It's very much my way to cultivate friendship with people that I'm going to be working with – to make sure, actively, that we know each other well, and that we get on before the rehearsals begin. Adam and Scott hit it off very quickly. They're good friends now, work together very well, and have got certain similarities. They both smoke like chimneys. They're both quite calm about performing; they're very relaxed. You go into their dressing room before a show and it's a very relaxed atmosphere: they just sit there, staring into space and smoking. They laugh quite a lot – have a good relationship.

Highland Fling had been designed as a vehicle for Scott. In some ways the Prince naturally followed on from that, using the acting abilities that Scott has.

AM: *In what ways is Scott like yourself?*

MB: He is like me in that we have good ideas together, perform well together, and have similar ways of viewing performance. His knowledge of other forms of performance is similar to mine; and he sees the potential in the projects that I suggest – whereas a lot of other people don't. If I was to say to him, '*Giselle* – let's think about *Giselle*', he would say, 'Good, right,' and he would read the scenario and come up with a whole series of ideas: 'You could do this, try this. If we put it in this setting . . .' He visualizes things in a similar way, so he's very good in that respect.

He is unlike me in many other ways. He's a hopeless case in terms of the way he lives: he smokes a lot, eats really badly, doesn't look after himself, is a workaholic, can't relax, has to be working all the time – performing, or, if he's not performing, doing something else in there. He flogs himself to death when he doesn't need to. I'm not really like that. It's easy to take advantage of someone like that when they're there all the time. My job mainly with him is to tell him to go home, to rest, to make sure he keeps fit, to be sure to look after himself. That said, he never misses a show – and, unlike me, he has the same body he had ten years ago!

AM: *Are there any ways in which you, consciously or accidentally, projected yourself into the role of the Prince?*

MB: Not as a character. I don't think the role has any characteristics of mine about it. I'm not that sad a person! I know that I visualized the Swan – but not in the way the Prince does. I was presenting a character – the Swan – that I felt was meaningful to me; but the Prince was someone else who was reacting to that character; and I was seeing the possibilities of that.

As it happens, all the dancers playing the Swan to date have been straight, and both the Princes gay. That may have added to the original shape of our production. Still, our next round of castings, for New York, could change that pattern.

AM: *Are there any ways in which you find any aspects of the Swan in you?*

MB: Strangely enough – if only I could dance it! – that would be the

43 Anna Pavlova (1881–1931), famous for dancing *The Dying Swan*, with one of her famous and beloved swans at Ivy House, her London home.

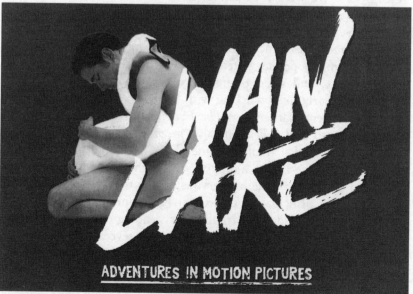

44 *Swan Lake*. A publicity image of Scott Ambler as the Prince with a live swan. This Prince/swan photograph was one of a series taken before rehearsals, and was inspired by those of Anna Pavlova and by the famous obsession of King Ludwig of Bavaria with swans. Although photographs of nude men had become standard advertising ploys since the late 1980s, this connection of a naked man to a bird was sufficiently controversial to be dropped from publicity for the production's seasons in America.

part that I would feel comfortable doing. Apart, that is, from the Queen, which is the role I'd love to do most. I have no great desire to get into drag, but I like playing characters that are in control of things. I don't mind a little bit of repression, but not to the point our Prince is at; and it's too emotional a role for me as well. I like to be the commanding presence.

AM: *Is that why you'd like to be the Queen?*
MB: No. The reason I like that role so much is that I love the revealing of the character as it goes along. I love being one thing and then another. There are little comic points in Act One where she's attracted to some of the young cadets; you have that really dramatic duet with the Prince, which is real tragic drama; you get to be sexy in Act Three, then tragic again at the end. It's just got everything in it, that part. You get to be funny, sexy – it's a great part for anyone who enjoys acting, dance acting. It's the part that I like directing the most.

AM: *At what point did Adam suggest Fiona Chadwick to do the Queen?*
MB: We were trying to find someone for that role, and I talked to a couple of people. Kate Coyne, from London Contemporary Dance Theatre, was one I talked to; and the Royal Ballet's Sandra Conley was the other person we were considering. Both Scott and I absolutely love Conley's performances in the Royal Ballet's character roles. She knows that we love her too, and she wanted to do something; but she was very concerned about just dancing at that time: she has had bad arthritis.

Then Adam Cooper suggested Fiona Chadwick. This was late 1994 or early 1995, and she'd recently lost her job at the Royal Ballet. Adam particularly liked working with her. He had danced with her a fair bit at Covent Garden – in *The Firebird*, for example, and in her farewell *Romeo and Juliet*, but also in other ballets – and thought she'd be very good. I think that they have a definite musicality that works together, and I think a rapport with each other.

I was, I suppose, a little bit nervous of her, to begin with. She had been a leading principal of the Royal Ballet for quite a number of years. I had seen her dance virtually every leading role in its repertory, she had worked with Kenneth MacMillan and several other important choreographers; but she was obviously a very good idea. Once she was on board, I organized a lunch with her, Adam, Scott and Etta – to make sure she would get on with everybody and they with her. Needless to say, we all ended up loving her.

AM: *I remember at one point you said, 'I can't really tell you the story of my own* Swan Lake.'

MB: I can't tell you the story of Act Four completely; I couldn't tell you exactly what was going on.

⌊ I consciously wanted to make *Swan Lake* about a man – very much a man, who happened to be a prince as well – who had trouble expressing himself and couldn't, for whatever reason, be who he wanted to be. He was also a needy person: that was the centre of it. And the swan was a symbol of what he needed – rather than some tragic figure who's been magically transformed into something else – I didn't feel it needed that. Once the decision was made that the Swan was in the imagination of the Prince and then projected on to a real person in Act Three, it made sense that other things were not relevant to our story.[4] ⌉

So with no Rothbart and with everything in the Prince's imagination, Act Four is another kind of drama – I know that much – but I really don't want to specify exactly what it means as psychological narrative at every point. It means more if I leave it ambiguous, if I leave certain options open.

AM: *How much do you think of audiences when you're planning a work?*

MB: I've always thought about the audience completely at all times.

Perhaps that seems to be going a little too far, a little too populist; and certainly I do have to please myself as well. But when I say that I'm ⌊very audience-conscious, ⌉I mean that, all the time when I'm making a piece, my questions to myself are all about whether the audience will get this; whether this will be conveyed to the audience in the way I want it to be. 'Will the audience be lost at this point? Does the audience need signals as to how to react at this point? Do we need the audience to applaud at this point? Even for ourselves, do we need some response here from the audience? If so, how do we get it?' Particularly with humour in the pieces: that's an on-going process of trying to get the audience to react in the right way. 'Maybe it's timed wrong: so try

4 Performers are, however, allowed some freedom with this. In September 1998, after performing the Prince for nearly three years, Ben Wright decided that, in Act Two, his Prince does see the Swan in real life. Will Kemp, however, who has played the Swan to the Princes of both Ambler and Wright many times, said in the same period that he tried to adjust his Swan to each Prince and that he sees the Swan in Acts Two and Four as the projection solely of the Prince's mind.

it a different way' – until the audience does react. The relationship of a show with an audience works two ways.

I've always felt that I was audience-conscious while I was making work. Not necessarily at the outset. When I say, 'I'm going to do this piece or that,' at that stage, maybe, to some people some of the choices I'm making don't seem very commercial or popular; but then I try to make them accessible – or understandable to anyone.

AM: *As you talk about individual works like* Swan Lake, *you're always trying to communicate – to get expressive ideas across – however ambiguous they may be.*

There is another attitude in some dance-makers' minds: that they make dances about dance, about movement – and here I include some very popular choreographers, such as Ashton and Balanchine. Is that any part of your thinking when you're making a dance show? Are there parts of Swan Lake, *for example, where dance – movement – becomes your subject matter?*

MB: I think that there are, but I suppose that, in my case, those are just parts of a larger show. In British dance today, that's the most obvious way in which I differ from, say, Richard Alston or Sue Davies; but I do look for those sections where we can just dance. Maybe, in some of those sections, the dancing is based on a single dramatic idea – but basically it is about dancing. To have those passages in a dance show is obviously important.

AM: *In* Swan Lake, *I presume, you're talking particularly of Act Two, the first lakeside scene.*

MB: Yes. If it were true – as I sometimes claim! – that everything in it is story-led, I would have cut the dance for the four cygnets and the four big swans. But those are really there purely as the dance interest. They have character, and musicality; but they don't add to anything that's going on plotwise at all. The Prince and Swan aren't even on the stage. I do treasure those moments as well within a production. They're a sort of challenge for me too: I like to try to make those moments work. Pure-dance choreography is not my strongest point. So if I can make something like that work, I'm more pleased with it in the end than with something that comes more easily that everyone else thinks is very clever. It's the dance choreography, more often than not, that I'm trying to make richer or more interesting.

Preparation

ALASTAIR MACAULAY: *How did you prepare for the production itself?*
MATTHEW BOURNE: I had such a long time to think about *Swan Lake*. I played the music a lot, daily: first, to decide which music to use and to familiarize myself with the structure of the music.

AM: *I would assume, from having seen* Swan Lake *and much of your previous work, that, while you were preparing this show, you found yourself going deeper into the music than you ever had with music before: that you were giving rein to your own musical imagination or response.*
MB: Yes, I'd really listened to it a lot, but completely divorcing myself from images of the ballet. I am able to do that when I'm just listening to it. I wander around; I visualize situations; I shape a story in my head. When I've got a basic situation – the ball in Act Three, for example – and I've got the relationships between characters, I just go off into the story, listen to the music, see if the music does something with that story. Sometimes it leads to nothing, but it is a good way of working: just to let a scenario shape itself musically in your mind.

I had CDs and tapes of different recordings of the music; but all the versions that had ever been recorded up to that time were of the original 1877 version: which made it very difficult to get a feeling of the whole piece, because almost no stage version of *Swan Lake* uses that version of the score. I had grown familiar with the 1895 version in the theatre, and I wanted to keep some of the 1895 ordering of the music; but that involved a lot of dotting to and fro around the 1877 version, since there had never been a recording made of the 1895. In fact, when our recording came out in 1996, it was the first one based on a version that was being actually performed. Since then, one has at last appeared of the 1895 version; but I can't say that I take to all the Drigo emendations. I was very happy to get to know the 1877 score so well; although we re-order it at several points, I think that there are passages where it works very successfully in our production. I'm proud of those.

AM: *When you were researching it – thinking about the music – you read, or reread, Roland John Wiley's 1985 book* Tchaikovsky's Ballets?
MB: Yes, I read it.

AM: *One of the points he makes about the 1877 score is that there is an inner family (my word, not his) of* Swan Lake *music. Much of the music – by reason of either melody or orchestration or tonality – is connected to Odette, the swans, Rothbart or Prince Siegfried.*

In the lakeside acts, Acts Two and Four, this is hardly surprising. Some of the music in Acts One and Three, by contrast, has little or no connection with this family, and therefore was surely designed simply as divertissement music. But some of the other music in these non-lakeside acts is 'family' music – by which I mean that it belongs to the 'inner family' of Swan Lake *musical material – and (since documentation on the 1877 stage original is fairly thin) it's hard to say just what dramatic or narrative purpose Tchaikovsky and/or the original production team assigned to these individual parts. Maybe the musical connections are accidental, or were just part of Tchaikovsky's ambition to give his score more overall coherence than was required by the narrative. Two examples: the theme of the Waltz in Act One corresponds with that of Odette's recitative in Act Two; the Russian Dance in Act Three, which Wiley presumes was danced by the 'Black Swan' Odile by virtue of its solo violin (an instrument often assigned to the ballerina), may have been 'the dance that won Siegfried over to Odile'.[5] I would also say – though Wiley does not – that one of the other national dances in Act Three, the czardas, sounds as if it is somehow related to this* Swan Lake *musical family. By contrast, the Neapolitan Dance, Spanish Dance and mazurka never sound part of the story, part of the* Swan Lake *inner world.*

I don't know whether you were inspired by Wiley, or if his book gave you confidence in your own instincts; but, as soon as I first saw your Swan Lake *in 1995, I was amazed to see that, in Acts One and Three, you distinguish dramatically between this 'family' and 'non-family' music.*

MB: I can't say that I consciously absorbed that point from him. He doesn't make that point forcefully; and I wasn't thinking hard of my textual decisions when I read his book. I would say that I made my

---

5 Roland John Wiley, *Tchaikovsky's Ballets*, Oxford, 1985, p. 285 (n. 16). See also chapter 2, 'The Music of *Swan Lake*', passim, esp. pp. 68, 80–3, 88–90. Also pp. 43, 50.

Bourne's own copy of this book is inscribed '1992' in his own handwriting, which suggests that he bought it while preparing his production of *Nutcracker*. There are several passages of chapters 1 and 2 that he (or, conceivably, a colleague) has underlined, but at no point do they particularly address the point under discussion here.

choices from musical instinct. Still, it's possible that my instinct may have been subconsciously guided by having read Wiley; I don't know.

AM: *Who was the first person you brought on board to help you plan the production?*

MB: Lez Brotherston. Funnily enough, he hadn't been my first choice as designer, although we'd had a good working relationship on *Highland Fling*. The reason was that he'd recently done another *Swan Lake* for Northern Ballet Theatre, again, a modernish version. He had said to me, 'I think I could do it differently for you, but I understand. Still, if you are interested, I'm interested.' So instead I asked Anthony Ward to design it. He had done *Nutcracker* and *Oliver!* I told him the story of my *Swan Lake* but – I'm not sure what his reasons were; perhaps he felt it was not the right piece for him at that time – he decided not to. I was quite upset by that at the time. I then pursued Stephen Brinson-Lewis, but he wasn't available. So then I thought, 'Let's get Lez to do it', because we'd worked well before.

He was soon on board, and he was invaluable. He had an enormous

45 *Swan Lake*. Costume sketch by Lez Brotherston for the Private Secretary. Bourne, who has sometimes played this role, says that his interpretation is closer to this sketch.

amount to contribute in terms of ideas, and obviously in the way it looked. It plays with time so much all through Act One and then Act Three; it's a mixture of timeless costumes, 1950s and 1960s costumes, and very much modern-day costumes. All that was intentional. It wasn't the world that I initially had had in my mind, but it really worked. I had wanted something more abstract-looking, a strange world that had this kingdom within it, where he pushed it more towards something that was British-looking.

AM: *Did you draw up your idea of the musical text first and then your scenario? Or vice versa? Or both at the same time?*
MB: I would go from one to the other. I would have a dramatic idea, and then see if there was the music to support it. Or I would just find myself in love with some piece of *Swan Lake* music – maybe one that wasn't in most stage versions of *Swan Lake* – and wait till I knew how I could use it dramatically.

Eventually, I sat down with our then Musical Director, David Lloyd-Jones, and we worked through the music together. I knew David from our *Nutcracker*, and knew him to be an authority on Russian music, and on Tchaikovsky in particular. I would ask him where we could use, or could cut, repeats in the music. We would listen to it; and he would say, for example, 'Well, yes, this is just a repeat here, you can cut it perfectly all right.' Or I would ask if I could shift an item from this place in the score to that without violating the harmony. All that was very useful: to achieve the musical structure, and then to record an edition, a collage from various recordings, in the order that we wanted to do it.

Meanwhile I gave Scott specific research to do, mainly around the Prince character. He would read a lot of books – as I did myself, and so did others later on – and he would bring back what he thought was relevant information. That helped. We did a lot of reading around all the princes and monarchs of this century and last: virtually anything relevant that we could get our hands on. So the Prince in our *Swan Lake* is an amalgamation of characteristics of different kings and princes.[6] The one thing they all seemed to have in common – the royal

6 Relevant books on Bourne's shelves include: Craig Brown and Lesley Cunliffe, *The Book of Royal Lists*, Routledge and Kegan Paul, 1982; Desmond Chapman-Huston, *Ludwig II (the Mad King of Bavaria)*, Dorset, 1990; Vivian Green, *The Madness of Kings (Personal Trauma and the Fate of Nations)*, Alan Sutton, 1993; Paul James, *Prince Edward (A Life in the Spotlight)*, Piatkus, 1992; Christopher McIntosh, *The Swan King (Ludwig of Bavaria)*, Robin Clark, 1986; John van der Kiste, *Childhood at Court, 1819–1914*, Alan Sutton, 1995.

men we chose to research – was that they all seemed very unsuitable for the job that they were born into; that they were not complete people. The actual job seemed to make them worse. We used the nervous twitches and the stammering of various kings. George VI was quite an inspiration: he was so unsuited to public life.[7]

AM: *Any foreign ones?*
MB: Ludwig of Bavaria, of course, because he was so obsessed with swans. In fact, he seemed too obvious a link. Still, we did read books about him, and a certain amount of him went into it.

AM: *Well, another book on your shelves that's extensively lined is* The Swan King (Ludwig II of Bavaria) *by Christopher McIntosh (1986). I can't begin to quote all the underlined passages to you, but let's pick one or two. There are areas of Ludwig's diaries that were destroyed decades after his death, and McIntosh asks why.*

What was in the diaries that was incriminating? Why were there so many secrets about Ludwig? . . . The explanation, I decided, lay in one or more of the three areas of his life over which there had been intense speculation . . .
The first of these problematic areas concerns his sexual life. It has long been known that Ludwig had homosexual leanings . . . The second sensitive point has to do with his death. The 'official' version is that on the day after his dethronement he drowned himself in Lake Starnberg near Munich . . . I believe, as I argue later, that though the cause of death was technically either suicide or manslaughter, the responsibility for it must ultimately rest with those who engineered his deposition . . . The third and most controversial area in Ludwig's life centres upon his supposed madness. Again, the official claim that he became insane is widely disputed. But there can be no denying that towards the end of his life, he developed very strange habits which were combined with a marked physical deterioration. (pp. 3–4)

So was it your study of Ludwig that decided you to make your Swan Lake *a study in madness or psychological distortion?*
MB: I think so, yes. Of all the princes and kings who we read about, he was closest to the character that we ended up portraying. But also he confirmed ideas that I had already had.

I think, initially, we were thinking that the Private Secretary, the Rothbart figure, was partly responsible for the Prince's madness, and created situations that would make his mental situation worse. The

---

7 An undated three-side paper in Bourne's handwriting, presumably from this period, is called 'Royals and Madness'. (AMP/Bourne archive.)

way a prince is constantly watched and followed and observed all the time: that could contribute to madness of some form. The original idea of the Private Secretary was to show him engineering situations that made the prince feel he was going mad and eventually doing so. The Stranger was the son of the Private Secretary and was brought there in the knowledge that the Queen would go for him – and also maybe in the knowledge that the Prince might fancy him too. There was some kind of power-struggle there: a question of loyalty, trying to maintain the Queen's position.

All that was Ludwig-related, though probably not consciously. But the political sub-plot got too complicated after a while, and we simplified it.

AM: *Then McIntosh writes of Ludwig's childhood fascination with swans.*

'Ludwig loved the swan not only because of its beauty and regal aloofness, but because it was associated in his mind with the other things that Hohenschwangau offered him . . . The murals that his father had commissioned the artist Moritz von Schwind to design . . . depicted scenes from stories and legends, such as those of Tannhäuser, the Holy Grail and the Grail knight Lohengrin, who travelled in a boat drawn by a swan.[8] *Not surprisingly, Ludwig came in his fantasies to identify himself with Lohengrin. Part of his was the knight in shining armour. Another part was the swan itself, aloof, majestic and pure. He knew that one day, the swan in him would be able to take flight, but before it could do so, it was to spend frustrating years in a gilded cage.' (pp. 15–16)*

This connects to your idea that the Prince in Swan Lake *starts to contain the Swan within his own mind.*

MB: Yes: the symbol of freedom. Another thing, in some descriptions of the symbolic associations of the swan, is that it's a sort of phallic symbol. The long neck: a sexual idea.

AM: *Then there's a whole chapter on Sophie, who I imagine is the nearest to a prototype for the Girlfriend in your* Swan Lake. *Among your underlinings here is: 'A natural reticence, even primness, in sexual matters was exacerbated by his cloistered upbringing . . . It could*

---

8 In 1895 a St Petersburg critic remarked on the resemblance between the *Swan Lake* theme and Lohengrin's warning. See Wiley, op. cit., pp. 37, 282 (n. 35).

*be said that fire and ice contended in his soul, with the ice usually
winning.'*

Then he gets engaged to Sophie. Extreme confusion.

*From the start there were hints that all was not as it should be . . .
In the photographs of the pair standing arm in arm, Ludwig looks distant, awkward . . . As soon as he came to his senses and realized the
full implications of the course he had embarked on, he began to draw
back . . . Physical signs of passion were restricted to a few chaste
kisses, which he placed on her brow. When she grew tired of this
restraint and once kissed him on the mouth, he was so shocked that he
nearly broke off the engagement there and then. (p. 85)*

MB: Our Prince does kiss the Girlfriend, but it has the feeling of his trying to prove something. It's rather sudden: something he feels that he
has to do, rather than something that comes out of passion.

AM: *Another volume here is* The Madness of Kings *by Vivian Green.
Its subtitle is:* 'Personal Trauma and the Fate of Nations'. *There's one
whole chapter here called 'The Swan King', about Ludwig. Lots of
underlinings in your copy.*

*'Certified as mad, he drowned himself or was drowned in June
1886 . . . His imagination was more especially gripped by the image
of the swan, an emblem which was to haunt him throughout his life
. . . Ludwig was very tall and radiated immense charm . . .' He also
had 'extraordinarily expressive eyes'. He was described as being 'mentally gifted in the highest degree, but the contents of his mind were
stored in a totally disordered fashion'. (pp. 226–7) During his engagement, Ludwig wrote in his diary: 'I longed for, am athirst for, freedom.'
(p. 228)*

MB: There are so many parallels. The fact that he drowned, for example. He is quite a magical character. I remember seeing the Visconti
film *Ludwig* in my late teens in London; it made a big impression.

AM: *And, in Ludwig's fascination with Wagner, isn't there a parallel
to your Prince's longing for a soulmate?*

MB: Yes. But it was Wagner's music that was the passion, not the man.
He didn't find Wagner a thing of beauty. If he found him a soulmate, it
was because of the music he had made. He found it physically overwhelming; and it was the freedom he felt to listen to music that's the
parallel to our Prince.

AM: *Wagner wrote about Ludwig: 'He is also so beautiful, spiritual, soulful and splendid that I fear his life must run away like a fleeting, heavenly dream in this common world.' (p. 230)*

MB: It was reciprocated quite strongly, wasn't it? It's very strange to read those letters now. Very romantic; they're like love letters. But Ludwig was also a prince; so there's a lot of flattery involved.

We really might have gone more for the Ludwig connection, but we were aware that he had been used as the Prince in some previous production of *Swan Lake*. Was it John Neumeier's? Not one I'd seen. But the idea had already been used.

Scott also read a lot about Prince Eddie, Queen Victoria's grandson, who has sometimes been thought to have been Jack the Ripper. And that whole period.

AM: *On to the actual planning of the structure and scenario: I imagine that the tricky act to work on was Act One. I remember seeing you in July 1995. You told me that you were working on the scenario for Act One, and you said with slight alarm, 'It's got seven changes of scenes so far!'*

MB: I wanted to tell the Prince's story as much as possible in Act One, to take it beyond the usual point of him just walking around, looking moody and a bit sad and dreamy. Before we got to the swan scene in Act Two, I wanted you to feel a lot for him and to know that he needed some sort of affection or love; and so I tried to fill Act One with two things. One was the life of duty and how he seemed unsuitable for that and bored by it. The other was his need for some sort of affection. So he's constantly being rejected or betrayed, one way or another, through Act One – by mother, by girlfriend, by society. So he's desperate. That's why he conjures up such a thing in his mind as the Swan. He also needs to have enough reasons to be veering towards a certain kind of madness. He can't just go mad. You have to know why. You have to think, 'This man is a desperate person.' So I wanted to show all those things in Act One as much as possible, so that we felt for him by the time we reached Act Two.

AM: *How early on did you conceive Act One beginning right back in the Prince's childhood?*

MB: Quite early on. It emerged from my concern that the hero should be more complex; that his feeling for the Swan should not be only something sexual. I wanted to show him in innocence early on as a child, with the vision of the swan – so that it was a vision that was there from childhood, but was also something that took on new meanings for him as he got older, something that he desired, wanted to emulate. Our first *Swan Lake* poster, or logo, made before we ever choreographed it, was of a naked young man (Scott) kneeling with a swan folding its neck around his – a young male version of the famous photos of Pavlova embracing her pet swan at Ivy House. But in our version it's altogether more intimate.

I think also it helped to show that he was a troubled child, having nightmares, alone in this great big bed – this tiny boy who's surrounded by adults all the time.

AM: *One of the main musical items of Act One is the waltz. Usually this is some kind of divertissement dance; Ashton choreographed it as such in more than one version for the Royal Ballet. In some other versions, such as the one choreographed by David Bintley for the 1987 Royal Ballet production, the Prince joins in the festivities. But you make the waltz an absolutely central part of the continuing narrative. How come?*
MB: It's terribly long. So I thought we should obviously employ some kaleidoscopic story-telling procedure here, and I also thought that we could actually say a lot within it.

AM: *You say 'obviously'. It's not obvious usually. But I find your version musically satisfying because that waltz never sounds like a divertissement that's irrelevant to the plot; as I've said, its whole sound seems to make it part of the core 'family' of* Swan Lake *music.*
MB: By listening to the way it was musically structured, I just felt that it was episodic, with different themes coming into it. Also, because it repeats, I felt that it had a sense of time moving on as well. So there's a sense that you could repeat something and comment on it again later; which is what we do in the first section, in which the Queen remains ageless while time and routine move on.

I also think that the beginning shows very nicely the progression of the Prince's age, and also the boredom of royal duty. When he was a boy, they were going round, doing all these openings; then, when he's grown up, years on, there's a repeat sequence. It's as if years and years of royal duties have gone on.

AM: *You actually have scene changes during this one waltz.*
MB: This is the sort of area in which Lez's contribution as designer was

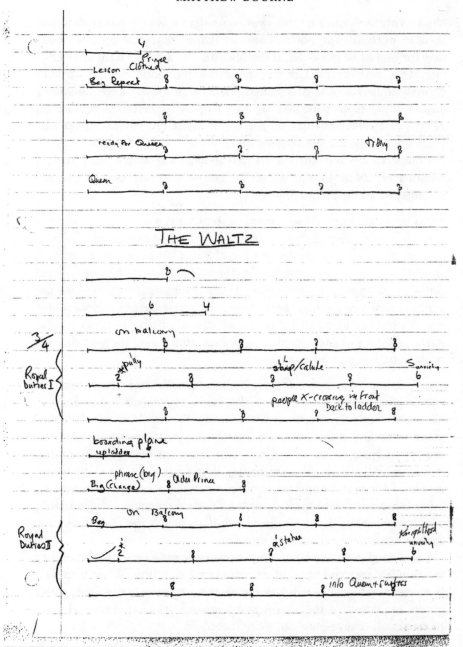

46 *Swan Lake*. From Bourne's annotated breakdown of Act One of the score: the beginning of the Waltz.

terrific. The set develops. It starts off with the Prince's bed, which turns round to become the royal balcony; then that disappears. We decided that we wanted to do something very fluid. So that's why the idea of ropes came in. We used red ropes, which would rein back the crowds wherever these Royals – the Queen and Prince – were going; then the ropes would create gateways for the Royals to walk through. The ropes created places without loads of set moving around. So you get all the unveilings, the ship launch, the pulling of cordons, and the banners coming down. Then we go into a sequence where she's giving medals: a sort of military occasion with mothers and fathers watching. We're pleased with that rope device.

Next we get the introduction of the Girlfriend, and her first meeting with the Prince. When she drops her bag, it's obvious that she's done it on purpose to meet him; so that sets it up nicely. Then we keep moving on in time. The whole thing is like 'episodes in the life of the Royal Family'. Next we're into another occasion in the palace. We open up the back wall, the big crown comes down, the red carpet comes out. The Queen and Prince come in again . . . and it all ends with the Girlfriend re-entering his life at some later point, now having developed a relationship with him.

So it actually tells a lot of story in seven minutes. You get the growing up of the Prince. And you get plenty of the Queen's character: the fact that she does all her Royal duties, finds someone that she fancies, and has her little dance with the cadets, where she's obviously into all those younger men. We see the Prince's disapproval of that; and we get introduced to the character of the Private Secretary a bit more, the way that he seems to be involved in all these things. And the Girlfriend is introduced. The Queen disapproves of her, but the Private Secretary is very much behind her liaison with the Prince. So the Private Secretary has motives and plots of his own, not all of which we fathom – certainly not yet.

It does a lot of things – but the idea was always that there should be some kind of movement going on, to keep the feel of the waltz going all the way through. So there's background material going on, with various aristocrats or military people or court ladies or whatever. I saw the waltz as a really flexible thing that could do a lot and say a lot.

AM: *During Act One, you stage a very funny mock ballet, the Moth Ballet, to the divertissement music that is used, in the traditional* Swan

Lake, *for the pas de trois. This Moth Ballet is in part a send-up of the corniest aspects of traditional – or just bad – Swan Lakes. The enchanted Moth heroine is very dolorous; she even attempts suicide (a direct quotation from the traditional Act Four of* Swan Lake *here); she finds love; but her lover has to combat the evil Troll who controls her destiny. How did you arrive at this little scenario?*

MB: I knew it was going to be one of those stories with good and evil, a hero, a heroine and a villain. I did want it to have some parallels to *Swan Lake*, but not in any way to be literally *Swan Lake* – just something that had parallels to some dreadful version of it. I was thinking that, in one way, our Prince goes to the ballet and later on re-imagines the ballet's events in his own mind. I even remember, early on, thinking of it being a beautiful ballet, one that made his mind go off into some sort of romantic reverie that led him into other things. But it went off in a different direction.

AM: *When was it that it turned into a joke?*

MB: By necessity. I felt that this was the way that we could make it work; largely for musical reasons: the music lends itself to comedy.

AM: *The coda is pretty brassy, as even the most devoted Tchaikovskians admit.*

MB: Yes: it's circusy. It's designed as an entertainment for the Prince, which is what it is in the original, except that here he's sitting in an actual theatre.

Originally, it was going to be like the early Sadler's Wells Ballet *Swan Lake*, with the Helpmann–Fonteyn look, tutus and tons of make-up and so on. But I decided that that was a bit too close to home; also, we didn't really have the people to do it. Another idea was to do a sea ballet like *Ondine*; I can't remember now why we chose not to. Eventually, she became a Moth; and the villain a Tree-Troll.

If we went further back, into pantomime-like Victorian ballet, and gave it those really awful Victorian stage effects – puffs of smoke and all that – then, I thought, we wouldn't be offending anyone. Even so, one critic did complain that we were sending up traditional ballet; but never mind. None of these dancers are supposed to be any good, and the characters on stage all think that they're marvellous: that was our idea. It's one of those awful, tacky ballets that probably played the London music halls: that was the feeling that I wanted from it. Once I knew the story we were telling, I found we needed one other short piece of music to help me tell it; and what we took was from the Act Three pas de six.

AM: *And you make a different sense of the pas de trois music. In this Moth Ballet, your hero enters to a very blithe and lah-di-dah piece of music; it's perfect for his silly, dancy, happiness.[9] The bit that you then interpolate from the Act Three pas de six is just a fifty-second dance, to express the lovers' conventional love-at-first-sight.[10] Then, to the music that the man usually has for his solo in the pas de trois, you bring on the villain – the Tree-Troll, which actually fits the brassy, rather martial nature of the music very well. (It's not far from the brassy martial music associated elsewhere in the ballet with Rothbart.)*

Now, another volume on your shelves is The Ballet Called Swan Lake *by Cyril Beaumont (1952).[11] Only two sections bear notes in pencil – possibly not yours, since it's a second-hand copy. Still, these have to do with sets and costumes for the 1895 St Petersburg production. I wonder if you drew Lez's attention to them for the Moth Ballet.*

'Prince Siegfried, as interpreted by Pavel Gerdt wears plumed cap, doublet and parti-coloured hose. The doublet is decorated with a qua-trefoil design, and is scalloped at the lowest edge; on his breast is a small appliquéd shield decorated with a heraldic swan – perhaps an allusion to the Knight of the Swan – which seemed a little previous, since he has not yet encountered Odette. His waist is girded with a knightly belt, supporting on the left side a wallet, and on the right side a dagger. Note the long hair and beard and moustache, which hardly accords with a youth who has just attained his majority.' (p. 61)

MB: I may well have lent that to Lez. It was certainly him that had the idea of putting the hero into old-fashioned hose – a lederhosen version

9 The music is Variation III of the original *Swan Lake* Act I pas de trois. The information accompanying the Adventures in Motion Pictures CD recording of *Swan Lake* erroneously names it – Number 5 of the first half of the AMP score – as 'Tempo di valse'. It is, in fact, 'Allegro Semplice – Presto'.
  Likewise the CD recording misdescribes its Number 7 as 'Allegro Semplice'. In fact, it (Variation V of the original pas de trois) is 'Moderato'.
10 Part IV of the Act III pas de six, also 'Moderato'.
11 Literature on *Swan Lake* on Bourne's shelves includes: Cyril Beaumont, *The Ballet Called Swan Lake*, C.W. Beaumont, London, 1952; Mark Helprin, Chris van Allsburg, *Swan Lake*, Ariel Books, Houghton Mifflin, Boston, 1989; Wilson Strutte, *Tchaikovsky – his Life and Times*, Paganiana, 1981; *Le Lac des Cygnes*, L'Avant-Scene Ballet/Danse, Paris, 1984; Maurice Moiseiwitsch and Eric Warman (editors), *The Royal Ballet on Stage and Screen – the book of the Royal Ballet film*, William Heinemann, London, 1960.

of the kind of costume that leading male dancers actually wore until Nijinsky. He certainly did his research into that.

AM: *Even the fact that the villain is a Tree-Troll connects to Rothbart, who – in the traditional* Swan Lake *– appears in the guise of a baleful owl.*

Immediately after this Moth Ballet, there occurs the biggest dramatic number of Act One: the bedroom scene between the Prince and Queen; based, I suppose, on the Closet scene in Hamlet. *Here you've brought a superb piece of music originally written for Act Three by Tchaikovsky and yet very seldom used there in any stage version. It's the second variation in the pas de six, the andante con moto.*[12] *Ashton used it in his version of Act Four, in 1963. He may have been the first to use it there; at any rate, since then, several other producers have followed suit. What Tchaikovsky meant by it is ambiguous. Certainly it is very momentous music, and again it seems to be central to the dramatic sound of* Swan Lake.

MB: This is where two separate ambitions of mine coincided. I wanted a duet for the Queen and Prince at that particular place. This was partly a desire to build up her role into a bigger dramatic figure and give her a pas de deux, or something like one, in each half of *Swan Lake*, and partly for reasons of story-telling. You've seen the Queen and the Prince publicly; here you see them privately.

I also always wanted to use that music. In fact, there are two pieces of music in the 1877 score that I particularly liked and wanted to include but that were omitted from the 1895 version. The other one – the adagio for the alternative pas de deux he wrote for Act Three – I didn't manage to fit in.[13] This one I had always loved since I first heard it in the theatre. Moving it to Act One may have been our most radical

---

12 One of the few *Swan Lake* productions to use this in its original Act Three location is Yuri Grigorovich's version for the Bolshoi Ballet. For other discussions of the usages of this music, see Arlene Croce, 'Swan Lake and its Alternatives' (*Going to the Dance*, Knopf, 1982, pp. 182ff.) and Alastair Macaulay, 'Wiley's Tchaikovsky' (*Dancing Times*, March 1985).
13 This is the four-section pas de deux composed by Tchaikovsky to accommodate the alternative choreography interpolated (originally to Minkus music and choreographed by Petipa) for his second-cast Odile (the ballerina Anna Sobeshanskaya) and Siegfried (see note 2). This music has no connection to the sound-world of *Swan Lake*; Roland John Wiley does not even deign to discuss it in his analysis of the score. However, the choreographer George Balanchine choreographed a virtuoso pas de deux to it in 1960, which has no connection to *Swan Lake* either in Balanchine's own one-act staging or in any other production, but which has been widely danced ever since – with the result that it is known in the dance world under the name Balanchine gave to his version: the 'Tchaikovsky pas de deux'.

musical decision, and David, naturally, wanted to check whether it would work there harmonically. It was my idea, but I wouldn't have made that kind of musical decision without his approval and help.

AM: *After that, the Prince – like Prince Rudolf at the start of Act Two in* Mayerling, *by the way – goes to some shady dive: a loud club.*

MB: He's in despair; he wants to drink; he's looking for his girlfriend – not because she's his soulmate but because he feels at least that she gives him some friendship. It's our parallel of the Peasants' Dance that usually occurs at this point in *Swan Lake*: same low-life idea (but taken further), same music. We call this scene 'Soho', and the club it's set in is meant to be a retro club – The Swank Bar, of course! – full of sixties characters: Sister George, Joe Orton, Cliff Richard, the Krays, Phyllis Dixie.

AM: *Who on earth was Phyllis Dixie?*

MB: She was the most famous British stripper of the 1950s and 1960s; the Gypsy Rose Lee of Britain. In our version, she becomes the fan dancer. The idea, you see, wasn't just retro; it was to create an idea of scandal. All these were scandalous figures from a certain period. Scandal entering the Prince's life: that's what that scene's about. The Prince doesn't know, though the audience has already seen hints of it, that the Girlfriend has been set up by the Private Secretary. The Private Secretary, you see, wants to discredit the Prince. The unsuitable girlfriend is one part of his plan; the Prince getting thrown out of the Soho club is another.

AM: *Then you give your Prince an expressive adagio solo when he's thrown out of the club.*

MB: Yes. But I'm not claiming to be original. I put this solo there because it occurred there in the first Royal Ballet production I got to know.

AM: *Well, it works there musically. Tchaikovsky composed it in an earlier stage in the action, as part of Act One's main divertissement, the pas de trois. But, again, it is the one part of that section that doesn't sound like divertissement. In orchestration, melody, everything, it's absolutely part of the central* Swan Lake *sound-world.*

MB: It had always mattered to me. I knew I wanted it in my *Swan Lake*, and I had always associated it with the Prince's romantic loneliness and need for something beyond the world he knew.

47 *Swan Lake*. From Bourne's annotated breakdown of the score for Act One: the Prince's solo.

AM: *Tell me about the lake in your* Swan Lake.

MB: At present, we're thinking of how to make it more visible for the New York production. Lez did design a layer at the back that sparkles, but so far the lighting or the staging has never made that show up well. We're using a curved mirror, which should pick up quite a lot of light and give an effect of water in the background.

It is really intended to be St James's Park. This is a good example of how Lez helped to give our *Swan Lake* a much more specific location than I had originally envisaged. Because of him, Scott and I went round St James's Park before we started rehearsing. We took a lot of photos. That's why there is a suggestion of gates there. St James's Park just seemed so perfect, because Buckingham Palace is there in view – and there are lots of swans there. I don't mean that it's a literal reproduction of that park, or that the audience should recognize it as such; but that was the idea in our minds. That's why the park bench is there and the sign – with the little royal crown on – that says, 'Please do not feed the swans.'

AM: *How did you and/or Lez devise the look of the swans?*

MB: Quite early on, I found a picture of an Indian dancer, leaping in the air. He had trousers that seemed to be made of fringing or something; they moved very well and looked good in mid-air. I took Lez this picture and said, 'I think it should be something like this, very simple'. I also said, 'Whatever we do, it's got to be very simple', because I didn't want it to be in any way comic: no beaks, not too much make-up – something that had a pagan feel about it. It ended up with a half-man, half-creature look. Years and years ago, I saw Roland Petit's *Hunchback of Notre Dame*, and the only piece of make-up that the Hunchback had was a black line across his eyebrows – just a straight thick black line, but it did do something to his face – and that was all. So I said to Lez, 'Why don't we just try a triangular beak-shaped dark line, from the hairline down to the tip of the nose?' We also decided very early on that the hair should be very, very short. The point was to get long, swan-like necks with the smooth lines of the head, neck and shoulders.

AM: *You always wanted the swans bare-chested and barefoot?*

MB: Yes. I would say that, of all the costumes, that was the one that I developed the most myself.

48 *Swan Lake*. Costume sketch by Lez Brotherston for the male swans.

AM: *Do they powder their chests white?*
MB: They use a sort of water-based pancake make-up.

AM: *Did you ever ask them to shave their chests?*
MB: Never. I felt that one of the things we were trying to show was a masculine image anyway. We weren't pretending that they looked like swans. It was like creating a creature of our own that suggested swan in some way, but also very much suggested maleness. The same goes when we've had different skin tones among the swans: that just has never been really a problem or an issue.

AM: *Do you ever look at a finished work of yours and spot something you wanted to put in it all along? Is there in* Swan Lake *any moment when you've thought, 'I always wanted to put that in my version before rehearsals'?*
MB: There are always moments or movements I imagine or envisage. I don't ask for any help on them; I just put them in.

AM: *OK. What swan movements did you already have in mind?*
MB: I wanted that Nijinsky-type use of the arms crossed over the head

– as in the photographs of *Spectre* or *Narcisse*. It has nothing to do with swans in particular. It just has a draping, hanging flow to it, that position. In *Town and Country*, during 'Shallow Brown', there's a bit where the chorus group comes on shuffling with their arms like that. There are some tree images that are a bit like that, like blossom on trees. I like having the hands very relaxed, just hanging. Either that or very cleanly straight, with fingers all together. I didn't like the spikily separated fingers you often see in ballet. I'm always getting people to close their fingers if they're taking a strong position: clean lines.

So the arms draped over the head does reappear quite a lot in my work. It feels sensual to me, and sexy as well, because it's about touching your own body, which is another thing that I like to use on stage. In *Swan Lake*, there's a bit where the swans wrap their bodies: like taking a T-shirt off – that type of movement.

A lot of those movements came about because Adam and I had to do a photo-shoot with Hugo Glendinning long before rehearsals and we hadn't any movement at that stage. All we had was a costume. It was easy to call upon some of those images, to play around with arms, looking through features, shielding the face. Having come up with these photographic images, we had a starting-point when we went into the rehearsal studio.

A lot of dancers, when we teach them *Swan Lake* material now, don't want to be having contact with their own bodies or heads. They're always leaving space between their arms and their head, or between their arms and their bodies. Constantly the shout from our end of the floor is: 'Arms on heads!' But it's an alien thing to a lot of dancers.

AM: *It also connects to a famous way that Pavlova had of wreathing her arms around her head and neck; which Ashton remembered and put into several of his ballets.*
MB: Movement works so much better if you actually make contact, rather than just keeping it in no man's land.

AM: *Did you also find yourself fascinated by the photographs of, say, Fonteyn in* The Firebird *and* Ondine, *where she is again wrapping the arms and hands around the head and torso in very picturesque ways?*
MB: I love those pictures; and I also think that *Firebird* was going through my mind in *Swan Lake*. I was probably thinking of several bird-like pieces that I'd seen. That *Firebird* image of shielding the face is in there somewhere.

AM: *Once you'd made the two major decisions about your lakeside scenes – that there would be no Rothbart and that the swans would be male – the general outline of Act Two seems to have fallen into place. A few of your choreographic motifs and patterns are adapted from Ivanov's choreography in the 1895 version, and in general you use the 1895 ordering of the score.*

MB: Actually, there were plenty of factors we had to reconceive from scratch. I talked about tempi quite a lot with David, about the tempo of virtually every item in *Swan Lake*. He said that a lot of the score had been slowed down far too much in modern times. We found some recordings that he felt were more appropriate as to how it should sound. The most interesting point was the pas de deux in Act Two, which he felt had been played slower and slower over the decades. We found a recording on Naxos, which played it rather fast, particularly the middle section. To begin with, it was a shock to hear it that way; but, after listening to it a couple of times, he said, 'Actually, this really is how it should be. This is how it's written and how it was intended.' The central section in particular, he said, was really quite lilty. Playful, even. Those aren't words people apply to any part of that pas de deux in the traditional *Swan Lake*, are they? But David drew us into hearing those qualities in the score. He said there's variety within that adagio that we should address. So that's how we choreographed it, with that central section as a jumpy section of movement.

That's often one of the challenges when someone who's conducted it a lot for the ballet comes to conduct it for us. They want to slow those parts down, and we have to say, 'This is the way we do it.'

That wasn't the only example, by the way. There were a lot of other changes of tempo to which he drew our attention and which shaped our idea of the show. So it was good to feel that we were doing something that was even more authentic musically than the traditional ballet.

AM: *Was it Lloyd-Jones who helped you solve the ending of the pas de deux? The 1877 version ends – very surprisingly – with a brisk allegro passage, which very few twentieth-century versions employ; Balanchine's one-act* Swan Lake *is one of those few. The 1895 version, arranged by Drigo, ends it on a beautifully prolonged diminuendo, and that version, as choreographed by Ivanov, is the ending we usually hear and see in the theatre.*

MB: We did try the allegro ending in rehearsals; but, whenever we got to that point, the music just made everyone laugh. The 1895 version wasn't on any recording – and that, too, just felt alien to me. So we ended up with the more straightforward diminuendo ending, which Tchaikovsky himself had written. It's from his '*Swan Lake* Suite'. I liked its simplicity.

AM: *And the fact that he used that version in his* Suite *suggests that he himself had come to the conclusion that it would be a better ending to the pas de deux that the original 1877 allegro.*

Another departure you make from the 1877 score is in the order of musical items. Tchaikovsky ordered the dances in 1877, after the entrance of the swans and the scene with the Prince and the huntsmen, as (i) tempo di valse (the waltz for all the corps de ballet of swans) (ii) moderato assai–molto piu mosso (the solo dance for the Swan Queen) (iii) tempo di valse (a return to the waltz music, but now for the big swans) (iv) allegro moderato (the dance for the cygnets) (v) pas d'action (andante–andante non troppo–allegro) (the music for the pas de deux or – in dance terms – adagio for the Swan Queen and the Prince, often known as the White Swan adagio) (vi) tempo di valse (another return to the swan waltz material) (vii) coda (allegro vivace) (for all the swans).

However, in 1895 Ivanov and Drigo re-ordered these numbers as (i) (v) (iv) (vi) (ii) (vii). Your ordering is something along these lines, except that you put the solo dance for the Swan (ii) directly after the cygnets (iv) and before (vi), the dance for the big cygnets.

MB: The 1877 score uses that waltz music once too often, wonderful though it is; and it builds up to the pas de deux as an expressive climax, whereas in the theatre there's more contrast and sense of development if you let the other dances seem to develop from what the pas de deux has established.

AM: *Act Three of* Swan Lake *is often referred to as the 'black act', because the ballerina usually wears a black tutu here. Odile, Rotherbart's daughter, looks so like Odette the Swan Queen – being danced by the same ballerina! – that the Prince takes her to be one and the same. He swears eternal love to her, and so breaks his vow of love to Odette; which is all part of Rothbart's evil plan.*

But this act is also a ball, given by the Queen to present her son with a number of potential brides. And there are a number of national dances, most of which – but perhaps not all – seem to have been designed as sheer divertissements.

Your Act Three is still a ball given by the Queen. It still has national dances. The principal dancer still reappears as a Black Swan, or as 'the Stranger', and, to the Prince at least, the identity of this new character is absolutely locked into that of the Swan. That said, your Act Three is a very different kind of drama; and it deepens the whole Swan Lake experience considerably. How smoothly did your preparation of this act go? Were you able to get the scenario pretty clear?

MB: A lot of it fell into place once I'd fixed the central idea, which is that – yes, it is a Royal Ballet ball; yes, the Prince is expected to pay his respects to these various women or princesses, though his heart is elsewhere. Then the Stranger arrives and attracts everybody: the Queen, the Prince, everybody. Originally, you see, I thought of the Stranger, or Black Swan, as the Private Secretary's son; and Act Three is where the Private Secretary's plot became more apparent. He wanted to discredit the Prince and to marry his own son off to the Queen.

There were certain problem numbers to address. Those show-piece national dances, for instance.

AM: *Yes. Most hair-raising of all, you start off the whole series with the Russian Dance: which is almost always omitted from twentieth-century stage productions of* Swan Lake, *despite its irresistible music. (Tchaikovsky added it to the 1877 production at a late stage.) Its use of the solo violin makes it very much the first soloist's dance; and Wiley shows that it was probably danced by Odile in the 1877 original. You give it to your Black Swan – or the Stranger – and a series of women.*

MB: I don't remember reading that in Wiley. As far as I knew, I was working from instinct. I certainly knew the Russian Dance, and I loved it so much as music. It's certainly an extremely lengthy variation for one dancer to dance, if that's what happened in 1877. I have seen it done like that, but as a Russian character solo, in heeled shoes, out of the context of *Swan Lake*. Also in one production of *Swan Lake* – Northern Ballet Theatre's, I think – as a solo variation for the Russian Princess.

I felt that it had such a lot of feeling in it; but what I'm especially pleased with is that we use it straight after his entrance into the ball, rather than going from his entrance into the Spanish Dance; which is what often happens at that point, but which immediately takes you away from the situation.

There's a tremendously dramatic musical effect that happens when you put the Russian Dance straight after the Black Swan's entrance. I don't know whether it's ever been done before. When I heard it, it just felt that that's how it should be. It actually comments on the situation, because it's like a little exclamation mark just after his meeting the Queen. Then it brings in that violin solo, which creates this atmosphere of tension amongst everyone. I was really thrilled with that. It had been one of the suggestions that I wasn't sure that David would approve. But he did.

AM: *What about the other national dances?*
MB: I put them in this order: Russian; Spanish; Neapolitan; czardas.

AM: *You omit the mazurka.*
MB: There's always one national dance too many! I've always thought that in watching most *Swan Lakes* at that point: 'Get on with it.' But cutting musical items is difficult, just because they're all so good. I knew the Spanish Dance was going to be like a floor show, so that wasn't a problem.

AM: *The Spanish Dance, here as in* Nutcracker, *is for one woman and a clutch of men. Is that format – one girl and two or more men – one that you're fond of for this kind of divertissement? I think it's almost the rule in* Swan Lake.
MB: Yes. The task there is to try to feature each Princess in some way or another.

AM: *It's also a touch of comedy, because it gives us a showbiz idea of the male chorus.*
MB: Yes. But I didn't want a whole series of different floor shows following on from that; I wanted some situations. With the Neapolitan Dance, I had an idea for a very Italian sort of lover's quarrel: some embarrassing situation, triggered off by the man's jealousy. The czardas was quite difficult, because I wanted to make it part of the central story; we only solved that in rehearsals.

AM: *Again, I think that you reveal that the czardas somehow – because of its orchestration – belongs to the inner family of* Swan Lake *music.*
   That leads, in your version, straight into what's usually known as the 'Black Swan' pas de deux. This raises some musical issues. Even in 1877, Tchaikovsky composed alternative versions of the main suite of dances for Odile and the Prince. The first was a very extensive and

musically elaborate pas de six, which may have included dances for Rothbart and/or his entourage, and which seems to deepen the mystery of Swan Lake *in fairly inscrutable ways. The second is a musically much more straightforward grand pas de deux which has virtually nothing to do with the sound-world of* Swan Lake.

Very few current versions use either. Tchaikovsky wrote another dramatic-virtuosic pas de deux in Act I – probably for the prince and some other female character, but we can't be sure – that, for a reason we no longer know, contains some very ominous pre-echoes of the later 'Swan' music. It was this music that, in 1895, the choreographer Petipa and composer Drigo inserted into Act Three as a grand pas de deux for the Prince and Odile. And this interpolation from Act One, this mysterious pas de deux, is the music you use here too.

MB: Yes, but what virtually nobody has ever mentioned is that we use the music as Tchaikovsky originally wrote it; and it's very interesting that way. In 1895, they not only reorchestrated it, they also chopped it up and cut out some of the most interesting passages. If you play it as written, as we do, there's only one point where the music really stops at all. In particular, the first section just continues right through, despite all kinds of very suggestive dramatic changes, for about seven minutes. The tension never lets up. We were talking about the difference of the two halves of *Nutcracker*: that in the second half there is almost nothing but a long series of separate numbers with definite finishes, whereas the first half runs almost continuously. Well, this sequence of music in *Swan Lake* has that kind of momentum you find in Act One of *Nutcracker*.

AM: *How clear were you just from listening what you wanted to do with this music?*
MB: Because it was drama-led, I had the whole thing mapped out in my head about what each piece of music was doing; and I was very clear on the ideas for each section – not necessarily on the actual steps, but the dramatic structure was very clear in my mind.

AM: *So was it clear, early on in your conception, that you were going to go in and out of reality? In and out of the Prince's mind? It seems to come out of the extraordinary changes in the music. But it's also helped by exceptional changes of lighting. Was that easy to achieve?*
MB: The lighting was not a problem. I did say to Rick Fisher, our lighting designer, that we would need a dramatic snap change of light to

make it at least somewhat clear to the audience that we'd gone somewhere else. But there are still people who don't see that and who think
it's reality. However, we know what we're trying to do! It all came out
of the music. Nobody has really picked up on the fact that the music is
different – and more authentic.

The first section happens in reality. It's for the Queen and the Stranger. I knew it wouldn't be a problem to do in rehearsal and it certainly
wasn't; I'm sure we did it in about an hour or so, very quickly.

But when this first part of the music changes into its second section,
that's when suddenly we switch into the Prince's mind. What I tried
here – a filmic device – is to make the Prince put himself in the Queen's
place. This dance is for the two men alone together, and it's where the
music is suddenly at its most Black Swannish. I had a problem in my
mind for a while about exactly what to do in this part. Then I saw one
of those Argentinean tango shows that came to London: *Tango Argen-
tino* or *Forever Tango* – it's all the same and it's all wonderful – where
two men were dancing together. I thought their style of movement
would work very well: that sort of dark intertwining of bodies. You've
got a formal partnering style built in, which says something straightaway; and it allowed for us to develop something that got more violent
and antagonistic between them after a simple start. It brought an older
memory into my mind, of the film *Valentino*, where Nureyev as Valentino dances with Dowell as Nijinsky. They're just partnering each
other in a ballroom in dark suits, observed by someone from a distance, and they do a whole tango.

There are two points where the music is really interesting and helpful.
The first is at the end of an adagio section, in our version just as the
Stranger leaves the Prince. The music continues – in the traditional ballet
there's a dramatic break for applause here – into a kind of sarcastic ren-
dition of the Swan music. It builds up; it has a definite edge that we tried
to pick up on. For us, it's the business of taunting the Prince. It's a paranoia situation. It's just as the Stranger leaves the Prince; he walks out as
everybody else walks in, all staring at the Prince, and the Prince acts as
though the Stranger's still there. So it's as if it's going on in his mind,
with his arm locked behind his back. He turns round and they're all
looking at him, mockingly. He's been acting strangely; and they continue to look at, stare, and talk about him. His paranoia grows; and
we're playing with what's reality and what isn't, and how much is in his
mind and how much isn't.

49 *Swan Lake*. Left to right: Scott Ambler as the Prince, Adam Cooper as the Swan (or Stranger), Fiona Chadwick as the Queen, rehearsing Act Three, in 1998.

The second is the fantastic violin solo that follows. In the ballet, it's all reorchestrated, and you don't get the incredible ending at all. In our version, they all laugh on stage there, and that came out of the amazing violin solo music that races over the orchestra. The company calls this the Sarcastic Dance; it's to do with taunting the Prince.

Then the Stranger re-enters with the Queen. Now, this situation is partly where we've left reality again, with the Prince's exaggerated view of his mother, the Queen, with the Stranger; but they probably are there together in reality too: we see that heightened through his eyes to the point where they are flaunting their affection for each other at him. It's a great piece of music, and yet it's generally not used.

As that long piece of music finally ends, the Prince runs out. There again we go into a very snap change of lighting, back into reality, with the Stranger downstage watching the Queen and princesses dance for him. We're back to the ball there; and this dance carries musically straight on into the coda (including the music usually associated with the ballerina's thirty-two fouetté turns on pointe), which we call the

Competition Dance. This is a sort of male-female competitive affair: a *West Side Story* type of dance. Anything you can do, I can do better – that idea.

Then the dramatic dénouement, in which the Prince goes hysterical and tries to fire a gun. Some of the details here took a while to fall into place, but the general gist fell into place in my mind out of the story so far and the music.

AM: *On to Act Four. What about the scene where the Queen and doctors officiate over whatever dreadful medical deeds are done to the Prince? When and how did that idea come to you?*

MB: Almost all of Act Four is the delirium of the Prince. After the incident at the ball in Act Three, he's been dragged off. That situation's partly real, but partly seen through his eyes. It's the Queen overseeing over all these awful treatments, but actually he's probably receiving some drug to calm him down. However, what we see is his horrific view of what's happening to him at that point.

AM: *And you've got multiple queens.*

MB: I remember that that was Lez's idea. It was the sort of idea I thought you couldn't pull off. I probably said, 'I want the mother to be officiating over this, and I want him to feel that she's doing him no good.' And he must have said, 'What about if they've all got the same face?' – a nightmarish thing – 'this face that keeps coming over you with all these different medical instruments and treatments is the same person'. He said that we definitely could do it using queen masks, so that they could all be the mother. I thought it was a great idea. They're all white, as well. That makes them some sort of half-way house between the swans and the court. They're also part of the second white act. So is the Queen. She's dressed in white, and so is the Private Secretary. That leads into a nightmare version of the swan world and of the swans themselves. They, when they reappear, are more sinister than they were before.

AM: *There were several 'white' opera stagings at English National Opera in the 1980s, I seem to remember.*

MB: Yes, the Pountney *Hansel and Gretel* was like that. I do remember those.

AM: *And, of course, that* Hansel and Gretel *had the horror witch-mother.*

249

Who decided to make the drama of Act Four largely a bedroom drama?

MB: One of my design ideas early on was that I wanted outsize, larger-than-life objects. I could see the Prince's room as enormous, with just two enormous things in it – like an enormous bed and a very big chair – so that they made him look very small. The idea was also to empha-size this with perspective, since the stage wasn't enormous. Eventually, it ended up just being the bed; and there's a big mirror-cum-window at the beginning as well.

AM: *The extraordinary entrance of the swans from under the bed . . .*

MB: Again, that was part of my whole idea for Act Four. The Prince having been in their world in Act Two, I now wanted them to enter his world in Act Four; but I wanted to feel that they were coming out of the walls. If I was to do a film of it, they would just walk through the walls, and through the bed.

It just seemed to make sense – something of the imagination – because he's asleep on the bed at the time. It's a way of showing the sort of world he's gone off into, but also showing that it's now con-fined to his world. He can't escape.

In the middle of the act, it actually goes into a sort of halfway house sort of world, where the bed seems to be suspended in mid-air almost, because the back wall disappears when the swan appears, and there's a starry background and a black floor. If you squint a little in the theatre, it appears that the bed is just suspended in a starry sky. It's as if the swans have come to get him, rather than him going to them.

Rehearsals for Act Two

ALASTAIR MACAULAY: *How did you structure the order of rehearsals?*
MATTHEW BOURNE: A funny order, actually, but practical. We began with the swans. Before the rehearsal period, we had already choreo-graphed quite a lot of the basic ideas and phrases for swan movement. I worked with Etta and Scott; and Adam was involved too, to a lesser degree. We watched swans in a park; and we watched a fair amount of documentary video material of swans, showing the differences of beha-viour – flying, coming into land, attacking fishing boats – and we iden-tified where we thought those kinds of movements would work. For example, we used the kind of movement that swans have when they're

coming down on to the water, with the weight very much backwards, to slow themselves down. We wanted to put some ungainly things in, you see: we didn't want it to look all beautiful and serene; because, when swans are out of the water, they're very awkward, and slightly turned-in. So within the swan choreography, there are two contrasting elements. Sometimes they scrunch up, sometimes they open out again.

To a certain extent we were remembering the traditional ballet, but we were trying to get away from flapping wings all the time. Obviously you can't get entirely away from that in *Swan Lake*, but we wanted to find some variations on that: with birdlike head movements and twitches.

There also came a point when we decided to make the swans creature-like, at times, as well as bird-like. Also semi-human.

AM: *In your notebooks for* Swan Lake, *there's a section just called 'Ideas', in which – before rehearsals, I think – you've put down your conceptions for each of the four acts. But you've also added other ideas – especially movement ideas – during the early rehearsals. Here are some notes for Act Two. 'Notes for swan motifs. Head nestling.'*
MB: That's very much out of the traditional *Swan Lake*, isn't it – but then it's also what real swans do.

AM: *'Clean into luxurious.'*
MB: That means type of movement. A good example of it from Ashton's choreography would be in *The Dream*, where Titania strikes a firm arabesque in Oberon's arms and then melts throughout all her limbs.

AM: *'A gesture carried through the torso creating a curved shape. Dying swan position. Folded right over.'*
MB: There are quite a lot of passages where they lean right forwards while crossing their arms at the wrist – the 'wings folded' position.

AM: *'Hands framing head à la Adam.'*
MB: At the photo-shoot with Adam we had come up with some basic swan motifs that I decided would become part of the choreography. In particular, the Nijinsky-like motif of crossing the arms around and above the head.

AM: *'Feeding, flying, swimming, gliding.'*
MB: We didn't use all that in the end; I don't remember them feeding.

50 *Swan Lake*, Act Four. Arthur Pita leading one row of swans. The arm position is taken from the Nijinsky-inspired motif created by Bourne for Cooper in their pre-production photographic session. (See illustration 36 and pp. 240–1, 251.)

AM: *Then there are extensive notes for the entrance of the swans: notes about structure, basic movement ideas ('Beak', 'Low to high', 'Abandoned', 'Clap', 'Round wings', 'Canon'), floor-patterns, and so forth. 'Scott's material, reworked. Canon. Etta's, Matt's canon.'*

MB: Another thing these notes show is that we were thinking of all the elements. Water and air in particular, of course. 'Grass blowing.' 'Trees, changes of position, blown.' This was about being blown from one position to another. 'Rocks.'

AM: *'Waves.'*

MB: That's a water idea, which we use at the end. Perhaps nobody's ever noticed this, but at the very end of Act Two, the Swan and the Prince turn around and run into the water; then the other swans all start to do pas de chat and to cross the stage with wave-like arm movements – first one line of swans, then the next. The image is of them running into the water.

We worked out the zigzag swan entrance beforehand, with about

51 *Swan Lake*, Act Two. The corps of swans. The zig-zag pattern entrance.

four of us doing it. Adam was involved, though he never danced that bit on stage. The formations were based on those from the ballet; I think I always wanted that entrance to have that zigzag pattern; but we used different steps.

AM: *You've mentioned the traditional* Swan Lake. *What other choreography was in your mind at this period?*

MB: Nijinsky's *Faune*. The general look of the costume, the intensity of the eyes, the two-dimensional feel to a lot of the movement. Particularly earlier on, when we started, I had the pictures of *Faune* in my mind for the atmosphere of what we were trying to create.

Also I felt an early modern dance influence. At this stage, José Limòn was in my mind. I had done a lot of Limòn classes at one time, and I took class for a few weeks with the Limòn company in New York in about 1988, 1989. What I remember is the feeling of the movement. Those classes are very long, about two hours, starting with barrework and centrework, and then with movement based in Limòn repertory. I enjoyed that style very much. Also for *Swan Lake*, I was looking through all the photos of Denishawn group pieces from the 1920s, trying to get ideas about group designs.

When we started company rehearsals, we had a week or two just for the male swans first, working entirely on Act Two. Again, we started with the zigzag entrance of the swans, and we encouraged them to reshape the material, to characterize it from within, to contribute to it.

52 *Swan Lake*, Act Two. Scott Ambler as the Prince, Adam Cooper as the Swan, and corps of male swans.

53 *L'Après-midi d'un faune*. Lydia Nelidova and Vaslav Nijinsky in Nijinsky's ballet. The contact of arms, the distance between the bodies, the profiled angle of the head, and the Faune's headdress all influenced Bourne's *Swan Lake*.

We worked in bare feet, with an approximation of the look they would have in costume, with rolled up trouser-legs. So we had plenty of swan style going before Day One of official rehearsals. The challenge for Act Two is that the story doesn't continue non-stop. So several dances have to be entirely character-based and dance-based. Within the overall group of swans, we worked on making each one feel the character of his particular swan.

AM: *'Phrases. All do an upper-body phrase, two eights. All do a lower-body phrase, two eights, jumps, one of each, then swan.'*
MB: This was a way of getting to work in rehearsal.

AM: *You've got further suggestions here. '(1) Quite nippy, more curves and changes. (2) Adage, four eights longer than each movement. (3) Jumping, look at adage phrase from audition.'*
MB: All these things meant something to me at the time! I wonder what. We especially worked to give specific characters for the four big swans and the four cygnets. The cygnets were to be young and wild. For that rehearsal, we put the music on, and I just said, 'Start moving around.' There were certain types of movement I wanted from them: a shunty movement, a picking up of the feet. And I wanted them to be the most gauche, the ungainly fledgelings of the group. So I said, 'Let's all make up a couple of eights of movement using those few ideas and see what we come up with.' We would learn each other's phrases; then there'd be something to play with, and I would start manipulating it. We developed little partnering ideas, making connections between the four; and then I structured it.

AM: *Here are some more notes. 'Entrances and Exits and Wings in Groups.'*
MB: I'm not sure what that specifically refers to, but I always like playing with ways of coming on and going off, to make entrances and exits more interesting. Because the set has pillars, we decided to use a lot of false entrances from them and exits into them.

AM: *'First waltz phrases all have up and down, swingy quality, flat-footed walk.'*
MB: That was an idea of how swans are when just out of the water. We played with it in rehearsal, and it's there on stage in the dance of the cygnets.

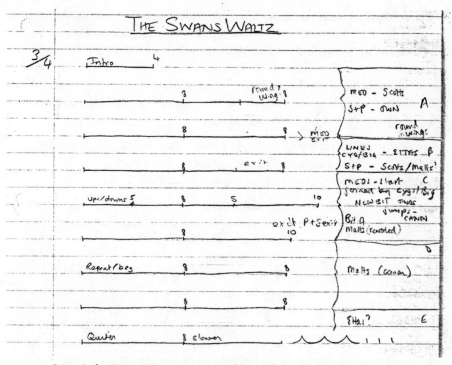

54 *Swan Lake*. From Bourne's annotated breakdown of the score for Act Two: the Swans' Waltz.

AM: '*Infernal Galop: wings beating.*'

MB: That was from the idea that I had had in *The Infernal Galop*, from the Cocteau painting where he drew Charles Trenet with wings. We had the dancers hold a splayed hand at the small of their backs, like wings; and we use that again in *Swan Lake*, but in Act Four only, as their basic still position.

AM: *So you have your swans fold their wings both before and behind. When they're behind, they turn out the wrists and slightly flex the elbows, creating a new shape. When the wings are folded in front, the wrists and elbows are left in calm lines.*

In your notes during the waltz for all the swans, where there's a brief duet for the Swan and the Prince, you've written, 'Duet and Relationship in General. Searching, wanting, imitating, following, journeying towards yearning, waltz. Duet in waltz about physical reactions to each other.' Then, 'Lifted off in different directions at the end of the

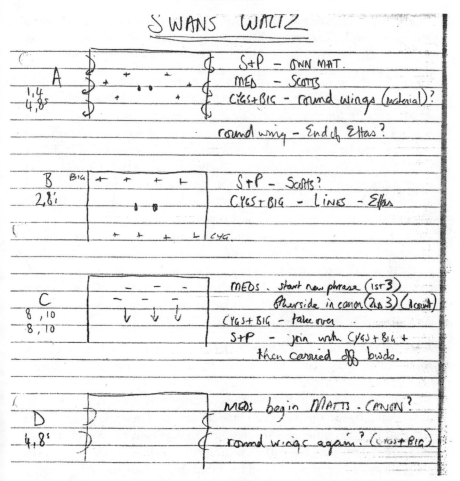

55 *Swan Lake*. From Bourne's choreographic notes for floor-patterns and phrases in the Swans' Waltz. 'S + P'= Swan and Prince; 'mat' = material; 'Meds' = medium-sized swans; 'Scotts' = Scott Ambler's phrases; 'Cygs and Big' = 'Cygnets and Big swans'; 'Ettas' = Etta Murfitt's phrases; 'Matts' = Matthew Bourne's phrases.

swans' waltz, (dream ideas), facing each other as contact is about to be made.'

MB: A lot of these things changed. Certainly not the lifting off. I'm not sure now what 'the dream ideas' were.

AM: *'End of entrance of swans. Runs involve lifts of Prince and Swan until they are face to face.'*

MB: That doesn't happen. What happens instead of that is that there's an attack of the swans on the Prince. They lift him in the air. The Swan isn't involved; he has exited. Then the Prince is saved by the Swan's re-entrance. They do end up face to face, but it's initiated by the Swan.

AM: *One of the four big swans in your original rehearsals was Will (William) Kemp. Within two or three months, you had him dancing the Swan. Was he the only dancer in the original company – apart from Adam Cooper and Fiona Chadwick – to emerge from ballet school?*

MB: Yes, and he was the only Royal Ballet School product to audition, too. At that point, we couldn't get anyone from the ballet world at all. It certainly wasn't considered a viable option at that point for anyone at the Royal Ballet School. It was entirely Will's initiative that led him to audition for us; he was still just seventeen. Since then, we have had many trained ballet students and many professional ballet dancers audition for us, probably owing to his example; but a high proportion of them aren't right for us. They're too 'ballet' – too precious and refined – and they don't use their torsos enough, or their weight. Those we take into the company tend to be the exceptions in those respects. As a dancer, Will fitted right in from the first.

AM: *Did the presence of Adam and Fiona have an effect on the class-work the company did? Did any of them start to take ballet classes? Or just to work harder in the classes they did?*

MB: I don't think so. In Britain, the contemporary dancers refuse to be intimidated by anyone who's a classical dancer. They take pride in the fact that they're contemporary dancers. In America, the worlds of ballet and modern dancers collide more. Here, there's much more resistance. It was more of a problem for Fiona and Adam and Will, coming from the ballet background; they were the ones that had to show everyone else that they belonged; and they did, of course.

But the entire level of technical accomplishment rose considerably with *Swan Lake*. After its première, one dancer, who had done leading roles with AMP years before, re-auditioned for us, and he honestly didn't have the technique to be one of the swan corps.

AM: *At what stage did you bring in second-cast performers?*

MB: They were there all the time in rehearsals. It was made very clear who was second-cast; most performances in the Sadler's Wells season would be first-cast. The second-cast were to have two matinées and two evenings in the initial run of two and a half weeks; and, once the

tour began the following year, they would have many more performances. But they were learning it along with the first cast. Credit has
to be given to them: they were equally involved in the creation of a lot
of the movement and the ideas. David Hughes was the second-cast
Swan; Ben Wright was the second-cast Prince. David Hughes left us
after the tour, on which he performed the majority of first nights. He
couldn't handle the situation of being second-cast to Adam, especially
after the amount of press and praise that Adam received. He felt –
rightly – that he'd brought a lot to the role and that he had influenced
the way the role developed; and it was hard for him that his creative
contribution received little acknowledgement. I have to say that Adam
had been an important part of my conception of the ballet. I spent a
few rehearsals with Adam alone, and I found that Adam was a very
good member of the AMP company. But, to do David justice, when the
show was in rehearsal, he was more animal-like, with greater fluidity;
the movement came through the whole of his body more; he was down
into the ground more. All this in turn influenced the way Adam did the
role.

AM: *Ben Wright, however, has stayed with AMP, and performed the
Prince frequently in the West End, in LA, and on Broadway.*
MB: Yes, and it's difficult to create the role along with Scott – who,
because of his position in the company, tends to feel, of his own way
with a role, 'This is exactly how it's done.' But Ben handled that very
well; and he helped the whole show by developing a very different way
of telling the story. He is a more vulnerable, younger-seeming Prince.
Both interpretations are very valid. I think Ben feels that Scott's Prince
isn't emotional enough; and Scott feels that Ben's Prince is a cry-baby
character. That's fine. I'm sure it'll be done another way when somebody else does it.

A great deal of the relationship between the Swan and the Prince
became clear only through rehearsal. There's a certain amount of fear
to begin with on the Prince's part. The Swan has been quite frightening
at the beginning of the piece, behind the window or the mirror; and he
retains a bit of that as well. You're not quite sure which way he's going
to go at any point; but I didn't start out with a really clear idea of
where to go with it. I knew that would come from working on it, and I
wasn't worried. I knew Act Two was all movement, so I knew the
drama would clarify in rehearsal with the dancers.

AM: *Here you've divided the Swan–Prince duet into five sections. (B) is called 'Lyrical'; in brackets, you've put 'Swan Solo'. (C) is 'Nippy'; in brackets, you've put 'Jumpy duet'. (D) is 'Very slow,' and (E) is 'Very upbeat'.*

MB: At this stage, I was still trying to use the upbeat 1877 ending – (E) – to the pas de deux. One solution I thought of was to bring in all the swans again; but, because of the way the duet developed, this felt completely wrong. The dancers kept laughing!

AM: *In more than one section of the pas de deux, Tchaikovsky is using some of his most long-phrased adagio composition. Did you have to work to find dance phrases that long?*

MB: It wasn't something that came automatically. But I had a feeling for this music; I did respond to it. It was a challenge to try to make it work. Although it wasn't so easy to organize the movement, I was helped by the fact that there was already a very strong idea about swan movement, about being something other than human. So the possibilities of what you could do with that seemed endless. I was certainly helped by having Adam to work with, because he is very musical, and because he was more used to moving like that to that kind of music.

There were certain problems we had to work through to make the Prince–Swan adagio work. All the lifts seemed odd, awkward, wrong, between two men. We were very concerned about that for a while. Then, very late on, we suddenly remembered that this is a dance between a human and a bird, or a human and a non-human creature. So it was about two different ways of moving, one more palpable than the other. Once we went back to thinking: 'What is this actually about?', to remembering that we weren't trying to create some great pas de deux, everything fell into place. We decided, for example, that the Swan couldn't hold with his hands, because they were wings: he had to lift the Prince up under the arms, with his hands still free so that there was a feeling of flight about it as well; and we decided also that at times the Prince must feel like a small child, vulnerable, as small as he can. But Adam found it difficult to give his weight to another dancer when the Swan is lifted or supported: he wasn't used to that at all.

The jumpy sequence during the pas de deux was particularly influenced by David Hughes and Ben Wright, the second-cast Swan and Prince.

AM: *During this adagio – in the musically very intimate moment when the cello and violin come closest together – the Royal Ballet version of the Ivanov (unlike the Kirov) has an especially affecting passage of choreography, when the Swan Queen is rocked in the Prince's arms. You have something both similar and different: it's the Swan who approaches the Prince from behind.*

MB: He wraps him in his wings, and lifts him up. It's like, 'No, you've got to accept me.' It's to bring the Prince back to his true nature. He literally clings to the Prince, leans back, and so can lift one leg up while the Prince lifts both his legs off the floor.

AM: *Is it an accident that this lift is related to a lift that the Queen does in the Stranger's arms in Act Three?*

MB: No accident. We were, in the Act Three duet, trying to find a few parallels, for jealousy's sake. At that point in Act Two, we had spent a lot of time wondering how far to go physically with the two men. Every time we came to that point, it felt awkward, too literal; but I think we hit it right in the end by keeping it quite ambiguous. The height of the physical relationship is the Swan's wrapping up the Prince with his wings and cradling him, which is quite moving. It's just what has never happened to the Prince before. He's been trying to get attention from his mother; you can feel that that's what he wants, and it's what he gets from the Swan. That's all he needs at that point: affection of some kind.

AM: *The feeling is literally an ambiguous feeling, because it is the Prince's longing for something unattainable, for a wild winged creature, but at the same time he wants to be held by it. There's an active-passive feeling.*

MB: Because the whole act is seen through the Prince's eyes, you have to make the audience feel the same as the Prince. That's why the role is quite difficult to cast. You want the audience to feel that they would be drawn by this Swan person as well – that they want to be in the Prince's shoes, basically.

AM: *You keep the Prince on stage during the Swan's solo.*

MB: Originally, we weren't going to; but, it made sense that the Swan was performing for the Prince. The Swan's a bit of a peacock here! Suddenly the solo worked, because you're seeing it through the Prince's eyes, which you need to.

With the dance for the four big swans, we started off by using some phrases from the swans' waltz. In their rehearsal, Will Kemp and Mark Mitchell suggested that we just jumped these phrases, and they got very carried away. It was a great rehearsal; I loved it, and laughed so much, they were working so hard. But they made it difficult for themselves! – to the point where the big swans' dance is not much liked by people who do it now: it's exhausting. So much so that, recently, we've taken out some of the jumps.

AM: *You've noted, 'Swan re-entry, big Swan solo'. Then, interestingly, 'Pleading.'*
MB: That was a feeling in the music at that point.

AM: *At the end: 'Swan lifted up by big swans, followed by Prince.'*
MB: That has happened in the production, or has been cut from it, at different stages. It depends whether the swans feel they're into lifting. We decided to do away with it last time, because it was such a hassle.

AM: *Did you do all of Act Two before moving on to the other three acts?*
MB: I think so, yes. It took the longest, and it was hard to get going.

Rehearsals for Acts Three, One and Four

ALASTAIR MACAULAY: *With which bits of* Swan Lake *did you already know how you wanted the movement to look?*
MATTHEW BOURNE: Quite a lot of it really, but there are some specific choreographic things, like the part of Act One when the dancers are all under the balcony at the beginning. I knew I wanted a sequence that looked like a crowd waving and that there was dance. Because I was so clear in the simplicity of what I wanted, I just did it, before the rehearsal – worked it out, taught it to people and then staged it which developed it a bit. That was a clear idea that I could just get on with, which is best when there's a lot of people involved; but the cygnets' dance, for example – I really didn't have any ideas at all about it until we got into the rehearsal room.

AM: *At what point did you give your dancers things to research?*
MB: Quite early on. They would know their role, or their line-up of roles, and I gave them different things to study or watch. Fiona Chadwick went away and read some books about the Queen and said, 'I'm

56 *Swan Lake*, Act One. Left to right: Fiona Chadwick as the Queen, Barry Atkinson as the Private Secretary, Emily Pearcy as the Prince's Girlfriend. The programme clutched by the Girlfriend shows that they are about to attend the gala performance of the *Moth Ballet*.

more Princess Margaret – Princess Margaret as she would have been if she had become Queen.' Since Princess Margaret is patron of the Royal Ballet, she had probably met her many times, and Fiona requested the tumbler for the gin, or whatever it is she drinks – not an elegant glass, but a tumbler like the Princess's. Saranne – who played the Italian princess – I sent away to watch Anita Ekberg in *La Dolce Vita*. I said, 'I want that business of kicking the shoes off – an Italian woman getting up on a table and getting a bit of sexual energy going – that sort of feel.' So she went away and watched that. The Princess of Monaco (Kirsty Tapp) went away and watched a documentary on Grace Kelly. In the Soho scene, Will Kemp was the Pop Idol. Because it was British retro, I asked him to play Cliff Richard. That foxed him; he would rather have been Elvis Presley. He enjoyed playing the Italian Princess's lover in Act Three, because he had been having a relationship with an Italian girl in the Royal Ballet and had visited Italy, so he knew the way of life and enjoyed the Mediterranean jealousy of the character. Each had their thing. Maxine Fone, who was going to be the ballerina in the little Moth Ballet, watched the oldest choreography we could find on video.

AM: *Which was the Kirov Ballet dancing* La Vivandière.

MB: Yes, we used a bit of that. She has a great sense of humour – we laughed a lot doing that – affectionately – and she really understood what she was doing there.

AM: *The Prince's Girlfriend: did she continue to be modelled along Fergie lines?*
MB: No. Although Lez and I had very much seen her as Fergie, Emily Mortimer researched her and made her Texan. She's called Terri-Belle Pratt! Emily wanted to create her own person.

The next act we made in rehearsal was Act Three.

AM: *You begin it with the autograph-collectors. Is that a reference to your own past?*
MB: I suppose so.

AM: *Then the scene changes to the ballroom. After the first dance in which we see the assembled royalty and guests, you have the Swan or Stranger enter in black leather trousers. And the music goes straight into the Russian Dance.*
MB: Yes: as soon I heard the introduction to the Russian Dance in rehearsal, I just knew he had to sweep forward and kiss the Queen's hand in an outrageous way.

AM: *Then – more outrageous – he produces the riding-crop.*
MB: That was Adam's idea: one of several first-rate ideas he had for his role. Where he got it from, I don't know! It suggests at once that the Stranger is into kinky things, that anything goes with him. As for the leather trousers: Lez and I had instantly thought that black leather was a good idea for the Black Swan. People think Adam's like that character. That's what they expect him to be like when they meet him: so that either there's an almost visible disappointment that he's not like that, or they're scared to say much because they assume he's going to behave in that way. There's a side of Adam that is like that, or that certainly enjoys acting that way onstage.

AM: *The whole set-up for the Stranger's entrance and the Russian Dance, however, reminds me of one of Ashton's last ballets,* Varii Capricci – *which you and I both saw during its first British performances in 1983 and which was led by Antoinette Sibley and Anthony Dowell. She played a glamorous older woman, La Capricciosa; he played a sexy stranger, Lo Straniero, who has quite an effect on her, and then departs as mysteriously as he came. At one point, she stands closely in front of him, and puts her hand back right on to his thigh.*

His response is ambiguous. Much the same happens during your Russian Dance, when he launches into a steamy duet with the Hungarian Princess.

MB: That's just the kind of reference that I can't discuss usefully, I'm afraid. I saw *Varii Capricci* several times; and, when you describe it, I remember it. But if it went into my unconscious memory and has influenced my *Swan Lake*, I can't say. It's interesting you bringing these references up; it's not that I'm denying the influence of other choreography on me or claiming that everything in mine is original; but sometimes I'm conscious of my sources and sometimes I'm not. And sometimes, when I see a piece again myself, I suddenly realize that it has had an influence on me.

AM: *You've said that the czardas was a problem to choreograph.*
MB: Yes, because I wanted to keep some story going on there. Eventually we came up with an idea to do with partnering, where the Prince and the Black Swan are partnering different women, but looking at each other all the way through. This would lead up to the Stranger's flirtation with the queen as well. So the dance became all about looking, and about various lusty situations. The whole stage feels that way during that dance. It leads up to sexual things.

AM: *How was it working with the dancers on the role of the Queen?*
MB: Fiona just came and got on with the work; she enjoyed being in a more relaxed atmosphere. To begin with, people took her to be quite aloof – which they soon found wasn't the case. Her approach to the second cast was that it was rude even to watch someone else, let alone to comment. (Sarah Wildor was the same when she came from the Royal to rehearse *Cinderella*.) Fiona had her head in a book – which some people thought was rude – but it was her way of not interfering. She had her own very clear idea of what she was doing in the part, which she didn't want to impose on others or to have interfered with. She was so calm, and such good company during the run of the show, that she fitted in very well. She's a very intelligent dancer, and a much more remarkable actress than she probably realizes; every time she comes back to rehearse the role, she slips right back into it at once. When the show was performed and friends came to watch her, she was always telling them how nice it was to be around relaxed people – the fact that we'd all go for drinks after the shows, that we all spent time talking to each other.

AM: *Your second-cast queen was Isabel Mortimer.*

MB: Isabel was the easiest person to deal with in many ways. She knew that the role would be a completely new challenge for her and that she would have to learn a whole new regal way of behaviour. She learnt a lot from watching Fiona, and showed no ego. She never minded picking up from what other people did. Her relationship with Fiona was good, as it was later with Lynn Seymour. They talked about the role together, and sometimes she would come to me and say, 'I saw Fiona or Lynn doing this in the part. Would you like me to do it?' Sometimes I would say, 'No, do what you're doing, that's fine', and sometimes, 'Yes, I think that is a good idea.' More than any other dancer – even more than Adam, who's very open in this respect – she's learnt from watching others: which, I feel, is a valuable thing for all dancers.

AM: *We've spoken of how you planned the 'Black Swan' dances: the Stranger's duet with the Queen, his tango duet with the Prince, the women's dance for the Swan, the 'sarcastic dance'. How much of that just evolved in rehearsal?*

MB: Because it was story-led, I had the whole thing mapped out in my head musically. I was very clear on the ideas of what each piece of music was doing, and the kind of dance style I wanted. The first section, the Stranger's duet with the Queen, I knew wouldn't be a problem to do. To have Fiona and Adam just letting rip, doing all these things, was a shock to the second-cast dancers at first; but the more permanent members are very good in that they don't kick up much of a fuss about it. They watch and learn from other people, and find new ways of working and moving; but that process works two ways. I know that Adam certainly picked up a new way of moving from contemporary dancers, a great fluidity. The second section was the two men, but once I had the Argentinean tango idea – that sort of dark, intertwining of bodies – I thought that would work for the music and provide a formal partnering device; it says something straightaway and allowed us from a simple start to develop something that grew more violent and antagonistic between them. It seems to be a form that's almost open to anything.

AM: *I know that you were influenced by Hitchcock's* The Birds *in Act Four, but the whole drama of jealousy and alarm that builds up in Act Three also seems very Hitchcock to me.* Vertigo *comes to mind, and other films of his.*

MB: Yes, Hitchcock is definitely there, in the Prince's character and in the way we light the scene. A lot of Hitchcock's characters are in situations where they don't quite understand why they're wrongly accused; or where they have some reason to be paranoid about the way people treat them. Hitchcock also had a lot of strange mother–son relationships, didn't he?

One of Adam's most brilliant contributions came during the duet for the Stranger and the Prince. He had the idea of the Stranger walking to one side, dipping his thumb in the Private Secretary's ashtray, and tracing down the centre of his forehead the dark line the Swan has. So – this is the Prince's fantasy, remember – the Stranger is saying, 'Yes, I am the Swan.' But in a taunting, sinister way. It's the Prince's dream, touched with nightmare.

AM: *In the coda, you capture the music's competitive spirit. In the traditional* Swan Lake, *the way in which the ballerina does her thirty-two fouetté turns over a drastic change in the music is always horridly unmusical.*
MB: I definitely stole one thing there. The way the Swan lifts the Queen over his hoisted leg over a series of tables; Fred and Ginger do that in the 'Yam', in *Carefree*. I'd always wanted to put that in somewhere! I think we tried to do something similar in *The Percys*, but it's quite difficult to achieve. However, when Fiona and Adam tried it, they just did it straightaway – it was great – and that helped other people to do it in turn. It's just a shame that we don't have as many tables as they had!

The interesting thing about all Act Three was that it felt dreadful in the studio. It never felt that it had any life to it whatsoever. I thought it was a disaster. It was only the first time we did it on stage, with the lighting, that it actually ever worked.

The next act we rehearsed was Act One.

AM: *Here are your notes for the prologue:*
'Boy (Prince) writing in bed having a bad dream. Awakes in a sweat on big chord; at same time, the Swan appears in large mirror above bed (it quickly fades) as the Queen enters the room (as if disturbed in the night). She comforts the young Prince. The Private Secretary appears at the doorway.'
So straightaway you've got that idea of a boy dreaming of a swan; it's the idea you used in the original poster image. But what kind of a dream does this boy Prince have of a swan?

MB: It's frightening when he's young. He's not yet worked out what the Swan is. We also ended up having the Queen a lot colder than that description; and the Private Secretary didn't appear there.

AM: 'Act One, Scene One. (The Private Secretary is directing all of this.) It is morning. Lines of footmen and maids are going about their business as if along corridors. They're regimented, almost clockwork. They carry things: towels, a basin, aerosols, a screen?, etc. How high bed? . . . Six or so servants prepare the Prince for his day of royal duties. They form staircase for him to walk down out of bed, they wash him, dress him, etc. He uses their bodies for seats, support, etc., eats breakfast? He is given a lesson in royal protocol with blackboard: how to 1) walk, 2) wave, 3) posture, 4) salute (use trolley maybe as substitute coach). Show Prince's rebellious/creative/imaginative side . . .'
   Did you show that aspect of the Prince?
MB: We got in as much detail as we could. Sometimes there wasn't enough music. He doesn't eat breakfast, for example.

AM: '. . . Perhaps the Queen interrupts his fun, takes his hand, and leads him into or through a doorway with flashlights. He resists . . .'
MB: That didn't quite happen there, but the feeling is true to what we did.

AM: Next you've put 'Toy swan?'
MB: This was an Equus idea really. In the play Equus, the horse image was triggered off by a picture of a horse in his room that was staring down on him from above the bed. So we were wondering whether, if our Prince had a toy swan, that might, from a very early age, have started all the nightmares.

AM: 'Act One, Scene Two, The Great Hall: waltz. Dancing lesson for young Prince? Maybe with Queen. Appearance on balcony.' Note in the margin: 'How does all this work? Balcony/bed . . .'
MB: On stage the bed reverses to become the balcony. We didn't have the dancing lesson.

AM: 'Line ups, walkabouts, unveilings, investiture, ropes to form barriers, red carpet, cutting ribbons, smashing a bottle to launch a ship . . .' Pretty much all of that happens on stage.
   'Transformation of young Prince to the Prince, using flash bulbs . . .'
MB: We did that, but not so literally.

AM: *'Note: dance possibilities (sections). Quintet, the Queen and four young admirers. Group dance, seven couples led by Prince and the Queen. Two solos, the young Prince and the Prince . . .'*

MB: We had the quintet, but the rest we either never tried, or changed. Originally the Prince did a solo; then we changed it to have him meeting the Girlfriend instead.

AM: *'Mixed group of dignitaries. Stiff, snobby, elegant . . .'* That's attached now to another note down the page: *'Girlfriend arrives on her own looking (common) and different from everyone else . . .'* Between that, you've got: *'Duet for Prince and Girlfriend. Somewhere in here we need to show Prince's personality/rebellion/fear, etc.'*

MB: We did away with the rebellion. We showed his fear of people and cameras. He flinches every time there's a camera flash. He looks a bit out of it most of the time.

AM: *'Act One, Scene Three, continuation: the scene following the waltz . . .'* You've got a note in the margin: *'How long do women need to get ready for ballet?'* Main text: *'Prince tries to introduce his new girlfriend to the Queen. This she avoids at first (she has some men with her). She exits (first fanfare) to prepare for evening engagement. Duet, Prince and Girlfriend interrupted by Private Secretary.'* In the right-hand margin, in capital letters: *'NO MIME.'*

MB: I meant, in general for the whole scene, that we weren't going to have any kind of formal ballet mime as such. We were going to act it in a naturalistic style.

AM: *And you've got a note about the duets: 'Does Girlfriend have a wrap. Can she move?' Next thing: 'Queen returns ready for Evening Out, with her escort. Prince introduces her, "She's not good enough." Prince: "But you've got that toyboy." She gives in.'*

MB: Because we didn't use mime, we couldn't be that specific. But we did give the dancers some motivation.

AM: *'They arrive in Royal Box and stand as if for the National Anthem. As they sit, curtain opens . . .'* You've got a note: *'Do we need a curtain?'* Then:

'Act One, Scene Four: The Ballet.' (You've got a note saying: *'Use lots of mime and bows to box.'*) Then *'First Section. Introduction to Idyll: first two butterflies, then other two. Two twos. Finally that Ballerina.*

'*Second Section, Hunter's Entrance and Solo. Chases butterflies, falls in love with the white one when she appears, and chases her.*

'*Third Section. Declares his love. She says she's held captive by evil forest ogre/troll, and cannot leave the forest. He vows to release her, etc.*

'*Fourth Section: ogre appears. Big fight. Hunter, dizzy spell in middle. He defeats the ogre.*

'*Fifth Section: they all celebrate. She dies at end?*'

Then you've put '*Twist needed.*'

MB: She collapses at the last minute. She withers away with excitement.

AM: '*Act One, Scene Five: Private, a room in the palace. Starts solos in 2 rooms. Could be with valet (boy) a maid (cover) . . .*'

MB: The idea was to have one room on each side of the stage, with the Queen in one and the Prince in the other, being undressed after the night at the theatre. Eventually, she was going to go into his room, but the beginning of the music was going to be them both thinking their private thoughts.

AM: '*She can sense him in his room. They're both distressed. He needs a bit of sympathy. His girlfriend has walked out . . .*'

MB: She storms out of the theatre. After this duet with his mother, he goes off looking for her.

AM: '*Queen becomes too intimate. He pulls away. She becomes angry. "Be a man." "I'm sorry," he says, "I just want a mother." She is incapable of that kind of love. She leaves. He feels betrayed and lonely, dons a disguise, and leaves . . .*' *Needless to say, in the margin you've written, 'Psychology.*'

MB: I'd forgotten the Queen getting intimate; we never used that. What we eventually felt was best was what we did on stage: to do with her not being able to touch him, and him trying to make her touch him, to bring her arms around him – things like that. If there's any sexual element to it, I don't think it works so well. It could work, but we didn't go for that.

AM: *Well, in a different ink, you've written, 'She is cold . . .' Take us through the action for this scene. What's the Prince doing here?*

MB: He's got a bottle; he's drinking in his mirror in his room, and she enters, but not seen by him, because he has his head down. All this is straight after the incident in the Royal Box during the Moth Ballet; the

Girlfriend has gone off in a huff. Now the Queen has come in to try to talk to him. She sees that he's in a fairly desperate state. It looks at first as if she's going to try to be a bit more human about the state of things with him. She tries to touch him, but doesn't feel very comfortable about it. As soon as his eyes meet hers, he turns round and looks at her. She can't meet his look. There's something about him and her that doesn't work, doesn't connect in that way. Then he tries to explain, saying that all he wants is a bit of love in his life, that that's why he had the girlfriend. But it gets out of hand. The thing that changes her way of looking at things is that she suddenly sees the bottle, and she starts to bring up something that she's obviously brought up before: 'You're drinking again.' Whereas she was going to try to be tactful and sweet and human about everything, now she starts ranting again at him. So it's the same old story, and he, in turn, gets more violent with her. But for him it is more desperate. He tries to make her be physical with him. That's the idea of the duet; that was how we talked about the movement. It's all about him trying to bring her to him, trying to get her to hold him, and about her resisting that and getting upset by it. But there is also the sense at the end – once they end up on the floor together and she gets up – that this is not the first time this sort of thing has happened. He crawls over to the mirror. She's about to leave; she sees him slumped there; she just looks at him. She goes over to him, brings his shoulders up, makes him look at himself in the mirror, and meet her eyes – in the mirror. What she's saying is: 'Be a man. This is your job.'

AM: *Was all this in your scenario before rehearsals?*
MB: In the scenario, it's just one line about the Prince needing affection from his mother; but it's one of the ideas you knew would take care of itself once you got going on it. It was a simple idea that then became, as we knew it would all along, more complex. Of course, working with all four of them on that, with Fiona and Scott and Isabel and Ben, was very good. They all think very much from an acting point of view and were very uninhibited in the way they approached the whole thing. I remember asking Fiona to turn and look back at the Prince in three different ways. She did them all brilliantly, and it was the one she devised that worked best. I wish it was a bit longer, actually. It comes at a point in the show where you've had quite a lot of humour, and to get into this new mood takes a while. Although it can be very powerful, it's

57 *Swan Lake*, Act One. The 'Soho' scene, set in a 'retro' club and peopled by figures of scandal from the 1960s. Eddie Nixon as the Club Owner, and William Kemp as the Pop Idol. Bourne told Kemp to base this character on the young Cliff Richard. Kemp, who only knew Richard as a much older performer, incorporated aspects of Elvis Presley: such as the knee-wobbles shown here.

over before you really have a chance to get into this separate scene musically. Then you're into Soho. But it went down particularly well in America, that duo. It always got applause there.

AM: *Your notes for the end of this scene: 'The Private Secretary enters. Has seen the whole thing and contacts someone on his mobile phone. (Fade) . . .'*

MB: The idea was that there was never any privacy. Even at home in his own room, the Prince was always watched.

AM: *'Act One, Scene Six: Soho Club. Several situations going on at once, Girlfriend is with the sailors. Fan dancer puts on a show. Little repeated group dances. Prince works his way around club trying to win back girlfriend. Sailor makes a pass at him. Fight ensues. Bit of jiving. Not necessarily all period dance. Go through relationships and groups.'*

MB: Details like 'The sailor makes a pass at him' are there so as not to make the whole situation too sexually clear-cut for some members of the audience. I wanted to show that the Prince can't handle an advance from a man.

AM: *He wants the Swan/Stranger in his mind, but he doesn't actually want the sex. But could it be played either way? As I think Scott perceives it, the Prince is straight at this point, and then the Swan hits him as a sexual revelation in his own mind. But could the Prince be actually a closet gay who won't admit his sexuality to himself?*

MB: I don't think he should be consciously seen to be comfortable with flirting with men in a Soho club.

AM: *So it becomes a drama about repression of some kind.*

The next page is all counts. Eights and fours, mainly eights. Do you reduce all music to eights?

MB: No. But dancers are happier with eights than with any other counts. Obviously, if something is definitely in sixes, then you have to go with it. Later on, we've got tens, twelves, all kinds of other counts.

AM: *Here we've got floor patterns for your idea of the waltz; and you've worked on the casting here in some precision.*

MB: The floor-patterns we probably used. It's a case of sometimes dealing with the number of people you've got, and working out what shapes you can actually make with that many people; what your options are really in terms of formations.

AM: *We've got notes here for Soho material. 'Wobbly legs, head to head, jive, v. close.'*

MB: 'Wobbly legs' are Elvis Presley knee-trembles. Will Kemp did those as the Pop Idol.

AM: *'Prince's Solo, Act One . . .' Lots of sixes here. 'The Private Secretary. Trapped, rejected, alone, yearning.'*

MB: My idea for the Prince's solo was partly the solo the hero of Ashton's *The Two Pigeons* does when he's at his lowest ebb. Like our Prince here, his solo is in front of the drop-curtain; he's been thrown out of one milieu and he feels that he's lost. I know that it seems a lot of work to divide Act One into seven scenes. But I think that it's easier to do that than to have one great long Prince's birthday scene as usually happens in the traditional *Swan Lake*. There's much more music for Act One than for Act Two, and yet usually it has less plot. Once we knew what we were doing for each scene, it was more straightforward. In fact, it was the least problematic act to create.

AM: *What about Act Four?*

MB: To be honest, the scenario was very, very weak in that area, when we went into choreographing it. We were trying to get Act One finished and had little time left to do Act Four. In some ways, I thought, 'The basic idea is there.' It didn't need very specific organizing in the sense of this scene being about one thing and that scene being about another. The whole thing had one overall feeling, and it was driven by the music. So I thought that, once we got going on it, it would create itself. Still, I was getting worried time-wise. So, while we were doing Act One, I used to send Adam and David (Hughes) up into a studio, because they weren't needed in Act One. I told them, 'Just listen to the music and see what ideas you have. Just think it through.' I knew that there were things I wanted to pinpoint; but the problem was that the music had so many climaxes. Just when you think it's all over, it starts up again. And your first thought is, 'What on earth can we do with this next climax?'

AM: *You solve the climaxes. You've got more plot than most Act Fours ever have. What moments do you think you pinpointed in advance?*

MB: The Swan coming out of the bed (I love that; I think it's very significant); the reconciliation of the two of them; the regret. Then the point where the swans turn on them: there seemed to be a real change in the music that made that clear. It was definitely going to be the swans turning on their leader; but, until rehearsal, I thought that they might be attacking the Prince as well at that point.

One theme in Act Four is betrayal. The Prince must feel the Swan has betrayed him in Act Three. The Swan has to win him back by saying, 'I am the true one.'

AM: *Were you changing any of the musical text once you got into rehearsals?*

MB: We use the original 1877 Act Four, without any supplements, which virtually no production does. When I was worried about finishing it in time, I think I went to David Lloyd-Jones in desperation and said, 'Are there any cuts we can make in the first dance, without it sounding as if there are cuts?' The answer was yes: there were repeats that we could take out. That helped quite a lot.

AM: *The whole act is the climax to your whole conception of* Swan Lake *as psychodrama, and it has several turns of the screw. The first hair-raising moment is when the first swans appear from under the bed. As you've said, this came from your idea that Act Four was Act Two in reverse: the Prince had entered the swans' world, now they enter his. He had stretched his mind to include them, but now they invade his mind and his privacy.*

MB: There's the section where the swans are all attacking the Prince – they turn on him because he has turned against nature (going with a Swan – or with a man) – and leave him for dead. Then the Swan interrupts them, on that fantastic climax in the music. The swans all leave, and the Swan is left with what he at first thinks is the dead body of the Prince, and he's griefstricken.

AM: *At first, the way that the Swan seems to be left destitute by the corpse of his companion evokes Act One of the Peter Wright Royal Ballet production of* The Nutcracker: *little Clara thinks the Nutcracker is dead, and she's desolate; but when your Swan grieves, he opens his mouth in a howl. Were you thinking of 'swan song'?*

MB: Absolutely. Then, as he realizes there is life left in the Prince, he picks him up. Here we repeat the wrapping-of-the-wings motif from Act Two; at which point I remember thinking in rehearsal, 'Now here comes another whole piece of music that leads up to the end. Where do we go from here?' Then I remembered the idea I had had of the swans re-entering to destroy their leader. So their first attack really was on the Prince, to get rid of him. They don't quite succeed; and now, since he's still alive and since the Swan's obviously sticking with him, they turn on the Swan – because he has betrayed them – and attack him. At an initial stage we hadn't quite separated the two out. I had been thinking that they would attack the two of them; but, because of those two separate climaxes in the music, we divided it into, first, the attack on the Prince – whom the Swan saves, somewhat like *Giselle* reversed – and, next, the attack on their own Swan leader. Now, the way they attack him, the image that we had was from Tennessee Williams's *Suddenly Last Summer*. I only knew the film, in which the young Elizabeth Taylor gives a vivid, painful description of how the hero was ripped apart. It is very over the top, but I remember seeing it when I was in my teens and being terrified by the idea of someone being torn apart; I found that very shocking. I haven't seen it since, though I think I've seen clips from it. I don't think I even saw the sexual connotations that were slightly hidden in the film at the time; what I remember was the horrible image, even in verbal description; and also – as I've said earlier – I was thinking of Hitchcock's film *The Birds*. The bed is centre stage. The swans come on from the wings, and they jump on it. Some of them come from round it and hang on to it; they all have a different way of getting on to it. They jump, they slide across the bed. It's quite a powerful moment: a build-up of power and menace, in which the swans are obviously angry and about to attack.

AM: *Then comes the heroic big dive by the Swan into their midst. This connects exactly to the Swan Queen's suicide in the traditional* Swan Lake, *which occurs at the same point in the score, and it catches the note of Romantic despair in the music. But how did this Swan's dive emerge?*

MB: It was Adam's idea. I was a bit suspicious of it, to be honest; at first I thought, 'It feels a bit clichéd.' But I liked the fact that we saw the Prince downstage, blocked by all the swans, and the way this let them reach out to each other before the Swan was devoured. Anyway, it was one of those ideas Adam had devised upstairs while we were doing Act One, and he wanted to do it. Once I saw how very well it worked, I left well alone!

58 *Swan Lake*, Act Four. Adam Cooper as the Swan, throwing himself from the bed into the chorus of swans. This self-sacrificial leap on the part of the Swan into the arms of the now cannibalistic and frenzied swans was one of Cooper's own original ideas. It occurs on the last great climax in the score.

It was amazing how quickly Act Four fell into place. We really had very little time left, but everything solved itself fast. I think that says a lot about the whole rehearsal process; by that stage everyone was deeply committed to what the show was all about. Normally, the final stages of completing a show are absolutely desperate for me; but in this case, despite the rush, I remember no panic. We had had a wonderful rehearsal period, and there was a lot of trust and devotion about.

Changing Casts

ALASTAIR MACAULAY: *We've spoken of the casts with whom you created* Swan Lake *in 1995. During these following three years, in fact, the role of the Prince has always been played by one or other of the same two dancers: Scott Ambler or Ben Wright. However, there have been a few other interpreters of the roles of the Swan and the Queen. Of these, perhaps the two most important were Will Kemp as the Swan and Lynn Seymour as the Queen.*

MATTHEW BOURNE: Will was around from the beginning, and was in the background for a lot of rehearsals involving the Swan, though not

59 *Swan Lake*, Act Two. Will Kemp as the Swan; Ben Wright as the Prince.

participating. He injured himself just before *Swan Lake* opened at Sadler's Wells, and was devastated by not being able to participate in the production he'd worked so hard on; but he watched every performance from the wings, and just lapped it up.

At the start of 1996, he then learnt the role fully from Adam; they had a very good relationship, and still do. Will was eighteen, and, as a recent graduate of the Royal Ballet School, he felt very much the excitement of learning this big role from Adam, who was still then a principal of the Royal Ballet, and who had received great acclaim for his performance in *Swan Lake*. Will also recognized Adam's generosity and practical good sense; but, even at that age, he found it natural to start doing things his own way. By the time he did his first performance, during the British tour in spring 1996, he seemed to have worked out for himself how he wanted to do it and what he wanted to bring out in it. Obviously, the differences in their techniques and in their styles of dancing make the role feel different anyway; but there were individual inflections and strokes of interpretation in Will which I found very impressive; it never felt like a copycat performance. We didn't change anything choreographically at all for him; he worked within the existing framework of the role.

AM: *Can you say what the difference in quality and movement was?*
MB: Adam is more over-powering and more dominant and has a much more powerful presence than Will does overall. His dancing has more strength and power and, therefore, seems to dominate the Prince much more easily, much more casually. Just by his presence, he can dominate the whole stage; and he actually looks much taller on stage than he is. When he walks on, in both Acts Two and Three, he looks enormous – and yet off stage he's the same height as me – not even six foot. I don't understand that at all.

AM: *This is what the critic James Monahan used to call 'the gift of tall-ness'. He was particularly fascinated by how the dancing of very petite ballerinas such as Fonteyn and Makarova registered colossally in huge theatres. It's something that a few people – actors and singers, for example – have naturally. But I think that ballet training – ballet is all about large-scale projection, after all – helps several people (though a minority) to acquire these heightened dimensions on stage.*
MB: Will, by contrast, is slight and boyish, a very different presence. He's only half an inch shorter than Adam, but that's not how it feels

on stage. His presence is something he has to work at. His style is more gentle and fluid, and his intensity is something he worked on – whereas Adam's is natural. Adam has an incredible sexual magnetism for people, because it appears that he's not trying very hard – and probably he isn't – in terms of projecting the image that he does. What Will has is a quite different kind of mystery. It is perhaps a different kind of erotic appeal, but Will's is projected with greater innocence and a certain spiritual quality that's really remarkable.

AM: *I also think that they use the music differently.*
MB: Yes. Adam has a great way of playing with music. The music's really inside him, in the sense that he knows what he's doing, so that he goes for one chord or beat or sound in the music, or holds back from one. He's in control of it, because he's got great resources of technique, and he brings some very strong dynamic qualities to individual phrases. Will's technique isn't such that he can exert that freedom; but he has a physical response to the music that feels more emotional; I think his style has a basic grace and fluency that complements the whole current of a phrase.

It's important to remember that Will has learnt all his professional skill and artistry with AMP, whereas Adam was already an established actor-dancer when he came to us. Adam is one of the world's great partners; women have complete trust in his hands. I'm sure that's the virtue of his they must miss most now at the Royal Ballet, where ballerinas so often feel terribly exposed unless they have an absolutely strong and reliable partner. Will has learnt a vast amount through sheer experience. There was at least one week in the West End when, because of injury to other swans, he had to dance all eight performances. And this is a role that Adam says is more exhausting than anything except Prince Rudolf in *Mayerling*. Will was just nineteen, but he always sustained the role.

As for Lynn Seymour, the thrill for me was that she saw *Swan Lake* at Sadler's Wells three times and asked me if she could be in it. I would never have dreamt of approaching her.[14] To be truthful, I missed almost all her career as a ballerina – though I knew much about her and I remember how often, as our teacher at Laban, you yourself would talk of her individuality and power. Certainly I had seen many

---

14 It is true that Bourne had never approached her. Nonetheless, in an early note on *Swan Lake* casting (dated probably 1994), Seymour's name is one of the ten women Bourne lists as possible for the Queen.

60 *Swan Lake*. Act Three. Adam Cooper as the Swan (or Stranger); Lynn Seymour as the Queen.

61 *Swan Lake*, Act Four. Final tableau, with Isabel Mortimer as the Queen holding the body of the dead Prince (Scott Ambler), while Adam Cooper as the Swan (above) holds the young Prince (Andrew Walkinshaw).

of the ballets that Ashton and MacMillan had choreographed on her: *The Two Pigeons, Romeo and Juliet, Concerto, Five Brahms Waltzes in the Manner of Isadora Duncan, A Month in the Country, Mayerling.*

Once we decided to use Lynn for several performances during the West End run – Fiona, Isabel and she shared the majority of performances of the Queen – she was a brilliant colleague. I regard Fiona's performance as definitive, but Lynn did more than any other AMP performer to show how a newcomer to the cast of a show can stamp her own way on a role; and she had a very good relationship with Isabel. Certain passages – particularly the Act One duet with the Prince – had to be rechoreographed on her anyway, because there were certain things that were simply designed on a younger dancer, but it was great working with her in rehearsal; she's absolutely committed. Even though she's a great star, I really think she's happiest in rehearsal. She loves being part of a team, she laughs about herself, is very unpretentious, and the whole company loved having her around. She loved the AMP way of working, which draws extensively on the performer's own idea of a role. But she's also amazing during a run of a show. She's extremely inventive, and at almost every performance she'd have some new idea; usually she'd ask me what I thought, but occasionally she'd suddenly try something outrageous on stage without having told anybody else that she was going to. She wrote me a letter to say that she felt like the Sleeping Beauty awakened – which made me feel very proud.

During the West End run we launched two other performers in the role of the Swan: Floyd Henricks and Adam Cooper's brother Simon. They were both really good – and it was interesting to see how all of them quickly won a number of devoted admirers. Just now we're preparing Keith Roberts, from American Ballet Theatre, to dance the role during the Broadway run. On a purely technical level, he's very beautiful to watch. Finding people who can dance both the White and the Black Swan is not easy. Dancers are usually good at one or the other!

9

The West End, Los Angeles
and Broadway

ALASTAIR MACAULAY: *In autumn 1996 your* Swan Lake *was transferred to a West End theatre. There it ran for 120 performances: the longest run ever known in London for any production of a full-length dance classic. Of course, certain plays or musicals enjoy unbroken runs for years on end. But dance shows seldom command that kind of drawing power, and their expenditure of physical energy is, of course, infinitely larger. Your West End run of* Swan Lake *broke various precedents established by productions of Tchaikovsky's* The Sleeping Beauty *(or* The Sleeping Princess*) such as the Diaghilev staging at the Alhambra Theatre in 1921, the Sadler's Wells Ballet's opening production at the Royal Opera House, Covent Garden in 1946, and the London Festival Ballet production which launched the first Nureyev Festival at the London Coliseum in 1976.*

You brought in a new audience to dance, and did it in part by appealing to the audience that might usually go to musicals. Since then, AMP has produced shows much along Cameron Mackintosh or Andrew Lloyd Webber lines. Like them, an AMP show has a logo for mass publicity; it has merchandise; it has a story that the audience more or less knows already; it has an album they can buy and play at home. What do you feel about this?

MATTHEW BOURNE: Selling a show as we do is something quite deliberate. It wasn't brought to us by the Cameron Mackintosh organization. I remember us saying, very early on in the original planning stage for *Swan Lake*, 'We need a Cameron Mackintosh-type logo for this piece,' something that very much stamps an image on the production. In fact, that logo's changed a fair amount as we've gone to different places.

AM: *You began, in 1995, with a naked man (Scott Ambler) embracing a swan. Ballet people may connect that with famous photographs of Anna Pavlova in her garden embracing one of her pet swans; but this image very obviously had intimate psychosexual suggestions.*

MB: Yes. When it went into the West End, there was a lot of nervousness about a naked man. I don't know why! Naked men are used in advertising an enormous amount these days; and, as far as I'm concerned, ours was a quite innocent image.

Still, that became fainter for the West End publicity. He became less obviously a naked man; he sank more into the water-like background. In the foreground, however, we put the eyes – Adam's eyes – staring out at the camera from under his brow like a swan. Next, for Los Angeles, he disappeared altogether. They were nervous of it looking like a ballet; to make it look like a musical, they wanted Adam Cooper in the black leather trousers as their main image, set against a red background. And now, as we're going on to Broadway, I've insisted on going back to the eyes. The naked man holding a swan has disappeared altogether. The lettering of *Swan Lake* is similar to the original lettering, but now with water beneath it.

AM: *Did you ever think of logos before* Swan Lake?

MB: Yes, I think we always tried to stamp our pieces with a kind of single image: either a logo or a very strong poster. (See *Deadly Serious*, for example.) The lettering for the name Adventures in Motion Pictures was itself a logo, and we've retained that more or less the same over the years. So we were always very image-conscious.

As you know, the logo's only one of many things that go towards making a production more commercial. You mentioned subject matter, stories people feel they already know. There obviously is a nod to commercialism there. There are certain titles you feel you can sell. What you actually do with that title can be any number of things: you can be creative within that structure. But if we'd retitled *Swan Lake* or *Cinderella*, it probably wouldn't have sold so well. That's a problem for a lot of ballet companies and for people presenting musicals. I'm sure *Phantom of the Opera* sells well partly because it's got an exciting title: it sounds great before you even buy your ticket, and it's a story you're vaguely familiar with.

I think that, if you're presenting a completely new story, that shouldn't put you off. But you have to consider that it should be a less expensive production, something that's less risky and maybe at a smaller venue. You can still make a success of a more experimental production, but you have to bear in mind that maybe you won't get the bigger audiences that you might with a well-known title. Recently I've been having conversations with Katharine about possible future projects, and at one point she remarked, 'I don't think I could sell, in the West End, a production called *Giselle*, for example.' If we were to do a version of *Giselle*, either it would be retitled, or we would do it in a smaller venue or in a repertory house.

AM: *Is this why you re-titled* La Sylphide *as* Highland Fling?
MB: We'd always invented our own titles. Because that was designed to be a small-scale or middle-scale touring production, it seemed to go along the same lines as our previous work; and so I didn't feel nervous about it. *La Sylphide* wouldn't have been a title that would have sold very easily to a general audience. *Highland Fling* sounds more colloquial, accessible, and has a nice double meaning.

AM: *Ashton found that his 1961 ballet* Les Deux Pigeons *did a lot better business when he anglicized the name to* The Two Pigeons.
Tell me: when you're planning a new show for AMP, how much do you think, 'I want to go back to the old story' and how much do you think, 'I've got to do a completely different take on it'?
MB: I don't really see the point in recreating things that have gone before. We're not a ballet company, choosing to do a new production of *Giselle* or *La Bayadère*, because in that context you have the choreographic text. You can dress it up in different costumes and sets, but basically you're producing *Giselle* – whereas our mission and our job as a company is not to do that. We're not maintaining any kind of tradition. I would never feel that anything we do had any boundaries as to what we could do with it. We would choose something simply because it had a good story, structure, music, whatever – and then we'd work with that.

I'm consciously trying to appeal to an audience that doesn't have background knowledge about what they're seeing. You may feel, 'When I go and see *Les Misérables*, I know the book', but most people who go and see it don't know the book. There isn't the assumption there that we're all going to see that favourite old story of ours.

In some ways, with our shows, the problem is getting people to actually buy their ticket, come and sit down and watch it. Once they're there – though I don't feel I've got to make it easy for an audience, necessarily – I do want to make it clear enough for them to feel comfortable watching it. I don't want something that mystifies them in any way. Obviously, a more sophisticated dance audience will accept a lot more in terms of abstraction than your average West End musical audience; but you can satisfy both of those sets of people, if you're clever and careful about what you do. I'm conscious of that.

AM: *What you do to* Cinderella *could, I suppose, be compared to a show like* Miss Saigon. *That's a reworking and updating of* Madam Butterfly; *your* Cinderella *is taken out of fairyland and put into the 1940s.*

MB: I think it is a similar approach, yes. But, when I saw *Miss Saigon,* I didn't know it was based on *Madam Butterfly.* I only realized that towards the end – and only because I'd seen *Butterfly.* It just seemed an original story to me at first, as I'm sure it does to many people; and that has new music, whereas we are using an established score.

AM: *But I and many people have certain qualms about big commercial West End shows. To me, a Lloyd Webber or Boublil-Schonberg musical doesn't just tell me a story I'm likely to know beforehand; it's also going to make me feel things that I've felt before. It sets out to press feel-good triggers in me: which I resent. It feels synthetic.*

Now that is not my reaction to Swan Lake *or* Cinderella, *or to musicals of the 1920s, 1930s, and 1940s. Am I being unfair to Lloyd Webber and Cameron Mackintosh? Do you like their shows more than I do?*

MB: It's difficult for me to say, because I admire so many of the people who have created them. I think you yourself would except certain Cameron Mackintosh shows from that 'synthetic' label. I'm interested in what draws a big audience, and I can see why these big musicals do. If you let yourself go with them, they can be highly entertaining and emotional. But yes, I find several of them manipulative in many ways. I call them 'push button shows'. It feels as if there's no human involvement, because the technical wizardry going on is on such a scale that the human aspect of the show disappears. You've got these enormous sets and these miked voices and great sound; you can kill a show through doing that. *Martin Guerre,* for example, was actually a small-scale show, with some very fine music at times; but it was overblown into a big West End production, with enormous moving pieces of scenery. It's really very folksy, and probably would have worked better in some-where like the Cottesloe. A Théâtre de Complicité type of production could have worked equally well for that.

One of the charms of an AMP show, I think, is that we don't have that enormous amount of money to spend. We don't make things over-blown; we don't lose the charm of Lez Brotherston's designs. His work does make you feel that you're going places, and he allows for us to do a lot, but actually it's done quite cheaply – and, inevitably, more inven-tively, because he has to make the most of limited means. Eventually, I think that's more theatrical: making something out of nothing, or mak-ing something spectacular out of limited means and limited possibilities.

AM: *Elsewhere we've been talking of dancers as mainly drawn from two trainings – ballet or modern. But there is almost a third genre: showbiz dance. Dancers who work in this category may be chiefly trained in jazz dance style. Some dancers work entirely in musicals, with a probably more hybrid training that will help them get through the varied requirements of this genre. Do you get any of those dancers coming to your AMP auditions?*
MB: We have had, but we've never yet accepted anyone whose prime experience is in West End musicals. This may change on Broadway, where the crossover of dancers is much wider. There you get dancers with very good dance training, ballet and/or modern, who've just moved into that area.

What do I admire in those dancers is their doing eight shows a week and giving it their full professional attention at every performance. This is something we've had to learn to do, and it's been a hard slog, actually. You go and see a West End show, it's some way into the run, and you're amazed at the enthusiasm and energy that's coming from the stage. Yet these people have been doing this for months and months, eight shows a week. At AMP meetings many times, I've said: 'I realize you're all here with various talents and for various reasons; but what you have to ask yourself, having done the West End, is: do you personally want to be doing eight shows a week? Is that something that suits you as a perfor-mer?' Because we have experienced a lot of problems with people get-ting tired and depressed, never having done a show that many times. It's a special skill that needs to be learned. In ballet companies, maybe you do a role three times in a year if you're lucky, and it always feels like a special occasion when you dance a particular role. To do it many times requires a different skill – that's what those commercial dancers have got.

They also have a performance ability that is very useful for certain aspects of what we do. So I don't rule out that kind of dancer at all; but they need the appropriate training to do the kind of work we're doing. It can't just be a jazz training; it needs to have covered other things.

AM: *Do you find that you've now got a company that has developed a West End style, a commercial-theatrical style?*
MB: I don't feel we're especially West End in style; I don't feel that we've changed in that respect. The performers have changed and have learnt how to project and how to maintain a long run. They know that they have to find ways of making the roles work for them, time and time again, and the dancing as well. They're mentally more prepared for it and are happy to find new things in what they're doing.

At times, I must admit I do wish for more presentation and style in the movement. There are things like the blue couples in *Cinderella* where I've often felt, 'I wish it was danced for the audience a little more; I wish it wasn't so internalized.' That's purely about just grabbing the audience. We talk about this quite a lot, but it's not something that comes very naturally to a number of the dancers. Early on, when doing *Swan Lake* in the theatres bigger than most dancers were used to performing in, we had to keep reminding them that there were people sitting way up there in 'the gods'. Often in *Swan Lake* it was 'the gods' that was sold out at every performance, because a lot of our audience were quite young and bought the cheapest tickets in the Upper Circle; so we had to acknowledge them. But you forget when you're used to performing in small theatres with people all in front of you on one level.

AM: *We've been talking largely of your appearances in Britain. What appearances did AMP make abroad before it took* Swan Lake *to Los Angeles and Broadway?*
MB: Very few. I've told you about our unsuccessful trip to Holland back in 1988! And that was the only foreign appearance in our first five years.

Unlike several British modern-dance groups of the same kind of size and experience, AMP never used to appeal to the producers who put on modern dance around the European continent. This was to do with our emphasis on humour. We were seen by the Europeans to be light-weight, entertaining: therefore not good. One exception was in 1995 when we took *Highland Fling* to Italy; that went down moderately well there. But anyone who ever came to see us, from France in particular, invariably hated our work.

AM: *The Channel can still be wider than the Atlantic.*
MB: But that situation – of European presenters not being interested in us has all changed since *Swan Lake*. We've had quite a number of invitations, including several from France, to take the production there; and in 2000 we plan to tour it around Europe. I'll be interested to see how it goes down there!

We always felt, mind you, that we were likely to be more appreciated outside Europe. In 1993, we took *Deadly Serious* to the Hong Kong Festival, where it had quite a success.

AM: *How did your association with Los Angeles come about?*
MB: Soon after *Swan Lake* opened at Sadler's Wells, Gordon Davidson, the artistic director of the Center Theater Group at the Ahmanson in LA, came to see it; and we began to develop what has proved a brilliant relationship with him. He felt a great affinity for our work straight away. Because of his enthusiasm for our production, LA was the first place that *Swan Lake* visited, straight after its season in 1996–97 in the West End. We had a wonderful season there in spring 1997. Then, early in 1998, Gordon came to see *Cinderella* during its final week in the West End. We told him straight away how we wanted to work further on the production; and he worked with Katharine Doré to enable us to do just that – to spend six weeks early in 1999 rehearsing it afresh, and to spend money on revising the sets and costumes.

Cinderella in LA – here we're speaking in June 1999 – was a very happy experience for us. The dancers really began to love doing the show for its own sake; they also really enjoyed the accommodation they had there; and, once it opened, they felt very appreciated there too. Currently, we're hoping to present our *Nutcracker* in LA over Christmas 2000; and, as with *Cinderella*, we hope to be able to reconsider the whole production this time and revise it as we see fit. To have people like Gordon and Katharine who'll work this way is the best news.

AM: *Before* Cinderella *in LA, you took* Swan Lake *to Broadway. Then, after* Cinderella *in LA, you won a whole series of New York awards for* Swan Lake. *But what did New York mean to you in advance?*

MB: You know, New York and Los Angeles were the first two cities I visited in America, in 1979, when I was nineteen. I went to theatres in one and to movie studios in the other. I especially remember the things I saw in New York: Angela Lansbury in *Sweeney Todd*, Patti LuPone in *Evita*, Bob Fosse's *Dancin'*, and the opening night of *Sugar Babies*, with Ann Miller and Mickey Rooney (the first-night audience included Andy Warhol, Shirley MacLaine, Eartha Kitt, and – rarest of all – Rita Hayworth).

When I began training as a dancer, New York took on another meaning for me – because it's known as the dance capital of the world. In 1986, when *Transitions* appeared in Hong Kong, we made friends with dance students from the Juilliard School, who were also performing there. In February 1987, I went over to stay in New York for four weeks with one of them, Kirk Ryder, who's still a good friend today. That was when I began to sample the dance life of New York. I took class with the Limòn company; I went to as many dance performances – ballet and modern – as I could; and I even performed in a new piece (choreographed by another Juilliard graduate friend, Torbjorn Stenberg) at Dance Theatre Workshop.

Since then, I've made several visits to New York, and today it's both a theatre city and a dance city for me. Early in 1997, I went there with Sam Mendes and Scott Ambler for auditions for *Cabaret*. I hadn't choreographed Sam's original London production of *Cabaret* at the Donmar Warehouse, but now, after working together on *Oliver!*, we were hoping to work together on the New York production. In the event, because of making *Cinderella*, I just wasn't able to do *Cabaret* as well, but, a year later, Etta Murfitt and Iain Webb and I were able to attend the first night of *Cabaret* on Broadway; we were in New York at the time to do auditions for *Swan Lake* on Broadway.

So I had quite a sense of New York by the time we took *Swan Lake* there in September 1998 – but I'd never presented any work of my own there.

AM: *Do you think there is a difference between the West End and Broadway? Between theatre in America and in Britain?*

MB: The gap between British performers in the West End and American performers on Broadway has narrowed a lot in recent years, owing to the growth of the large-scale Mackintosh/Lloyd Webber musical. The standard of singing is certainly much higher. Because the shows are so long-running, there is a variety of shows for people to perform in. You can make a very good living from just show-hopping. People will do a year in *Cats*, then a year in *Saigon*. So there's work there, and the training and performers have come up to scratch.

The interesting thing in America – having auditioned a lot of people – is that the community of dancers in New York is much more integrated than here. Here it's very much the three camps – contemporary, ballet and commercial – and there's very little mixing between them. In New York there seems to be a mutual respect between dancers. There is a greater respect for dancers all round; ballet dancers there have respect for contemporary and commercial dancers, and contemporary dancers are interested in watching ballet. We don't have that here.

AM: *That's partly because the two leading ballet choreographers, Balanchine and Robbins, had both worked extensively on Broadway. Agnes de Mille is actually more famous for her work on Broadway shows than on her ballets for American Ballet Theatre. The leading modern-dance choreographers – Martha Graham, Merce Cunningham, Paul Taylor, Twyla Tharp, Mark Morris – all have shown immense respect for Balanchine's work and for some other areas of ballet; and some have worked on Broadway: Tharp, Morris, Lar Lubovitch, for example. So there is a long tradition of crossover there. Many of the leading modern dancers take class with the ballet teacher Maggie Black – and are proud to say so in their programme biographies.*

MB: Yes; that's another thing. A lot of American contemporary dancers, if they're going to do a class, would rather do a ballet class. Here, there's a lot of discussion about where you can find a good contemporary class, which is very difficult to find. You do all this contemporary dance training in college – and then suddenly you're out and you find it's actually a lot easier to find a ballet class. To keep your training going is very difficult if you're a purely contemporary dancer.

AM: *What about Los Angeles? Did you find that LA audiences reacted to* Swan Lake *differently?*

MB: They did. The LA audiences had no preconceptions about us; they had no preconception of what we would be like at all. Our big fear was that the humour wouldn't work, but actually it worked better than it had done in London. I think they find the Royal satire aspect of it very funny. The little ballet in Act One they found hilarious; it went down much better there than it's ever gone here in London. Of course, they're very happy to react vocally, and they're very emotionally easy with things, in the sense that they're quite happy to cry at the end and not be ashamed. I think we also get more applause breaks there, because they're more readily reactive. As soon as any lights are lowered or something finishes, there will be applause.

AM: *Many Royal Ballet dancers remember that, particularly on the big tours of America in the 1960s and 1970s, there were passages of choreography which won applause – right through the music – that never would at home. (One was the 'cow-hops' in* Giselle; *another was the concentric rings revolving in opposite directions in Ashton's old garland dance in* The Sleeping Beauty.) *The roar of applause always made the dancers much more proud of the choreography.*

MB: That has happened to us too. In the West End there was always an 'eggy' moment after the Act One duet for the Queen and the Prince: no applause, though we'd have liked it, to cover the scene change. But in LA they'll fill any gap for you with applause, and that keeps the show flowing. However, applause for particular steps, which is common in New York dance performances, I find a little crass, particularly in more profound or serious work.

A lot of the audience in Los Angeles came as part of a subscription system, and hadn't specifically booked to see our *Swan Lake.* They can be quite conservative as well, but we found them very open-minded.

At this point, I'm still viewed in this country very much as a choreographer; in America I'm viewed as a director. Here I get offered choreography on shows where they've already got a director on board; but I'm really not interested in that any more, despite my pleasure in working on *Oliver!.* I need the whole vision, the whole piece, to come from me. This isn't a vanity thing. It's just because, otherwise, I know I can't do the choreography I'd like to do.

AM: *So what was your feeling about being on Broadway?*
MB: New York doesn't have London's variety of theatre. And theatres there are less characterised, less individual. There's a generalized theme-park feeling about New York theatres that I don't enjoy.

On the other hand, New York audiences can be very warm. To have a hit there is just as exciting as you might hope. I have to say that, for those of us involved in administration, there were some terrible technical problems backstage that at first spoilt our pleasure in working in New York. We presented the show with a mixed British and American cast, and the British dancers had a very good time there. And in due course, we all did.

Adam Cooper, Will Kemp and Floyd Hendricks all had great successes as the Swan – as did Scott and Ben Wright as the Prince, and Fiona Chadwick and Isabel Mortimer as the Queen. Some company dancers took leading roles for the first time: Ewan Wardrop and Tom Ward as the Prince, Detlev Alexander as the Swan. We'd hoped, during the run, also to present both Lynn Seymour and Natalia Makarova as the Queen, but both of them were injured. So Marguerite Porter, whom I'd often seen in her career with the Royal Ballet, joined us at quite short notice and ended up staying with us throughout most of our run: she was great to work with, and made the role her own.

AM: *Unlike the theatre world, the dance world in New York is larger and livelier than London's. Less so, however, than it used to be. I don't mean that smugly; London's dance world has not generally grown in scale or consequence, though it has become less narrow-spirited. New York used to be a Mecca that gave added vitality to the whole dance world. The deaths of the choreographers George Balanchine, Antony Tudor, Martha Graham and Jerome Robbins during the 1980s and 1990s have cast a pall.*

Meanwhile, largely for economic reasons, it becomes no easier to put on a dance production in New York: so that even the choreographers who live and work there can only present their work in New York very occasionally – often after presenting it a good many times on tour. What is it like being a foreign choreographer bringing a big dance production to New York?

MB: In *Swan Lake*, our experience was simply that the production – wherever we've done it – just got better each time we did it. The Moth ballet, the duet for the Prince and the Queen, the Soho scene: these went down better than ever in New York. This was partly to do with the audiences, but partly also because we'd kept learning how to get reactions.

At first, during previews, there was something of a 'Come on, show us' feeling in the audience. We felt we had more to prove. But that changed.

It was wonderful to be in New York for months on end. Several former Balanchine ballerinas – Allegra Kent, Merrill Ashley, Lourdes Lopez – were very enthusiastic about the production, and expressed a lot of interest in performing the role of the Queen. And Mikhail Baryshnikov was very supportive. He threw two parties for us: one during our period of previews and one on closing night. He'd already loved *Swan Lake* when he'd seen it in the West End. To have him – one of the greatest dancers of the century, and an inspiration to all dancers – behaving as a friend to the company in New York from the first meant a huge amount.

AM: *How did the American dancers in the company prove in performance?*

MB: Most of them were terribly professional in approach, and most or all of them loved doing it. They were a real mixture. One man had been in the Martha Graham company, and another, Krissy Richmond, got leave from the US touring production of *Chicago* to perform with us. (She played the Queen at the end of our run, and we nicknamed her 'The Fosse Queen'.) Keith Roberts, who played the Swan, was much more animal in his interpretation than we had anticipated – we had been awed by the purity of his dancing in audition – and I have the feeling that he surprised himself.

But I learned just how unusual, for all of them, our style was. Not just its acting demands; its dance style too. They were used to attack, to projecting the movement with lots of bite. And they found it hard to pace it, and to catch some of its fluidity.

Mind you, I wonder: could anyone else spot the difference between our British and our American dancers? If so, I never heard people talking of it.

AM: *Let's talk about all the New York awards you ended up winning. You won the Best Choreographer and Best Director of a Musical awards from three different bodies: the Outer Critics Circle, the Drama Desk, and the Tonys. That's six; and the Drama Desk also gave* Swan Lake *a Unique Theatre Experience Award. Also, for his contribution to* Swan Lake, *Lez Brotherston won an Outer Critics' Circle Award for Best Costumes, two Drama Desk Awards, for Best Costumes and Best Set, and a Tony Award for Best Costumes. Did any awards mean more to you than others?*

MB: Yes: the Astaire Award, for Concept, Direction and Choreography.

I was thrilled to win it, and I had really wanted to win it. What a lovely thing to happen! Obviously Fred Astaire has always meant a lot to me. His widow was there for the award ceremony, and it was presented to me by Shirley MacLaine, who'd made a special trip to New York for the event. Of all the awards ceremonies, it was the most modest and the most pleasant. And I was very touched that Shirley said that my choreography represented the past, the present and the future. Adam won an Astaire Award too.

Obviously, the Tony Awards receive the most attention of all, and, coming last, there's a special sense of climax about them. The Tony committee, however, had deemed *Swan Lake* ineligible to win an award as a musical, or as a special event, or as a revival. So we were in an odd position. That was why, when I won Best Director of a Musical prize, I said in my speech, 'I'm astonished to win the award for Best Director of a Musical that's not a musical!' and then I made a face. I just meant it with gentle sarcasm; I meant that *Swan Lake* is musical theatre in the same way that dance shows like *Fosse!* are. The audience got my point, but I was reported in the press – in New York and London – as if I was simply astonished to have broken a category.

There was so much surprise that I'd won the Tonys that I almost felt I had to defend myself. If that makes me sound arrogant, please remember I'd just won the Best Director and Best Choreographer prizes at two other ceremonies. So I couldn't be *that* surprised to win the Tonys. I was, however, very proud.

10

Cinderella

1997

Idea

ALASTAIR MACAULAY: *You had choreographed* Cinderella *at the age of eight or thereabouts. What would* Cinderella *have been to you then? Had you seen a pantomime of it? Or the Disney film?*
MATTHEW BOURNE: At that point, the Disney film. *Cinderella*, as a pantomime, I remember seeing later: one, in the late 1970s – at what is now the Prince Edward Theatre – with Twiggy as Cinderella, Steptoe and Son as the ugly sisters, and Christopher Gable as the Prince.

AM: *As a stage dance work,* Cinderella *must have entered your life with Ashton's 1948 version for the Royal Ballet? It's still in repertory today.*
MB: Yes: around 1980. I saw it many times in that decade. The performances of Antoinette Sibley and Anthony Dowell – both then in their forties, and both glorious – were particular events. One of the things that was rewarding about seeing it again and again was getting to know the music, because at first the Prokofiev score seemed very difficult to me. It didn't seem like the kind of music I'd been used to in other ballets, but it grew on me. I loved Ashton's daring in having male performers as the Ugly Sisters; it was a surprise to see that in ballet at the Opera House, especially in a work otherwise along the lines of a fairytale classic.

But I was also very taken by Ashton's dance choreography in his *Cinderella*. I was fascinated by the changing patterns and intricate construction in the Star section; and I loved the Seasons solos, which seemed to express the four seasons so well. That, in a way, was an inspiration: expressing the essence of an idea – Spring, for example –

295

in short pure-dance solos. I also loved the little theatrical strokes, such as Fairy Autumn throwing leaves at the beginning of her solo. Particularly in *Cinderella*, I loved Ashton's use of the upper body and the back. In Cinderella's solo, there are little tips or arches backwards on pointe that are like nothing else in ballet. I thought that was so odd; I took great pleasure in things like that. He also made amazing theatrical effects by pure dance means. When Cinderella entered the ballroom coming down the staircase on pointe, looking straight into the air ahead of her – that made a big impression on me, as did the way, at midnight, that the whole population of the ballroom seemed to become like the mechanism of some chiming clock, with her trapped in the middle. I think now that getting to know that music was a big reason – maybe the main reason, as I go over it in my head now – for going back again and again. There's some sort of mystery, there's a dark side, to that music – which I tried to capture when I did eventually do it myself. I think it brought to Ashton's version a depth that made you want to see that again. There's a seriousness in the music that makes the choreography more alluring and mysterious.

AM: *In the meantime, during the 1980s or 1990s, had you seen any opera or theatre versions of* Cinderella?
MB: I saw the National Theatre pantomime during the mid-1980s, with Robert Stephens. During the last five years I've seen, on video, the Rodgers and Hammerstein musical. But nothing very inspirational.

The story itself has all you need. When you're looking for ideas, you just have to go back to the story, to make parts of it touching, parts of it magical: the transformation of Cinderella, her leaving for the ball.

AM: *Did the idea of choreographing* Cinderella *yourself – after your childhood version – only come to you after the success of* Swan Lake?
MB: Because I love it as a story, it's something I certainly would have decided to do sooner or later. I think the fact of the Ashton version being around always put me off doing it. It took the success of *Swan Lake* to give me the confidence, to feel that I could make any impression in a work that had already been done so well. In some ways, *Swan Lake* gave us a big problem: how could we follow a success like that? I wanted a production that would take us back to the old company way of working, with everyone intimately involved in their characters at the rehearsal stage, and I felt *Cinderella* would be good in that respect.

62 *Cinderella*. Publicity poster. Two famous photographs of the 1941 Blitz in London show St Paul's Cathedral silhouetted, as here, against the surrounding destruction, and the empty ballroom shoes outside the bombed Café de Paris.

All of us felt a great pressure on us after *Swan Lake.* There was a sense that we should do something on the same scale and should try to equal or surpass its success; people had already forgotten that our previous most successful productions, *Deadly Serious*, *Nutcracker* and *Highland Fling*, had been much smaller-scale, with far fewer performances. Once I thought of *Cinderella* as our next production, the idea of setting it in London during the War came quickly; and then a lot fell into place. The 1940s setting would make it just different enough, would make it my own. The story included plenty of different characters, which would be good for the company; and I would just use the music to inspire me.

AM: *Where did the wartime setting come from?*
MB: I read a book on Prokofiev and started reading anything I could find on *Cinderella* itself. What stood out was the time when it was written – that made me listen to the score again. Now I heard it very much as a 1940s piece, a wartime piece, and very filmic too. Prokofiev wrote famous film music, and loved films; you yourself have argued that some of his ballet music is really the best film music ever written. There were some bits that quite strongly put into my mind the idea of air-raids and bombings, especially just before she goes off to the ball. There's a section that sounds very much to me like lights flashing on and off, a feel of sirens. When I listened again to the end of the music for the nightmare chimes at midnight, I could feel, in the music, things crashing down, as if after a bomb. I thought, 'If we've got those strong points within the score that can say those things, then I think certainly we could build the rest of it around the idea.' Our *Cinderella* is still a story of romantic love, but it's romantic love set against a dark period in history, against all kinds of twentieth-century adversity; and it's not a story of Miss Perfect meeting Prince Perfect.

It also helped me that Ashton hadn't used all the music, especially in Act Three; I became very interested in the ideas that I got from the music he hadn't used. The deeper I went into it, the less I heard Ashton's version in the music. Now there are several sections in which I really can't remember what exactly he did with the music.

Apart from the music, I got more and more ideas just by thinking about and researching the War. I knew quite suddenly that my *Cinderella* would occur during the London Blitz, and I thought more and more about that. My parents were young then, so I'd heard about it from them; and I'd seen films. Certain images became very important, like the famous photograph taken after a bomb had dropped on the Café de Paris and, on top of the rubble, you see a pair of ballroom shoes. When you're working on a version of *Cinderella*, you have to think carefully about all kinds of crucial plot details: the shoes, the strokes of midnight, and so on. The more I reconceived these in the context of the Blitz, the more of an inner life and momentum my *Cinderella* began to have in my own mind.

AM: *I can think of one other Ashton ballet that connects to* Cinderella: *namely,* La Valse. *In 1996, I remember coming across you at a ballet evening at Covent Garden that ended with that 1958 Ashton ballet to Ravel's score; and you said to me, 'Yes, I love it so much, and I'm going to come back and bring Lez Brotherston to see it because I want part of my* Cinderella *to look like that.' This really surprised me, because many people complain about André Levasseur's costumes for Ashton's ballet – very old-style* Come Dancing, *they say; not many people find it, choreographically, one of Ashton's top-drawer ballets. Yet Anthony Dowell must share your taste, because it has been revived a surprising number of times during his régime as artistic director of the Royal Ballet.*

MB: It's a glorious piece. Very MGM, I find! It uses so many people and it's such a spectacle. But I also love anything waltzy. I don't think it's great choreography. I know people think it's a bit throwaway, but I do think it's a wonderful, glorious experience, and I feel that the atmosphere it creates is something quite special, especially the smoky atmosphere at the beginning.

AM: *It's not throwaway at all. It's very tightly choreographed.*
MB: It always feels like the best thing in the evening for me when I see it. There's an extraordinary doom-laden feeling amid all its jubilation, and that was what I had in my mind with *Cinderella* in the ballroom scene. I wanted it to look somewhat like a 1940s ballet in costumes, to look Beatonesque.

AM: *You eventually cast three dancers in the role of Cinderella, since the show ran for eight performances a week, but most publicity went to the first-cast Cinderella, who was Adam Cooper's partner, the Royal Ballet's young soloist, Sarah Wildor. At what point did you decide to use her?*

MB: Quite early on. I had liked her dancing very much in a lot of pieces at the Royal Ballet, and she stood out in a lot of minor roles, with an individual approach to movement. I always felt she was a star, and had seen her do leading roles in several ballets: MacMillan's *Manon*, where it was good to see her handle the sexuality so well; MacMillan's *The Invitation*, which she danced so well with Adam. And I loved the quality of movement she showed in Ashton roles: Titania in *The Dream*, the ballerina in *Rhapsody*. Having met her, I felt that she was not your average ballerina type. She's from Southend; she can be quite plain-speaking and down-to-earth. Things like that impressed me about her.

AM: *So, as you're starting to cast your production, you decide to use Sarah Wildor and Adam Cooper from the Royal Ballet, the Royal Ballet School-trained Will Kemp – whom you liked so much doing the Swan that you decided to give him the role of the Angel – and the famous dramatic ballerina Lynn Seymour, who had worked so well in your company in* Swan Lake. *That means that the four leading roles in your work, in the first cast, are taken by dancers from the Royal Ballet or Royal Ballet School stable. This is quite a change of dance material for you.*

MB: I can't say I was ever conscious of trying to get more ballet people, let alone more Royal Ballet people, into the company. It has been misinterpreted quite a lot, both in and outside the company. 'What is this company then?' people have said. 'I thought that we were building up something to do with a certain type of dancer doing the kind of work that we do; but then we bring in all these guests. Why can't you build up people from within and create your own stars?'

I can understand this feeling, but I didn't see it like that. For one thing, I think I have always built up people within the company, where it seems appropriate: Scott Ambler, Etta Murfitt, Maxine Fone, Ben Wright are just the leading examples. Will Kemp may have come from the Royal Ballet School, but the Royal Ballet wasn't going to give him a job. He took the risk of joining our company – nobody there encouraged him, quite the opposite – and now he has achieved greater fame and larger roles with us than any of his contemporaries whom the Royal Ballet School favoured more. Probably, he wouldn't have been right for the Royal; and almost certainly none of his contemporaries would be right for Adventures in Motion Pictures. As I've said before,

63 *Cinderella*. Sarah Wildor as Cinderella; Lynn Seymour as her Stepmother. Pre-production photograph.

most of the ballet people – Royal or otherwise – who now audition for us are just wrong for my work, whatever their strengths may be in other directions.

I remain very interested in ballet and hope there will be other ballets to follow; but the heart of my work for the foreseeable future is with Adventures in Motion Pictures, and I'm quite clear that there is a strong distinction between what it does and what ballet companies do. My work with Adam, Sarah and Lynn came about because they expressed an interest in my work. They happen to be the kind of exceptional artist who can commute between the two genres.

Lynn, after all, is the prime example – being the foremost dance actress of the last forty years. I always think she's one of those few dancers who's completely accepted by the whole world of dance, like Baryshnikov. Whereas a lot of contemporary dancers don't get the point of such ballerinas as Antoinette Sibley or Darcey Bussell, they do with Lynn Seymour. They completely respect and admire her, and it seems to me that her home now is in this kind of work. If any company can assure further life on stage for Lynn now, I hope ours is the one. Likewise, Adam and Sarah are known as the up-and-coming dancer-actors of their generation.

Sarah apart, much of my policy in casting *Cinderella* was to give roles – find roles, invent roles, in some cases – for performers who had made an impression with *Swan Lake* or other AMP works. I knew I was going to have the character of the Pilot (the hero) played by Adam and Will, just as they had worked on the same role in *Swan Lake*. I also tried to have Simon Cooper in that role: we needed three casts, and he had worked very well as the Swan. He had had real rapport with Saranne Curtin as the Queen in *Swan Lake*; he's very tall and would have been, temperamentally, a good partner for her; but I think he didn't want to work on a production alongside his brother Adam and endure the inevitable sibling comparisons from the very beginning of the production.

Then, because Will had had particular success in *Swan Lake*, and because Emily (Pearcy) had become very popular with audiences as the Prince's Girlfriend, I wanted to give them roles in the first cast of *Cinderella*. We had won a new public, who had favourite performers, and I wanted to make a show that would give them a reason to come back and see it with multiple casts. So I purposely put Will in that first cast, with his own role; likewise Emily as a sister, and Scott Ambler, Ben Wright and Andrew Walkinshaw (who's not really a dancer, but had been such a good performer as the young Prince in *Swan Lake*) as brothers. Whether or not everybody noticed, *Cinderella* was to do, not with me moving in the direction of the Royal Ballet, but with returning Adventures in Motion Pictures to a more intimate, ensemble way of working.

AM: *At what point did you decide you were going to have a male angel?*
MB: Oh, quite early on. I knew I wanted something a bit different, and I was conscious of everyone expecting, after *Swan Lake*, some kind of gender-reversal. I can't tell you how often I heard the question 'Is Cinderella going to be a woman?' when we first said we were doing it. Well, I wanted the heroine female and the hero male. But when I realized that I didn't like the idea of a fairy godmother as a character, I thought of changing the gender there. I knew I did like the idea of a guardian angel.

AM: *Well, you're in good company. Rossini's Cinderella opera, La Cenerentola, has a male guardian angel too: a bass role.*

MB: I also wanted to create something that was, in a way, asexual. I didn't want the audience to feel that there was any kind of competition between this other man in her life and the man she falls in love with. So we tried not to make him of sexual interest to her. But there is in him a sort of a caring, guiding force that's ambiguous: it could be for good or ill, but it's fateful. He saves her from the bombing, but then he is also around when the bomb does happen; and he enables her to find out new things about herself.

We thought of having him turn up in several different guises. That proved too hard to manage throughout; but in Act Three he also appears in the guise of the psychiatrist. I also wanted to give the sense, at the beginning of Act Three, that he's like the Angel of Death, and, at the end of Act Two, that his dance is bringing down the buildings all around. So there are two sides to the Angel, and that's what we worked on when we first started to do the movement for him.

The first time he appears, in Act One, is when Cinderella is being tormented by the family. The scene turns into a sort of nightmare, where they've all got invites that they're waving at her and pretending to give to her only to snatch them away. So she screams. I said to the three girls playing Cinderella, 'It's as if you're crying for help', and the Angel appears, suddenly, at the top of the fireplace.

AM: *Does it occur to you that – as you describe it – that's rather like what happens in some traditional* Nutcrackers? *Clara has been pursued by the mice, she screams for help, and then Drosselmayer appears – in some productions (including the 1892 original) at the top of the clock.*

MB: I hadn't thought of that. But it's true.

He then hypnotizes her, in a way, and leads her to the door – whereupon the Pilot enters and breaks the spell. We return to real time, and Cinderella looks after the Pilot; but we sense that it's the Angel who's brought him to her.

AM: *Cinderella always has stepsisters, but you chose to make a big role for her stepmother, who is not in all, or even most, versions of the story. You also gave her stepbrothers. How come?*

MB: One of the reasons behind the casting of the show was to go back to what I'd done in AMP's smaller shows, by having more intimate, family scenes. At the same time, I wanted in other scenes – the ball-room, for example – to use the larger scale and big dance impact we'd shown in *Swan Lake*. So I wanted, in the family scenes, more roles than just the usual two stepsisters. I had a lot of people to cast, and I thought it'd be good to surround Cinderella with a bigger family than usual. It would give us more characters and more ideas to play with, and would provide the chance for more people – with two or three casts in each role – to have a go at creating and playing a character; and a large, noisy family would create a context in which Cinderella would keep being submerged.

AM: *When did you decide on such wartime details as the fact that the hero is a pilot?*
MB: At one point, we thought of making the Angel look like a pilot – because of the connotations of the air, the sky, from which he comes and through which he travels. But then, as we thought of the various armed forces in the war, we decided to make the hero a pilot because the Air Force was the most glamorous. Think how many World War Two movies are to do with the Air Force. We were looking for who

64 *Cinderella*. Adam Cooper as the Pilot. Pre-production photograph.

would be Cinderella's dream man, and we thought a pilot would be the sort of person she might idolize. The Nureyev version of *Cinderella* is all about film history and film stars; and I think that, if that version hadn't existed, I – with my interest in film – might well have made Cinderella's hero/boyfriend a film star. It's a logical idea, which Nureyev – although I don't enjoy his actual choreography – pursued intelligently as a producer.

I was also inspired by the film, *A Matter of Life and Death*, which furnished my *Cinderella* with quite a lot of ideas. David Niven was the model, costume-wise and look-wise. The Pilot's moustache and whole persona come from Niven.

AM: *You mention Nureyev's version. Tell me what other versions of the Prokofiev ballet* Cinderella *you studied.*
MB: I saw Nureyev's version on TV or video. Likewise Maguy Marin's version, which I thought was so beautiful. There's not a great deal of dancing of any kind in it. It's like a dolls' house come to life. The whole thing's done with masks. It's terribly endearing. The characters become like children in a way, and the whole production has a wonderful childlike quality to it; but the Prokofiev music is edited a great deal, and an echo is put in at times. I'm not keen on the Nureyev version; I think it's overblown, and there are whole sections I really dislike. There's an incredibly long pas de deux in Act Three – when Cinderella and the hero have met again – that's just waffle; and the story doesn't make complete sense either.

AM: Cinderella *was originally a Soviet ballet. Did you do any homework on any Soviet productions?*
MB: I had a video of one odd little version. It was quite fun, but I didn't really get much from it. What I haven't been able to see is the original Lavrovsky production. Prokofiev composed his music with Galina Ulanova in mind, and – even though no Soviet version of *Cinderella* has had the impact the Lavrovsky/Ulanova version of *Romeo and Juliet* has had – I'm sure many features of the music would fall into place if one could see the original production.

AM: *Still, your production is often most successful when it hears something quite new in the score. Perhaps the individual biggest hit dance of your production occurs in Act One. It's a dance conceived by Prokofiev for Cinderella alone in the kitchen: it's always known in British*

*ballet circles as 'the broom dance' because Ashton has her dancing
with a broom as if it were her imaginary partner. You, however, have
her dance with a tailor's dummy – who suddenly comes to life as the
Pilot. Now he's as stiff and immobile as a dummy, now he's partnering
her as a dream lover. It's nicely ambiguous, and it goes like a dream in
the theatre. Did you conceive that beforehand? Or did it just emerge
that way through rehearsals?*

MB: The Dummy Dance, as we call it, emerged out of a conscious decision to build up the part of the Pilot. Adam was cast in the role, and he
was, with Lynn, our big star. He didn't demand anything, but I was
conscious that he needed more to do. So we thought: 'Well, how can
we introduce his character into Act One – when it normally appears
only in Acts Two and Three? And how can we give them a duet early
on, when they shouldn't really even meet until Act Two?' So we came
up with that idea of an image that was in her mind – the image of the
man that she's dancing with rather than him himself.

The logic of it is that she's already met him briefly, when he took
shelter in the house, earlier in the act. He has obviously been injured,
comes to the house, and knocks on the door. She shelters him in a side
room. Meanwhile the family come back, put on the gramophone, have
the dancing lesson and all that business; and then the stepmother finds
him in the house. She's suspicious of Cinderella and realizes something's going on. So the Pilot comes out and introduces himself.

The stepmother throws him out of the house; she's livid that Cinderella has been harbouring some injured member of the armed forces;
and that's when she's left on her own. She sees him in the dummy, does
the Dummy Dance; and the dummy comes to life. Now, when Cinderella's alone, she dreams of him, not as a sick man but as a romantic
hero. This dream image of him will return throughout Act Two. Only
in Act Three do we again see the Pilot as he really is.

AM: *You never thought of having a Buttons in your* Cinderella?
MB: Cinderella's friend? Well, one of my original ideas was that she
had imaginary friends. She was a lonely child whom everybody
ignored, but she had imaginary friends that she would conjure up.
Maybe they were friends from long ago who were now evacuated to
the country or to other countries. They would have been in white and
grey, dressed as wartime children; and they would have appeared in
the room from time to time and would have played with her, or danced

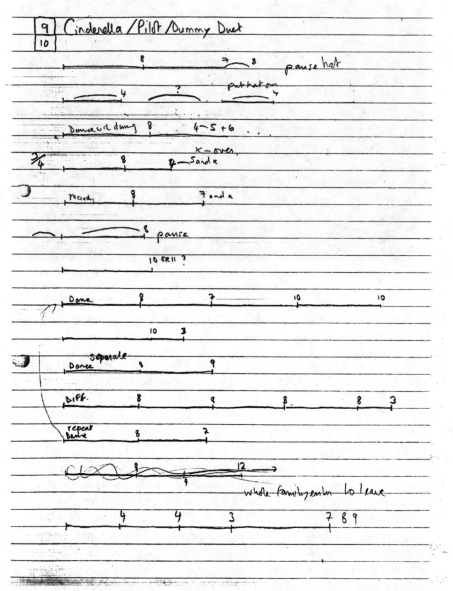

65 *Cinderella*. From Bourne's annotated breakdown of the score for Act One. The 'Cinderella/Pilot/Dummy' duet takes place to what is often known as Cinderella's 'broom dance' in more traditional versions of the ballet, notably Frederick Ashton's.

66 *Cinderella*. Adam Cooper and Sarah Wilder in the Act One 'Dummy' duet. Rehearsal photograph.

with her. I really liked the idea, but it would have been one, possibly confusing, element too many on stage.

AM: *As you describe it, it sounds rather like another MacMillan ballet – Solitaire – in which the heroine has these companions, who may be dream figures but who always leave her alone in the final resort.*
MB: I haven't seen that, but another piece of his that has grown-ups playing children, *Playground*, was one of the earliest pieces I saw, and I very much enjoyed it. I loved all the psychology of it, and it was brilliantly performed; but, in particular, it made me interested in adults playing children. It had a definite influence on my *Nutcracker*; and in *Cinderella* I saw these evacuee children a bit like that – in shorts and little dresses.

It's really the Angel who brings the fantasy into her life. Once I'd given her the dance with the dummy, I thought, 'Well, we can't have another thing that happens in her fantasy life before she goes to the ball,' which is then followed by the family, having dressed to go to the ball or New Year's Eve party that they're invited to, all leaving the house – leaving her alone again. Now the Angel returns and entices her to follow him outside into the street; but at some point within the dummy duet she has lost her glasses. She doesn't see so well.

AM: *Had you always conceived her as bespectacled?*
MB: Yes – we wanted her to be quite frumpy.

AM: *The ballroom in which she – transformed into a glamorous dream image herself – dances with this dreamy war hero in Act Two gets bombed.*

In Act Three, she's had a breakdown; and the Pilot, who has a breakdown himself while looking for her, finds her when they're both in hospital. You make a lot of the hospital scenes, in which Cinderella is isolated from all her former life. Somehow, as we're talking about it, this connects to the third act of another ballet, one that Sarah Wildor has danced at Covent Garden: MacMillan's Anastasia. *The girl, who is the child of an important family – in this case, the Romanov dynasty – is seen in hospital. She's lost her home, everyone questions her identity, she's in torment. Was MacMillan's final hospital act anywhere in your mind?*
MB: I think it was, a bit. Especially since I'd seen Sarah in it fairly recently beforehand; but I'm always drawn to hospital and medical scenes with doctors and nurses, and I think MacMillan has been as well. We've got a bit of that in *Swan Lake* – the Prince having sinister treatments at the beginning of Act Four – which I choreographed before I ever saw *Anastasia*.

I do hate hospitals. I'm very frightened of going to the doctor or the dentist – anything like that. So probably that's why they keep reappearing in my work.

AM: *The words* film noir *were often bandied around in the publicity and reviews of your production. Did you really mean that genre as an inspiration for your* Cinderella?
MB: No. I'm not an enormous fan of *film noir* as a genre – though I'm not sure precisely what I understand by the term. I know a few, like *Double Indemnity*; and, if this qualifies, *Mildred Pearce*. I like them – but they're not an area I'm particularly drawn to. Usually *film noir* has a sort of dark, murderous or sinister storyline. I know my *Cinderella* has bleak elements, and certainly it has strong cinematic elements, but I don't think they're what real film buffs would call *noir*.

Several war movies did shape my idea of *Cinderella*. I've mentioned

67 *Brief Encounter*. Celia Johnson and Trevor Howard in David Lean's wartime film (written by Noël Coward). The railway-station setting recurrent in the film helped to inspire the final scene of Bourne's third act, and near the end two minor characters are briefly seen to be re-enacting Johnson's and Howard's last farewell.

A Matter of Life and Death; there were others. Another idea I wanted to make at the end of the show is that Cinderella and the Pilot become part of the bigger story of the War. Their story begins to fade, and what takes over is lots of other little stories of other similar couples on the same railway platform. Well, this was a cue – as in *Town and Country* – for a replay of *Brief Encounter*, of course! Celia Johnson and Trevor Howard, or the characters they play in that film, are just another couple on the same platform as Cinderella and the Pilot.

The whole feeling of the War – as I've understood it, partly from movies – led me to stress the intense, fleeting, dreamlike quality of wartime romance and fantasy, but also to show that these people were not really glamorous. They were ordinary mortals under stress in difficult circumstances. At the end, Cinderella and her Pilot – married – go off on the train together; but, though we've seen them be glamorous in their dream lives, they really aren't starry people now. They're just people at the station with a lot of other people. Cinderella's final scene with her father is emotional, but not a big demonstrative number. The feeling should be that she and the Pilot are perfect for each other. Nothing heroic about either of them. He's pleasant, but dressed quite drably; and so is she. They don't have to be a prince and a princess to have a happy ending feel to it. It's more touching, in a way.

Then the Angel returns. She more or less thanks him, and he is happy to have brought them together; as happy as a not-quite-human Angel can be. Whereupon he promptly sees his next charge – the next girl he's going to look after – a similar-looking girl. Hopefully, you haven't noticed her until that point. She's been downstage, reading a book very quietly, for ages. She's quite sad-looking – and the Angel is advancing towards her. The train bearing Cinderella and her Pilot is just departing, as the curtain falls.

Scenario

ALASTAIR MACAULAY: *When did you start to prepare the production?*
MATTHEW BOURNE: I was working on it over the 1996–7 Christmas period while *Swan Lake* was still in the West End, and then when we took it to LA. But I think the initial meetings with Lez Brotherston – whom I always knew I wanted to design it – had begun in the summer of 1996. There were four of us involved in planning this production, and I had regular meetings with the other three: Scott Ambler, Adam Cooper and Lez.

I think that at first Lez thought it was odd to have Adam around. He thought of him only as a dancer; but I had several reasons. One: Adam had quietly had some very good ideas on *Swan Lake*, ideas that played very important roles in the eventual production. Two: he really seemed to enjoy that aspect of it. Three: since he was making a decision, at the time, about whether to leave the Royal Ballet or not, I thought that this – because it would give him something he could get his teeth into – would help him discover whether there was some kind of life outside the Royal that he could enjoy.

Meanwhile, I spent an equal amount of time working on the production myself. I would then present the ideas that I had to the other three, and see what they felt. Sometimes what I gave them, in fact, was not my ideas but my problems: 'I don't know what to do with this piece of music.' Again, that's where Adam can be very helpful. Whereas Scott and Lez had to get to know the score before they could be equally helpful in that area, I had only to say, 'What are we going to do with the Seasons music?' for Adam to understand completely what was concerning me. Largely because of the Ashton production, he knew the music well already. In the case of the Seasons, for example, he knew straightaway that they were a suite of four variations composed for solo dancers, he knew the nature of each piece of music. So he understood – because we weren't going to bring on a divertissement of Season fairies, and because we were going to keep the story going through this music that was essentially plotless – all the specific problems. Straightaway he would discuss the tempo and character of each piece of music with me and start to come up with ideas, or with further questions.

AM: *Take me through the basic narrative structure that you arrived at.*
MB: Act One is divided up a lot, because the music demands it. So we started with a Prologue. Then 'Meet the Family': a basic introduction to each character. A first solo for Cinderella follows, when she dances with one of the sister's fur jackets. Cinderella tries to get her father, who is wheelchair-bound to recognize her and to give her some attention for the problems she has. Then comes the nightmarish sequence when the Stepmother and stepsisters and stepbrothers all torment her with their invitations to the ball. When Cinderella cries for help, the Angel appears. He brings the Pilot into the house.

Now all the various sisters' and brothers' boyfriends and girlfriends arrive. There's a whole scene using those characters. The mother puts on the gramophone, and gets them to dance her way. (We don't use recorded music here, of course – it goes on being played by the orchestra in the pit – but the characters on stage behave as if it was coming from the wind-up 78 record-player. All this is to the 'dancing lesson' scene that Prokofiev wrote for Cinderella's stepsisters.) The Stepmother finds the Pilot and throws him out. When Cinderella is alone again, she has a fantasy duet with a dummy. The family leave for the party.

The Angel reappears. The sequence which follows – which we call 'the blackout' – includes gas-mask dogs, as we called them (characters with snout-like gas masks on); a dance for airmen and planes that becomes more aggressive and turns into a dance of bombers; various imagery of the Blitz; then the air-raid itself, which goes into the 'departure waltz', in which Cinderella finally leaves with the Angel in the sidecar of his motor-bike.

Act Two starts with a 'back to life' dance. A bomb has dropped, and now the bodies are coming back to life. They're couples who've been in the ballroom. Then the family makes its entrance; the Stepmother's drunk. Several dances emerge from this situation. The Pilot, now glamorous and confident, enters with two colleagues; they do a 'heroes' dance'. The Stepmother is very keen on him now, and makes him dance with her, in which everyone else follows. Cinderella arrives with the Angel: the grand waltz. Because it's all a dream scene, Cinderella's father now appears; he too is upright, composed and dignified. The ballroom couples – the blue couples, as we call them – dance, and Cinderella dances with the 'blue' men. There's a 'Refreshments' episode – which is basically the drunk dance of the family.

Now, outside the club, Cinderella and the Pilot have their big duet; and finally, back in the ballroom, the famous waltz comes in again. This leads up to midnight and the falling of the bomb. The Pilot finds Cinderella's shoe by the wrecked entrance to her house.

Act Three starts with the Angel of Death's dance. The people of London are living in fear, and the Angel passes amongst them, signalling their deaths. Most of the company are in the scene. As the Angel touches or passes these people in the street, they leave the stage. It suggests that, when he's touched them, they're dead.

We see the Pilot on the street with Cinderella's shoe, looking for her. There's an underground scene in which he's accosted by a prostitute. Up on the Embankment, he gets into trouble; then to the hospital. Cinderella has a memory solo, and the family comes to visit her. The Pilot is brought into the room next door. They find each other.

Finally, the Railway Station. You see various individual stories, then the family farewell, particularly between Cinderella and her father. She and the Pilot (newly-weds) depart on the train as the curtain falls.

AM: *You mentioned the idea you had of the Angel appearing in the Prologue. This wasn't the only idea you dropped, was it?*
MB: There was quite a big sub-plot at first, which we rehearsed and took into the preview performances before scrapping it. It was mainly a red herring. According to this sub-plot, beginning several years before the piece starts on stage, Cinderella, as a young girl, had seen or suspected that the Stepmother had killed her mother at a New Year's Eve party in her house; and that the Stepmother had got away with it, and had married Cinderella's father. The shock of this incident had

made Cinderella lose her voice. She'd then blotted it out of her memory. This created a relationship of serious antagonism between Cinderella and her Stepmother; but we also thought that it could explain why the Stepmother kept Cinderella away from society and wanted to hide her away when guests came round.

So we had a different prologue originally, which was great – except that nobody understood it! It opened with a gun-shot. Then through the gauze you saw the Stepmother (Lynn Seymour), standing halfway down the stairs in a fur coat. The picture you had was of her on the steps with a sort of smoking gun – while the mother was dead on the floor, by the fireplace. The clock was at midnight. Then the midnight chimes really rang out, and you saw Cinderella, as a little girl in a nightdress, in the background. Obviously, she had run in and seen this. It was a very tight scenario, which explained all kinds of details throughout the story. We'll talk about how and why we changed it later on.[1]

There were several other details that I wasn't always sure about. Having the father come to the ball in Act Two, for example: I thought that might be confusing, and I considered cutting it at one point. I kept it, largely for the reason that I wanted things to keep happening to Cinderella in the ballroom. I didn't want it just to be a scene of dancing without story; in my version, events have to keep occurring, even in the ballroom. In the event, it works well and helps to clinch the dream-like nature of the whole scene.

Something else that I want to make clearer when I stage *Cinderella* again in 1999 is the whole blackout sequence outside the house towards the end of Act One. The idea of it was that she is following the Angel through the streets of London. We see it through her eyes – but her eyesight is bad. She hasn't got her glasses on, and we're in the blackout. So things that she would normally see on the street now become frightening. They take on different meanings to her. She feels threatened, that she's being attacked, perhaps. But we didn't make that clear enough in the London production, and I think it could be done a lot more clearly. We had people with torches to begin with. They were like wardens – that's fairly straightforward – but at the next stage, in which the people in gas masks appear to her like dogs with snouts, we need her to see their transformation. I think that can be done. We'll see. The whole blackout sequence should be more frightening.

1 See pp. 349–51.

AM: *Now, here you were working in opposition to, or despite, Prokofiev's intentions for this music.*

MB: Very much so. There are passages when I think *Cinderella* is hard to choreograph even when you are following Prokofiev's intentions; but this is the passage when it was at first hard to proceed because we were going against them.

AM: *It can't help that Prokofiev has anyway a peculiar conception of Spring and Autumn in particular: both quite aggressive and harsh.*

MB: But what I began to hear in the music was his emphasis on time. Those two Seasons have a quality of hectic speed; and since the whole ballet attends to the importance of time, leading up to the huge chimes of midnight at the end of Act Two, I began to hear how these scenes could have a different meaning. I also heard the qualities of flight and aggression in certain parts of the Seasons' music, and I began to see how I could use those.

I'm still not satisfied with what we achieved there. During previews, people kept saying to me, 'Cut it! If it doesn't work, cut it!' But, stubbornly, I was determined not to cut anything.

AM: *Instead, you not only use all four Season variations, you also use all the intervening music that Prokofiev wrote which is often cut in stage productions of the ballet.*

MB: Actually, those sections were quite helpful for moving the story on. I found it easier to hear them as action music rather than as clean-cut dances.

At the end, in the coda music, the Angel takes her on to another level, to a beautiful place, perhaps somewhere in the sky. They're journeying; but then reality breaks through again. We have an air raid, a realistic situation with people running for shelter as she tries to get back to her house. As the street clears, she's at her front door again, but she can't get in. You have a sense of the planes coming towards her house, and she can see them in the sky. Just as she gets into the house, a bomb hits it. We have an explosion with lights flashing. Just as the doorway in the house moves away, you're left with the image of the Angel having caught her, having saved her from death.

The idea – as in *A Matter of Life and Death* – is that she's suspended between living and dying as Act One ends. The music continues, and we've gone into some kind of half-life world in a starry place, with the moon in the background. She has been knocked senseless and we're

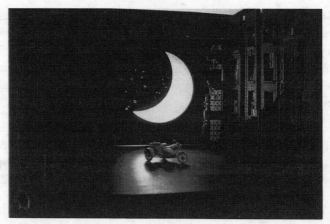

68 *Cinderella*. Set design by Lez Brotherston for the end of Act One.
The Angel drives the motorbike, with Cinderella radiant in his side-carriage,
around the stage and off as the curtain falls.

suddenly going off into her unconscious world; but the Angel has saved her, and then we go into the final waltz sequence. This again involves the airmen, who are part of the Angel's world – they could be dead pilots – and she ends up, in her fantasy, being driven off in the sidecar of the Angel's motorbike. I thought it was important to have some kind of vehicle; for me, it wouldn't be *Cinderella* unless she was driven offstage magically into a new world.

AM: *Act Two starts with the noise of a great bomb going off.*
MB: Yes. A snap blackout and a very big, surprise explosion, which makes people jump quite considerably – they're not expecting that. It's a very effective start to the act.

The Angel is soon visible. He's seemingly in control of all these goings-on. We did ask ourselves, 'If all this act is Cinderella's dream, why isn't she there at the beginning? Or why isn't she there with the Angel?' The answer was that, when you're in a dream, you're not necessarily in it yourself. You don't see yourself in a dream; you are within it.

Now the couples, who, seemingly dead, are lying on the floor and up against benches – come back to life. The sense here is that these blue couples are the spirits of dead lovers who have been killed in the war. The men are dressed like soldiers and the women have versions of 1940s ballroom dresses – which also look rather like 1940s ballet costume, with lots of tulle. I didn't at first want them to seem grotesque, but actually people liked that aspect of the production, and we gave them a more grotesque make-up. When we do it again, we may break down their costumes even more, to make them seem more dusty and to hint more at the bombing.

Then the family enters. Originally, they entered wrapped in blankets and holding little mugs. In her mind, they had been on their way to the New Years Eve party but had been ushered into this ballroom for shelter from the bombing on the streets. It was a nice image, but, after a while, we realized we didn't need it. It seemed to make more sense, in a dream, that they'd turned up to this ball, which they had an invitation to; but there was no one there, it was all destroyed. So they're wondering whether they've come to the right place, but they decide to make the most of it. The Stepmother's had a few drinks and she encourages them to get to know everyone – 'Since we're here, we'll have a good time!' – and there are various flirtations that go on, not least a one-way one between her and the Pilot. There's a feeling that another bomb might be about to drop at one point and there's a lot of frightened running around. Especially for the people who are already dead, there's quite a lot of fear; or rather a memory of their deaths. The fear came out of the music. One piece of the score begins with a sort of rumble, which leads into a series of false entries. So all the blue couples keep running up to the stairs – waiting for the entry of the Prince, the Pilot – but there's no one there, at least the first time, so they come back and go into a dance. Then they run to the stairs again, but – cheap joke! – it's just one of the family coming in, doing up his flies. The third time they run to the stairs, the Pilot finally does enter, with two other heroes, one from the Navy and one from the Army. Everyone applauds. The Stepmother and the sisters take a liking to them, the stepmother particularly to the Pilot. So then we get a duet – to a mazurka – for the Stepmother and the Pilot.

The Angel enters, and this previously ugly place becomes magical, with lots of twinkly fairy lights – and now Cinderella enters. The blue couples elaborate on the feeling of this situation by doing a series of partnered moves to do with covering the eyes and then having things revealed to you. What's revealed to Cinderella at the end of this is the Pilot. There's a fade from the Angel into the Pilot: the Angel backs away into the Pilot; they turn around, back to back, and then she's looking at the Pilot. The idea is that the Angel can become, or conjure up, the Pilot: that he can provide Cinderella with what she really wants. This leads into the waltz and back to a form of reality within all the non-reality; and, for Cinderella and the Pilot, a 'getting to know you' kind of dance. We wanted to have quite a realistic relationship, some real sexual chemistry between them, but starting off formally. He's smoking at the beginning, to make it fairly casual.

Then the father enters. He is in his wheelchair, as he has been all through Act One. We characterized him as someone who'd been a hero himself in World War One – and was injured in that war or had mental and physical problems resulting from it. In Act One, he'd stopped recognizing Cinderella any more. He becomes lost to her in many ways; but now, in the fantasy world of Act Two, the Angel brings him on, back to his former self as a dashing father-figure in full uniform; and he dances with her. It's all as if her dream has come true: a wish-fulfilment fantasy within a fantasy. As I said, I did worry that this didn't forward the plot – in fact, it interrupted it, since she and the Pilot had only just met – but in the end, this scene stayed because otherwise she and the Pilot would leave the ball too soon.

AM: *There's a subliminal psychological connection of all the male elements in her life falling into place at the same time: father and lover; which all works because of having a male guardian angel.*

MB: Yes; and, during her dance with her father, the family re-enter and start to wonder, 'Who is she? Who is he? Do we recognize her? Or him?' But they've all drunk a lot by that point, so they're not thinking clearly, and it's all: 'Oh no, it can't be him. Or is it?' She eventually flaunts her relationship in their face and exits with the Pilot, to which the family do a drunken 'reaction' dance – to the galumphing music that Ashton uses as the 'runaround' music for the two Ugly Sisters in his version. In our version, it's a drunken kind of jive, led by the Stepmother. Basically, when she's had a few, she's nicer than she is normally! She lets her hair down and has a good time.

That gives us another 'wipe', because we have to do a scene change there. They come downstage, then move across; and, as they leave, we're somewhere else. The set has moved, and a few things have gone: the piano and the side benches. A sign that was outside the ballroom has come down inside, in front of the stairway. Cinderella and the Pilot are seen coming down the stairs – with fewer clothes on now. We did originally have her dress coming off in the ballroom – which was interesting because, in the dance before she leaves the ballroom, she was surrounded by blue couples, and when they disappeared again, she walked out of the dress, left it behind, and made her exit. The top half was obviously the same. But it didn't quite work: it didn't feel in character.

AM: *Is that true in general? That, even if a theatrical effect you've tested works on stage, you will jettison it if it doesn't have emotional or psychological truth?*
MB: Yes, absolutely. So then there's the pas de deux outside the ballroom. The idea here always was that this was something intimate that happens in a private place. It becomes sexual; they end up on the ground, with signs of a post-coital feeling. He was even going to light a cigarette at the end, originally, though we dropped that when we found it looked a bit crass. Instead, they both start to go to sleep. One of my original ideas for the set here included an old bed with springs hanging out of it. The idea was that they were going to go back to this place; but it just wasn't possible to design a set like that.

Then the Angel re-enters, looking more menacing, as if to say: 'This isn't the right time for this.' He brings her back to some form of reality about her situation. She tries to wake up the Pilot, but she can't wake him up: it's the beginning of some sort of nightmare. She's asking for help but, instead, the Angel lets her relive bad memories: originally these included the shooting of her mother; her father being pushed back into his wheelchair, feeble again; and all the family showing their invitations and snatching them away. The Angel even shows her an image of the Pilot with one of her sisters. 'It was all a joke, and not true.' At the same time, there's a macabre business going on with the blue couples: lots of killing gestures, and bodies hanging on things and being carried: all Blitz-type imagery.

Actually, that material was one of the things in the production I'm very pleased with, but in the London production we never lit it well enough to show all the images that are going on. There's a bit where they all become wheelchairs, for example. Eventually, after all this nightmare, the Angel brings down the set. The buildings start crashing in. Smoke and bombs are going off. At the very end, where we really have gone back to reality, the Pilot is back looking the way he did in Act One – rather than the cleaned-up version. His uniform is dirty, he's injured again, and he's coming back to the house where he met her –

only to find that it's been bombed. He finds her shoe in the rubble of her front door: the place she was when we last left her in reality. He's left wondering, as we were at the end of Act One: is she dead?

But you do see a body being carried away on a stretcher behind him. It is her, and she has got the other shoe on. Again, this could be better lit, but at some performances it caught the light perfectly. Meanwhile, in the background there's a homeless woman in hysterics (Etta Murfitt giving an Oscar-winning performance – worth the price of a ticket alone).

Images of mother with gun, brother with toy gun, Pilot with other woman, father in wheelchair, family with invites – those were all ideas.

AM: *Ideas you used?*
MB: Yes, we used all of them; they were all there.

AM: *Right at the end of Act Two?*
MB: Yes, but this will change now.

AM: *You used the music for the chimes of midnight for all of the Blitz scene. Is there any emphasis on midnight in your production?*
MB: Yes, though there could be more. Our original plan was that it wasn't just any midnight; it was New Year's Eve. Part of the set for the ball was a very big 'Happy New Year' sign, but it was so dominant and ugly that we cut it. The programme says that it's New Year's Eve. Originally, we wanted to establish that her mother had been killed on New Year's Eve, at midnight, years ago.

We have clocks throughout, including the face of Big Ben: I love how that looks, and it feels all the more wonderful to have achieved it on a limited budget; but there's no sense of 'You must be home by midnight', or any of that sort of thing. The sense that time is limited for her is expressed in other ways in our production: because this is the Blitz, because life itself could end any moment, there's the constant possibility that 'Your time is up'.

At the end of Act Three, the clock in the railway station is just past midnight. We've moved on.

AM: *As I think you know, there are a few anachronisms and errors in your account of the War. I'm no expert on these matters, but it's amazing how many people, even of my generation, know very precise details of the life of those years.*
MB: Yes. With some of these, I suppose I knew I was taking a slight

historical liberty. For example, I wanted to have one stepsister involved with an American GI even though the Americans weren't actually over here at this period of the War. *Cinderella* is set during the height of the Blitz, which was 1941 – though the Blitz returned in 1944 for a while when there were GIs around, and you could claim it is set in that year.

In general, though, I try to be correct. However, we had a huge post-bag from people – even old generals – correcting us about insignia and things on hats. Actually, what we heard most about was the railway carriage. It has 'Second Class' written on it, but, during the War, there were only First and Third. I just passed them all on to Lez: 'You've done this wrong.'

AM: *You begin Act Three with several musical items which Ashton cut from his version.*
MB: Act Three of Ashton's *Cinderella* has always felt too short to me, especially as the story resolves itself fairly early on. So it was good to use all the music he didn't tackle but that Prokofiev composed for the Prince's journey around the world in quest of Cinderella – I really liked all that music as well. I thought it had such a lot of drive and energy. We had to spend some time, obviously, on how to adapt the music to our London version, since one part of the music describes the Prince's oriental journey and another part his trip to Spain.

Ours starts with a dance for the Angel and the people on the streets of London: the image of him as the Angel of Death. There's a 'Who's next?' feel to it: 'Who will he touch next?' At the end of that section, the Pilot reappears with the shoe. He's obviously a bit disturbed. There's a dance on the street – originally it was going to involve pas-sers-by also – as if he is some madman getting strange reactions from other people; but, to be honest, we ran out of time, so that it ended up being a solo. That worked well too, because it suggested that he was addressing imaginary people in his mind, like someone talking to him-self out loud. (Rick Fisher did some very nice lighting effects to heighten that effect. All the windows that surround the stage had a suggestion of fire in them – like flashing lights. So it was all a bit oppressive. The rain was coming down too, so it had a nice atmo-sphere at the beginning. Actually, the visual atmosphere throughout this act worked very well.)

Then the Pilot runs down into a tube station. This is to the Spanish music – which has a castanet effect that we ignored. We turned it into

69 *Cinderella*. Set design by Lez Brotherston for the London Underground scene
in Act Three, in which the Pilot searches for Cinderella.

a kind of London Wartime underworld, with lots of prostitution and
cheap sex. It's interesting how the castanets stop sounding relevant
when you take away anything that looks Spanish from the stage picture! They just merge into the general orchestration. The scene is basically about his temptation by other women. There's also a sequence –
Guys and Dolls thrown in, for no good reason except that it's a good
joke – where the Salvation Army come down and try to save the souls.
Now, we had a great deal of discussion, as to whether he should have
sex with one of the women down there, or whether he should stay true
to Cinderella. The thing that made us agree to it was our sense that he
is only human – part of him thinks she's dead anyway – and that it
doesn't give him any serious fulfilment. A similar thing happens in
Waterloo Bridge, actually, but the other way round. (That's a fantastic
film, with wonderful music.) When Vivien Leigh is told that Robert
Taylor is dead, she becomes a prostitute. When he does return, she's at
the station. She's there to pick up the new soldiers off the train, but he
thinks she's there to meet him. She's now a prostitute, with a tarty
beret on and a low-cut blouse.

Anyway, the Pilot does the business; but just before doing that, he
looks at Cinderella's shoe and hides it – as if she shouldn't see what
he's about to do. Afterwards he runs out, disgusted with himself, to the
Embankment. (Lez does a nice scene change there, very simply.) He
throws up into the river; and then, to the oriental music, he has a solo.

The original idea was that this was going to be set in a Lyons Corner House. It was going to be about a misunderstanding between an oriental woman and her lover that ended up being a similar situation. The idea came from a Fred Astaire movie (*Ziegfeld Follies*) – but it wasn't relevant. As with the Spanish music, we realized that it would work perfectly well without having to illustrate some foreign colour. So in this solo on the Embankment, he imagines Cinderella in the shoes and tries to kiss her. He's watched by a woman – the Woman from the Savoy, according to our cast list. She's been at a party at the Savoy, she's had an argument with her husband, and she's come to have a coffee and calm down on the Embankment. She sees him and comforts him. There's a misunderstanding when her husband comes looking for her. A couple of thugs join in for the fun of it, beat him up and taunt him with the shoe. He's left a desperate man. He crawls off stage.

We 'wipe' that by bringing on the hospital screens – which is a nice filmic effect. It overlaps one world into another, without doing a scene change. The screens are moved around, the lights come up, and the whole sequence of the hospital scene is created through screens – forming rooms, corridors and doors. This is the re-introduction to Cinderella. We haven't seen her since the end of Act Two. Now she's here in hospital recovering, but having psychiatric treatment; and she has one shoe on: the other shoe. She's talking to her psychiatrist – played by the Angel in a white coat and glasses – and obviously the shoe is connected with her obsession. So she does a solo, telling her story and how she is. Finally, she throws the shoe to the ground. He comforts her and takes her back to her room. The screens re-form to another part of the hospital. The family – processing through the hospital – are coming to visit her! Basically, the Stepmother is trying to butter up Cinderella in case she spills the beans – or actually to do away with her. This is confusing in our current version, since the murder of the mother has been excised. Why would Cinderella's family even come to visit her? But we will resolve this before staging it in America in 1999. Anyway, here the Stepmother is. She has brought the others along – they're very reluctant – with gifts and flowers and chocolates. She says she doesn't want to see them, but they barge their way into her room. For once, she stands up to them and to the Stepmother and tells them to get out. So she has moved on and is changing as a person. They are thrown out. However, the Stepmother somehow gets back into her room again – Cinderella's asleep – and tries to smother her with her pillow.

The Stepmother is caught. Cinderella is saved, and points to her, accusingly. She could be saying, 'She tried to kill me!' or 'She killed my mother!' Then comes another wipe with the screens – and, along another corridor, by complete Dickensian coincidence, we see the Pilot. He's ended up in the same hospital, and has also been brought there for psychiatric help. He's got his suitcase and he's coming in, with a nurse. We see him, but Cinderella doesn't.

There's another quick change of scene with the screens. Now we have the Stepmother carted off by a couple of men in white coats, and the family rejecting her or feeling guilty. Then we're back to two parallel hospital rooms, with Cinderella in one and the Pilot in another – stage right and stage left. He is brought into his room to have some electric-shock treatment: some device that's put on his head and by which he's given this frightening treatment to the very violent banging music to which, in the traditional *Cinderellas*, one of the stepsisters tries on the shoe as hard as she can. Cinderella wakes up to the screams of someone in agony from the room next door; she rushes from her room to see what's happening, and arrives just as the doctors have left. She recognizes him, and wakes him up; but just as you're expecting the big recognition scene of true love, you have a little hiccup. He doesn't recognize her, initially, because he doesn't have his glasses on – we haven't found out till this point that he wears them. So they turn around: he's put his glasses on to see her, but she's taken hers off, so he still doesn't recognize her. Then they turn around again; she puts her glasses on this time, and now he knows her and she him – finally.

AM: *Some critics have said that your frumpy Cinderella who only becomes beautiful when she takes her glasses off in Act Two is just a rehash of the corny old 'Why, Miss Jones, you're beautiful without your glasses' situation. But this pay-off (non-)recognition scene is really the reverse of that. They may have dreamed of being glamorous, but in real life what they're looking for is an unglamorous fellow spirit.*

MB: Yes. The whole point of our conception was that these characters were ultimately very ordinary people: Mr and Mrs Ordinary; but with so much distorted reality and nightmare earlier on, it's only in the third act that you find out who the real Pilot is, and that Cinderella is more than happy with the way he really is. It's amazing how well this all fits into the music; or, rather, how easily it seemed to take shape from the music.

And then the final scene on the railway platform.

Film ideas easily floated into mind, like the quotation from *Brief Encounter*. I know I've already quoted from that in *Town and Country*, but here I couldn't resist. A railway scene seemed a perfect solution for all the leave-takings we had in mind; the music just called, emotionally, for one tear-jerking moment after another, and so *Brief Encounter* was just begging to be used again. But I decided to lift the whole energy of the act by putting in a sort of dance bow at the end. We use the big Waltz of the Stars, but in the version with extra repeats that Prokofiev arranged in his *Waltzes Suite*. All the dancers come on and dance, taking their bows at the end of their dances; and it's a Victory dance, with Victory-V salutes.

Preparation

ALASTAIR MACAULAY: *You've not only referred to several films (A Matter of Life and Death, Waterloo Bridge, Brief Encounter, and others); you've also used the word 'filmic'. Do you find, in envisaging a ballet, when you're going through the music and imagining a show, that you're seeing it as a film as much as a stage work?*

MATTHEW BOURNE: At times. What excites me, however, is the theatrical aspect. I never see it overall as a film; but, yes, I see sections of it coming from film and I gain inspiration from film.

AM: *Both in* Swan Lake *and* Cinderella, *you've touched on moments that could almost belong more easily in a movie.*

MB: I suppose I often think in terms of movie techniques – like 'fades' and 'close-ups' and 'wipes'; but my instinct is theatrical, and musical.

AM: *To me, what you often bring out is a filmic quality in the music. Tchaikovsky is one of several nineteenth-century composers who sometimes seem to be composing music for film before film had been invented. Berlioz is another. Their music has long-shots and close-ups and travelling sequences: they are picturing poetically a view more complex than any nineteenth-century theatre could have staged, and they sometimes do it in their works for the concert-hall – writing music that is meant to conjure up a kaleidoscope of images. Arlene Croce called* Swan Lake *'the greatest unstageable ballet ever written', and part of the reason is that, in 1877, Tchaikovsky's vision far outpaced what any theatre could realize. Even later, when Tchaikovsky was working for the most sophisticated opera house in Russia and with a highly skilled team of theatre professionals, there are passages in his scores that must have taxed them to the limit and that still tax any theatrical producer. The second half of Act Two of* The Sleeping Beauty, *with the journey to, and arrival at, the sleeping palace is one example; as is the latter half of Act One of* The Nutcracker, *with all its transformations of the Party scene into the Mice scene and then again into the Snow scene. The same goes, at times, for Berlioz's* Damnation of Faust, *and Wagner's* Ring Cycle. *These composers were composing as if they could already see what film directors would be achieving in a few decades' time. Virtually no stage then or now could provide the changing series of visions, landscapes and close-ups that they were assembling in their scores. This is also true for such concert-hall pieces as Tchaikovsky's* Manfred Symphony.

I even believe that you bring to the surface a buried filmic quality in Act Four of Swan Lake. *As for Prokofiev, he really did write movie music. Often enough in* Cinderella, *he really is writing very definitely for dance; but I always say most of* Romeo and Juliet – *his most popular score – is the best film music written in the twentieth century.*

I, however, say all this from the perspective of one who sits in the auditorium. Does it ever feel like film music as you're trying to make it work in the theatre?

MB: Yes, it does: the more scenic music particularly feels as if it's written to accompany action and lend atmosphere. There are sections when it's very hard to find any real dance impulse in the music.

AM: *Which sections of* Cinderella *feel that way to you?*

MB: Act Two is where it feels most like a ballet – with both dance and theatre on its mind. Much of Act One and parts of Act Three feel very filmic. The music for the underground sequence in our piece changes a lot, as film music does, to accompany different action and quick changes of scene, place and character.

AM: *To me, one of the hardest bits to stage in* Cinderella *is the ending of Act Three, because there's very little rhythmic vitality.*

MB: It's not hard to stage, but it is hard to dance. I solved it by deciding not to dance it! The music has such enormous feeling in it, but it's difficult to choreograph to. As you say, there's nothing to hang the

movement on, beyond the feeling of the music. It was a conscious decision early on – rather than a desperate 'haven't got much time left'
decision – to dare not to dance through that long piece of music. Actually, we suddenly give the Angel a tiny dance around Cinderella and
the Pilot as he's completing his mission.

AM: *One canny thing you did was to time your big emotional
moments surprisingly. Following your* Cinderella *the first time round
as an Ashton fan, I was more or less waiting to see what you did with
certain cues in the music. There's one cue where I thought, with sudden disappointment, 'Oh, he's not playing on our emotions at the
moment when Ashton's Cinderella makes her very touching farewell to
her sisters.' I had thought you would do a fond leave-taking between
Cinderella and her father there, but no. Then, however, when, from an
Ashton point of view, you're not expecting it, but on the next little
spurt of emotion in the music, you suddenly give us the last big recognition scene between father and daughter. It affected me all the more
because the timing took me by surprise.*
MB: But that really didn't come out of my trying to differ from Ashton.
By that point, I didn't remember precisely what he did to all that
music; and, meanwhile, the music just told me what should happen
where.

AM: *You have here some of your preparatory notes.*
MB: Yes, for the Act Two pas de deux. Interestingly, in the light of
what you've just been saying, I got lots of ideas from watching videos.
'Roberta', my notes say. As you know, that film contains the classic
example of Fred and Ginger starting a dance duet by just walking. I
was also thinking of aspects of the 'I'm Old-Fashioned' duet that Fred
dances with Rita Hayworth in *You Were Never Lovelier*. ('Holding
both hands, face to face and shuffle backwards and forwards with
turn', say my notes.) Then 'Let's Face' – that's the Fred and Ginger
duet 'Let's Face the Music and Dance' from *Follow the Fleet*. 'Pass
from hand to hand at waist as she turns', I've written. Then, for the
Angel and Cinders, I've written 'Hypnosis Dance' – that's 'Change
Partners and Dance' in *Carefree*.

Lots of notes on film dance duets, actually! The last dance in *The
Barkleys of Broadway*. 'Between You and Me': that's a number from
Broadway Melody of 1940 with Eleanor Powell and George Murphy,
which I've always liked. Some of these things we used, some we didn't.

The only one I'm sure we used is the walking side by side from *Roberta*.

If I'm at a loss in a duet rehearsal for what to do, we might look at some of my favourite musical numbers on video. Then we'll try out something like that, and it will lead us on to the next thing. It's something to fall back on if we get a bit lost. I keep trying to add to my stock of knowledge – I've been buying a lot of videos of less-well-known musicals. There are some Debbie Reynolds and Donald O'Connor films, Esther Williams films, and films with Gower Champion or early Bob Fosse choreography that have fantastic numbers, absolute treasures of choreography, but that haven't passed down into the established pantheon of 'Great Moments from the Musicals' – *Give A Girl A Break* and *I Love Melvyn*, to name only two. Not to mention more famous dances that I often go back to, such as 'All Of You', which Cyd Charisse and Fred Astaire dance in *Silk Stockings*; or their big duet in *The Band Wagon*, 'Dancing in the Dark'.

It's easy to see what my notes mean when they refer to films. Elsewhere, even I can't tell what my notes mean: 'Use victims phrases', for example, later in Act Two. Here I've got 'Use *Late Flowering Lust* dance here'. That's the actual dance of the poem 'Late Flowering Lust' on our 1994 video, in which women are thrown over men's shoulders, and look grotesque and fall to the floor. This is part of what the blue couples were doing late in *Cinderella* Act Two, when the men were carrying them as if they were carrying bodies from rubble.

AM: *How much does it actually re-use your choreography from* Late Flowering Lust?
MB: I don't think it does at all, but we used the idea behind it. That dance in *Late Flowering Lust* looks like marathon dancing, with people collapsing in each other's arms, but still trying to dance. In my notes for Act Three, I've got a section called 'People living in fear'. This is the Angel of Death section near the start of the act. I was looking for ideas for dance phrases that I would then give to different members of the company, ideas for them to make movement. 'These are the people of London – on the streets of London – watching something or several things in the sky – possibly a plane or planes – suspicious of other people – hiding in shop windows – things dropping from the sky (avoiding them) – hearing things – lights in face – torches – car lights – not daring to look up – confronting things because of this' (I don't know what

that means) 'Protective of each other – keeping out of danger – looking for cover – rain – can hold umbrella.' There was an idea that a lot of people were going to have umbrellas at one point in that sequence, because the stage picture has it raining. But, obviously, they get in the way. 'Angel – look at whole group at end. And all look back at him.' Yes, we do do that. There's a little phone box at the back of the stage and at the end of the number he disappears. He opens the door of the phone box, looks back at them all, they look at him, and then he goes into the phone box. A bit like *Dr Who* – as if he lives in this phone box.

Here's a brief outline of one little scene – the family visit to the hospital. A lot is to do with nurses. '1, nurse on another journey. 2, nurse into room. Other nurse outside. 3, Cinderella says "No". 4, nurse says "No". 5, they barge in.' (That's the family.) 6, all smiles, because nurse is there. Give gifts, get bored. 7, nurse says "Time is up."' This is just to give me guidelines for what to do before going into rehearsal.

The scene with the hospital screens – because it was so complicated in terms of where those screens went – was done on the spot, because it was impossible on paper to keep track of where the screens were going.

Here I just have a breakdown of casting for the railway station: 'Maxine, Cinderella look-alike, sitting on suitcase.' She's the one the Angel ends up going to at the end of the piece. 'Etta and Ben, *Brief Encounter*. Just a series of couples, woman with baby, husband injured.' And then notes for the final 'Victory' dance. 'Knees up, conga . . .' Actually, what we ended up doing is a lot better than these notes. We did this dance quickly, and that proved a good idea. 'People running in and around phrases, chasing people for a kiss or a lift.' You know that famous picture of the sailor kissing the woman in Times Square, where she's really twisted over? I wanted that sort of impetuous feeling – of just grabbing anyone and kissing them with joy.

Rehearsals

ALASTAIR MACAULAY: *For how long did you rehearse* Cinderella *in the studio?*

MATTHEW BOURNE: For about ten weeks with everyone, and more time with individual people beforehand. However, I was ill for more than a week during this rehearsal process, and that led to a few problems we could have done without. It took about a week setting it up in the theatre. However, because I'd been ill, we had to cancel a couple of previews – when we went into 'tech-ing' the production, there were still bits of the show that hadn't been choreographed. So there was a lot of catching up to do.

AM: *I want to compare the way you work to the ways used by other choreographers. Can you understand how Frederick Ashton could make his* Cinderella *in six weeks? Or his* Fille mal gardée *in four weeks?*
MB: I don't know, no. I suppose that, if that's all the time you have, then that's what you do. We made *Nutcracker* in five weeks. It helps, obviously, if you are working with a company of people who are very used to the way you work, because they do half of it for you – they give you the performance straightaway. Strangely, the bits that need adjusting most in *Cinderella* now are the bits that we spent most time on.

AM: *Let's talk about choreographic method. As you know, some chor-eographers turn up to the studio and have worked out every movement beforehand. You yourself tended to work that way early on in your career. Other choreographers, like Ashton or Balanchine, certainly give everyone the impression that they have no movement ideas when they walk into the studio. They get the rehearsal pianist to play the music, they say, 'Now, let's see', and then they set to work.*

When Ashton was younger, he would sometimes rush around the studio in response to the music, and then ask his dancers to copy what he'd just improvised; but he had more methods than one even then. Once he turned up with a hangover and sat there with his hand over his eyes. 'Move around, keep warm,' he said to his dancers, but he didn't look. He was due that day to create a pas de trois – in Valenti-ne's Eve, *his first choreographic version of Ravel's* Valses Nobles et Sentimentales *– and one of his three dancers, Peggy van Praagh, kept herself warm by doing particular exercises from the Cecchetti ballet syllabus. Suddenly Ashton, still with his hand over his eyes, said, 'That'll do, we'll use that.' Van Praagh said, 'But you weren't even looking.' Ashton said, 'Can you do it again?' She could; so Ashton took those movements, fitted them to the music, changed the rhythm and the angles, and set them for all three dancers as the pas de trois! Later he would sometimes say, 'I had a dream last night of a fountain,' and his dancers – in that case, Antoinette Sibley and Anthony Dowell,*

working as Titania and Oberon on their pas de deux in The Dream –
*would say, 'A fountain?' and had to try to 'make' a fountain in dance.
In making* Cinderella, *he had the music for* Fairy Spring *played, and
said to the dancer Nadia Nerina, 'What do you hear in it?' She said,
'Bursting of buds', and that image was what propelled the whole solo.
Now, it may well be that Ashton had a more definite idea of what he
wanted – at least its highlights and its overall shape – than he ever let
the dancers know; and certainly, when he made* Rhapsody, *Lesley
Collier said that all the movement for the ballerina role came out of
him and that she – not feeling inspired that way – told him he'd have
to invent all her movement himself. She claims she contributed no
ideas or movement herself at all to what is an elaborate and extremely
virtuoso role: Ashton was seventy-five at the time.*

*Still, in general, his method was to invite the dancers to contribute
to the creative process. But what you're talking about seems to go
further, because, before the movement, you're asking them to help conceive the characterization and even details of the plot.*

MB: Of course I do plenty of work before going into the studio. But it's
often to do with structure or sense. Or music. When I go home in the
evenings, often what I spend time trying to solve is how to make a piece
of music work. It's usually not to do with the specifics of steps – it's to
do with the ideas that are going to help create the steps. 'OK – we've
got a piece of music. Maybe we've got a solo that needs to happen
here. Now, I have not a single idea about why this solo is happening.'
So, out of the studio, what I dwell on is all the whys and wherefores of
that solo being there. 'What things are going to get us motivated into
making the movement?'

It's taken a lot of confidence to get to that stage, but it seems to
work for everyone, because it gives everyone an involvement. They
know they're going to have to work and use their own minds when
they get there; and the majority of performers relish that side of working with us.

I think that what I can do now is react quickly to movement that's
given me. Even if I'm given the most awful phrase of movement by
someone, I've got a way now of changing it without it seeming as if I've
said, 'That's dreadful!' I can start from the beginning and make it into
something else. I work best by making one thing into another rather
than having to make something out of nothing; but I don't want to leave
too much up to chance. With ensembles in particular, and curiously

often with dances for women, I find I have a clearer idea of what I want to do. There are sequences like the underground scene in *Cinderella* where I made most of the movement just because I knew so surely what I wanted. Solos you can leave more to chance, and you can mould the material that emerges in the studio without too much problem.

AM: *As you say, your gift is in shaping the material into something of your own. That being so, can you say what your dance style is? What movement do you accept or reject? How do you shape the material you're given?*
MB: The first contribution I make is in rhythm and dynamics. The material you get tends to be even.

I also try to make it more full-bodied, to get the dancers to go further with each move. Often, I will add something more fluid in connecting one movement with another – to make things more sensual.

What else? I just look to see if there's a phrase of movement. I look to see what I feel's missing from it. Often it's a sexiness, and that's to do with the way the back is used; also the shoulders and the head.

AM: *And you're looking for a current that will connect the movement?*
MB: Yes. Occasionally it's good to surprise with a connection that doesn't seem to make sense, but it needs to be musical and as full-bodied as it can be; and dancers often pull away from that, you know. It's lovely to see dancers who go for everything, but by no means all of them do. So I'm usually pointing out how it could go further, lower, higher, deeper, whatever.

Sometimes I will add more gestural interests to movement that looks a bit ordinary. I'll say, 'Try it with a different arm', for example. Another thing that works really well is to tell people to go away and give it focus – but take their focus to the most unorganic, the most unexpected place – because everyone naturally falls into certain patterns. As soon as you take the head in another direction, as soon as you look the opposite way or are looking down when it feels that you should be looking up, it takes on different meanings. We start to see the human aspect of the movement. A great deal is to do with the use of eyes – but as the focus of the whole body, not just as a set of facial expressions, and not looking conventionally in the direction you're going in. It always works, that device, to give something more interest.

Unadorned classroom-type movement – which is often the first thing in the mind of the dancer – is often what I most readily reject. I also reject humour that's thrown in your face. Some ideas we work on do have humour, and I try and make them more subtle by disguising it. I don't like things that seem to say, 'Aren't we funny!' or 'Aren't we clever!'

AM: *Dance people often talk of a dancer 'creating' a role. How do you feel about this?*
MB: I wouldn't want anyone to believe that, in a show like *Cinderella*, first-cast people created a role without any contributing influence from other second- or third-cast performers.

When AMP began, there weren't two interpretations of an idea being presented to me at any one time. It was always the individual, and I worked with that person. He or she created that role with me, and there was no question that it was anything other than theirs. Later on, when we started to re-do shows, sometimes a dancer wasn't available and, for the first time, we encountered a new interpreter of the role. That was when we started to allow a certain amount of re-interpretation. Basically, the choreography already existed, and there was an idea of character obviously in that, but it made sense to allow the new dancers to bring a bit of themselves to the role.

In each case, I had to work out how flexible I was going to be. This is quite an issue. Certain things – you feel very firmly – work the way they already are. It's not always easy to work out whether this is to do with what you think the character should do, or whether you just want to impose on the next person the quality you loved so much in the original dancer.

In the shows we do now, however, we start off with two, three or four individuals preparing each role, working in the studio together to create movement. They must all understand that they can bring something of themselves to it.

When someone says that Sarah Wildor 'created' the role of Cinderella, in many senses this is true, because she was the chosen person to do the first performance. She was obviously there at all the rehearsals, a lot of her thought went into the role, and she interpreted the role in the way that she felt was right for it. But alongside her were two other people, Maxine Fone and Saranne Curtin, who were also dancing the role, feeding into the movement and ideas, bringing their own slightly different interpretations of those ideas and movements. So it's wrong to say flatly now that any one person creates an AMP role.

Each role is an ensemble creation involving more people than me and one dancer.

AM: *So you start rehearsals. You take everyone through the story and the main ideas. Then you give everyone their character or characters, and then set them their homework.*

MB: At the beginnings of the *Cinderella* rehearsals, we watched a lot of videos together. We had at least a couple of days' worth of videos, with me showing Pathé newsreels with general background, so that people knew the specific historical world that we were going to be in. This method is used by directors in plays and musicals, and I have used something like it on most of my work with AMP for several years. We show the set, the costumes, the background material. On the second day of *Cinderella* rehearsals, we had a class in authentic swing dance from the 1940s, taught us by a Lindy Hop expert, Louise Richards. It was fascinating to see who, of our dancers, was good at it and who wasn't – and often surprising. (You feel some of the ballet people might be a little stiff with it, but not at all – whereas people who are more into jazz dance look terribly awkward.)

We then did more specific character development: getting people to do their own research. I had a big video library in the rehearsal rooms and lots of books that people borrowed, like a library. Obviously, the Stepmothers were watching Joan Crawford movies! – *Mildred Pearce, Possessed, Harriet Craig* – but Lynn decided that she wanted to be Bette Davis as well: that suited her more. I could see what she meant – she wanted to be more animated than Joan is. Isabel Mortimer was much more true to Joan's stiffness: the broad shoulders, and the 'hardly-moving-at-times' quality of her acting. Lynn wanted to move more, which she found with Davis rather than with Crawford.

AM: *How did Sarah, Maxine and Saranne develop their Cinderellas?*
MB: They talked to each other quite a lot; but I think the essence of their chats was to do with their decision that they would all have different ways of doing it. It was important to them to acknowledge amongst themselves that they would do that. Maxine's way was to make her character more in control, someone who was active in doing things, who would fight back. She doesn't like playing a wimp; she would never be meek or frightened. So she was more of a troubled person, disturbed rather than timid. Saranne probably gave in more to being put upon and being a victim – which was so interesting, quite a

70 *Cinderella*: rehearsal for Act One. 'The Dummy Duet': Will Kemp as the Pilot; Maxine Fone as Cinderella.

challenge, because she is brilliant at playing very alluring, sexy women. She had been very good as the Queen in *Swan Lake*, especially in Act Three. She has a very good sense of glamour and deviousness and sexuality. So this part was not something she'd done before; but she's a very intelligent actress – quietly gets on and does her own thing. Whereas Sarah Wildor, I think, probably fell somewhere in between. She was very enquiring, constantly – lots of questions, lots of new ideas all the time about the character, sometimes even working too much on the logic of the role, needing too many reasons for why she was doing things. Sometimes, however, she wouldn't ask – would just find solutions by herself. I'd say, 'Why aren't you doing that?' She'd reply, 'Oh, because she wouldn't do this because of . . .' Eventually, we talked about a lot of things, some of which the audience didn't need to know; but these things really mattered to her, to give everything complete logical sense. She was never hard to work with, but things would often stop because of that need to know. Obviously, logic is of major importance to me, and so are explanations of why a character is doing something. Still, she cottoned on to the way I worked – and was, ultimately,

335

71 *Cinderella*. Rehearsal for Act One, with Saranne Curtin as the bespectacled Cinderella and Ewan Wardrop as the Pilot, as the Pilot is about to be thrown out of the house.

very creative to work with. They are actually all three very creative people in terms of developing character.

AM: *In the event, the performance Sarah Wildor gave had more heart-catching star quality than anything I'd seen her do at Covent Garden. Are you able to explain the radiance she had in the role? Was it just a smaller theatre?*

MB: Well, she really believed in what she was doing. She'd had the chance to study, create and work with the character for ten weeks of rehearsal, which she never gets at the Royal. She used to talk about it at home all the time, so she was obviously living this person. I think she also felt very confident in terms of working with Adam – who is famous as a rock-solid partner and stops his partners from worrying about any insecurity.

I think maybe the smaller theatre did help. I know what you mean about the radiance that she had, but what surprised me was how far she went to de-glamorize herself. I expected that of Maxine, for example, because she's used to acting all kinds of characters; but Sarah even hunched her back over. I had said I wanted it to be a bit like that, but I hadn't expected how much she really took to it. It took her time: during previews, we didn't see just how strong her performance was going to be; but she, along with a lot of great dancers, has complete and utter trust in the choreographer. If you say something, they'll really go for it.

AM: *The bleak, unglamorous side of Cinderella is what astonished people when Fonteyn danced the role. When she'd been injured, Ashton had made it on Moira Shearer; but Fonteyn, coming to the role a few months later, made the fireside scenes more bleak and hopeless, and thereby the ballroom scenes all the more radiant.*
MB: I think it's one of those roles where you can save yourself for that. Our Cinderella is certainly gorgeous at the ball. I don't know how much of that we talked about.

AM: *How did they find dancing (a) in heels (b) in bare feet?*
MB: I remember the first movement I ever asked Sarah to do, she said, 'Is any of it on pointe?' I said, 'No.' She said, 'Oh, thank God!' For Sarah, bare feet weren't a problem at all. The heels were a problem, simply because they weren't the easiest of shoes: a bit big, with all those jewels on.

AM: *Did the three Cinderellas learn from each other?*
MB: That's certainly not something anyone will admit to! I feel there is much to be gained from watching fellow performers in your role. There is always something to learn. Maxine and Saranne would have seen Sarah's performance, because they were on stage in other roles most nights. Why I made them do that, I don't know. As well as learning Cinderella and helping to create her, they were learning other roles in the piece as well for other nights. They had a lot on their plates. But they were all very good – and Maxine and Saranne should have won more attention and recognition for their performances than they did. They're really remarkable performers.

AM: *How did the two contemporary-trained dancers take to the more ballet-related material? And vice versa?*
MB: I think it's harder for a ballerina, once she's off pointe, to get into the ground at all, to feel grounded in that way. Ballet dancers, especially the women, take all the emphasis upwards. And so there are certain types of movement that Sarah found quite difficult to do; or, when she did them, they looked like something else.

Another funny thing – I really don't know why this is – is that, when I'm working with male dancers, I can get quite a lot from the material they're giving me; but, when I'm working with female dancers from whatever background, I tend to choreograph it completely from scratch myself.

AM: *Do you have any character sketches for Cinderella, the Pilot and the Angel?*

MB: Not written down, but we'd discussed their characters in some depth. It was fun to ask Adam, after all his heroic roles, to play the Pilot as if he were really a bit of an accountant. The first rehearsal that we did with Cinderella and the Pilot was the beginnings of the dummy duet. This happened very early on, because Sarah had to go off on tour.

We spent a lot of time on the Angel with several people who were going to be playing the role. We tried to come up with less of a character, more of a way of moving, a feeling as to what that character was capable of, some parameters: Who was he visible to? Could he make himself visible at times and other times not? Could he become other people? Was he a friendly presence or a mysterious presence? Was he always for Cinderella's good? Maybe he was just her fate and wasn't necessarily always a good thing, but was there to see her through her life.

AM: *It occurs to me that the Angel may be the most curiously and perhaps successfully hybrid role you've made. Adam Cooper was recently laughing and saying, 'I was very much aware four or five men contributed to the making of that role' – you being one of them. It's movement has ballet and it has contemporary and it has sheer AMP eccentricity. How did all this emerge and then merge in rehearsal?*

MB: Will Kemp, Arthur Pita, Adam Cooper, and Theo Clinkard – all the people who danced it – were equally involved, and they all contributed material to it.

We tried to find a way of moving that was like floating, hovering; and we watched the film with Alec Guinness as Jacob Marley in *Scrooge*, when he appears to hover, all covered in chains. A very odd way of moving – bits of his body float away at times – but it didn't feel right to keep that up the whole time. Then we had an idea that he was a bit Fred Astairish, or that he had a Cary Grant type of angel's presence. There's a film we watched called *The Bishop's Wife*, where Cary

72, 73, *Cinderella*. Will Kemp as the Angel, showing the character's various characteristic movement motifs in a studio photo session.

Grant plays an angel who does good for the bishop's wife, who's married to a clergyman played by David Niven. Our Angel wasn't going to have wings; he would be like an ordinary man. But maybe he would need to look different for the stage. So we identified him as a bit odd, but nothing outlandish. And we had books of angel paintings that we looked at: gestures from medieval paintings and from sculptures. We used quite a lot of those within the Angel's solos and developed movement from them.

Then we worked on the two sides of the Angel. One side was the caring guardian figure. The other side was the Angel of Death. The midnight section should, we thought, have a different vocabulary of movement. Will and Adam have ballet training, Arthur and Theo have contemporary training, and you can see aspects of both kinds within the material. There are some strong positions and jumps from ballet; and there is also some fluid movement. There are some almost body-popping moves – which came from that Alec Guinness example of initiating movement from one place and carrying it through the body. Men are good at working together in my experience; and these four did. We not only took material from all the dancers, we also spliced it: adding the upper-body movements of one dancer's phrase to the lower-body movements of another.

If two dancers played a role, they discussed it and then gave us a little

339

talk on their character. The Stepmother was played by Lynn Seymour and Isabel Mortimer. Lynn really amazed everybody by the detail she brought in, and how logical it was straightaway, how much it helped the story. Hers was a very elaborate story – of her life with her various husbands. She had five children, and she explained which children were by which father, why they were like they were, and why she'd moved on to the next husband each time. What I remember being impressed by at the time was that it very logically made sense of the story that she already knew we were telling.

AM: *She was always revealingly logical in her career as a ballerina at the Royal Ballet. She made all kinds of new sense of MacMillan's Manon when she stepped into that role, making new decisions that explained all kinds of things about the character and gave new impetus to the story.*

MB: My notes from the Stepmother don't include everything Lynn came up with, but here goes. She's called Sybil, in her late forties. She's an ex-hooker. Four previous husbands. The first was a customer. The second was a tycoon, by whom she had the two sons. She was married to a politician, by whom she had the girls; and then to a spiv, with whom she had the younger brother. She is dangerous, stealthy, plotting, selfish, greedy, unpredictable, ritualistic, jealous of daughters.

I love people who bring that kind of logic to what they do. I'm forever asking: 'Well, why did they do that? What was the point of that?' and I really love it when someone has the initiative to make the whole piece more logical through their thought process. People who don't do that tend to annoy me after a while, in their acting choices. Sometimes, when we're into a run, you can really get someone who bugs you, because their performances show that they're not really thinking about it properly.

Cinderella's father is called Robert. 'He's fifty. Ex-public school, Cambridge, First World War officer, hero of trenches. Drafted early in War, Dunkirk. He was injured in some way, on a war pension; at one point he had a lot of money, which is why she went for him. Dashing, brave at one point, loving parent, now distant, periodic displays of interest, confused by other kids, her family.'

The dancer is Barry Atkinson, who came to dance extremely late. He's had an odd life – he's a world-renowned expert on earthquakes and has written books on them. He decided he wanted to learn to

74 *Cinderella*. Rehearsal for Act One. Lynn Seymour, as the Stepmother, approaching Sarah Wildor, as Cinderella.

75 *Cinderella*. Rehearsal. Lynn Seymour and Andrew Walkinshaw as Elliott, her youngest child.

dance in his thirties, went to The Place and trained. He was never really a technical dancer, but he performed in some people's work. He choreographs operas as well. Yet he still has this earthquake expertise on the sidelines and is often contacted internationally about certain issues. He's now in his late forties and he does full company class every day. He entered AMP as Dr Dross in *Nutcracker*; then he was the Private Secretary in *Swan Lake*.

Brother One is called Malcolm, and is played by Scott Ambler and Colin Ross-Waterson. He's mid-to-late twenties, prissy, obsessive, cold, resentful, creepy, decorous, unfit for military service, claustrophobic. Wants to know everyone's business, obsessed with cleaning, appearance. Into knitting and sewing. Has a fear of the blackout.

The second brother is Vernon. Ben Wright and Theo Clinkard played him. He's lazy, calculating, still, slow, intellectual. He has a death obsession and a sick sexual relationship with Cinderella. Politically he's ambiguous, possibly a spy or wants to be a spy. Everything is an experiment for him. Appears suddenly without warning.

Sister One, Vivien, is played by Heather Habens or Michela Meazza. She's twenty-one to twenty-two. She's into fashion magazines, she copies poses from magazines, does facial exercises, uses Cinderella as masseuse. (I tried to get them all to find things that Cinderella could do for them – but we didn't really do much of that.) She's self-centred, pretentious, into trends, house-proud. The war is an inconvenience. She draws line on legs to look like stockings; in fact, that's one of Cinderella's duties.

Sister Two is Irene. Emily Piercy and Vicky Evans play her. She's in her mid-twenties, stroppy, moody, a martyr, bitter, neurotic, depressed, disappointed with her life, irritated by family. She resents not having a father. She's an ex-tomboy, wanted to be a racing-car driver, she hates chores, takes Valium, despises mother, dominates Stan, her boyfriend, flicks ash in Cinderella's hand, sends her out for pills.

Young Brother, Elliott – played by Andrew Walkinshaw – is fourteen. He hero-worships the GI. He's got a toy plane, picks his nose, is spiteful, vicious, a mummy's boy, hypochondriac, has tantrums.

Girlfriend One, Maggie – Etta Murfitt or Teresa Barker – is twenty-seven or twenty-eight. She's socially adept. She holds court, lets hair down from time to time, she's uninhibited, middle class, has brains, is active, upwardly mobile. Possibly she's protective of Cinderella, a little like Judy Garland in *Me and My Gal*.

Girlfriend Two, Betty, is played by Jacqui Anderson and Valentina Formenti. Her husband has died in the War. She's embarrassed by her appearance, wears glasses, was once active, is now getting over her loss.

The GI, called Buster, is played by Neil Penlington. He's twenty-three or twenty-four, well-hung, a womanizer, well-groomed, charming, arrogant, flirtatious, sexist, good background, has an easy life, is a jock. He uses chewing gum, has a constant beat going in his body all the time, like he's listening to music, checks his appearance in the mirror, has a high sex drive. He has a shallow relationship with the Stepmother, and no time for Irene. He makes advances on Cinderella.

Boyfriend Two, Stan, played by Phil Hill, has done it all. He tells lies, he's working class, he used to run market stall, met Irene in an air-raid shelter, is a Jack of all trades, clumsy. He bangs into things, is not well hung, slouches, doesn't understand his girlfriend. The Stepmother disapproves of him, but tolerates him, he supplies her with things on the black market. He uses the betting office, is a slob, a wheeler-dealer, absent-minded, leaves things behind, a dreamer, scruffy, not socially adept.

AM: *What a crew! Some of these aspects you dropped, of course, because you couldn't portray them without your show's narrative. Were there features, however, when you said, 'I'm sorry, that just won't work, it's wrong'?*
MB: That has happened – for example, with Ben Wright's brother. The character that he began to develop for it was obsessive, and what was coming across was that it wasn't physicalizing itself enough. He got stuck at one point and decided he wanted to change the emphasis of the character. He didn't really get into it the way he would have liked until some way into performing it, when he really found a way of doing things with it that worked for him.

I was trying to help. My problem was that it was too much in the head, with not enough coming out in movement. One task was to try to make the two sisters and the two brothers different from each other. Ben's character originally was going to be very bookish and intellectual, but there wasn't much you could do with that. In the end, we made him much creepier and a bit deviant sexually. He has nasty thoughts about Cinderella; he molests her – which is a serious moment, because you assume that he has done this before and that she just puts up with it.

AM: *What you're describing is a method of working adored by actors; but actors are generically an articulate lot. Many dancers, however, are far less articulate, and would be shy of contributing to an original conception of character.*

MB: This is why I'm so careful about people I pick to be in the company. Even then, maybe between ten and twenty per cent of them find it difficult; but often you can't predict who will take to it. Most of them do take to it very enthusiastically. They get carried away, and sometimes provide much unnecessary information; but you have to let them go with it, because it's giving them so much. It's time well spent. Mostly they are quite happy to talk to the whole group about what they've found – it's easier in groups. If it was left to the individual, I think each one would feel much more nervous about saying, 'This is who I am', but, having discussed it in a group, one of them will represent the others. It gives an initiative to people, which most people like.

AM: *I'm curious about the sources of movement for certain dances. For example, the big pas de deux in Act Two – where did those movements come from? It goes down well with ballet-goers – you've had it performed at a gala or two – and various observers are convinced that Sarah and Adam contributed all the moves from their own Royal Ballet repertory. Some older AMP members or followers have felt that this pas de deux is where you show strongest – to them, alarming – signs of moving towards real ballet choreography and away from AMP character-based and narrative-based style. Adam, however, has remarked to me that there are numerous absolutely contemporary-dance features to it that both he and Sarah had to work hard on. Still, there is one lift, when Cinderella is scrunched up around him, that does remind me strongly of MacMillan's* Mayerling; *and I had to smile when I saw it, because, when* Mayerling *was new, in 1978, we had seen nothing like several of its most strenuously acrobatic/erotic/morbid lifts before – but now here they are recurring in, of all things,* Cinderella.

MB: Actually, in a number like that, I do get the dancers to contribute, but in a different way. I'll have a strong overall idea of what I want, and I'll say to them, 'I want something like this where . . .' I just explain it very vaguely, and they all have a go at doing something like what I've said. When I've got all these options to inspect, I can choose what feels right. In the case of the pas de deux, the problems were solved very democratically between the three couples that were doing it a lot of the time. At times, you're aware that one couple is pulling in one direction and others in another.

It looks different when Sarah and Adam do it, yes, and it looks like something only they could do; but that's simply their emphasis in performance. And yes, they contributed movements, though I don't think I could identify their sources, whether from *Mayerling* or elsewhere. Certainly when I look at the pas de deux now, I can still see just how many of its problems were solved by Saranne Curtin and Ewan Wardrop. I am also reminded just how much of it was material that I myself had given them.

Looking at my notes, I remember that one thing Sarah and Adam changed was the way I had organized the counts. As usual, I had counted out the music in the way I heard it, often an irregular sequence – here a 3, a 3, a 12, an 11, a 4, a 6, a 12, an 11, etc. Adam and Sarah studied these, listening to the music, and said, 'Could we just count this in 6s?' And here are my revised counts – all 6s and the odd 3. It was the first time, I suppose, that I'd been contradicted in my way of counting – and it was a lot easier for everyone once we'd counted it their way.

I learnt a lot, of course, while making the pas de deux. I wasn't sure sometimes how high a lift could go; or where one lift could go once it was in motion. But I always had an idea in mind, an image that I was aiming towards – though sometimes it would go off at a tangent. Those rehearsals for the duet work were what I loved the most, actually; they felt the most creative. The solo work, and the ensembles, involved a different kind of contribution, in which I was often getting up and helping them do it. I always knew that I wanted the duet to be both intimate and sexually passionate. We were always talking about it from an acting point of view while we made it. I'm sure we'll fiddle around with it further, but I was always happy with it. What I would work towards now is to make it more natural-looking in its passion, rather than hitting spectacular positions.[2]

A lot of my work later on is to do with directing the action, and this is what my rehearsal notes show. They look like a director's notes for rehearsing a play. 'Sarah – more horror at gun.' 'Lynn – too much reaction to shoes, don't show it to audience.' Pages and pages of notes like

2 Bourne did indeed revise this pas de deux in 1999 for the Los Angeles production, having Cinderella and the Pilot alone in a bedroom, evidently after sex. The beginning and end of the pas de deux in particular were revised.

that. Here are some notes for the third version of the Prologue: 'Lynn stays on. Sarah comes from party, sees her, gets father. Father distraught, holds body. Lynn comforts, Sarah drops teddy, Lynn and Sarah look at each other, Sarah accusingly, Lynn half smile.' As I've said, we ended up not using any of that.

AM: *During this rehearsal process, you got to know this large group of dancers well, and a number of them were new to the company. When you'd made* Swan Lake, *Will Kemp was the only Royal Ballet-School-trained dancer to audition (some other ballet dancers auditioned). With* Cinderella, *however, you had had scores of ballet dancers to choose from; and likewise from contemporary backgrounds. How do you feel about the dancers you chose? And those you rejected?*

MB: The best dancers to work with, certainly in audition, are those who have a way of looking at the movement and just doing it, without bringing any in-built affectations or stylistic tricks to it. What happens with a lot of classical-ballet dancers that come to auditions – even dancers who, you think, should be able to do anything, dancers you've seen in many productions of different ballets by different choreographers – is that they can't actually string the movement together or make any sense of it. It's too alien to what they know, and you just know you're not going to get anywhere. With student dancers from some of the ballet schools, it's certainly no better. Even at that stage, they're not open-minded enough to be able to take on something new.

That's a big problem with dance schools at the moment – not ballet schools alone. We've recently been round all the British schools, both ballet and contemporary, and there's something missing from the training. Dance students are set in the way they move, so that it's very difficult to get them to do anything else.

AM: *Is that partly to do with your strong emphasis on the torso and upper body?*

MB: Yes, but the main problem is to do with connecting movement together and not just hitting positions; they want to hit positions constantly. Dance, as far as I'm concerned, is going through positions, but to them it's about stopping in them. I know that Ashton and Balanchine would tell their dancers to hit positions – but they would also make a strong emphasis on a through impetus and on connective phrasing. Today's student dancers, to an alarming extent, are making no real phrases.

I wish, too, that there were drama classes within dance colleges and that there was more opportunity for dance students to create characters through movement. This isn't just because colleges are now very technically orientated. When I was a dance student, we did lots of non-technical things, but I think that only once in all our many choreographic sessions was I set a task that was anything to do with character.

Another problem is: Where does a movement start? You try to explain that, in anything that involves the back more, the shoulders always need to be kept down. The impulse should come from lower in the spine and torso, but they find it hard. As a result, they find it very difficult to live in the movement, to become something beyond themselves.

AM: *How has the feel or direction of your company changed?*
MB: I certainly try to improve the technical standards. The big difference is that a lot of them now are doing things beyond anything I could ever have done myself as a dancer. Whereas once I could always show the choreography and it all came from my body, that's no longer the case. When I look at some of my old works on video now, they seem so grounded; I'd make the dancers jump more if I was working on them now.

Something that's still an issue for us is partnering. A lot of the men in the company don't have a great deal of partnering experience or strength. There's some resistance – 'Not another lift!' – amongst a lot of the male dancers. But there are now about ten boys from a ballet background, who don't seem to have a problem with it – it's part of what they've come from. For some of the contemporary dancers, lifts are a problem. It's always 'These lifts hurt the back' – which I'm afraid becomes boring after a while. This is an area where I could get more creative in time to come; I'm not making monstrous demands in that direction, and dancers really can train themselves to acquire the strength to cope with what demands I do make in this direction.

I've tried to get better dancers generally, both ballet- and contemporary-trained: by 'better', I refer less to technique, I think, than to spirit. Certainly someone like Adam has brought a certain integrity to the playing of a role that people have admired and learnt from. When we were rehearsing *Swan Lake*, he always gave the full performance, so that I could see what was going on. He acted full-out at people, so that they had to react and act back. Scott is similar. And Fiona also had this commitment to performance, to showing in the studio what her full performance would be like. Very inspiring. Elsewhere in the company, I had been getting a lot of, 'Oh well, we'll see it on the night' – especially for reactions. That's why Act Three in *Swan Lake* felt a bit dead in the studio.

Lynn is Lynn and she does what she does, but what people admire in her is her total involvement in character on stage. You have to rise to the occasion to work with her; but hers is a different form of acting. She doesn't connect so much as you might expect in terms of the eyes. Her style comes from a certain era of dance acting, which is much more operatic and larger than life. Some of our performers probably think more of it as film acting, but Lynn takes naturally to playing to large houses. Her much more out-front style took some adjusting to, even by seasoned performers like Scott – who in due course became devoted to her; but her commitment to performance is always an inspiration. As a result, both Saranne Curtin and Maxine Fone in *Cinderella* gave fuller and fuller performances in rehearsal – so that I could actually see what they were going to do.

Previews

MATTHEW BOURNE: I learnt from *Cinderella* just how invaluable the whole process of preview performances can be, and the danger of opening a big production in the West End straightaway. So many of our old shows opened in Bristol, and I missed that this time around. We weren't even opening at Sadler's Wells, as we had with *Swan Lake* – we went straight into the Piccadilly Theatre. Many musicals have been performed there, but most of them would have opened out of town first.

ALASTAIR MACAULAY: *How many previews had* Swan Lake *had at Sadler's Wells?*
MB: Just two performances before we allowed critics in. At the time, that seemed like a lot! Most dance productions open to all the press on their first night, but my whole experience with *Oliver!* was so much about previewing that – fortunately – I had that model in my mind when I was doing *Cinderella*. I had learnt that previews were a form of rehearsal, and I made sure the company of *Cinderella* knew that as

well – that these were rehearsal days until a couple of shows before the first night. Partly because I was ill for more than a week during the official rehearsal period, we had to cancel two previews and were rehearsing and revising things right up to the first night. The pressure was intense.

One thing that happens during previews is that – for two or three weeks before the first night – all kinds of people feel the need to tell you how to fix the show. Sometimes this is useful, and sometimes it's dreadful. What was most useful and interesting to me was what Sam Mendes did. He came to the very first preview performance, we had dinner afterwards, and he simply told me what he thought he'd seen – told me the story as he'd understood it on stage. And that's what you want to hear – not 'This bit was good, that bit wasn't very good.' I'll say, 'What do you think you saw there?' and that's how I find out what's coming across.

You start to hear some odd things! I suddenly realized that the original Prologue, with its big emphasis on the mother and Stepmother, confused people. Many of them thought at first that one or other of them was Cinderella. Then, when Cinderella did appear, they weren't sure, until some way in, that this actually was Cinderella. So I listened to this, realizing that I needed to make Cinderella more central right from the beginning. She originally started at the side of the stage, just reading a magazine, completely anonymous, with all the brothers' and sisters' business going on. I had thought she would emerge from the group eventually and that we'd all know that that was Cinderella; but you've got to be more obvious with an audience sometimes. So we placed her centre stage – so that everything reacted around her – and then we all knew that she was Cinderella.

Another problem was that, even for those people who realized which character was the Stepmother and which was Cinderella, the point of the Prologue – Cinderella's real mother being killed, with Cinderella a witness of sorts – just didn't fall into place until well into Act Two, if then. 'Why have we seen this murder?' they'd say. 'What's it got to do with the main story?' Some of them thought that the main story was, in fact, a flashback to the past rather than the opposite. One detail whereby we managed to confuse people was to do with shoes. We wanted Cinderella to attach so much significance to this one pair of shoes because they had been her mother's; but the audience, seeing her mother die in those shoes, began to wonder if she too was Cinderella.

I realized that we all understood the story as if we knew the words they were speaking; but the audience doesn't know which character is which, or how each one feels about any of the others, until you make it clear. This sounds obvious as I say it, and most of our *Cinderella* was perfectly clear. I'm actually very proud that we made such a completely new version of the old story clear in so many respects to so many people. We didn't give them the Cinderella narrative they knew; we gave them one they'd never imagined. But there were features, especially to do with the Prologue, that didn't make sense to an audience at first. In fact, there still are, although only minor ones. I'll go on working on this production until I feel I've got it right.

Then there were people like Cameron Mackintosh. He had put some money into the production, and he had ideas, and – because he's such an enthusiast – he has to tell you all of them. He does it in a good way – but it's a hard time. You must listen to people's opinions, but when people, even people like Cameron, tell you, 'This doesn't work – cut it', you have to stick to your vision for the piece yourself and you mustn't lose sight of it. I've been told to cut things quite a lot, but I was determined to do the complete score. I felt I would be letting myself down if I didn't.[3]

Katherine (Doré) wrote me a letter after some of the first previews to make some suggestions. She didn't really know the show – she was just reacting as an audience member. She knew just how to handle the situation.

Likewise, certain members of the company who were not performing every night would go out and watch – and I would listen to some of them. Ben Wright was very useful in this respect after an early preview – mainly to do with passing on what people actually were or were not seeing from the story.

Still, I discovered that an audience will accept certain things without needing to make full narrative sense of them. Even when we reduced the Stepmother's pre-history, the audience was just happy to accept that *Cinderella* contained a bad character. People didn't need to know why she had taken against her stepdaughter; that's merely what they expected when they came to *Cinderella*.

---

3 Nonetheless, Bourne later cut two short musical terms from the Seasons suite in Act One when reproducing *Cinderella* for Los Angeles.

AM: *So what changes did you make?*

MB: It was very hard when we decided to simplify the whole Prologue. We were removing things that, for some members of the cast, were the entire reason for what they then did throughout the rest of the show. Lynn, Barry, all three Cinderellas – to explain to them at this late stage that the old Prologue wasn't important and that it would be better just to introduce the characters at the beginning was really painful. We did show Cinderella's real mother, but just briefly, and showed the Stepmother taking her place; and at the same time we showed how Cinderella's place in the family declined. Extremely simple, and clear.

Achievement

ALASTAIR MACAULAY: *It impresses me that, while I've been doing these interviews with you and talking to Lez Brotherston, Etta Murfitt, Scott Ambler and Adam Cooper, all of you have calmly and openly talked about the various things in* Cinderella *you'd still like to 'fix'. Some choreographers refuse ever to make changes to a work.*

MATTHEW BOURNE: We're still making changes in *Swan Lake*! And I don't just mean the changes that most choreographers make as they adjust details to suit different dancers. There are still dances in *Swan Lake* that I think can be clearer or more entertaining. I know it's considered a big 'hit' – but, for us, it's always a work in progress.

The same goes for *Cinderella* – only more so, because there are still important details we want to adjust. The important thing will be to agree on which direction to revise it. One option could bring back the old Prologue but focus it and integrate it better. Another is to re-accentuate the role of Cinderella. The blackout scene needs revision, but we haven't decided just what we will make of it. These things are best discussed by a whole group of us: Lez Brotherston, Scott Ambler, Etta Murfitt, and, if he's available, Adam Cooper.

One very good suggestion that I'll consider came from Sam Mendes, after that first preview he saw. He felt that the whole thing should start with Cinderella in a hospital bed, having been in the bombing, and being on one of those sort of life-support machines with a beep going; there should be an enormous clock in the background; the Angel should come in, and the clock should stop just before midnight. Then the piece would start, like a flashback, but with this 'Will she die? Won't she die?' tension behind it all. Then we would get to that point again in Act Three, where she's back in the hospital. I loved it when he told me – very *Matter of Life and Death*, too – but it was so different from the story that we'd been pursuing at that point. We may not use it, but it's a terrific new angle on the whole story, isn't it? Few suggestions are that imaginative.

Another good idea – which we may well use when we revise it in 1999 – came from Adam. This would involve framing the whole show in the midnight section at the end of Act Two. The bomb goes off, the dream turns to nightmare, and the nightmare is Cinderella's recurrent memory of the Stepmother murdering her mother. This will explain why the Stepmother comes to the hospital in Act Three – to try and get rid of her.

AM: *Would you say there's any message to your* Cinderella?

MB: I'm not into messages.

AM: *I didn't think you were, but you spoke earlier of the message of* Highland Fling.

MB: But we didn't make *Highland Fling* to deliver a message. We simply found that, as we made the piece, it was saying something anyway. We were asking there, 'Why does James cut the Sylph's wings off?' The answer is that he wants to turn her into an ordinary woman. So the message is about a certain kind of accidentally destructive man who wants to possess and contain the thing he loves.

You could say that the message of this *Cinderella* is that each of us may have a guardian angel, that each of us may find love and fulfilment in surprising circumstances, that romantic love and glamorous fantasy can occur in very ordinary, unglamorous, or grim circumstances.

AM: Cinderella *is the fourth of your so-called 'classics'. As you look at the series –* Nutcracker, Highland Fling, Swan Lake, Cinderella *– do you think that you've got deeper into your music each time? It occurs to me that part of what makes your* Nutcracker *fun is that, from the overture on, there is an irony between what we see and what we hear. We hear wonderful innocence in the music, but we see these stock-still lost orphans. And that irony is there at one level in our minds right through your* Nutcracker. *In* Highland Fling, *that irony isn't so strong – but it's there from time to time. After all, it begins in a gents' toilet! Right in the middle of things, there are brief moments that look as if* *the dancers happen to be sending up* La Sylphide. *(Maxine Fone, in the middle of a dance, suddenly sends up a Taglioni pose; and, in Act Two, you do some of your most absurdly earnest mime to the music that, in the Bournonville version, accompanies the most tragic/heroic dance for James.)*

But with Swan Lake, *though it has plenty of irony, there's no point when you're seriously ironic about the idea of* Swan Lake *itself – except, early on in the Moth Ballet, which isn't really about* Swan Lake *but about bad old ballet. Likewise in* Cinderella, *you may do a completely new take on the old story, but it comes out of the music. You may sometimes go completely against Prokofiev's deliberate intention, but you're not making some ironic comment on his score or its scenario; you are responding to numerous aspects of the music.*

MB: I hope you're absolutely right to see that, because I think my approach has indeed changed quite a lot. I've steadily tried for a more generally serious approach to the score and to the subject-matter – the seriousness doesn't preclude humour – and I have tired of needing to comment on a piece in the way I used to. I try now to get to the heart of the piece emotionally – rather than show how clever I am. Some people find, particularly with *Cinderella*, that there are whole sections that don't seem like the older AMP. Yet, funnily enough, one of my intentions with *Cinderella* was to return to the old smaller-scale AMP style in the family scenes.

If I was to do *Giselle* now as a piece, it wouldn't be anything like *Highland Fling*. I've done my ironic comment on the Romantic era in that one. I would approach my *Giselle* through the music much more.

AM: *We may well find it ironic just to conceive that anybody might make a 'classic' anyway in our time. But – this is a favourite theme of mine, and was a point I made when teaching dance history all those years ago – the word 'classical' in its wider sense (or senses) can be applied to such non-ballet dancers as Fred Astaire, and even Isadora Duncan; and it can be applied to the work of such modern-dance choreographers as Merce Cunningham, Paul Taylor, Twyla Tharp or Mark Morris. So, when you call these four works 'classics', do you think of yourself as a 'classical' artist?*

MB: I was put into a 'Best of British' issue of *Vogue* last month. They'd grouped together various artists from different areas, and I was in a photo with a gardener, an artist, a clothes designer, a writer . . . We didn't know why we'd all been brought together, but apparently they'd put us under the banner of 'classicists'. It took several of us by surprise. I said at the time, 'I hope it doesn't look as if I'm calling myself this, because I think there'll be a lot of people that'll argue against that.' You being one of them!

AM: *I would, but I don't need to impose my views on you or on this book.*

MB: I don't feel as though I am. I do, as you know, acknowledge the past a lot; but it's for other people to say. I feel as though my approach is structurally quite similar to a lot of classical ballets in the way I approach work; but the actual movement, and the attitude to movement, is coming from somewhere else. Do you see this issue of dance classicism as something larger than the style of the steps?

AM: *Yes, I do. A dance classicist makes dances that are about dance itself, in a way that is as formally coherent as a piece of classical music. And dance classicism expresses a certain attitude to human energy and to artistic form, to the world and to connectedness of life.*

MB: As I've acknowledged before, dances about dance are not my foremost skill, though I try for that at times.

AM: *What surprises me in looking at your work – and particularly at* Cinderella *– is that it belongs to a genre almost now defunct, a genre formed in the eighteenth century: the 'ballet d'action', which is primarily about narrative and character and situation – about representation – and only incidentally or occasionally about pure dance values. In Act Three of* Cinderella, *you have virtually a whole act of mime – something that has hardly been attempted since the nineteenth century.*

MB: There are a couple of dance solos, but the emphasis is mainly gestural. It was instantly the most popular act, the act that completely worked for audiences and that needed least revision. It works straightaway for an audience that isn't used to looking at dance.

AM: *Are you proud of being able to make an entirely mimed act?*

MB: I feel it's part of the company's style, a style that we've developed for a long time now. In that sense, yes, I feel proud of that, because I know that very few people are choreographing this way today.

Performance

ALASTAIR MACAULAY: *When your company is performing in the West End, your leading dancers are commanding higher fees than they would if they were with the Royal Ballet – is that true?*
MATTHEW BOURNE: Probably, yes – some of them.

AM: *And the general ensemble members of your company are earning West End fees way above what they would in any contemporary dance company – and possibly more than if they were in the corps de ballet at Covent Garden.*
MB: Yes, that's true.

AM: *When their run is over, however, they go back on the dole queue?*
MB: Yes. They also have to take the risk – as many actors do as a way of life – that a West End or a Broadway run can close with two weeks' notice.

AM: *Taking that risk has worked very well for some of your company. It led Adam Cooper to choose between a secure contract at Covent Garden and an insecure but exciting independent career. Have there been other people who've chosen not to go into secure salaried dance jobs?*
MB: Yes, some of them from contemporary dance. People have chosen to work with us rather than going to Rambert Dance Company, for example, where they would have a secure job, probably for years. It doesn't always work to our advantage, mind you. There are dancers I'd like to attract who find that they need the secure job tenure that I can't offer them.

AM: *Although I missed all the brouhaha of the previews and the first night, I saw the production three times during its four-month run at the Piccadilly Theatre. I straightaway thought it told its completely different story very clearly (with one or two blips on the way). There were individual performances and dances that I loved more on each viewing. And I found that it cohered more each time. Was this growing coherence due to the company getting it under its belt? Or were you able to rehearse it and fine-tune it further during the run?*
MB: A bit of both. The more you perform any new choreography, the more you can get on and do the movement – which is in the body –

and then give a performance on top of that; but also, they had time to talk about their roles a lot in note sessions and in some smaller rehearsals.

AM: *How often do you do note sessions?*
MB: We have the possibility of doing it every day, after class and, if it's needed, we use that slot. We don't use it every day during a long run, but we do several times a week.

AM: *We've talked of how some performers developed during rehearsals and previews. In the three performances I saw, I was especially struck by the difference between Adam Cooper and William Kemp as the Pilot.*
MB: I was surprised at how logically Will had thought through the whole thing – he hadn't shown in rehearsal that he would be quite that thorough. I know now that he had thought it through with detail and feeling, but the naturalness of it was a very happy surprise to me in the theatre. Some dancers don't look as if they know why they're doing what they're doing. It looks like: 'Now I move here – and I look here – and I do this', which drives me mad. So, when I see someone who makes their performance work in that way, it's very exciting.

As with *Swan Lake*, there were several details that Adam just did naturally to perfection. Will had to work harder. At first, he made some of the English-smoothie character of the Pilot in Act Two funny in a way I hadn't intended. He got real laughs; it was witty. But I wanted to preserve the romance of the character, the real emotion behind it. He had understood the whole shape of the role, however, and he caught the nervous breakdown in Act Three with an intensity that was all his own. Adam has a relaxation on stage that works uniquely well at several moments: when he lights a cigarette and looks at Cinderella, he's so calm that it's a powerful moment.

They're both very good in the role, and for them it was good to be dancing the role of the Angel as well.

AM: *Etta Murfitt – dancing several roles, none of which took much of the limelight – has said to me that the fun of the run for her lies in doing three different roles each week.*
MB: Yes, it works for some people, and all Etta's performances were terrific. But it's much bigger sweat for other members of the company. The eight-show-a-week routine puts great pressure on everyone.

AM: *So tell me, what is the structure of a working week for a member of Adventures in Motion Pictures?*

MB: In the West End, there are six evening performances from Monday to Saturday, and matinées on Wednesday and Saturday as well. We try to give people one show off a week, if we can – but when some dancers get injured this often isn't possible. The dancers are contractually required to take a minimum of four classes each week out of six. Company class lasts an hour and a half; if they take class elsewhere, they have to clear that with us, the day before. We try to make classes as near to the show as possible – mid- to late-afternoon. Then, after that class, we put in a forty-five-minute 'emergency call' every day, in case we need last-minute rejiggings to cover things like changes of partner. This session is also when we give notes. When a larger rehearsal is needed, then the class may be shifted to midday or late morning. The rehearsal will take place after that. But if the rehearsal is smaller or less demanding, then we'll call in a few people before class and do a rehearsal from about midday onwards.

AM: *Tell me about company class. What range of teachers and range of styles do you draw from?*

MB: We try to vary it between classical and contemporary classes each week. We employ guest teachers for a week at a time.

AM: *Any particular kinds of ballet? Any particular kinds of contemporary?*

MB: In ballet, the dancers like a ballet class that's very dancy, that really moves: not one too tied to individual virtuoso steps. Much depends on the teacher, and we have found several good ones – such as Laura Connor – who are popular with the dancers. Also a few people within the company teach class sometimes: Iain Webb, Etta, Isabel Mortimer, Ben Wright, Vicky Evans.

The dancers who've been professional ballet dancers – Adam and Sarah, for example – do a few contemporary classes, but generally go to ballet class. There was some fuss made in the ballet press that Sarah was required by the Royal Ballet to keep up half-an-hour special pointe-work every day while she was with us. Maybe she was, but she didn't tell us about it. Lynn, of course, will only do ballet class, but she is very specific about what she likes. She has taught a few classes for us, but though they're good classes, the features that are, to her, articles of faith – the crossed-over fifth positions that she

357

learnt in Stanley Williams's class in New York – really aren't useful to most of our dancers.

The contemporary classes tend to be more Cunningham-based. Whatever style of contemporary it is, it needs to be quite technical and strengthening – not the kind of contemporary that's more to do with finding your body, and rolling around on the floor, and release. Those just wouldn't be useful to us.

Revisions

AM: *Tell me about the revised version of* Cinderella *you took to Los Angeles.*

MB: The whole experience of the Los Angeles production of *Cinderella* was great. I loved the collaboration involved in planning revisions – we really got back to the things we valued most in our work. The whole production had much more of a company feeling; the dancers enjoyed doing it and took pride in it.

AM: *So how did you change it?*

MB: Lez Brotherston, Scott Ambler, Etta Murfitt and I spent several days discussing what we wanted to change, and why.

As a result, we made the whole family household in Act One more domestic in scale. There was a large drape to separate the hallway from the living-room, and there were lighting fittings hanging down to stop the room seeming palatial in height. We kept the simple Prologue in which the Stepmother and her brood of kids replace Cinderella's mother and demote Cinderella. And we began the family scene by giving the audience what it expects to see in any *Cinderella*: the heroine busy doing the housework centre-stage, her sisters lolling about. Then we introduced the other members of the family. We also made the Stepmother less of a star role and a more completely integrated member of her family.

And we gave the Pilot much more to do in this act – or, rather, we made him much more of a fleshed-out character at this stage of the show. The blackout scene involved not just Cinderella's search but also his.

In Act Two, we made the ballroom less dreamlike and more specific: a club, a place where a World War Two story really might happen, with a waitress and a *maître d'*. It had a much more realized bandstand, with a piano, a double bass, and a mike; and (instead of banquettes) it had chairs and tables, to make it more social.

At the same time, we made the whole ballroom look much more wrecked. At the beginning, we had Cinderella (still dressed as she had been in Act One) and the Angel, taking in the bomb-wreckage to the ballroom; and then we made much more of the Angel bringing the ballroom back to life. We approached the 'blue' couples as individual characters. Each had a different hairstyle; and they all looked much less like the dancers in Ashton's *La Valse* than they had before and much more like real people in the 1940s. Two of the five 'blue' men were no longer in uniform: one was a bandleader wearing a tux, another a *maître d'* in tails. They were still mainly 'blue' couples (with red accessories), and the fact that they were dead couples who come back to life for the duration of this act was made more emphatic.

It was still a 'dream' act, but we located the dream in reality much better this time. And we introduced Cinderella's mother here, with her father, both alive and well. They're a vision, a part of Cinderella's dream. She can't communicate with them, but they're part of the sense that this is a ballroom where dreams seem to come true. Actually, Cinderella's mother here is the one area in which we still confused audiences. She was in a white dress, and the production had used publicity showing Cinderella wearing a similar white dress in the London production. Cinderella no longer wore that white dress in Los Angeles, but a few people in the LA audience had already connected her with the white dress and so confused mother and daughter.

Just about everything for the 'blue' couples was rechoreographed. We gave them more of a flavour of 1940s social dance: not so much as to re-create those dances literally, but just enough to place them in a period and an atmosphere. The Stepmother no longer had a separate entrance; she entered with her family. That made a big difference. Cinderella now was more clearly her own fantasy: a sexy woman, like a film star. And not goody two-shoes. When the Pilot chooses her in front of all her family, she shows just a hint of malicious satisfaction.

We changed the pas de deux considerably. It was now more plainly a separate scene in another place, with a bed in which the Pilot was lying, plainly after they'd had sex. And the beginning, the ending, and parts of the middle were entirely changed.

The strokes of midnight worked much better largely because we lit the scene far better this time, but also because we clarified: the audience can see Angel warning Cinderella about the time, and there's a sense of his unrelenting control of events. When midnight starts, Cinderella sees one layer of nightmare after another. First, her family taunting her with the invitation to the party and leaving her out. Second, the shooting of her mother by her stepmother. (Whether or not this had actually happened in the past is deliberately left unclear; this is a nightmare.) Third, the family joins the Stepmother around the body of Cinderella's mother. (It would be almost the same group-portrait scene as we saw in the prologue to Act One, but for the Mother's corpse.) Cinderella tries to shake her father and get him to react, but he doesn't respond. Fourth, he's pushed into a wheelchair. Fifth, Cinderella sees the Pilot with one of her sisters. Sixth, she – in hysterics – runs offstage (actually to do a quick change). Seventh, the Angel initiates the destruction of the buildings. Eighth, the 'blue' couples start to die again, in stylized movements, with images of bodies being carried like corpses and other people screaming. Ninth, on the final stroke of midnight, Cinderella reappears – dressed in her old drab clothes – and falls down lifeless amid all the bombing. Tenth, her body is picked up by air-raid wardens and carried off on a stretcher.

The whole show had much more logic.

AM: *How much logic does an audience need, though? We know this is a dance show; we know the hero and heroine will have a dance duet. Do we need to see the specific state they've reached in their sexual relationship?*
MB: I believe the audience does need it. Even when an audience comes expecting to see this situation or that in a well-known story like *Cinderella*, it helps if you give the world onstage such detail and motivation that each situation becomes unusually real.

Certainly it helps the performers. If you're going to do a long run of a show, you need to know why you're doing each and every movement if you're going to find satisfaction from performance night after night. In Act Three, for example, the West End audience may not have been bothered by the fact that Cinderella's family all went to visit her in hospital – but the performers were. They've never liked her, so why do they visit her? Now in LA we could make much clearer what we'd always meant to show – that all the members of the step-family have abused Cinderella in some way and that they're frightened, now that she's undergoing psychiatric treatment after being traumatized by the bomb, that she'll tell on them. They want to shut her up, the Stepmother above all. In the scene when she returns to Cinderella, she used to try smothering Cinderella in her sleep. Now she confronts her, threatens her. There's a struggle. Possibly the Stepmother tries strangling Cinderella; it's not entirely clear, because at that moment other people arrive. That was our main change in Act Three; otherwise it was the act we could leave much as it had been.

AM: *I testify how much better the show was in LA; I was able to see it there three times. Among other things, I could see many more filmic resonances now. In Act Three, after we've seen (to one side) the* Brief Encounter *couple at their railway-café table, there's an amazingly moving little moment when she (Philippa Gordon in the Celia Johnson role) is briefly centre-stage. She's alone now, and she turns and gazes at the table where they said goodbye. It's just a look, and it's absolutely laden with feeling.*

In Act Two, Cinderella now arrives in the ballroom with her hair flowing over her shoulders, in a sexy coloured dress rather than in debutante white. Sarah Wildor (blonde) looks like Veronica Lake; Saranne Curtin (redhead) looks like Rita Hayworth. Was that deliberate?
MB: No, that was just happy accident. We knew the look we wanted. Only when the dancers put those costumes on did we realize that they looked like individual film stars.

But there were other consciously film-related ideas we were able to bring off better this time. In Act One, we'd always had the idea that Cinderella tries to touch the Angel, but finds that she puts her hand through him, but we weren't able to put it into practice. This time, we really brought it off, entirely in movement terms. She gestures towards him. First, his body arches back before her hand in a concave arch, and then it suddenly snaps back into an upright position – with her hand sticking out now behind his back, and with her looking at it in alarm.

AM: *I met you in London just after you'd finished rehearsals, a few days before you flew to LA You told me how pleased you were with how they'd gone, and you said, 'I think it's only the second time around that you do the real choreography!'*
MB: What's interesting is that, this time, I did much more of the creative work. The first time around, I encouraged the dancers to come up with much of the material for the movement. This time I had a much

more precise idea of what I wanted. I've talked about 'we' as usual, and I don't think I would have been so clear in rehearsals if I had not been through those very productive discussions with Lez, Scott and Etta. They focused my mind.

There is no one sure formula in choreography. I'm lucky in that I work with like-minded people who help me to clarify what's in my mind; or to see the sense of what's in theirs. When work goes well, you just get deeper – it seems – into your own instinct. And into the music. I knew what I'd heard in Prokofiev's score all along, but this time I was able to bring much more of it to life.

I I

Past, Present, Future

ALASTAIR MACAULAY: *I'd like to ask you about how you like and/or dislike the new eminence you've achieved as an artist and as a choreographer. You've achieved this eminence in particular with first* Oliver! *and then* Swan Lake.

MATTHEW BOURNE: *Oliver!* changed my life in terms of finance. Just to have a regular income was great. I suppose I like sometimes being recognized, because I've always enjoyed that aspect of theatre. Anyway, because I'm a choreographer, not very many people know me – so when it does happen, it's very agreeable. It's different for a star dancer like Adam – or a film star. To walk down a street with someone as well known as Shirley MacLaine, as I did in the States, was just amazing: the number of people who spoke to her! Everyone shouts out, 'Hi, Shirley, how are you doing? You look great!' and she says, 'Hi!' all the time – to all these complete strangers.

What's strange, though, is that I do get a number of people who get obsessed with me, think they know me, think they understand me as a person. I don't like that much! I sometimes get overanalysed, and drawn into saying things about myself and my work – just to say something. I've started to understand why so many artists say, 'It's just a show', 'I did it to please the audience.'

AM: *If you put it into words, you destroy the spontaneity of it.*
MB: Yes. You're in danger of spoiling the magic – if there is any – by saying too much about it. I know that there is an interest in where ideas came from and how things develop – but I think often things are put to you that you didn't have any intention of saying. You can sometimes fall into the trap of feeling you must make some response.

363

Mostly, people are very nice, and I hope I'm always nice back. But some people suddenly hang around and become your 'friend' – and interrupt you when you're with your real friends. I'm having to learn how to be more firm in some situations, just because a lot of my time is taken up now with things that aren't particularly creative. I don't get enough time to listen to music or read to find new ideas.

AM: *Throughout this book, you've spoken in terms of 'we' in your work – and I have the feeling that you use your collaborators to help you along the lines they're best equipped to help. When I spoke to Etta Murfitt about Scott's role in helping you to conceive and plan a show, she said, 'Yes – Scott's useful in that way. I'm not. But get a show started and I'm very good at contributing to the making of it.' I also think you use several of your friends to help you find ideas, music, stimulus. How conscious are you of using the people around you? Is it instinctive?*
MB: It is. I sometimes feel guilty about this. When I feel I know what I'm doing, I don't want to involve anyone else; but there are times when I need to talk things through, and then I feel I can ask the help of people a little. Then, however, just as they get all excited and involved, I say, 'I know what I'm doing now, thanks' and carry on alone. It is, of course, my job to make the final decision on anything; but, yes, I have different people I go to for different things – sometimes just because I just want reassurance that an idea is a good one.

AM: *The sexual implications of your* Swan Lake *are much discussed. What about the performers? Are your male swans of mixed sexuality?*
MB: Yes, of course.

AM: *So is there any repression or sexual embarrassment at all in AMP? What's it like for straight and gay guys to mix together in a show that has attracted a great deal of gay interest?*
MB: No problem at all. I don't think there are in any dance companies, are there? Maybe sometimes in ballet companies, but even there such problems must be rare.

AM: *Do the women ever find it either a pleasure or a pain to be around a fairly high number of gay men?*
MB: I've never known a company of people where sexuality mattered less. There are no cliques in that respect, and there are all sorts of relationships and couplings within the company, gay and straight.

AM: *Do you ever win any disapproval in politically correct circles for not having offered any presentation of femininity as audacious as your Prince or Swan? Do you ever get accused of misogyny?*

MB: Yes, I did, the first time we went to the States. For the first time ever, I got asked questions about my treatment of women. The assumption was that I saw all women as either the bimbo girlfriend or the whory queen – that I saw all women as sexual animals, either as prostitutes or as sex-mad princesses. I just say, 'They're all *characters*.' There are as many male stereotypical characters in *Swan Lake* as female ones.

AM: *Your Sylph is certainly the least stereotypical character in High-land Fling.*

MB: While we were in Los Angeles – after a lot of good reviews had come out – we received one review from a gay critic that said, 'What a shame that this didn't depict a gay relationship in a happy way. Why does it always have to be tragic? What a pity it didn't have a positive ending.' Obviously he didn't know *Swan Lake* very well! The obvious answer to that is: 'That's the story'.

I showed a male couple being happy together back in *Town and Country*, as it happens, and one day I may do so again. Political correctness doesn't worry me that much, I must say.

AM: *But are there aspects of feminism that you do adhere to?*

MB: Yes. I try consciously to present women as equal to men. All the women in the ballroom scene in *Swan Lake* stand up to the Stranger. He doesn't just seduce – there's a lot of give and take. This is partly because I think that's the way things should be, but also because the women in the company want to be seen that way. Women today don't want to be swooning all over the place over a man. That's why many modern young women (including some ballerinas) find some ballets difficult – they want to assert themselves more than certain roles will allow. Sylvie Guillem does not play 'simpering and girly'. Some roles are now interpreted in new ways.

AM: *To what degree did* Swan Lake *come out of your lack of a partner and to what degree did* Cinderella *come out of your discovering a partner?*

MB: I find it very difficult to judge these things. It's interesting that those pieces came about like that. *Swan Lake* happened when I had

had a lot of rejection from various people, and I began to lose confidence; but I was very happy creating it. To a certain extent, my feelings go towards the dancers that I'm working with. I'm glorifying the person on whom I'm choreographing. To involve yourself in a story to the level that I try to do, you almost have to take on the various characters. At times, I felt as though I was the Prince in *Swan Lake* – though really I'm not like him at all.

It is wonderful to get to know your dancers as persons through the rehearsal process, and, in those circumstances, an affection may well emerge that feels like a form of love on both sides. Adam and I have felt very close since the making of *Swan Lake* because of the importance it has had for both of us. I don't want to deny that affection, but I also don't want it to be misunderstood or given a greater sexual emphasis than it has.

AM: *Have there been other dance relationships which have involved that kind of love/fascination on your part?*
MB: Quite a number – certainly with Simon Murphy in the early 1990s. It's fairly clear in the way I cast him. The first piece he did with us was *Deadly Serious* – and he was cast as my lover. He was also partnered with me in the short film we made called *Drip* – we had a revealing duet about two people having sex, but with a door of frosted glass between them. He's teasing me, things go on on both sides of the door, and eventually it goes into fantasy – we end up dancing in the Criterion Restaurant! Simon died in 1995; *Swan Lake* is dedicated to him.

The love I have for some of my performers includes some of the women, so it is not necessarily a sexual kind of love. Admittedly, if there is an element of desire there too, then the situation can grow a bit competitive.

AM: *Are the female roles you make to any degree any expression of the woman inside yourself? I don't mean that you're a drag artist – I mean that most men, straight men too, find there is a feminine aspect to them.*
MB: I would certainly look inside myself to try to identify with any character – with female characters as much as the male characters.

AM: *How do the women in the company change the chemistry of the company or your working process?*
MB: It depends on what I'm asking from people, what sort of production we're doing. To date, I think I've been happier working with

individual women than with an ensemble of women. Developing something for any particular female dancer is a real pleasure. Whereas I am quite happy choreographing for men as a group or as individuals. Partly it is for me – unlike a lot of choreographers – an aesthetic thing as well; it's to do with costume. I love seeing men's clothes danced in. I have problems with lots of dresses – there's something about that look which I find very covered up. In the kind of productions that I do, women's costume can often become a problem, getting in the way of the movement; whereas you put a man in a suit and everything works.

AM: *I think that you've said, when choreographing material for women, that you tend to go back to ballet, or to Isadora Duncan or to Ginger Rogers, in your mind as various models for female style.*
MB: Isadora, definitely. I like dancing with a lot of freedom in it; and there are particular female dancers whose freedom excites me. I love watching female dancing, and I've loved working with a lot of the women I've worked with, and using their personalities. What I'm saying is simply that I find it more of a challenge to do something original with a woman. So many brilliant, vivid examples of how a woman can dance on stage have already been established that it's particularly hard to establish a new one.

AM: *You've said that your choreography for women tends to come more readily from your own body. Do you want to talk about the whole business of who provides the movement in choreography?*
MB: Gender apart, I know people who feel that contemporary choreographers in Britain should go back to choreographing steps and choreographing movement themselves, and not rely completely on the dancers. I do agree with that to a certain extent. Often, the reason for letting others start off the choreographic process is time. There's just not enough time to initiate all the movement and to supervise everything else; but I would like to start doing more of the early stages of choreography myself again – I always used to – because I think you can lose touch with your own style and your own ideas.

AM: *As a performer, what were your favourite roles?*
MB: I enjoyed very much doing the Laurence Olivier part, Max de Wynter, in *Deadly Serious*. It was a character that had other sides. He had a secret male lover; he wasn't what he seemed.
    I went into *Nutcracker* the year after it was made, and I loved being

part of an ensemble, being one of the gang of orphans, and then having one little featured thing to do in the second half. And I always enjoyed doing *Spitfire* – feeling as if we were these great male ballet dancers, coming and taking the applause. If the audience entered into the spirit of the piece and cheered and bravoed, it added to the fantasy. When we did the Dance of Life gala that Gillian Lynne organized at Her Majesty's, back in 1991, in the interval we were literally surrounded by Irek Mukhamedov and Julio Bocca on either side of us. There was Mukh spinning around the stage, and there we were, warming up in our underwear – embarrassed even to attempt a plié! We were a big hit. It proved that you could achieve something through ideas, as well as through jumps and turns – which was what most of the evening was made up of.

For someone with very limited dance capabilities, to be on stage in that company is a lovely memory. That's why I want to perform in *Swan Lake* on Broadway – as the Private Secretary, a role I've already sometimes played – to enable a personal dream to come true. It's just a treat for myself – it's not something the production needs.

AM: *One of the ironies of doing this book is that I have to admit that I never saw on stage either the work you dedicated to me,* Greenfingers, *or the one whose score I had pushed you towards,* Boutique. *The score is the Rossini anthology that Diaghilev chose and Respighi arranged for Massine's 1919 ballet* La Boutique Fantasque. *You choreographed it in 1994 for the London Studio Centre. What did you do?*
MB: Because of *Boutique* in the title, I set it in a boutique in 1960s Carnaby Street. It follows the ballet scenario pretty closely. A young man comes with his flighty girlfriend to a fashion boutique. He falls in love with one of the dummies in the window. There are various scenes involving the designer who makes the clothes – he's there in the shop and he shows off various collections with various dancers, but it's all automated. He is a control freak. He brings the models to life, and they dance to show off the clothes for the girlfriend. After a while, the girlfriend makes the young man buy a lot of stuff. He comes back at night and breaks into the shop. All the dummies are now unclothed, but they have wigs still on. They all come to life.

AM: *Of their own accord?*
MB: Yes, it becomes more eerie. He finds a girl – the dummy he's fallen for – and there's a scene I'm very pleased with where she's all in pieces

and then put together again. They dance – to that lovely music for the pas de deux – a whole duet, she being dummy-like all the while. It's rather like the dummy duet in *Cinderella*, but the other way round: she's the dummy. He takes her hand at the end and kisses it – as they go behind a screen at the back, which is the entrance of the changing room. He's holding an arm, and she's not attached to it. Now there's a whole scene with the other dummies holding bits of her body. Someone's got the head, someone else the torso. Eventually she's put together again. There's a finale, which ends with the shop front coming down again.

We had quite an elaborate set, a shop front and an interior. It ends up with him stealing the dummy – the actual dummy – out of the shop. It was not an easy piece to choreograph, because it was made on students over a long period of time according to the spaces in their timetables so you lose track of what you're doing; and with students you really do have to do all the choreography. But it worked well. It's a piece I would consider restaging, in the right context. It felt very young, like a young people's ballet somehow. I couldn't imagine doing it with a very sophisticated company like the Royal Ballet.

AM: *Are there other Diaghilev scores, or Royal Ballet scores, that you are drawn to?*

MB: Several, especially the lighter ones. *Les Patineurs* is such a perfect ballet, and that kind of music appeals to me immensely. You once told me that the critic David Vaughan said, 'Whenever people say, "Oh, it's minor art", then I know I'm going to like it.' Well, I'm like that too.

I am vaguely considering several one-act ballet scores at present, because I've been invited to several different ballet companies to choreograph something. I'm interested by Stravinsky's score for *The Firebird*, and by the Arthur Bliss score for *Adam Zero*. I'd quite like to do something to the Chopin music for *Les Sylphides*.

The Royal Ballet suggested the Brecht-Weill *Seven Deadly Sins* to me (with Ute Lemper). I like the idea, but to me the music is wrong for the Royal Opera House, which was what was being suggested. I respond to the music, but I don't really like the scenario – it doesn't actually say those sins to me, very clearly. If I were to do Seven Deadly Sins, I'd want to do each sin completely, not some illusion of the sin. I've seen about three versions of it, and each time I always assumed it was going to be more full-on in terms of lust, gluttony, or whatever, and each time there were passages when I didn't know what was going on.

AM: *Any ideas for other full-length dance shows?*

MB: I have a whole notebook of ideas. One idea was *Sweeney Todd*. Apparently there's a full Malcolm Arnold score – this was an idea of Adam's. (He loves Malcolm Arnold – and I think he sees himself as Sweeney Todd!) It's got some good characters in it.

I had an idea for a *Carmen*, a sort of Almodóvar *Carmen*. Kinky Spanish sex, small-scale production, very raw, possibly set in a meat factory with flesh and carcasses, and using maybe a small-scale orchestration of the Bizet score with a lot of percussion.

Both *Lolita* and – especially – *The Servant* appeal to me as inspirations for small-scale productions.

What may happen with some of these ideas is that elements of them will go into another idea. The relationships in *The Servant* are interesting – a series of duets, with different pairings complicating it – because their relationships change all the time. It's almost like *La Ronde*.

Coppélia? I do find some of the score wishy-washy at times. Still, I have ideas for it – Dr Coppélius makes models from wax. It would be a bit like those Universal horror pics. *The Sleeping Beauty*, on the other hand, doesn't feel right, but I just love the score and keep playing it – not least the bits that are usually not used in the stage versions.

Dangerous Liaisons is another idea. And *Billy Budd*. *The Tenant* is a Roman Polanski film of paranoia about a man who rents an apartment where the previous occupant, a woman, has jumped out of the window and smashed through a glass roof. She's in hospital, virtually dead; then she dies. It's about him thinking that all the other tenants in the building are trying to get him to do the same thing – and it's all in his mind. Eventually, he buys a dress and a wig, turns into her and jumps out of the window. Twice! Because he doesn't kill himself the first time, and so he tries to drag himself up to do it again. It's one of the favourite films of my youth.

These are projects without scores, admittedly; but when I was in Hollywood just recently, I met with some film composers and agents of film composers. The sort of people who approach you to write music for dance tend to be serious composers – who write these long bits of music that just don't do anything for me – but film composers are used to working the way that Petipa and Tchaikovsky did on *The Sleeping Beauty* and *The Nutcracker*: 'One minute of this, and thirty seconds of that; then I want a fanfare here.' I talked to them about this, and they said, 'Absolutely, that's the way we love to work.' Many of the best composers are working in film, but are also looking for more creative outlets.

Another possibility is to find someone to arrange older music for me, the way that John Lanchbery did for Ashton. I'd love to develop my great love of Percy Grainger into a full-length work. For me, Grainger is a major composer – overlooked, though not so much these days. There's some beautiful, incredible music. Maybe this could work for *Billy Budd*, since Grainger wrote so much nautical stuff. What's so good about Grainger is the variety in the orchestration and the amazingly original sounds that come out of the orchestra.

I am considering *Midsummer Night's Dream*, but with a new score. I know it's been done a million times; but I think it could be quite good for our company. It has such a variety of characters. You've got the other world and you've the real world; you've got young lovers, you've got fairies and Puck. There's a lot of good roles there.

The Red Shoes as a full-length ballet. I mean the story of the Powell-Pressburger movie, not the Hans Christian Andersen story alone. *Peter Pan*: I've got some friends who've written a musical score for it that I like. *Dorian Grey* possibly. *Blithe Spirit*. *The Beggar's Opera*. *The Water Babies*.

AM: *Quite a few of your current pieces are on or over the cusp of 'camp'. Do you ever think about this? Are there some aspects of 'camp' in art that you enjoy? And others that you don't? And can you say why?*

MB: Well, I think I like the real meaning of 'camp' – if I understand it correctly. But there's a certain gay connotation – as in 'campness' and 'camp' behaviour and 'camping it up' – which I'm not a fan of. I also shy away from certain gay icons. To me, 'camp' is more to do with humour. I certainly don't think, 'Oh this scene's going to be camp,' when I'm choreographing. It's not a word I use very often. But I see how people often interpret what I've done in a very camp way that I myself usually have not initially seen. Like the character of the Queen in *Swan Lake*. You hear, 'Oh, she's so camp. We love her' – that sort of thing; and I just think, 'Well, I've never thought about it that way, and I never really conceived her in that way, as a camp figure.'

AM: *Yet you sent your wicked Stepmothers in* Cinderella *away to study Joan Crawford movies.*

MB: Yes, but that character was conceived as comic, and to me that's what camp is. I suppose I've enjoyed a lot of camp humour, but I'm very choosy about what sort I like. I don't really like drag acts. Whereas I very much enjoy Kenneth Williams, for example, who is quite over the top; but his whole personality, with its contradictory aspects, interests me. Just as some people think I'm into camp, so others say that what I do is parody and send-ups. I do think that there's an element of that within some aspects of what I do; but I certainly wouldn't set out for a whole evening of parody or send-up. We start with a serious base, and the humour creeps in.

AM: *You mentioned earlier your love of stars. I imagine part of what you love is their sheer projection, and that's what you're looking for in your own kind of dance. Now, do you have to work on projection in your dancers?*

MB: Yes, a lot. It doesn't come naturally to many people. I wish it were there naturally, because it's not the sort of thing I want to be dealing with, particularly in group dances. But even taking your focus out to the audience, acknowledging the audience's existence and where they are, is often ignored completely. So we talk about it quite a lot. And we talk about techniques of focus: if you're acting with other people on stage, really look them in the eye. I don't like it when a dancer flirts with an audience too much – but there are ways of connecting with the audience, of making sure that they've seen what it is that you're trying to say; and there are ways of turning your head to show the expression you want to come across, ways of doing it within a narrative piece. Scott Ambler is brilliant at this.

I know that, when I'm on stage performing, I'm conscious, in virtually every move I make – of where I'm doing it in relation to the audience; and how, and if it's coming across; or if it's making sense. We've even got to the point where we've discussed ways of engaging the audience by showing emotion facially, as when I taught everyone in *Nutcracker* to open their mouths a little when they jumped on the ice. It made an amazing difference. It adds height to the jump and it adds joy to the whole feeling. But some of the dancers I've worked with need imagery to get them to do this; it doesn't come naturally. So you have to say, 'If you're on the ice, you're looking out across the sky-line.' You give them something to look at as they're doing what they're doing; and then it comes alive more. For some people, it just comes naturally; they connect with the audience.

AM: *Have you found yourself working on what movement does project and what doesn't? Do you find some movement simply doesn't project when you've got it on stage?*

MB: Yes. A sort of fine-tuning process comes into action here on those things you don't think about when you're actually making movement. What helps a lot is to make sure that certain movements have a stop, an end to them.

AM: *Apart from choreography, your success in Los Angeles has led to a number of invitations to direct movies, which you're considering, cautiously. Since movies percolate through into your choreography anyway, let me ask you about your general taste in movies. We've spoken of Hitchcock, Walt Disney, Fred Astaire. What else?*

MB: Actually, someone in Hollywood has asked me to give him a list of movies I found inspiring – or the sort of films I'd like to have made – so here are some of the notes I've been making for it. Silent movies. I like a lot of Lillian Gish – *Broken Blossoms* and *The Wind*. The silent version of *Phantom of the Opera* – tinted – is beautiful to look at.

Disney's *Snow White*. Cocteau's films: *Beauty and the Beast* and *Orphée* and *Testament d'Orphée* and others. I've often wanted to do something with that atmosphere and that sort of look to it. To a certain extent, some of that went into *The Infernal Galop*, but not in a way that was evident. Jean Vigo. Jacques Tati, especially *Monsieur Hulot's Holiday*: a very big influence. The reason is fairly obvious: it's humour without words; but it's also observation of human madness and frailty. Everyone looking at one person doing something odd: I've used that idea quite a lot.

Hitchcock's *Rebecca*, *Strangers on a Train*, *Vertigo*, *Rear Window*.

David Lean, for epic story-telling, and for *Great Expectations* and – of course – *Brief Encounter*.

The Hunchback of Notre Dame, Charles Laughton. *The Night of the Hunter*, with Robert Mitchum, directed by Laughton.

Powell and Pressburger: *The Red Shoes* and *The Black Narcissus* – which I think would make a marvellous opera.

AM: *There are two important operas about nuns already.*

MB: This would be better! I like Visconti's films: *Rocco and his Brothers*, *The Leopard* and *The Damned*. And I remember seeing the film *Ludwig*, which made a very big impression on me.

Joseph Losey's films with the Pinter screenplays: *The Servant* and

Accident and *The Go-Between*. Dirk Bogarde chose to appear in many interesting films, especially *The Night Porter* – very controversial when it came out – which is a very good story.

Woody Allen films I love for their humanity: films that are about people and relationships, and not about special effects. I love the mixture of reality and fantasy that he uses very well in certain of his films, like *The Purple Rose of Cairo*, and a film called *Alice*, which is based on *Alice in Wonderland*. Putting fantasy in a modern-day setting – as in a musical he did recently, *Everybody Says I Love You*, where he does a dance with Goldie Hawn on the banks of the Seine. At one point, she flies up in the air with the music. It's a lovely metaphor for being in love, and it just happens for no reason.

Terence Davis films: *The Long Day Closes* and *Distant Voices, Still Lives*. They're all stories told primarily with the use of music. They are both nostalgic about his childhood and use a lot of popular music, and some favourite classical music of the time. Great films. Mike Leigh's films, very much, for social observation and humour and character. Some Tim Burton films: *Edward Scissorhands*, *The Nightmare before Christmas*. His interests include demonic children, and odd mixtures of fantasy and suburbia. But he's also mixing a modern world with a fantasy world, which very few people do these days.

Ian McKellen's *Richard the Third*.

AM: *No screwball comedy?*

MB: For pure pleasure, I would add things like *Bringing up Baby* and *The Philadelphia Story*. But I was thinking about a certain thing there.

No list can contain them all. I love *Citizen Kane*; and *Lady from Shanghai* is amazing. All Orson Welles' films are great. I forgot to write down, for example, Stanley Donen, who doesn't come straight to mind as an important director, but who is actually a very important director for me. The way he worked at MGM was an incredibly creative process, in that it was a real team of people. While they were working on one film, they were talking about the next, and that's why those films got better and better as they went along, and more inventive and clever. They had their great old stars, like Astaire, and they had the young stars they were training and promoting and giving opportunities to. If you couldn't sing, you were taught how to sing. If you couldn't dance, you were taught how to dance. If you couldn't act, they worked on that for two years before they put you in a film; and they had the best music department. A fabulous set-up. If only it existed now! But reading about it makes me see parallels to the way I'd like to work with AMP.

AM: *It's like the company set-up at Disney.*
MB: Yes, because they also seem like a real team of people – an ideas factory, which is a nice concept. I feel happier working surrounded by like-minded people who are gong to contribute to the idea. So that sort of set-up, as part of a team, is something I'm very happy working in.

AM: *Now what do you find inspiring in, say, Powell and Pressburger movies?*
MB: The freedom to go against the grain of what was being done at the time and to do what they wanted to do. So the films still look very much the product of their makers. I do like directors that you can 'see'. There's one school of thought that says, 'If you can see the director in the film, then he's not a good director,' and there's another that says the reverse. I like the directors you can 'see' and the choices they've made, what they've done with the camera, and how they've gone from one scene into another.

One particular bit sums up Powell and Pressburger for me – not necessarily the film as a whole. There's a wonderful transition from a scene on a railway platform in *I Know Where I'm Going*. Wendy Hiller is about to get on a train. The transition between her getting on to the train and seeing the train move is shown by the camera attending to the top hat worn by one of the men she's saying farewell to. Towards the end of the scene, it looks as if his hat's on fire – there's smoke coming out of it. Just as it looks silly, it fades into the train itself with the steam coming out of its funnel. It's an odd, pleasurable little detail that doesn't really mean anything but helps the fluency of the story and the movie. It's precisely that kind of thing that you can do on film and that you can't do on the stage.

AM: *You were in Los Angeles for eight weeks with* Swan Lake, *but evidently in that time you were encouraged a great deal to think in terms of making movies.*
MB: It was surprising just how many people came from the film world to see the show there; but then movies are many people's reason for being in LA. I think that anyone who seems a bit different in terms of direction and is getting praise is going to attract Hollywood interest,

because they're always looking for new talent as directors. Various meetings were set up for me, and people there often remarked that the work was very filmic, that it was narrative through strong imagery – which is what film-making is all about. To them, it seemed a natural progression for me to be making movies.

The problem that has arisen is that I've been sent scripts and, since I'm not a theatre director like, say, Nicholas Hytner, I've never dealt with a script. I've read them, and I have opinions on them. But the whole venture is just asking me to take on too many new things at once: dealing with scripts, thinking in terms of film, taking me away from the people that I'm surrounded with now. So, over the past year I've been thinking that what I would like to do is to look at some film ideas, but to develop them myself through the kind of work that I feel I'm doing now.

What tends to happen, when you're a choreographer, is that you get offered all the films with dance as a sort of sideline in them. *Dirty Dancing*-type or *Footloose*-like films, where there are characters who happen to dance. But that's not my thing. I don't do funky numbers – I express ideas and feelings through movement, which is not something that happens very often these days in films.

I'd love to do a film version of *Swan Lake* that was really conceived for the camera, so that it wasn't a theatrical concept – rethinking how those characters and ideas and that structure could work on film. Likewise *Cinderella*, and *Nutcracker*, and *Highland Fling*. That would be a great way for me to start, because I would be intimate with the material and passionate about it; and I would be allowed to make the decisions.

AM: *Other than actual film of stage dance, and other than the Astaire and Disney movies we've mentioned, what are your favourite examples of dance on film?*
MB: The ones that are most successful are the ones that are designed for film. The *Red Shoes* ballet works because it wasn't a ballet in the first place. It was designed as a film idea – and it actually incorporates the orchestra at one point and the audience. It's about what it's like to be on a stage performing a ballet. All as reconceived for film: no ballerina could ever dance that ballet straight through in live performance.

I think too many later musicals that were brought to the screen used an adapted version of the original Broadway choreography – and, therefore, didn't feel as filmic as they might have done. A lot of the pleasure in Fred Astaire and Gene Kelly is in the fact that it looks as if it's been made up on the spot using what's handy, with props that seem to just be there at the right point when you need them; and dances can travel across rooms or down streets, which is what the camera can do. Whereas in a film like *Sweet Charity* or even *West Side Story*, some of what you are seeing is a Broadway number and it's not the same as being in a live performance.

AM: *How about the Ashton ballet films?*
MB: I think *The Tales of Beatrix Potter* works well at times – but it's not always a lot to do with dancing. The outsize sets and the animal masks make a great contribution. What's good is how well most of it could only work on film: which was proved when they tried to do it on stage after Ashton's death. So it does have its strong moments. Sometimes, when it just goes off into a dance, it doesn't really go anywhere; they don't feel like tales. The Vegetable Ballet that Ashton choreographed for *Tales from a Flying Trunk* has some wonderful choreography, but it feels much more as if it's a stage production. That's why Ashton was happy to adapt it for the theatre.

AM: *We're speaking here in June 1999. What are your current plans for Adventures in Motion Pictures?*
MB: We are hoping currently to film both *Highland Fling* and *Cinderella*. Things look good at the moment, but where money is concerned you never know until you've actually done the work.

Onstage, I plan to do a new full-length *Carmen*, to have its première in Plymouth in August 2000. We'll use Bizet's music, but we haven't yet fixed what arrangement of it or if we'll also add music from elsewhere. At present, I'm thinking of a logo that will play on the title as *Car Men*. I want the production to be rough, sexy, realistic, and I may well set it around some petrol station. We'll see.

And – as I've said – a revised *Nutcracker* in LA for Christmas 2000. Just now, we're preparing a national tour of *Swan Lake* that will start in Sheffield in October 1999, which will then – we hope – become an international tour, visiting Europe, Japan, the United States, and possibly other countries too. There may also be a London revival. On a smaller scale, I hope to revive *Spitfire* for a Stonewall gala. It'll be good to see it again; it's eleven years old. I'd also love to revive *Town and Country* in time for its tenth anniversary in 2001. Who knows?

AM: *Most choreographers deny that they ever borrowed anything, unless from a great dead master. And they will sometimes go to great lengths to conceal most of their sources. There are exceptions to this rule. Richard Alston used to say, 'I quote Ashton without knowing it.' But you may be the prize exception for the degree to which you openly identify your sources. Sometimes you've forgotten some of them, but, if they're drawn to your attention, you never fight the possibility or fact that these sources influenced you. Would you like to discuss the subject of originality and unoriginality?*

MB: It has a lot to do with confidence. I know that, when I use an idea that I've seen somewhere else, it's never a complete copy. It's a starting point, and usually ends up looking completely different. So I'm quite happy to say where the beginnings of an idea came from. Maybe the issue of originality matters much more when you're doing a pure-dance piece, because all you're using is dance and musicality.

What I am afraid of is what I see as conventional movement. Everyone has their aesthetic – and there are certain dance movements or shapes that I just shy away from. I would sometimes shy away from a straight arabesque line in my own choreography; but I wouldn't be afraid of quoting from a picture I'd seen of an old ballet. For a start, I wouldn't know how, in the original choreography, that dancer had got in and out of the position in which they've been photographed. Anyway, it just sparks something off.

I'm not afraid of being accused of stealing other people's ideas – because that really isn't what I do. By the end of my choreographic process, something that set off as a quotation has become very 'me'. I always like that line of Stravinsky's, when somebody said to him, 'We hear all these little bits of Mozart in your music – what do you have to say about that?' and he said, 'I feel I have the right to steal it because I love it.'

76 *Cinderella*. Matthew Bourne (centre) directing rehearsals. Iain Webb is on
the left, Etta Murfitt on the right.

Choreochronicle

Professional Choreography by Matthew Bourne

Compiled by Alastair Macaulay, revising the 1995/96 AMP choreochronicle, with the generous assistance of Scott Ambler, Elizabeth Marshall, and Matthew Bourne.

ABBREVIATIONS

M	Music by	A	Actors
Dir	Directed by	Si	Singers
S	Sets	Pr	Première
C	Costumes	RV	Revisions
L	Lighting	TV	Televised
D	Dancers	NP	New production
F	Female performers	N	Note
Ma	Male performers	AMP	Adventures in Motion Pictures

1987

Overlap Lovers. An Intrigue in Three Parts.

M: Stravinsky, 'Tango' (1953); Man Jumping; Juan de Dios Filiberto. **C:** James McCloskey with June Bourne. **L:** Ken McComiskey or David Goldsworthy. **D:** Carrollynne Antoun, Keith Brazil, Emma Gladstone, Susan Lewis, David Massingham, David Waring, Catherine White. **Pr:** July 15, 1987. Bonnie Bird Theatre, Laban Centre for Movement and Dance, London
AMP.

N. Dedicated 'For Fred'. (Fred Astaire had died earlier that year.)

An early AMP announcement (1986–7) for this work says 'Matthew Bourne is working on a piece, for six dancers, using the films of Alfred Hitchcock as a starting-point.' Bourne now says that any specific references to Hitchcock were removed as he made the work 'more abstract', but that they helped to give the work its sense of intrigue and sexual ambiguity.

Bourne himself later danced Waring's role; and Joachim Chandler later danced Antoun's. In the 1987–8 season, Bourne and AMP colleagues 'directed' a number of other pieces for students at schools or youth dance centres where AMP was doing residencies. Bourne has no recollection of these.

1988

Buck and Wing

M: Steve Blake (commissioned). **C:** Pam Downe. Art work: Clive Mitchell. **L:** Tim Barwick. **D:** Emma Gladstone, Catherine White. **Pr:** August 22, 1989. The ICA Theatre, London. *AMP.*

N. Dedicated 'For JM and EP'. Bourne was inspired here by Jessie Matthews and Eleanor Powell.

Spitfire. An Advertisement Divertissement.

M: Minkus and Glazunov.
  1. Adage.
  2. Variation I. 'String Vest and Y-Front Briefs'.
  3. Variation II: 'Cellular Singlet and Thermal Pant'.
  4. Variation III: 'Interlock Trunks'.
  5. Variations IV: 'Single Flap Access'.
  6. Coda.
C: Matthew Bourne. **L:** Tim Barwick. **D:** David Waring (I), Keith Brazil (II), Jo Chandler (III), Matthew Bourne (IV). **Pr:** August 22, 1988 Institute of Contemporary Arts, London. *AMP.*

NP 1991. **S** and new **C:** David Davies. **L:** Rick Fisher. **D:** Scott Ambler (I), Ben Wright (II), Jamie Watton (III), Matthew Bourne (IV).

N. An early 1988 AMP announcement says 'Matthew Bourne's quartet for four men takes as its starting point Perrot's famous "Pas de Quatre" and places it in the world of men's underwear advertising. Music by Glazunov and "costumes" courtesy of Marks and Spencer.'
  There have been successive revisions to the third variation over the seasons.
  Other dancers who have danced in this work include: David Massingham, Stephen Kirkham, David Greenall, Phil Hill, Adam Cooper.

1989

The Infernal Galop
A French dance with English subtitles

Sound: Anthony Cowton.

1: 'Les Enfants du Paname'
M: song sung by Mistinguett.
2: 'Fruits de Mer'.
M: 'La Mer', sung by Charles Trenet.
3: 'Pret-à-Porter'.
M: Commissioned score by Philippe and Fredo Boyer.
4. 'Les Grand Duets d'Amour'.
M: Song 'Hymne à l'amour' sung by Edith Piaf.
5: 'Pistiere'.
M: Emille Prud'homme and Les Compagnons de la Chanson.
6: 'Le Grand Ecart'.
M: Jacques Offenbach, from 'Orphée aux Enfers'.

S: Clive Mitchell. C: David Manners. L: Simon Corder. D: Keith Brazil, Emma Gladstone, Stephen Kirkham, Susan Lewis, Jamie Watton, Catherine White. Pr: 17 August, 1989. The Place Theatre, London.

NP 1992. One additional number, 'Tristesse', added – after 'Les Enfants du Paname' and before 'Fruits de Mer'. M: Additional song, sung by Tino Rossi. SC: (revised) David Manners. L: Rick Fisher. D: Scott Ambler, Matthew Bourne, Ally Fitzpatrick, Andrew George, Etta Murfitt, Simon Murphy.
AMP.

N. This was a Place Portfolio Commission 1989.

Terrafirma

Opera composed by Steve Martland. *Innererklang Music Theatre.*

N. Bourne describes the choreographic style, laughingly, as 'experimental'.

As You Like It

Play by William Shakespeare. Dir: John Caird. M: Ilona Sekacz (commissioned). SC: Ultz. A: *Rosalind* Sophie Thompson, *Celia* Gillian Bevan, *Touchstone* Mark Williams, *Orlando* Jerome Flynn, *Silvius* Alan Cumming, *Phoebe* Cassie Stuart, *Jacques* Hugh Ross, *Duke Senior* Clifford Williams.

N. In this production, while the audience entered the theatre, the entire cast performed social dances for 10–15 minutes before the spoken beginning of the play.
   Phoebe danced a solo, in a vaguely Isadora Duncan style.
   At the end, the entire cast performed a hoedown.

Pr: Royal Shakespeare Theatre, Stratford-upon-Avon. September 13, 1989.
Royal Shakespeare Company.

N. This production transferred to the Barbican Theatre in March 1990.

Singer

Play by Peter Flannery. Dir: Terry Hands. M: Ilona Sekacz (commissioned). SC: Sanja Jurca Avci. L: Terry Hands. A: *Chorus* Joe Melia, *Stefan* Mick Ford, *Singer* Antony Sher, *Mani:* Malcolm Storry.

N. Bourne's choreography was for a brief 'play within the play'. It featured the actors Alan Cumming, Cassie Stuart and Mark Williams.

Pr: The Swan Theatre, Stratford-upon-Avon. October 11, 1989.
Royal Shakespeare Company.

N. In repertory into 1990.
   The production transferred in 1990 to The Pit, Barbican Centre, London.

Leonce and Lena

Play by George Buchner, translated by Jeremy Sams. Dir: Lindsay Posner. M: Stephen Warbeck (commissioned). SC: Julian McGowan. A: Bourne's choreography was for two actors – one male, one female – who performed as mechanical puppets. Pr: Studio Theatre, Crucible, Sheffield. November 9, 1989. Running until December 2, 1989.

Within the Quota

M: Cole Porter, 'Within the Quota'. **D:** Approximately 12–15 dancers, all female RAD dance students. **Pr:** Royal Academy of Dancing, London.

1990

Children of Eden

New musical. **M** and lyrics: Stephen Schwartz. Book: John Caird. **Dir:** John Caird. **SC:** John Napier. **L:** David Hersey. **D:** Anna-Jane Casey, Colin Charles, Brenda Edwards, Stephen Houghton, Vanessa Leigh-Hicks, Aaron Peth, Mitch Sebastian. **Si:** Anthony Barclay, Kevin Colson, Ruthie Henshall, Shezwae Powell, Frances Ruffelle. **Pr:** Prince Edward Theatre, London.

Greenfingers

M: Percy Grainger, 'Country Gardens'. Elgar: 'Chanson du Matin'. P. Grainger: 'Shepherds Hey'. **C:** Fenella Magnus. **D:** Carrollynne Antoun, Keith Brazil, Bill Eldridge, Susan Lewis, Catherine White. **Pr:** Farnham Maltings.
AMP

N. This choreography was incorporated in 1991 into the 'Country' section of 'Town & Country'. It was privately dedicated to Alastair Macaulay.

1991

Town & Country

Town: Louden Lots
1. 'Pomp and Circumstance'
M: Edward Elgar, arr. Paul Whiteman: 'Pomp and Circumstance'.
2. 'By the Sleepy Lagoon'
M: Eric Coates: 'By the Sleepy Lagoon' (the theme tune for 'Desert Island Discs').
3. 'Housewives' Choice'
M: Jack Strachey.
4. 'Dearest Love'
M: Noël Coward, 'Dearest Love', sung by Coward.
5. 'Brief Encounter'
M: Including Edward Elgar, 'Serenade' played by Alfredo Campoli and his Salon Orchestra; Noël Coward's spoken patter from another recording; Rachmaninov, arr. Matheson for 'Brief Encounter'.
6. 'Music Everywhere'
M: Eric Coates.
7. 'By the Sleepy Lagoon'
M: reprise of 2.

Country (More Clingingly)
1. 'Handel in the Strand'.
M: Percy Grainger.
2. 'Country Gardens'
M: Percy Grainger.

3. 'Gay but Wistful'
M: Percy Grainger.
4. 'Clog Dance'
M: J.S.Bach, arranged by Percy Grainger.
5. 'Chanson de matin'
M: Edward Elgar.
6. 'Shallow Brown'
M: Percy Grainger (sung by John Shirley Quirk, with chorus).
7. 'Shepherds Hey'.
M: Percy Grainger.
8. 'The Sussex Mummers' Christmas Carol'
M: Percy Grainger.
SC: Charlotte Humpston. L: Rick Fisher. D: Scott Ambler, Matthew Bourne, Ally Fitzpatrick, Etta Murfitt, Jamie Watton, Ben Wright. Pr: Arnolfini, Bristol
AMP

N. Dedicated to June and Jim Bourne.

A Midsummer Night's Dream

Opera composed by Benjamin Britten. Words from William Shakespeare's play *A Midsummer Night's Dream*. Dir: Robert Carsen. SC: Michael Levine. Si: *Oberon* James Bowman, *Titania* Lillian Watson, *Bottom* Roderick Kennedy.

N. Bourne's choreography was largely for the boys' choir, 20–25 in number. There was also some choreography for a hoedown for the 'mechanicals', and Bourne had some involvement with the staging as a whole.

Pr: Festival Theatre, Aix-en-Provence Festival.
Aix-en Provence Festival production

N. This production was revived by English National Opera at the London Coliseum in 1995 and 1996. Catherine (White) Malone rehearsed Bourne's choreography.

The Tempest

After the play by William Shakespeare. Dir: Nick Hedges. M: Various, including Noël Coward's 'Mad About the Boy', and excerpts from Paul Dukas's 'The Sorcerer's Apprentice', Richard Wagner, Harold Arlen, recordings by Billie Holliday. Musical director (live singing by the cast): Richard Balcombe. SC: Brian Lee. L: Kevin Fitz-Simons. A: *Prospero* Simon Bowen, *Trinculo* David Williams, *Stephano* Stuart Ash, *Caliban* Andrew Danezi. Cast also included: Sam Barriscale, Philip Goldsworthy, Clive Brunt. All the performers, approximately 25 in number, danced. (There were thirteen Ariels – a chorus.)
Pr: August 15, 1991. Running until August 24. The Place Theatre, London.
National Youth Theatre

N. There were some dance duets (for example, a tango, a sand dance and matador-and-cape duet for Stephano and Trinculo, to cha-cha music), and a big 'Hollywood fan dance' indicating water.

R: This production was revived in 1993.
National Youth Theatre

Show Boat

Musical. **M:** Jerome Kern. Lyrics and Book: Oscar Hammerstein II. **Dir:** Ronny Danielson.
A, Si, D: About 80 performers – actors, singers, dancers – in all. Some 30 members of the
Malmo Balletten dance company performed most of Bourne's choreography. **Pr:** Stadsteater,
Malmo, Sweden.
Malmo Stadsteater

N. Bourne set dances in particular to 'Make Believe', 'Can't Help Lovin' Dat Man', 'Ol' Man
River', 'After the Ball', 'Life Upon the Wicked Stage', 'Why Do I Love You?', 'Goodbye, My
Lady Love'.
The production was revived the following season.

Watch with Mother

M: Voice of Joyce Grenfell, beginning of nursery-school 'Moving to Music' sketch.
Percy Grainger, 'First English Waltz'.
Fauré, arr. Percy Grainger
P. Grainger, 'Children's March'.
J.S.Bach arr. Percy Grainger, 'Blithe Bells'.
C: Abby Hammond. **D:** Bourne originally choreographed this on nine dancers in the
Transitions Dance Company in autumn 1991. Three of these dancers – Saranne Curtin,
Maxine Fone, Andrew George – joined Adventures in Motion Pictures in 1992. However –
as a result of these defections – the work was never performed by Transitions.
In 1994, Bourne revived it for the National Youth Dance Company, rehearsing it at
Roehampton Institute. One of his dancers, Theo Clinkard, joined Adventures in Motion
Pictures later that year.
Pr: The Rambert School, London.

1992

Deadly Serious
'An Hysterical Double-Feature'

M: Songs: Cole Porter's 'You Do Something To Me', sung by Marlene Dietrich. 'Stardust',
sung by Ella Fitzgerald. 'Mr Wonderful', sung by Peggy Lee. Other music by: Charles
Gounod ('Dance of the Marionettes', as used as the theme for Hitchcock's TV series);
Bernard Herrmann, from the scores for *Vertigo, North by Northwest* and *Psycho*; Ferde
Grofé, 'Cloudburst' from his *Grand Canyon Suite*; Miklos Rosza; Jean Sibelius, 'Valse Triste'
(Sibelius's own recording); and 'Miranda' from his incidental music for *The Tempest*;
Franz Waxman, score for *Rebecca*; David Manners (commissioned).
SC: David Manners. **L:** Rick Fisher. **D:** Scott Ambler, Matthew Bourne, Ally Fitzpatrick,
Andrew George, Etta Murfitt, Simon Murphy. **Pr:** March 9, 1992. Arnolfini, Bristol
AMP

Nutcracker

New scenario by Martin Duncan and Matthew Bourne, after an original scenario by Marius
Petipa based on Alexandre Dumas *père*'s version of E.T.A.Hoffmann's *The Nutcracker and
the Mouseking*.
M: Pyotr Ilyich Tchaikovsky, *Nutcracker*. ('Mere Gigogne' was cut from Act Two.)
Dir: Martin Duncan. **SC:** Anthony Ward. **L:** Robert Bryan.
D: *Dr Dross (King Sherbert)* Barry Atkinson; *Matron (Queen Candy)*: Rosemary Allen;

Sugar (*Princess Sugar*) and *Fritz* (*Prince Bon-Bon*) (*their children*) Ally Fitzpatrick and Scott Ambler; *Clara* Etta Murfitt; *Nutcracker* Andrew George; *Orphans* Teresa Barker, Saranne Curtin, Misha Downey, Maxine Fone, Friedrich Gehrig, Andrew George, Mary Herbert, Phil Hill, Rachel Krische, Jason Lewis, Simon Murphy, Susan Jellings, Anton Skrzypiciel; *Governors and wives* Bruce Budd, David Owen Lewis, Angela Sorrigan, Gladwyn Taylor (members of Opera North chorus); *Cupids* Simon Murphy, Maxine Fone; *The Doorman* Scott Ambler; *Liquorice Trio* Teresa Barker, Misha Downey, Friedrich Gehrig, Saranne Curtin; *Knickerbocker Glory* Anton Skrzypiciel; *Marshmallow Girls* Maxine Fone, Mary Herbert, Rachel Krische, Susan Jellings; *The Gobstoppers* Phil Hill, Jason Lewis, Simon Murphy. **A:** From Opera North chorus. **Pr:** August 26, 1992. King's Theatre, Edinburgh. *Opera North with AMP.*

NP: This production was revived by AMP at Sadler's Wells Theatre in 1993 and 1994. The credits now read 'Devised and directed by Martin Duncan and Matthew Bourne. Choreographed by Matthew Bourne.' Slightly revised **SC:** Anthony Ward. **L:** Tina McHugh.
For this 1993 revival, an interval of 20 minutes occurred between Acts I and II.
D: As above, with the following main exceptions. Matthew Bourne danced an Orphan and Knickerbocker Glory. Stephen Kirkham danced an Orphan and a Gobstopper.
AMP

In the 1994 revival, Saranne Curtin danced Sugar.

The Percys of Fitzrovia. An Arty-Farce.

1. 'Still Life'.
M: Madame Florence Foster Jenkins's recording of the Laughing Song from Johann Strauss's 'Die Fledermaus'.
2. 'A Nest of Eels'.
M: Martinu.
3. 'Aural Pleasures'.
M: Franz Liszt.
4 'Militant Tendencies'.
M: Johannes Brahms.
5. 'Hard Backs'.
M: Bohuslav Martinu.
6. 'Writer's Block'.
M: Tchaikovsky (Piano Concerto No 1, arr. Percy Grainger).
7. 'The Object of Beauty'.
M: Louis Ganne.
8. 'Finishing Touches'.
M: Franz Ries.
9. 'Peculiar Vices'.
M: Bohuslav Martinu.
10. 'The Golden Hoarde'
M: Bohuslav Martinu.
SC: David Manners. **L:** Rick Fisher. **D:** Scott Ambler, Matthew Bourne, Ally Fitzpatrick, Andrew George, Etta Murfitt, Simon Murphy. **Pr:** Arnolfini, Bristol.
AMP

N. The programme says 'The choreographer would like to thank David Manners for suggesting the idea of Fitzrovia and the performers of AMP for their many contributions to the making of 'The Percys'.'

1993

Late Flowering Lust

TV film to poems by John Betjeman as set to music by Jim Parker and spoken by Nigel Hawthorne. **Dir:** David Hinton. Director of photography: Nic Knowland. Produced for Ecosse Films by Douglas Rae. 57 minutes. Filmed in July–August 1993. Broadcast by BBC2 on 8 May 1994. **C:** Pam Downe. Location: Bennington Lordship **A:** Nigel Hawthorne, Richenda Carey, Jonathan Cecil. **D:** Rosie Allen, Scott Ambler, Matthew Bourne, Ally Fitzpatrick, Maxine Fone, Andrew George, Etta Murfitt, Simon Murphy.
AMP

Drip. A Narcissistic Love Story.

Short film for TV. **Dir:** Frances Dickenson. **M:** Rowland Lee. **C:** David Manners. Produced by Caz Gorman. 11 minutes. Filmed: September 1993 Location: Brixton. **D:** Rosie Allen, Scott Ambler, Matthew Bourne, Andrew George, Etta Murfitt, Simon Murphy. Broadcast: BBC2, 9 February 1995.
AMP

1994

Peer Gynt

Play by Henrik Ibsen, in a version by Frank McGuinness. **Dir:** Yukio Ninagawa. **M:** Ryudo Uzaki. **S:** Tsukasa Nakagoshi. **C:** Lily Komine. **L:** Tamotsu Harada. Co-produced by Thelma Holt, Tadao Nakana, and Duncan C Weldon. **A:** *Peer Gynt* Michael Sheen; *Solveig* Catherine White; *Ase* Paola Dionisotti; *Buttonmoulder* Haruhiko Joh. 27 actors in all. **Pr:** Oslo (Winter Olympics).
Royal Shakespeare Company.

N. Bourne's choreography was for ensemble dances. He remembers a hoedown and a troll dance.
   The Catherine White playing Solveig is not to be confused with the former AMP dancer Catherine White (now Catherine Malone).
   This production was performed at the Barbican Theatre (March 3–12), in Manchester, and then in Tokyo, Japan.

Highland Fling. A Romantic Wee Ballet.

M: Hermann Lovenskjold (*Silfiden*, opus 1); Lerner and Loewe (overture to *Brigadoon*); 'Auld Lang Syne'. **SC:** Lez Brotherston. **L:** Tina McHugh. **D:** *The Sylph:* Maxine Fone; *James:* Scott Ambler; *Effie:* Emily Piercy; *Madge:* Etta Murfitt; *Gurn:* Simon Murphy; *Dorty:* Rosie Allen; *Robbie:* Andrew George. **Pr:** Arnolfini, Bristol
AMP

N. This production was revived in 1995 and 1997. Other, later, castings included: *The Sylph:* Jacqueline Anderson; *James:* Neil Penlington; *Madge:* Isabel Mortimer; *Gurn:* Phil Hill, Neil Penlington, Lee Boggess, Theo Clinkard; *Dorty:* Heather Habens; *Robbie:* Mark Mitchell, Neil Penlington, and Lee Boggess; *Covers/Sylphs:* Saranne Curtin, Lee Boggess, Jacqui Anderson.
There are plans for a revival and for a film.

Dedication: 'For James [McCloskey, Bourne's first designer who had died two weeks before the première]'

Oliver!

Musical. M, Lyrics, and Book: Lionel Bart. **Dir:** Sam Mendes. **SC:** Anthony Ward. **L:** David Hersey. Produced by Cameron Mackintosh. **A:** (alternate casts in brackets) *Fagin:* Jonathan Pryce; *Nancy:* Sally Dexter; *Oliver:* James Daley (and Gregory Bradley); *Artful Dodger:* Adam Searles (and Paul Bailey). **Pr:** December 8. London Palladium.

N. Most of Bourne's choreography was for the children (24 in each cast) and for Fagin. This production ran until February 1998.

Bourne was involved in revisions to the Palladium production with three of the four later actors playing Fagin: Jim Dale, Robert Lindsay, and Russ Abbott. He was also involved in revisions for the touring production.

NP. (revised for touring) **Pr:** July 1998. Theatre Royal, Plymouth.

N. This production is currently in an extended world tour.

1995

Watch Your Step

M and Lyrics: Irving Berlin. **Dir:** John Caird. **SC:** Sue Blane (adapted around the existing set for *The Phantom of the Opera*). **D:** Rosie Allen, Scott Ambler, Matthew Bourne, Maxine Fone, Andrew George, Gareth Griffiths, Heather Habens, Phil Hill, Isabel Mortimer, Etta Murfitt. **Pr:** Her Majesty's Theatre, London. Irving Berlin Gala.

N. This was for a single gala performance.

Bourne recalls the choreography, especially for the title number, as being 'in the style of Vernon and Irene Castle'.

Girls were made to Love and Kiss

M: Franz Lehar, sung by Richard Tauber. **C:** from AMP wardrobe. **D:** Etta Murfitt, Emily Piercy. **Pr:** AMP gala, Donmar Warehouse, London

N. There was only one performance.

The Swan

M: Camille Saint-Saëns ('Le Cygne', sung by Richard Tauber as 'Der Schwann'). **C:** provided by Adam Cooper. **D:** Adam Cooper (then a guest dancer). **Pr:** AMP gala, Donmar Warehouse, London

N. There was only one performance.

Boutique

M: Rossini, arr. Respighi (*La Boutique fantasque*). **SC:** Paul Edwards. **D:** *The Designer* Kenneth Pettitt. *His Assistant* Emma Northmore. *The Young Man* Xavier Pont. *His Girlfriend* Michela Meazza. *Barbie* Cecilia Madrazo. *Ken* Bernet Pascual. *Photographers and models* Mirko Battuello and Amy Edwards, Juan Rodriguez and Maya Sato, Daniel Adams and Maria Rowland.
Flowerpower Ruriko Al, Lorena Perez, Mariana Dias, Mariah Hamid, Nozomi Saito.
Bridalwear: Barbie Cecilia Madrazo. *Ken* Bernet Pascual. *Bridesmaids* Nozomi Saito, Naya Sato, Gemma Matthews, Ruriko Ai. *Male models* Mirko Battuello, Bernet Pascual, Daniel

Adams, Juan Rodriguez. *Pet fashions: Owner* Maria Rowland/ *Poodle* Marah Hamid. *Owner* Mariana Diaz/ *Poodle* Jane Lawrence. *Rave Up:* The Cast. *Adage:* The Cast. *Pas de deux:* Cecilia Madrazo and Xavier Pont. *Finale:* The Cast.
Pr: July 1995.
Images of Dance

N. This production was revived in July 1999
   Images of Dance, attached to London Studio Centre, is a company of graduating student dancers. Michela Meazza later joined AMP.

Roald Dahl's 'Little Red Riding Hood'

TV film. **Dir:** Donald Sturrock. **M:** Paul Patterson. Filmed: June–July 1995. Location: Elstree Studios. TV Broadcast: 1 January, 1996. **SC:** Sophie Becher. **A:** *Red Riding Hood and her Grandmother* Julie Walters; *Narrator* (seen) Ian Holm; *Voice of the Wolf* Danny De Vito; *Wolf* Peter Elliott. **D:** *Hyena* Andrew George; *Cat* Etta Murfitt; *She-Wolf* Scott Ambler; *Prussian Sow* Phil Hill; *Cow* Emily Piercy; *Sheep* Maxine Fone; Three child performers from the Sylvia Young School as Pigs.

N. Bourne's choreography was for Julie Walters and for the dancers.
   All the adult dancers were members of AMP.

Swan Lake

M: Pyotr Ilyich Tchaikovsky (arr: David Lloyd-Jones). **SC:** Lez Brotherston. **L:** Rick Fisher.
D: (two casts are given, since most roles were double cast in rehearsal)

The Swan	Adam Cooper (David Hughes)
The Prince	Scott Ambler (Ben Wright)
The Queen	Fiona Chadwick (Isabel Mortimer)
The Prince's Girlfriend	Emily Pearcy
The Private Secretary	Barry Atkinson
The Young Prince	Andrew Walkinshaw (Sid Mitchell)

Act I

Queen's escorts	William Kemp, Mark Mitchell, Simon Reglar, William Yong
Moth Maiden	Maxine Fone
The Nobleman	Phil Hill
Butterfly Maidens	Sarah Barron, Saranne Curtin, Heather Habens, Kirsty Tapp (Isabel Mortimer)
Evil Forest Troll	Lee Boggess
His Attendants	Jacqui Anderson, Teresa Barker
Club Owner	Eddie Nixon
Pop Idol	William Kemp
Hostesses	Sarah Barron, Saranne Curtin
Fan Dancer	Heather Habens
Barmaid	Jacqui Anderson
Barflies	Teresa Barker, Stephen Kirkham
Party Girls	Maxine Fone, Isabel Mortimer (Kirsty Tapp)
East End Gangsters	Mark Mitchell, Ian Wooller
Sailors	Greig Cooke, Simon Reglar
Schoolboy	Andrew Walkinshaw (Sid Mitchell)

Act II

Swans	Greig Cooke, Darren Ellis, Floyd Hendricks, Eddie Nixon, Simon Reglar, William Yong
Cygnets	Lee Boggess, Phil Hill, Stephen Kirkham, Quang Van
Big Swans	William Kemp (Colin Ross Waterston), Mark Mitchell, Pablo Pena, Ian Wooller

Act III

Doorman	Mark Mitchell
Press, Photographers	Lee Boggess, Darren Ellis, Simon Reglar, Ian Wooller
Royal Spotters	Simon Reglar, Kirsty Tapp
Autograph Hunters	Stephen Kirkham, Andrew Walkinshaw (Sid Mitchell)
The German Princess	Heather Habens
Her Escort	Pablo Pena
The Spanish Princess	Jacqui Anderson
Her Escort	Quang Van
The Hungarian Princess	Sarah Barron
Her Escort	William Yong
Princess of Monaco	Isabel Mortimer (Kirsty Tapp)
Her Escort	Greig Cooke
The Italian Princess	Saranne Curtin
Her Escort	William Kemp
The French Princess	Teresa Barker
Her Escort	Phil Hill
The Romanian Princess	Maxine Fone
Her Escort	Floyd Hendricks
Spanish Dancers	Lee Boggess, Darren Ellis, Mark Mitchell, Eddie Nixon, Simon Reglar, Ian Wooller

Act IV

Doctors and Nurses	Jacqui Anderson, Teresa Barker, Sarah Barron, Saranne Curtin, Maxine Fone, Heather Habens, Isabel Mortimer, Emily Pearcy

Pr: November 9, 1995. Sadler's Wells Theatre
AMP

N. This production has been extensively revived and somewhat revised. For the 1996 tour, and for performances throughout 1996 and 1997, a new orchestration for 25 players was provided by Rowland Lee.

Revivals: British tour, 1996. Piccadilly Theatre, London, 1996–7. Ahmansson Theatre, Los Angeles, 1997. Neil Simon Theatre, New York, 1998–9.

The most important additions to the cast were: William Kemp as the Swan (from February 1996), Lynn Seymour as the Queen (from October 1996), Floyd Hendricks as the Swan (from November 1996), Simon Cooper as the Swan (from December 1996), Saranne Curtin as the Queen (from November 1996), Keith Roberts as the Swan (from November 1998), Marguerite Porter as the Queen (from October 1998), Krissy Roberts as the Queen (from December 1998), Ewan Wardrop and Tom Ward as the Prince (from November 1998), Detlev Alexander as the Swan (from December 1998).

A TV film/video of this production (featuring the first cast in almost all respects) was made in 1996. **Dir:** Peter Mumford. **Broadcast on TV:** 26 December 1996.

Dedicated to Simon Murphy who had died in 1995.

1997

Cinderella

M: Sergei Prokoviev, *Cinderella*. At the end, the version of the 'Waltz of the Stars' from Prokoviev's 'Waltz Suite' was played during danced curtain calls. Orchestration: Daryl Griffith. Sound design: Simon King. **SC:** Lez Brotherston. **L:** Rick Fisher. Produced by Katharine Doré.

D: (multiple castings are cited to show which dancers were involved in the original creation of the roles)

Cinderella	Sarah Wildor (Saranne Curtin; Maxine Fone)
The Pilot	Adam Cooper (Ewan Wardrop; Will Kemp)
The Angel	Will Kemp (Arthur Pita; Adam Cooper; Theo Clinkard)
The Stepmother	Lynn Seymour (Isabel Mortimer)
Cinderella's Father	Barry Atkinson

The cast also included: Scott Ambler, Jacqueline Anderson, Teresa Barker, Andrew Corbett, Matthew Dalby, Darren Ellis, Vicky Evans, Valentina Formenti, Lucy Harrison, Ben Hartley, Floyd Hendricks, Phil Hill, Michela Meazza, Etta Murfitt, Neil Penlington, Emily Piercy, Colin Ross-Waterson, Tom Searle, Kirsty Tapp, Alan Vincent, Andrew Walkinshaw, Ben Wright.

Pr: September 26, 1997. Piccadilly Theatre, London
AMP

NP:

Cinderella	Sarah Wildor (Saranne Curtin)
The Pilot	Adam Cooper (Ewan Wardrop; Will Kemp)
The Angel	Will Kemp (Arthur Pita)
The Godmother	Isabel Mortimer (Emily Piercy)

AMP

Pr: 30 March 1999. Ahmansson Theatre, Los Angeles.
Choreography, scenario, and designs were extensively revised, especially in Acts I and II. Two musical items (score, end of no. 15, nos 16 and 23) were cut from Acts One and Two. At the start of Act Two, the Prelude to Act One was reprised. In Act Two, no. 24 was moved to after no. 30.

N. Bourne dedicated *Cinderella* 'to my late grandparents Mabel and Harry, Flora and William, who lived through the Blitz'.

Note on the Editor

Alastair Macaulay is chief theatre critic of the *Financial Times* and chief examiner in dance history to the Imperial Society of Teachers of Dancing. In 1983, he was founding editor of the British quarterly *Dance Theatre Journal*. In 1988 and 1992, he served as guest dance critic to *The New Yorker*. In 1998, his biography of Margot Fonteyn was published by Sutton Books. He lives and works in London.

Index

Figures in italics refer to captions.

393